A Short Guide to the History of South Africa

By

Dr. Damian P.O'Connor MA.

*

There are two dangers that face us in a situation such as ours today. One is the danger of over-simplification. In a world where the problems are so complex we may feel tempted to oversimplify and thus falsify the real character of the problems before us and miss the real solutions. The other danger is what I may call the danger of following slogans or catchwords, and so missing the real inwardness of the problems before us.

Jan Christian Smuts, 1943

There are those who, in the absolute conviction of their own rectitude, resent the fact that anyone should hold an opinion different from their own. When that does happen they ascribe it not to intellectual conviction, but to some form of moral turpitude. So they become impatient of the free expression of opinion – they want to put restraints on opposition and criticism – they desire to see created in support of their views and policies, that servile, standardised mass-mentality which is one of the instruments of dictatorship.

J.H. Hofmeyr, 1939

Cover image: The Blood River Monument

Also by the Author

Non-fiction

Books

*Imperial Defence and the Commitment to Empire*

*The Zulu and the Raj: The Life of Sir Bartle Frere*

*Between Peace and War: The History of the Royal United Services Institute 1831-2010*

Articles

'Imperial Strategy and the Anglo-Zulu War of 1879'. *The Historian, June 2006.*
'The Lion and the Swallow: The Somaliland Field Force 1901-20'. *Journal of the Royal United Services Institute October 2006.*

'In Praise of the Tail: The Land Transport Corps in the Abyssinian Campaign 1867-68.' *Journal of the Royal United Services Institute, February 2006.*

'The Political Uses of Lawlessness; Rhodes, Kruger and the Bechuanaland Field Force'. *Journal of the Royal United Services Institute, June 2005.*

'Privateers, Cruisers and Colliers: The Limits of International Maritime Law in the Nineteenth Century', *Journal of the Royal United Services Institute, February 2005.*

'Who Killed Cetshwayo? A Case Study of Ethical Foreign Policy', *Journal of the Royal United Services Institute, October 2004.*

'Defending Australia: Imperial Expansion and Local Defence', *Journal of Australian Naval History, March 2009.*

'Dragoons and Commandos: the development of Mounted Infantry in Southern Africa 1654-1899.' *Journal of the Royal United Services Institute. March 2008*

Africana Fiction

*The If Conspiracy*

*Pelly's Quest*

*Kruger's Millions*

*Veldt Ozymandias*

*The Oshadangwa Murders*

*The Capinga Questions*

\*

## Introduction

### Don't Skip It, It's Important.

This isn't what you might call a standard work of South African History. Although I've been studying the subject for several decades and have published several tracts aimed at the academic end of the audience spectrum, this time I'm going for a more 'Gonzo' style. What that means is that I am going to employ all the black arts of sarcasm, subjectivity, hyperbole, splenetic polemic and humour to pour scorn on a lot of the garbage that I've been asked to believe over the years. Do not expect detached objectivity because a lot of the aforementioned garbage has been shovelled down my throat under the cloak of a 'detached objectivity' that was anything but and, frankly, I'm fed up with it. That said, it is an accurate and reliable broad brush account and all the better for being openly and honestly subjective.

History is as much about Historians as it is about History and in these pages you are going to meet some of them and learn that many of them are not nearly as disinterested as they make themselves out to be. They have careers to make, politics to push, bonnets buzzing full of bees, a general aversion to upsetting apple carts, a willingness to argue over things far less important than the question of how many angels can dance on the head of a pin and are as guilty of groupthink, self-deception and wilful blindness as anyone else. But some of them are quite good.

There is no reason to fall out over questions or interpretations of historical events. If you are the sort of person who thinks that it's worth issuing death threats over the internet because I don't agree with your version of events or you think I'm (*insert your favourite epithet here*) then please confine your activities to buying several thousand copies of this book and holding a celebratory book burning. The only reason to get hot under the collar about History is when someone is using it to persuade you to vote, think or behave in a way that is harmful to you or your neighbours. Admittedly, that does happen a lot but the answer to it is not to throw your teddy out of the cot and Tweet something pithy but to read up on the subject, do your own thinking and, most importantly, assess the motivations of the person selling you the pony. Having your own point of view does not make you a bad person.

Finally, this book goes from 1652-1902 and I'm hoping to get a sequel out as and when. It cannot be comprehensive and a lot of events, people and places have been left out – sorry Langalibalele – but I think I've made a fair selection and I hope that you'll know a bit more about South Africa when you have finished the book than you did before you started it. If you think that's a modest ambition for an author, well, I've read books on this subject that are so bad that I've had to reach for the mind bleach before I've got more than half way in to them.

Finally, finally, some people like footnotes and long bibliographies. I'm keeping the footnotes to a minimum and skipping the bibliography because if you are a specialist, you'll recognise the sources and if you're not, you'll just be irritated by them. There are enough references to books in the text to provide you with some next steps if your interest is particularly sparked. Besides, the truth is usually buried in the archives and that probably isn't the best place for a beginner to start looking. (This book is though). That said, this is a list of the main abbreviations for the archival sources used in the footnotes; help yourself. Frankly, I live for a big pile of dusty archives that haven't been opened in decades.

ADM; Admiralty. BL; British Library, Kings Cross. CAB; Cabinet Office. CO; Colonial Office. CP; Carnarvon Papers. FO; Foreign Office. KCAL, KCM; Killie Campbell Africana Library, Durban. NAD GH; Natal Archives Department, Government House Records. NA ZGH; Natal Archives Depot Pietermaritzburg, Zululand Correspondence. OIOC IOR; British Library Oriental and India Office Collections, India office Records. PRO; Public Record Office, now 'The National Archives' at Kew. WO; War Office.

\*

## Van Riebeeck

Now it might seem odd to start off a History of South Africa with King Arthur but the fact is that History is as much about Historians as it is about dates and battles, and as we have in very many ways been ill-served by them, it's necessary to know something about how they go about doing their work to understand why I think this; so bear with me and you'll see where I'm going with it.

King Arthur and the Knights of the Round Table is a much-loved story of quests, Holy Grails, love-triangles, magic, heroism, betrayal and tragic defeat. It is set in the period 450-550AD after the retreat of the Roman Legions when the Saxons were invading Britain, and coincided with the moment when Christianity began to supplant the old Druidic beliefs. For a moment in History, before the old Britain was swept away and Anglo-Saxon Britain was established, so the story goes, King Arthur manages to create a peaceful, powerful, just kingdom based on his castle at Camelot before it all falls apart as a result of Sir Lancelot's affair with Queen Guinevere, Mordred's treachery and a Saxon invasion. Mortally wounded in the final defeat, Arthur is borne away to the mystical Isle of Avalon where he vows to return in the hour of Britain's greatest need as *Rex Quondam Rex Futuris* - The Once and Future King.

This has provided a glorious trove of raw material for poets, writers, painters and film makers ever since. (Tennyson's *Morte d'Arthur,* Robert Graves' *Count Belisarius,* Waterhouse's *The Lady of Shallot,* T.H. White's *Once and Future King* are fantastic, Marion Zimmer Bradley's *The Mists of Avalon* and John Boorman's *Excalibur* are guilty pleasures and of course, the heavily derivative *The Lord of the Rings* is a complete uplift; Bernard Cornwell's *Warlord Chronicles* are dreadful, in my opinion, but to be fair to him I read them in a dismal crap-hole in China and so might have had the balance of my judgement skewed).

Such is the interest and enthusiasm in the subject that the existence of Arthur has been held to be actual historical fact by many people and for many good reasons. They argue that the likelihood of a Romano-Celtic-British warrior leader, a *Dux Bellorum*, putting together an alliance which included Christian knights and Druidic shamans to resist the Saxon invasion is quite high and that the evidence for this is to be found in oral tradition, the names of landscape features such as Arthur's Seat up in Edinburgh, villages called 'Tye' in East Anglia, Welsh etymology and a variety of textual references. There is enough there to provide a basis for belief in King Arthur *if* you want to believe but the reality is that there *isn't* enough definite information to identify an actual person in a specific place and time carrying out a specific set of acts. There probably was a 'Camelot' – Roman Colchester, *Camulodunum* – but most Historians of this period tend to identify Arthur with South Cadbury or Tintagel Castle and the South West of England rather than East Anglia. Similarly, there probably was an Isle of Avalon which is now popularly associated with

Glastonbury, a town that might possibly have been an island in the marshes of the Somerset Levels during the period, and which contains the famous Abbey housing the alleged King Arthur's grave. Given the propensity of medieval monks to enhance the status of their monasteries with bogus relics, we can probably dismiss this as a fraud though.

This is important because in order to establish an historical account, we need to have convincing evidence in the form, primarily, of written records that can establish a definite time frame for a person or event. After that, notable artefacts – buildings, coins, tools, almost anything really - can be used to support or challenge those records and from this process of weighing the evidence, debating the conclusions and thinking carefully about the process, History is created. In all this, the records come first; they are the best and most vital evidence available. They may be incomplete, contradictory and sometimes misleading but they really are the best that we have.

Let me illustrate this; in my own village in England, a local farmer and History enthusiast armed with a metal detector dug up a beautiful Bronze Age axe head. Smooth, expertly crafted with the characteristic green patina of old bronze, it was a pleasure to hold and to feel the connection between the present and that distant past. What could be learned from such an artefact? Certainly, it revealed the level of technology available at the time and we could make plenty of inferences about its use and effectiveness but in terms of real, definite information about the events of that time and place we are at a loss. The Bronze Age in Britain – and we assumed that it was not brought here from elsewhere, though it is impossible to be even reasonably certain about this – lasted from roughly 2100 – 750BC so that axe might have been forged, used and lost by any number of people, at any time within that period and as such it is not very useful for an Historian who wanted to write a History of any single century during that period. It is rather like trying to write a History of Napoleon and beginning with *Napoleon Bonaparte was born sometime during the period after the birth of Christ and before the invention of nuclear weapons, although we cannot be entirely sure of this....*

The same farmer has also dug up any number of old coins and these we can trust as records, usually because they are stamped with the picture of a monarch, have the name written on it and are usually provided with a date to boot. So, if a coin is found with the portrait of King George III on one side, his name inscribed around the edge and a date placed conveniently under his glabrous face then we might assume with a high degree of certainty that there was a chap called King George III knocking around in 1792 and we can thus begin our History with the sentence '*In 1792, King George III of England....*'

Now this goes for any kind of History. We know a lot about the Egyptians because they wrote everything down in the form of hieroglyphs; ditto Aztecs and Mayans. Chinese people can read the inscriptions on the Terracotta Warriors at Xi'an because the characters that were used to record information remain the same today, which makes life a lot easier for them than those Classical scholars who have to learn Latin and Greek before getting to grips with their subject in European digs. After Homer wrote the Iliad, the History of the Trojan War, scholars long debated whether it was an actual record or just a piece of interesting fiction until, during the 1870s, Heinrich Schliemann decoded the clues in the book and found the site of ancient Troy under a hill in Turkey. There is a plethora of written records for Historians to get at when they want to study just about any major civilisation that has ever established itself on the Earth.

Except in South Africa. None of the indigenous societies of southern Africa had a written culture. They kept no meaningful records. There are no archives. There was memory and tradition but both these things are unreliable. Even when it comes to artefacts, there is a real paucity; a few pot shards, some Iron Age remnants, a sheep byre or two. Even the ruins of Great Zimbabwe, thought to have been built between 1200-1500AD yield up little to explain its rise and fall. This means that we *have* to rely on European records because for most of the period there are no others and this has led many people to think that our view of South African History is *Eurocentric* and therefore biased to such an extent that it is unreliable. There is a valid point here and we have to be aware that a point of view comes as part and parcel of any written source but, crucially, the fact that the sources were created by Europeans does not in itself make them unreliable. Records come in all shapes and sizes, have varying viewpoints, are created for very different purposes and are, despite the contortions of conspiracy theorists, notably difficult to fake convincingly. One skill that Historians try to develop is *empathy* which is the process whereby an attempt is made to stand in the other chap's shoes, see the world from his point of view and so interpret the written records in such a way as to build up a balanced picture. So, the records are the records. They are the best sources we have and if you take them out of the South African equation you have, literally, nothing to work with up until (roughly) the end of the 19th Century.

During the 1980s there were some attempts to substitute the records with 'oral' History, most notably by analysing the accumulation of titles that official praise-singers bestowed on Bantu monarchs in the hope that a record not dependent on those apparently biased and apparently inherently racist written records could be established. It went nowhere for obvious reasons; they were 'praises'; Bantu monarchs had the power of life and death over their subjects so it would be a very brave praise-singer who put in something a bit on the critical side; they also tended to leave out dates. Those working in the field of Oral History also noted how the accounts changed over time; veterans of the First World War were generally very proud of their actions until attitudes to war began to change after the 1960s; thereafter, the honourable discharge of a difficult and dangerous duty angle was toned down in favour of the 'isn't war ghastly and unnecessary' narrative being then established. So, the attempt to challenge the primacy of written records failed; if it had succeeded then we would have had to accept that King Arthur did actually exist because someone once sang a song about him to your great-grandmother.

I have been studying South African History all my life and I've visited the country many times over the past two decades. I've read just about everything - fact or fiction - I could get my hands on about the subject, pored over countless documents in plenty of archives, trod the red earth of battlefields, driven long, long miles over black top, tracks and the corrugated, plain old dirt of South Africa's back roads. I've published academic books and articles in the UK, USA, South Africa, Australia and Europe (in Flemish translation, remarkably). I've given talks and lectures at the National Army Museum in Chelsea, the US Naval Academy and most memorably for me at a conference in Dundee, Kwa-Zulu Natal where I had the somewhat un-nerving opportunity of explaining in person to Chief Mangosuthu Buthelezi why my country wrecked his. (To his credit and my relief, he held no grudges and awarded me a medal for Services to Zulu History). I've also done a bit of work on African development issues which won me an honourable second place in the Brenthurst Foundation/Royal United Services Institute Inaugural Nelson Mandela Prize Essay Competition back in 2006. I'm telling you this just so that you know I'm not some balloonist with a cargo of axes to grind come new to the subject and eager to impress with my erudition, or preen with self-righteousness, or signal my virtue for the benefit of the politically correct. I'm writing this History because - make no mistake – things in the great country known as the Republic of South Africa *can* go the way of Zimbabwe, but only if a false narrative of South African History can be created to justify the destruction of property rights, the abandonment of the rule of law and the dispossession and expulsion of white South Africans. And, yes, that false narrative has been under construction for a very long time and has gained a currency in politics and academia that it simply does not deserve. It is a narrative that claims that white people ripped off the land and wealth that properly belonged to indigenous Africans in an orgy of capitalist, imperialist exploitation; this is untrue, yet even to voice that opinion is to invite vitriol from those on the Left who are responsible for constructing that false narrative.

The existence of the records provides rich resources for the refutation of this false narrative and as such, the creators of the false narrative have had to find a way to destroy their credibility. They came up with a theory called *deconstructionism* which essentially held that the writer of the records was more important than the records themselves and that if the writer was white then he was instantly discredited as being part of the machinery of oppression. Never mind that the inventors of this gibberish were white themselves, what they insisted on was that any accounts created by Europeans can't be trusted and must be dismissed as unreliable because they are inherently racist. Having thus called into question the credibility of those records – pretty much the only sources we have – they created a vacuum which could then be filled by all sorts of twaddle whose reliability could not be tested because there was nothing to test it against. What was left was nothing but empty assertion, Newspeak and straightforward threats; *it happened because I, a non-white person or a white person who identifies as being 'on the Left', think it happened and you are a racist to deny the validity of my perception.* Think about that; if you accept that statement then you are saying that your perception is more important than the reality; that because you think (or self-identify as Avian) that you can fly, you actually can. You have just junked science, fact and the observation of your senses. Perception is not reality – that's why they are two separate words. It might make you feel virtuous but please don't take a running jump off that cliff.

No...wait....

\*

That there were people in southern Africa before the 17th Century is both obvious and well known. The problem is that we have only the archaeological record to refer to and archaeology tends to deal in the generalities of centuries rather than the specifics of decades or individual years. All we can say with any degree of certainty is that Stone Age cultures known as the Saan were established in South Africa sometime, probably a long time, before the Europeans turned up and that some of these cultures adopted a more pastoral way of life and became known variously as the Khoi, Khoe Khoikhoin, Khoikhoin and, when mixed in with Saan, Khoisan. (Take your pick which name you prefer to use; nobody seems to be able to agree for more than five minutes on which one to use). Even this is up for debate; *Saan* is considered by some Historians to be a Khoi term of abuse rather than their actual name and their modern-day descendants up in the Kalahari tend to prefer the term 'Bushman' which in turn, has some connotations of insult. For simplicity's sake, I shall use Bushman, Khoikhoin and where they are probably mixed, Khoisan.

Much the same can be said about the arrival of the Bantu peoples into southern Africa. Here linguistic evidence has been used to try to trace the movement of peoples through the spread of and interaction between different languages. This is evidence that is compelling only when supported by other, harder, sources but in this case, we can be more certain of a few more things because Arab traders came into contact with the Bantu as early as perhaps 600AD and recorded their arrival at Sofala in modern day Mozambique around 900AD. Again, we can say with a fair degree of certainty derived from both Arab and Portuguese records that the Xhosa peoples had settled the fertile strip along the Indian Ocean now known as KwaZulu-Natal and had crossed into the present-day Transkei by around 1700AD, with the Pondo and Tembu peoples following up behind them. This was possibly also the case with the Sotho and Tswana speaking peoples who settled along the Vaal and Orange Rivers in those areas that are known today as Gauteng and the Free State. Across in Namibia, the Herero and Ovambo peoples possibly arrived at the same time but again, the sources are patchy, and the evidence is derived from that weakest and most unreliable of evidence, oral tradition. As we have seen, by this measure, the story of King Arthur *has* to be accepted as fact when in reality it is no such thing.

Which brings us to Van Riebeeck. We know that Van Riebeeck arrived at the Cape with his ships *Goede Hoop, Dromedarin* and *Reiper* from the Texel River in Holland on 6th April 1652 with orders from the Dutch East India Company to set up a station for the victualling of ships heading to and from the East Indies. We know this because there are actual records. If you can read Dutch, you can find them in Amsterdam or Cape Town. If not, you'll need a copy of *The Record or a series of Official Papers relative to the Condition and Treatment of the Native Tribes of South Africa* which was compiled by Donald Moodie, a retired British naval officer who had filled several posts in the later British colonial administration of South Africa, including official Protector of Slaves for the Eastern Division of the Colony. He was tasked in 1838 by the Governor to investigate the treatment of Africans at the hands of Europeans since the arrival of Van Riebeeck and so dug up all sorts of stuff scattered around government offices from the time of the Dutch occupation onwards, beginning with Van Riebeeck's actual journal and correspondence with his bosses in Amsterdam and had it translated. So now we have actual, good, solid verifiable evidence, especially as he was put on oath to produce a fair record. Not odd items of metal ware, shards of property, bones, old wives' tales and wild guesses, but actual South African *History*. And because we can put a date on it, that *History begins with Van Riebeeck*. And, critically, it establishes the fact that white European colonists were living in the Western Cape long before the arrival of the Bantu colonists in the Eastern Cape. In 17th Century South Africa, just about everyone except the Bushmen were colonists and in 21st Century South Africa, just about everyone is the descendant of a colonist.

*

One of the many egregious nonsenses spouted about European imperialism is that it was a dastardly land grab planned sometimes hundreds of years in advance. One author charted the History of the British Empire with a chapter entitled 'Reconnaissance' and went on about the voyages of Drake, Cabot and those other Elizabethan explorers as though they were the advance guard of a determined plot to take over the world. I can't remember the author or the actual title of the book because I threw it out. The reality is that for an awful lot of the time the European governments made it quite clear that they did not want the responsibilities of an African empire, had no desire for the expenses of conquest and insisted that those of their subjects tempted to wander around that continent ought to stick entirely to the business of trade and should not expect the government at home to get them out of any mess that they might embroil themselves in as a result of their own cupidity or stupidity. Making money was fine; conquest and imperium was not. Probably the best exponent of this view was J.K. Galbraith, the Canadian-American liberal intellectual and diplomat who worked for Roosevelt and JFK and who is probably best remembered for his book *The Affluent Society*. We'll look at his 1963 book *Reluctant Empire: British Policy on the South African Frontier 1834-54* later on, though the title gives a bit of a clue to what his conclusions were. And if a wet liberal like Galbraith isn't convincing enough, what about taking the word of Rider Haggard, an arch-imperialist second only to Rudyard Kipling?

> The Rise of the British Empire in the teeth of the hamperings and opposition of British statesmen and the elephantine obstinacy and stupidity of permanent Officials, is and always must remain one of the marvels of the world.[1]

And please note: the basic idea that the primary value of the Cape from the minute Van Riebeeck set his foot ashore right up until the end of the British Empire was the trade and shipping that went *past* it to India and the Far East has *never been challenged by any serious Historian*. Even the Communist Brian Bunting, author of *The Rise of the South African Reich*, whose historical sketch of the Dutch Colony was exactly what you would expect from a Stalinist, admitted this.[2] As Van Riebeeck's bosses, the Directors of the Dutch East India

---

[1] Quoted in *The Cloak That I Left*, Lilias Rider Haggard (London, 1951).
[2] B.Bunting, *The Rise of the South African Reich*, (London 1964), p.8.

Company, declared: 'The Cape Castle is the frontier fortress of India.'[3] Interest in the *continent* of Africa was always *secondary* to the trade to and from the East. However, if you need proof of this reluctance the best place to start is indeed with Van Riebeeck because a more reluctant imperialist would be difficult to find.

Johan Van Riebeeck was thirty-three years old when he brought his three ships into Table Bay. An experienced trader, surgeon and administrator, he had served the *Vereenigde Oost-Indische Compagnie* (Dutch East India Company -VOC) in Tonkin and Batavia (now Vietnam and Jakarta) and was hoping that this posting would get him a decent promotion – it did, but it was a long time coming; he applied for a new posting after only a year and repeated the request to leave this 'lonesome and melancholy place'[4] several times. G.M.Theal, South Africa's first (and possibly best) Historian described him as 'a little, fiery-tempered, resolute man, in the prime of life, with perfect health, untiring energy, and unbounded zeal, he was capable of performing a great amount of useful work,'[5] but actually, he didn't much like him. His final judgement was that van Riebeeck wasn't very bright, apt to be tyrannical, had a chip on his shoulder about his origins, was inclined to be snobbish and had justly acquired the nickname *the little thornback*. Nevertheless, he recognised his ability as an administrator and as a good Company man and certainly rated him better than the chap who succeeded him, who he reckoned was bone idle. Actually, I think Theal was being a bit harsh; a certain amount of arrogance is sometimes necessary in a leader faced with tasks of great magnitude in situations where there is little guidance available and the stakes are life and death.

It was not his first visit as, like many others, he had spent nearly three weeks resting his ships in Table Bay on his way back homeward some years before. Like many other voyagers, he was impressed with the possibilities of establishing a base in the bay where fresh vegetables might be grown, cattle traded from the local people and ships repaired, watered and re-victualled. The Company, fearing that in the event of a looming war with England they would be beaten to the prize, reluctantly decided that the possession of such a station was a justifiable expenditure and so despatched an expedition with Van Riebeeck in command.[6] Thus began ten frustrating years for the reluctant founder of modern South Africa.

Not much was known about Southern Africa in 1652. What was known was that the passage around the Cape of Good Hope was a perilous one. Apart from some horrendous spring gales, the like of which turns normally balmy Cape Town and points eastwards into a bad night on the Solent, the prevailing circumpolar Antarctic currents clash with the southerly Mozambique current to create truly mountainous seas. Add to this terrible surf along most of the southern and eastern coastlines, thick fog brought up the west coast by the cold Benguela current and the lack of really safe and secure anchorages and you can start to appreciate the bravery of those seafarers who put to sea in boats that today wouldn't be licenced for a cross-Channel booze cruise never mind the circumnavigation of the globe. Luis de Camoes,

---

[3] G.M. Theal. *History and Ethnography of South Africa south of the Zambezi before 1795* Vol. II (London, 1909), p. 203.
[4] D. Moodie, *The Record or a series of Official Papers relative to the Condition and Treatment of the Native Tribes of South Africa* p.62.
[5] Theal. *History and Ethnography* Vol. II. p. 6.
[6] http://www.saHistory.org.za/people/johan-anthoniszoon-jan-van-riebeeck

Portuguese poet, soldier and adventurer who had been round the Cape more than once, wrote in his 1572 epic *The Lusiads* that the Cape of Good Hope was guarded by the Titan Adamastor and his rage at being defeated by Neptune was the reason for the dangers of the passage. Looking at the tumultuous wreckage of rocks, huge boulders and tortured stratum just beyond Plettenberg Bay, it is easy to imagine that they might indeed be the product of an angry Titan tearing up the sea bed, especially when the cormorants sit atop them, wings outstretched like eagle standards. Vasco de Gama, the subject of Comoes' poetry, went around the Cape in 1497 in a vessel thirty yards long and nine at its widest point; that's shorter than my back garden. There's a replica of one of his caravels in the maritime museum in Mossel Bay but if that's too far to travel, you might look at the replica of Drake's *Golden Hind* in Bankside, London and reflect that it's just a tiny bit bigger than the *Sao Gabriel*. By the time Van Riebeeck arrived at the Cape, the ships were a little larger but still nothing like the later East Indiamen such as the *Arniston*, which was 60 yards long and 14 yards wide, and still succumbed to a storm off Cape Agulhas in 1815. The event is commemorated today in the eponymous name of the bay and a decent little mid-range wine (well, mid-range by the measure of my pocket, anyway).

Navigation during Van Riebeeck's time was also something of a hazardous affair, it being a large part of a Captain's duty to work out just where he actually was; in 1653 one ship 'wandered about this Cape'[7] for three months after the only people who knew how to read a compass died. Although a Captain might be reasonably certain of his Latitude by measuring the height of the sun, the solution to working out a decent Longitude lay well in the future and estimating the speed of the ship by means of a log line tied off with knots was only a little better than rule of thumb. Creeping along the coast lines was not much of an alternative either because of uncharted rocks and shoals, especially the Agulhas bank, and the fact that if the Captain wanted to reach India without first starving to death or dying of scurvy or thirst, then he would have to trust to the trade winds and clear blue water. Nevertheless, there were some maps and charts to go off and though they could not be relied upon for accurate inshore navigation, they did provide some sort of clue for a Captain on his way to the Cape. What they did not do was give much indication of what lay in the interior.

Again there were maps drawn up, mainly from Portuguese accounts, but as a means to navigation they were virtually useless; Abraham Ortelius's 1570 map places Zanzibar somewhere in the Namib desert while Justus Danckerts' 1680 map is refreshingly free of useful detail; Joao Teixeira's 1630 map is a beautifully shaded and illustrated affair showing St. Lucía Bay in roughly the right place and indicating an awareness that there are some mountains inland from the coast that might just be identified as the Drakensberg. The colours of fiery orange and soft plum purple capture the actual colours of the mountains of the Namib, as do the green and gold tints for the verdant valleys; so well indeed that I'd be proud to frame that map and hang it on the wall of my study; but I wouldn't care to use it to get me from Cape Town to Colesberg because the Karoo desert isn't shown there.[8] It's a small thing, but important I feel, given it's a ten-hour drive across that desert and really quite hot.

---

[7] Moodie, *The Record* Van Riebeeck's Journal June 2nd 1653.
[8] Andrew Duminy, *Mapping South Africa* (South Africa, 2011).

As indicated, getting to the Cape by sea was no small achievement. The journey could take anything up to five months, especially if the Dutch ships were obliged by dint of English hostility to add to an already formidable distance by travelling via the North Sea, Scotland and Ireland; also, the Portuguese port at Luanda, Angola, was generally closed to any kind of trade or re-supply beyond essential watering. When the Huguenots went out to the Cape in 1688, one ship made it in a near record time of 87 days, but another took seven months. Any voyage from Holland therefore began with North Sea weather, followed by the misery of sea sickness in Biscay, to which was added the risk of being taken by Moorish pirates and sold in the slave markets of Algiers, storm and shipwreck anywhere along the way, weeks of sitting in your own filth in the doldrums, outbreaks of contagious diseases aboard and the almost inevitable scurvy. This debilitating condition was only dimly understood in the 17$^{th}$ Century; most captains knew that it was related to the lack of fresh food and that the typical sailor's diet of cheese, biscuit, dried or salted meat and booze had to be supplemented if the crew was not to weaken to the point of uselessness. Attempts to remedy the situation included the addition of apples and pears to the regular inventory of the ship but as these fruits did not contain the necessary vitamin C, the effort was wasted. The choice facing the Captain leaving the last watering places in the Azores was to risk putting in to the fever-ridden ports of West Africa or trust to speed and make a straight run down to the Cape but in either case, it was a rare voyage that didn't involve deaths on board; in 1662, the *Oranjie* arrived in False Bay with fifty dead and 150 sick aboard; in 1665, the *Rynlant* arrived with thirty-three dead, 170 sick and only five healthy men left standing; the following year the *Dordrecht* arrived, having lost 112 out of the 294 embarked. These were not isolated incidents either; many ships arrived in Table Bay with so few crew in any fit state that they were unable to anchor or even furl sails and it was common practice to drop the weak and sick off at the Cape and then fill out the complement with those invalids from the last ship who had since recovered.

When Van Riebeeck dropped anchor in Table Bay after a gruelling eighteen week voyage – which was actually regarded as rather quick (the captain earned a £50 bonus for any passage under 120 days) - and cast his eyes along that magnificent view from the Devil's Peak, up across the rising ground towards the sheer walls and flat shaved summit of Table Mountain and then down to the Lion's Head he might well have caught sight of actual lions as well as elephants, hartebeest and perhaps plentiful herds of springbok, the odd rhinoceros and a giraffe or two. Certainly, there were hippos (good eating!) and crocodiles in the rivers and if the lands looked like wide, open savannah, there were also thick forests just behind the mountain screeching with monkeys, baboons and every variety of bird. This has all gone now, of course, swallowed up by a great port and an expanding city, excepting the baboons that scavenge the bins on collection day and make a nuisance of themselves otherwise. Further out, around the other side of the Table, there were wide, flat valleys between mountains that seemed to explode out of the ground giving the land something of the feel of France and something of the feel of an alpine meadow. To Mrs van Riebeeck, young Master Van Riebeeck and his two cousins Elizabeth and Sebastiana, the outlook must have been one of mixed wonder, excitement and apprehension for this was their new home, for better or for worse, for an indefinite period to come.

For Jan Van Riebeeck, there was probably a greater emphasis on the apprehension bit because he knew that winter was coming on and the first challenge would be to survive it. No doubt the greenhorns in his crew were looking forward to a bit of decent weather after leaving the frozen canals and bleak, December skies of their Northern hemisphere home but the old hands would surely have put them straight on this one. Certainly, the climate of the Cape is more pleasant than that of Holland but the winters can be very wet; twenty rainy days is the average in July, but it has been known to rain continuously for eighteen consecutive days and unless you have actually lived in makeshift accommodation through a wet winter, it is difficult to understand just how miserable an experience this is. Wet, chafing clothes are the norm, keeping warm becomes an overwhelming obsession, lighting a fire with damp wood and no tinder is a trial in itself. Colds and flu become debilitating conditions, rheumatism a torture, exposure a daily peril and a high calorie intake a necessity which if not achieved, exacerbates all other dangers and discomforts. Add to this the routine diseases of an unhygienic age – dysentery, diarrhoea – means that to survive requires an effort of will, a cheerful acceptance that being wet, cold, damp and miserable is your natural state and any improvement on this a boon. The crews saw their huts washed away; food was scarce; lions were plentiful and apt to get into the livestock; and lions are terrifying – if the howl of a wolf is the sound of a lost soul falling to Hell then the rumbling growl of a lion is the sound of the devil driving him there; the woofing cough and horrible growl can come from a mile distant but still sound as though it is your bedroom; dysentery broke out; by June, sixty out of the 116 colonists were sick; nineteen of them would not see the spring.

Bad weather was not something that couldn't be overcome given some idea of what the seasons might be but it is one of the facts of life in South Africa that although there is a broad division into a Western, winter rainfall zone and an Eastern summer rainfall zone, the climate can be very unpredictable and given to extremes. In 2016, a three-year drought came to an end with a deluge that put Johannesburg airport under three feet of water within a couple of hours one afternoon. Summer in the Free State can see temperatures up in the 40°C range while winter in the same place can see the mercury down at -25°C; ('But it's only for a couple of weeks,' says my old pal, Thielman, cheerfully). Snow in Africa isn't usually the first thing one thinks of when planning a holiday but there are ski resorts in Lesotho, snow warnings on the passes going up to the Highveldt from the Karoo, periodical flurries along the Drakensberg into KwaZulu-Natal and a regular dump on the Langkloof, just an hour's drive up the berg from the holiday resorts of the Garden Route. In July 1652, the colonist's pit traps froze over; tons and tons of good hartebeest venison taunted the hungry colonists from just beyond musket shot (they were so quick, even the Khoikhoin couldn't catch them).

This posed a question for Van Riebeeck that the modern age has settled with satellite based, computer aided weather forecasting, but which he had only a guess and a gamble to guide him; when to plant? Van Riebeeck had arrived at the end of a drought when the earth was parched and the grazing dried up, but nevertheless impressed with the potential fertility, seeds went in to earth as soon as the gardens had been laid out; and as soon as they showed a shoot, terrible rains washed them away. The next planting would have to wait for the spring, but just when was that? And what if there was insufficient rain then to make them grow? Or too much? The storm drains in Stellenbosch and Tulbagh tell you all you need to know about that particular possibility. And in the Cape, wheat is harvested in the *spring*. Such anxieties are largely unknown where modern agriculture exists but they made up the everyday conversations of the 17th Century. Even when the spring planting went in and the harvest looked promising, the barley, peas and beans were flattened by the furnace hot blasts of the SE winds tearing down from the interior without warning and sending the temperature spiking; this was a problem solved by planting at Rondebosch, which is sheltered from the worst of the winds. The settlement had been established with the express aim of providing fresh meat and vegetables for the VOC ships but for that first year and long afterwards, Van Riebeeck and his men were reduced to scrounging what they could from any vessel that entered the bay, eating bird's eggs and penguins from the long, low bore of Robben Island and cursing the Khoikhoin herders whose fires they could see in the distance.

The difficulties of that first year were exacerbated by the absence of the local inhabitants that the VOC had hoped to rely on for supplies of sheep and cattle. These were the Khoikhoin, a nomadic, pastoral society dependent on their herds but supplementing their diets with game, roots and berries. They were divided into a series of clans and tribes, each with its own territory under the nominal authority of a chief who might or might not be obeyed according to circumstances, somewhat fractious, inter-related and generally following a nomadic pattern that took them to the Cape in spring, eastwards during the autumn and then towards Saldanha Bay to over-winter; sometimes the cycle was two years rather than one. In appearance, they were more Asiatic in skin tone than black Bantu, slight in build, usually under five feet high, with high cheek bones, heart shaped faces and epicanthic folds in the inner corners of their eyes. Rather more alarming was the fact that they smeared their naked bodies with animal grease as defence against the sun, hung sheep intestines around their necks as a portable snack, were quite able to eat the long rotten carcasses of seals and gave off an odour that even 17th Century seaman found difficult to endure.[9]

Their language was characterised by the five clicking sounds which gave them their European name – 'Hottentots'. This name has since been characterised as 'offensive' or 'racist' terminology but in reality, it is an innocent term guilty of nothing more than being a form of short-hand. Neither Van Riebeeck nor any of his party were able to speak the Bushmen or Khoikhoin languages and so were unable at first to discover their real names. Those Bushmen groups that they had observed along the coast, who were similar in appearance and language but, living off shell fish, appeared to be more in the hunter-gatherer line, they termed the 'Strand-lopers' – nothing more offensive than 'Beach walkers'. 'Ottentoo' is just onomatopoeic echoing of the clicks in the language.[10] As the Dutch learned more about the Khoikhoin, so their terminology changed; almost immediately, they began to refer to the clans they had expected to trade with as the 'Saldanians' or 'Saldaniers' after they were led to believe that these groups had gone north towards Saldanha Bay to escape the drought. The increase in knowledge was enlightening in more than one way; in 1668, Corporal Kruse came across a band of Bushmen who the Khoisan had informed him were

---

[9] N. Mostert, *Frontiers*, (London, 1992) pp. 108 – 109.
[10] Moodie, *The Record*: Journal of Commander Jan van Riebeeck, 8th, 9th April, 1652.

known as the Obiqua – *the murderers* – who tried to rob him and were roundly thrashed and relieved of their own cattle for their pains.[11]

Attempting to understand the relationships between the various clans and groups was something that gave Van Riebeeck a headache right from the beginning. Two days after he had arrived, he was obliged to break up a fight brewing between the Strand-lopers (the Goringhaiconas) and the Saldanians (the Chocoquas) and it rapidly became clear to him that the Khoikhoin lived in a state of petty strife, intermittent warfare, the abduction of women and near constant cattle rustling. This situation was not helped by the fact that he was forced to rely on a single interpreter in his dealings with the various clans and that the interpreter turned out to be a shifty, dishonest rogue who did his best to stir up animosities between the Khoikhoin and the Dutch from which he intended to profit.

As the first person to be incarcerated on (and escape from) Robben Island, Autshumao has been posthumously rehabilitated as something of a hero. Were you to visit Nelson Mandela's prison cell on that island, as so many tourists do, then you would probably travel there on the vessel *Autshumao* yet the picture that emerges from Van Riebeeck's Journal – the *only* source we have – paints him in a very different light; as an incorrigible crook who took full advantage of his position to deceive and bilk everyone involved in the nascent relationship between the Europeans and the Africans. Not much is known for certain about him and how he came to learn the broken English in which he conversed, but the proposal that he was taken to the Dutch East Indies on an English ship is perfectly plausible. It is also perfectly possible that he was returned to the Cape and promised some sort of payment as an interpreter for each ship that came in to trade for cattle. Van Riebeeck knew he was there before he left Holland and the first thing he did on landing was to seek out Autshumao – more popularly known as Herry the Strandloper - to help him barter for the cattle he wanted. Reading Noel Mostert's rather too sympathetic History of the Xhosa people, *Frontiers*, however, it would be possible to make the mistake of thinking he combined the intelligence of a Bismarck, the shrewdness of a Talleyrand and the negotiating skill of Thabo Mbeki when in reality Van Riebeeck nailed him for the petty crook he was straight away.[12] As a candidate for jail, Autshumao fits the bill perfectly; for many of the Khoisan leaders and a fair few of the Dutch settlers, he was a candidate for the chop; Van Riebeeck had the patience of a saint with him, forgiving him over and over again. When the old crook died, he did so reviled and distrusted by just about everyone.

It was not until the winter was over that the Chocoquas appeared, driving their huge herds of cattle and sheep, 10,000 head and more, before them but despite the Dutch being well prepared with trade goods of copper, brass and tobacco, business did not go well. Van Riebeeck wanted livestock in quantities that the Chocoquas did not want to give up and the Chocoquas had no need for the amount of copper and brass that was on offer. This, Van Riebeeck found extremely frustrating but there was little he could do to force them to part with their cattle in greater numbers. Struggling to understand just exactly who, what and

---

[11] Theal. *History and Ethnography* Vol. II p.174.
[12] Moodie, *The Record:* Journal of Jan van Riebeeck, 24th Nov, 1652.

where the various clans were,[13] who led them and what goods would be most attractive to them for trade was a conundrum that plagued the Dutch for years and which was made infinitely worse by Autshumao/Herry and his reservations about him were confirmed when Herry approached him with a novel way to get the Chocoquas to trade. Herry wanted to get hold of the Chief of the Vischmen clan ('Fishermen' or more properly, the *Soaqua*, who were possibly Saan) and kill him and all his people, an action which would so please the rival Chocoquas that they would be more disposed to trade. Van Riebeeck would have none of it; for one thing, he feared an attack by the English and had no intention whatsoever of complicating his situation by getting mixed up in local wars and rivalries; for another, his two hundred men were massively outnumbered by the Khoikhoin; more importantly though, this was no way to do business.

*

> The Court of Justice was assembled for the trial of the Hottentots; when the culprits were, according to the sentence of the Court, for their repeated crimes of violence and cattle stealing, committed upon the persons and property of the Company and good inhabitants, condemned to be hanged upon a gallows until death ensues. It were much to be desired, and would be most praiseworthy, could all such villains be deterred from the commission of crime by this example. But the commission of crime is (God mend it) so implanted among many Christians, and so habitual to them, that, notwithstanding that they are fully aware of the attendant punishments, of which they have examples every day—still these are not sufficiently powerful to divert them from their evil courses, and to lead them to improvement ; and this holds good independently of that class of criminals to be found in every country, and in every quarter of the world, that has yet been discovered, who are entirely incorrigible, and, with respect to their disposition, education and conversation, appear to be more brutes than men, &c
>
> *Extracts of Resolutions of Council. Sept 14, 1678.* Moodie, *The Record.*

There was another reason for Van Riebeeck's frustration; the Khoikhoin were incorrigible thieves. Anything not nailed down was lifted. Metal tools such as knives, saws and hoes were particularly sought after but anything would do. Anyone not armed was robbed with menaces and it quickly became impossible to send out any sort of work party without an escort. Work on the construction of an earthwork fort and stockade was speeded up; in theory it was to protect the station from the English, but increasingly the Dutch were eyeing up the Chocoquas as the most likely foe and itching to get their revenge. Van Riebeeck insisted on a policy of turning the other cheek in the hope that he might persuade the Chocoquas to a more profitable trade, but privately fumed that he would lift their whole herd

---

[13] Moodie, *The Record*. Van Riebeeck's Memorandum to Wagenaar 5th May 1662.

in an afternoon and round the whole tribe up as slaves for the Indies to boot given half a chance.

His restraint however was simply interpreted as weakness; Herry led the thinking on this by murdering a herd boy, lifting his forty-two head of cattle and decamping for the interior, only to return shortly after to flaunt his robbery in the face of Van Riebeeck who insisted that no notice or reprisal be taken for fear of frightening off the other clans. This was October 1653, but as the summer proceeded, Herry realised that perhaps he had just killed the goose that laid the golden eggs; for the rest of that summer, it became increasingly apparent that Herry's new intention was to convince the Khoikhoin that he held the monopoly on trade with the Dutch while at the same time offering the Dutch a resumption of the cattle trade in return for a pardon. In short, he was playing both ends against the middle,[14] a game that resulted in the VOC's authorisation of a death sentence for him and permission for Van Riebeeck to confiscate as many cattle from the Chocoquas as they stole from the Dutch. Thus, the first clash. Thus, the first fundamental clash of cultures.

For the Europeans, the right to secure ownership and enjoyment of property is one of the main supports on which a settled society rests. It is a fundamental tenet that property might only be taken from the citizen with that citizen's consent, under lawful arrangement according to established and agreed custom and practice. It is the rock upon which a civilised and prosperous society is built. It provides the motivation to go out to work in a grim morning in November for by it the workers gain a secure roof over their heads that cannot be taken away at the whim of a tyrant. It gives the boy racer his dreams of a superbike, the inventor and the artist the certainty to bring their dreams to fruition to the benefit of all. It gives the doting parent the chance to give a hand up to her children, the caring citizen the ability to fund a charity. It is the universal incentive for people to make their choices wisely, to create, to build, to achieve and provide. It is the sum of an individual or a family's labour and to steal property is the despicable act of stealing the sweat of a person's brow and the shirt from their back. It is the reason why economies based on collectivisation and the expropriation of property fail; no property rights = no incentive to work or create = no nothing.

This is what Magna Carta is about. This is what taxation and representative government is about and in the 17th Century Dutch Republic the right to the ownership and enjoyment of private property was doubly sacrosanct because the Protestant Reformation had established the principle that ownership of property was proof of Godly virtue. Everyone was bound by this belief in the sanctity of property; everyone from the lowliest peasant to the haughtiest aristocrat; even – *especially* – a King was so bound and those rulers who tried to ignore it did so at their peril. Only four years before Van Riebeeck landed at the Cape, the English had made the point that there would be no taxes without the approval of the people in the most forcible way possible by cutting off King Charles' head in Whitehall.

---

14 Moodie, *The Record*, Jan. 27th 1655 Riebeeck to Chamber XVII.

This was not how the Khoikhoin and the Bushmen understood property at all. They lived a wild and natural life and by that I do not mean the sort of wild and natural life imagined by Greens, animal rights activists, hunt saboteurs and fans of Walt Disney. Nor do I mean the sort of wild and natural life imagined by those 17th Century 'romantic primitivists' who put forward the idea of the 'noble savage' living in an Eden of unfettered freedom and bounty. I mean the sort of wild and natural life that is nature 'red in tooth and claw'. It was a brutal, pragmatic life in which there was little room for sentiment, where the prize went to the strong and the devil really did take the hindmost; children would be strangled or buried alive if they were disabled or a burden;[15] the old were simply abandoned with an ostrich egg full of water and a bit of meat when they could no longer keep up; (these observations on Bushman life were made by the Reverend Kicherer, a sympathetic observer from the London Missionary Society).[16] The popular image of the Bushmen scrabbling about in an arid desert landscape is only part of the story; in reality, they would have been just as much at home in the mountains, savannah grassland and forests of the Cape and just as exposed to the dangers that went with those landscapes, like elephants, leopards, hippos and crocodiles. The essential questions that dominated their lives was *is it food and how do I kill it?* Or, *am I food and is it going to kill me?* Actually, many of them would probably never get to ask this second question until it was too late; I speak from experience when I say that when the grass is long you can be within three yards of a lion without ever being aware of its presence; the evidence gleaned from the skeletal remains of the earliest Hominids indicates that they were the preferred menu option for the big cats that they shared their caves with and there isn't much to argue that this option diminished until evolution provided mankind with guns. Nor did the Bushmen entertain the syrupy notions of today's vegan bunny-huggers; everything was food, including grubs, beetles, insects and ant eggs (known as 'Bushman rice') and no feelings were wasted on 'humane' slaughter. When the writer, columnist, food critic and travel writer AA Gill went hunting with the Kalahari Bushmen, (he contributed a toad to the feast) he was surprised when one of them snapped the back legs of a new caught but still very much alive buck. He questioned the cruelty, only to receive the reply: 'The first rule of hunting is make sure you never have to catch your prey twice'; Bushman ostrich traps work by slowly and agonisingly decapitating the unfortunate bird.[17] The Bushmen do not cry when Bambi's mother is hunted down but hang around to see if they can get a share of the kill.

Living the life of the hunter-gatherer often involved a great deal of travel and although Bushmen groups asserted vague rights to territory, this never really hardened into the assertion of territorial integrity or land ownership. Similarly, the superabundance of game available meant that scarcity was rarely a problem that needed to be addressed by asserting a right to particular food sources or the development of an economy beyond the most basic of barter. Property rights beyond the ownership of personal items were unnecessary and so undeveloped. Instead, a more collective approach developed; in times of scarcity as in plenty, it made more sense to share – no-one can eat a whole zebra in one go and there are no fridges in which to store the surplus - and from this we can see the origins of the African

---

[15] Theal mentions this in *History and Ethnography* Vol II p.175. Mr. JLB Matekoni of Speedy Motors has a disabled child rescued from Bushman infanticide.
[16] Quoted in Nigel Penn, *The Forgotten Frontier* (Cape Town, 2005) pp. 242-43.
[17] Peter Godwin, *Bushmen.* Jan 2000. http://ngm.nationalgeographic.com/ngm/0102/feature6/fulltext.html

philosophy of *uBuntu*, a belief that all Humanity is in some way connected and so, in a sense, imparting a collective responsibility that takes precedence over individual property rights.

'Theft' as a legal or judicial concept was probably unknown in Bushmen society because there was little to steal and even less chance of getting away with it. In a very real sense, whatever was required could be taken from the wild and so the act of taking something from a weaker clan was probably seen as more akin to culling a buck from a herd rather than violating someone's property rights. It certainly could not be said to constitute a moral wrong or evil because the lifting of cattle or the taking of Dutch property was so persistent and prevalent over such a long period that one might expect a moral revulsion to be eventually effected in even the most hardened recidivist. Even when opportunities to purchase such objects by working for wages became more widespread, 'theft' still remained a notable feature of South African life. That the strong should take from the weak at whatever opportunity was just a fact of Bushman life; there was no 'right' or 'wrong' to it. This might sound a bit like moral relativism; in fact it does, especially as punishment for theft among the Bushmen was sometimes observed but it is possible that this was a consequence of violating the Eleventh Commandment rather than the Eighth. The only other answer I can come up with is that, based on anecdotal evidence and my own unscientific observation and experience, that the lack of any form of formal education produced in many southern African peoples an attitude of short-termism, of instant gratification and an unwillingness to accord possible future consequences much importance. In Africa, so the saying goes, so many things can kill you today that it makes no sense to worry about things that might kill you next year – so help yourself.

We might imagine something similar being the case with the Khoikhoin with the proviso that their vast cattle herds probably did constitute 'property' and were jealously guarded. The extent to which cattle were owned individually or whether they were owned collectively is a moot point. Bantu cultures, still far from the Cape at this time, featured both individual and collective aspects of ownership. A man might own any number of cattle while at the same time being required to tend the cattle of his chief, for which he gained the use of the milk in payment. Certainly, the Khoikhoin understood the seriousness of Herry's thieving and understood that retribution was likely to follow, yet at the same time it is possible to assume that they held similar attitudes to 'theft' that the Bushmen held. If you could take from the weak, that was fine and really not very different than hunting a buck out of a herd. Similarly, they understood the concept of territorial possession, if not the idea of land ownership, because they asserted their rights to grazing and pasture.

This was the cause of the second clash. Initially, the Khoikhoin had regarded the Dutch as temporary visitors and expected them to pack up and leave just as other ships' crews had done in the past but as time went on and the fort was built, crops planted and livestock put out to graze it began to dawn on them that something was different about these visitors; they were here to stay. In February 1655, this realisation had hardened into a determination that the Dutch were not going to be allowed to stay and threats were made by one clan known as the *Caepmen* (the Goringhaiquas), that unless the Dutch started making plans to go back over the sea, then the fort would be burned down, the trade goods stolen and Van Riebeeck's people killed by overwhelming forces brought in from the interior. Trouble was brewing and Van Riebeeck began to ask his masters in Holland for both reinforcements and permission to attack the Goringhaiquas.

In June of that year, Herry reappeared and with astonishing aplomb insisted that he had had nothing to do with theft and murder – perish the thought! – but it was really all the fault of the Goringhaiquas and that the Dutch should attack them forthwith. By this time, some of the Dutch had acquired a working knowledge of the Khoikhoin language (if only to chat up the women and barter for *dagga*) and vice-versa but Van Reibeeck was in desperate need of a more competent interpreter than a doped-up matelot with a vocabulary limited to pretty compliments and lewd requests and so, through gritted teeth, hired Herry back. This happy situation lasted until December when another Dutch speaking Khoikhoin, named by the Dutch Doman, arrived to break Herry's monopoly and imparted the news that Herry was indeed responsible for the crimes that he was accused of and, furthermore, was distrusted by both the Chocoquas and the Goringhaiquas, both of which clans were hoping to establish their own monopoly on the trade with the Dutch. It was also revealed that he was also a person of some status, with large livestock holdings somewhere in the interior (which van Riebeeck suspected had been bought with brass stolen from the Company). His cover blown, Herry decided to decamp once more only to reappear six months later demanding to be recognised as the paramount chief of all the Khoikhoin clans in the area. Once again, Van Riebeeck entertained him for the sake of trade's increase and once again, Herry broke the deal. Turning up like a bad penny once more, he reappeared in December, now in some sort of hostile alliance with the Goringhaiquas, and then decamped once more. The following year, he reappeared and proposed an attack on the Chocoquas but by then Van Riebeeck had understandably had it up to here with him.

While this charade was being played out, several important decisions regarding the settlement had been taken. The first was that it was to be expanded into a full colony; secondly that those VOC employees who so chose could apply to become free colonists – 'Freemen' or 'Burghers' - in the hope that by breeding cattle themselves dependence on the unreliable supplies of the Khoikhoin would be reduced; and thirdly, the colony was to be so fortified as to exclude the Khoikhoin clans from interference with the expanding orchards, crops and pasture. Thus, had attitudes hardened and conquest begun.

During the winter of 1657, Van Riebeeck sketched out a plan to confine Herry and his Goringhaiquas allies to the southern part of the Cape peninsular by establishing batteries across the flats from (roughly) Rondebosch to Muizenberg. This was thought to be a feasible plan because in those days Muizenberg was a crocodile and hippo infested swamp that no one would be foolish enough to drive cattle across, but like many other schemes to fortify the Cape and keep it separate from the interior, it was soon found to be unworkable. More importantly though, Van Riebeeck, now armed with a new, reliable interpreter named Eva, intended to get on with trading with the Chocoquas.

Eva, daughter or niece to Herry, had been brought up in Van Riebeeck's household and quickly blew the gaffe on Herry. For the first time, proper information about the people of the Cape became available; the Chocoquas were actually called the *Qeuna* and were made up of several separate clans, which included the *Charigrina, Chorachouqua* and *Chocona*; there was an 'overlord' for the Cape too, whose name was Chory – not Herry; to the North were the *Namana* clans, to the North East were the *Oengayqua*; and farther out to the East were the *Chobona*. Not only that, but Eva was able to give a fair picture of the relations between the various clans which revealed that there were several rivalries, some violent, and a very great fear of the Chobona – the Bantu, the Xhosa (possibly). She also revealed that Herry was telling all sorts of lies to the Chocoquas to prevent them from trading with the Dutch so that he could establish a monopoly. The knowledge that Eva imparted was knowledge that could be put to good use in building up trading relations but the tragedy was that it came too late. Relations had already deteriorated and attitudes had already hardened on both sides and poor Eva became the target of some scathing criticism from her fellow interpreter, Doman, for being disloyal to her people.

The immediate issues that brought things to a head were twofold. To begin with, in May 1658, the lifting of cattle by the Khoikhoin, then an attempted raid on the Company kraal ended in the dogs being set on Chainhantima, an important clan leader, and Van Riebeeck despairingly declaring 'that whenever they perceive any opportunity of injuring us, they do not suffer it to escape.' He wanted both the Company and the Burgher's cattle returned. The second was the issue of escaping slaves, a steady stream of whom took their chances with the climate, the geography, the lions and the Khoikhoin rather than spend their lives in humiliating servitude. The Dutch were convinced that the Khoikhoin were harbouring them or, according to Eva, enslaving them in their turn and demanded that the slaves be returned. When neither of these things were forthcoming, Van Riebeeck acted. In June 1658, the sons of the Caepman chief Gogosoa were seized and taken hostage.

Could this situation have been avoided? There are some reasons to believe that it might have been. Fraternisation between the Dutch and the Khoikhoin at the everyday level had already produced some forms of co-operation and the co-existence necessary for both sides. In June 1656, a mixed gang of Dutch and Khoikhoin had conspired to steal a quantity of cotton cloth from the Company, which suggests that there was both a community of interest, regular contact and routine communication (however criminal) on at least one level; pilfering of Company stores by both Khoikhoin and Dutch had been a problem from the beginning. By 1657, a vigorous (and illegal) trade in cattle had grown up between people discharged from the Company service - the Freemen - and the Khoikhoin which the VOC struggled to regulate and control and which built contacts still more. Some Khoikhoin were working, intermittently, as labourers for the Dutch. There had also been some co-operation in the matter of slaves escaping from the colony and, given that the Dutch population was small (144) and almost entirely male, and four years out from the fleshpots of Amsterdam, it seems reasonable to suppose that a certain amount of sexual tourism had been engaged in on both sides; no doubt under the watchful eye of Annetje de Boerin, landlady of Cape Town's first tavern. There had been no armed conflict as yet and Van Riebeeck went to great lengths to avoid taking offence at Herry's enormities in order to keep things this way.

On the whole though, these promising developments could not outweigh the forces that made conflict more likely. The settlement had been established to victual VOC ships and so far, it had signally failed to achieve its aim because the Khoikhoin would not trade the livestock required in sufficient quantities. This compelled the Dutch to provide their own supplies and this meant the occupation of land which the Khoikhoin regarded (however nebulously) as their own. Similarly, from the outset the Company had intended to occupy such land as was necessary for their purposes if the Khoikhoin could not be persuaded to co-operate and this, in the last analysis, meant dispossession at gun point. The issues of petty theft and cattle rustling meant that a bedrock of hostility and distrust was formed, which was routinely reinforced by Herry's behaviour. This latter point is important because what continually comes through from Van Riebeeck's journal is frustration at not being able to get any accurate picture of the real situation vis-à-vis the Khoikhoin and thus establish some satisfactory trading relations. Believing that control of such information made him powerful, Herry was exceedingly close at giving it out; it was not until 1658 that Van Riebeeck found out his real name of Autshumao and by this time fear of an attack from England or France had pushed the VOC into the decision to fortify the Cape and push the Khoikhoin off it.

Some writers have claimed that Doman the interpreter was the first indigenous South African resistance leader, a man of intelligence and perception who was outraged at the taking of Gogosoa's sons as hostages and so made a principled stand against this dreadful act of colonial, racist oppression but this just isn't borne out by the sources. Intelligent and perceptive, Doman very probably was; the Dutch had picked him out as a bright spark and invested a fair number of guilders in sending him all the way to Batavia to be educated and trained in their ways but was he really outraged at the taking of hostages? Only in so far as the hostages came from *his* clan; all the other clans could go hang. As soon as he was back at the Cape from Batavia he had pressed for an attack on one of the clans that had previously robbed and beaten the crew of a boat sent off to Saldanha Bay. The day after the hostages were taken, Doman was pressing that some of Herry's people should also be rounded up along with some of the Gorachouqua clan who had robbed a tobacco field. Some days later, Doman reported that the clans were quite willing to give up Herry as a hostage in return for the release of Gogosoa's boys – they had already returned several of the runaway slaves, probably on Doman's prompting. Not content with this bit of double-dealing, when Herry was tricked into appearing at the fort and duly incarcerated, Doman complained that he should have been executed on the spot. What Doman was doing was his own bit of *divide et imperia*; by taking the part of Gogosoa, whose clan he belonged to, against Eva, who was part of Herry's clan, he hoped to get Herry executed, thus leaving him to inherit the vacate slot of chief interpreter and broker because, of course, Eva was only a woman and the clan leaders would not be willing to accord her any sort of equal status. Some resistance leader; in October 1658, he proposed an attack on the Chocoquas clan, which was no more than a ruse to cement his position as chief broker, as Herry had done.

With Herry out of the way, Van Riebeeck was able to sit down and do the deal with the hugely corpulent Gogosoa – he was known as the 'Fat Captain' - and the Goringhaiquas that he so desired. In return for the release of the hostages, Gogosoa would trade livestock, keep his cattle out of the cornfields, help return runaway slaves in return for due payment and shelter under the walls of the fort if the Chocoquas threatened them. And, it was made clear, they would get 'powder and lead'[18] if any more attempts were made to lift Dutch cattle. Herry was finally brought to book for the murder of the herd boy and the lifting of the Company cattle by having his own herd confiscated, getting himself banged up on Robben Island and his people handed over to the authority of Gogosoa. A further boon was that the mutual antagonism of Eva and Doman allowed Van Riebeeck to finally get a better picture of things by interpreting their varying accounts.

For a little while there was a certain amount of co-operation but this soon fizzled out probably because Gogosoa's authority was probably nominal rather than absolute and also because Doman was up to his scheming tricks: 'The interpreter Doman like a rogue endeavours to thwart the Company in everything,' wrote Van Riebeeck. 'And is three times worse and more mischievous to the Company than Herry ever was.'[19] Slaves continued to desert, illegal trade continued between the Khoikhoin and the Freemen, petty theft remained a serious irritant, Doman continued to urge an attack on first one clan then another, while several other clans demanded that Van Riebeeck have Herry, now safely out of the way on Robben Island, executed - a request that however tempting to accede to was refused. Nor would Gogosoa abide by the terms of the deal done during the hostage crisis. By 1659, Van Riebeeck had had enough and under pressure from plundered Freemen, still worried about an English attack and frustrated by the lack of definite orders from Holland, the desertion of Doman and his involvement in a series of farm attacks along with the murder of a Freeman was the last straw: permission was given to shoot any Khoikhoin coming near to crops or cattle, a price put on Doman's head and a plan to take hostages put in motion.

> '…we had now borne the insolence of the Caepmans too long…and that God therefore allowed us, not only to offer all possible resistance, but to do them all the injury in our power, in order that, as they would not be influenced by kindness, they might be brought to a better understanding and behaviour by force.'[20]

Thus, did the First Cape Frontier War begin. Not that it was very much of a war at all and it wasn't recognised as a war at all by GM Theal, the first real historian of the early Cape. Though it lasted ten months, fewer than perhaps fifteen people were killed and despite attempts to paint it as a war of resistance, it was no such thing; the 16,000 strong Chocoquas clans led by Oedasoa, Eva's brother-in-law, and Ngonomoa were quite happy to see the Caepmen (Goringhaiquas) humbled, and after initially offering the Dutch an alliance stayed out of it, eager to play both ends against the middle; Herry was brought from Robben Island to peach on his people (and on being returned there, promptly stole a boat and escaped).

---

[18] Moodie, *The Record*. Van Riebeeck's Journal, July 18th 1658.
[19] Moodie, *The Record*. Van Riebeeck's Journal, Aug 26th 1658.
[20] Moodie, *The Record*. Van Riebeeck's Journal, May 20th 1659.

Doman, who had usurped Gogosoa's authority was shot through the lung and then reviled by the Caepmen for starting the war; he begged Eva and the Chocoquas to broker a peace for him; he was forgiven and returned to work as an interpreter. Herry turned up again too and was duly forgiven. Van Riebeeck didn't get much credit from his bosses though and was told in no uncertain terms that his job was to grow crops and provide cattle for the Company ships and not get mixed up in irritating and expensive wars.

Much was solved; a lasting peace was achieved and a certain *modus vivendi* worked out; the Khoikhoin grudgingly accepted that the Dutch were here to stay and the Dutch accepted that the best way to achieve their ends was to avoid giving any excuse for war to break out again; although they finally got some horses to form a mounted troop, the Dutch were still hopelessly outnumbered. Word of the conflict and subsequent peace spread into the interior and more and more clans began to contact the Fort with a view to trade; the beads, brass, copper wire, iron bar and tobacco were flying off the shelves. Oedasoa of the Chocoquas thought to do exactly what Herry, Gogosoa and Doman had done - establish a monopoly of trade with the Dutch in return for help against his enemies, this time sweetening the proposal with the offer to supply slaves, but the Dutch stuck to the principle of trading on friendly terms with anyone who could bring them cattle, sheep, ostrich, feathers, hides and – from Monomatapa – gold and diamonds. Generally speaking, relations between the Europeans and the Khoisan were very good; of the fifty criminal convictions in the ten years of Van Riebeeck's posting, none involved violence between the two peoples[21] although everyone knew that, out of sight of the authorities, the settlers would defend themselves and their property when necessary.

The most tangible result of the war was a determination on the part of the Dutch to properly fortify the Cape against the Khoikhoin as well as the English. A small part of this fortification can still be seen in the botanical gardens at Kirstenbosch today; Van Riebeeck's famous almond hedge, which he left behind when he went back to Holland, exhausted and eager to shake South Africa's dust from his heels. It was decided upon because a scheme to dig a canal across the peninsular and turn it into an island was reckoned to be impractical.

In 1899, Cecil Rhodes paid for a statue of Van Riebeeck to be erected in Adderley Street in Cape Town and in 1952 the Portuguese and Dutch governments respectively contributed statues of Bartholomew Diaz and Mrs Van Riebeeck to mark the city's tercentenary celebrations. Under Apartheid, Van Riebeeck's landing at the Cape was celebrated as a public holiday and from 1980 it was also known as 'Founder's Day'. Although we have to accept that his arrival does actually mark the beginning of South African History and Cape Town is still widely referred to as the Mother City, to claim him as the Founder of all things South African, it has to be said, is over-egging the omelette and it was perfectly reasonable for the post-Apartheid government to get rid of that particular holiday. So far, they haven't pulled down any of these statues – unlike the one of Rhodes situated at the university that was built on the land he granted to it.

---

[21] Moodie, *The Record* p. 220.

So, what can we say about van Riebeeck? In August 1660 came the news that he was to be relieved of command which, judging from the tone of the despatch, was pretty much the sack – though it is unlikely that Van Riebeeck was particularly disturbed by this welcome redeployment. In the event, he had to wait another two years because his successor died on the voyage out. More than three centuries later, I can still hear him grinding his teeth. From the point of view of his mission, he had done pretty well in establishing a viable victualling and trading post, had introduced plenty of new crops, built up a reasonably good picture of the clans in the immediate vicinity and navigated their politics. Although there had been conflict, he had kept it within bounds and when war had broken out, he had brokered a peace just as soon as he possibly could. His greatest failing, in the eyes of his cavilling employers, was that he had failed to discover Monomatapa, a city that didn't exist.

What can we say about the longer term impact of his arrival? This is obviously more complex; as a young man I travelled to India in the company of a very irritating girlfriend and while eagerly drinking in the sights and smells of that remarkable country, I mused openly on what the impact of British imperialism on the country had been. (Answer: some good, some bad but mostly positive, all in all, of course, *probably*). 'We shouldn't have been there in the first place,' was her acid response. 'Wouldn't they have been far, *far* better off without our involvement?' The complexities of three centuries of contact were thus dismissed in 140 characters or less (and before *Twitter* had even been invented) but translate the question into the context of South Africa and it is deserving of an answer; would South Africa have been better off without Van Riebeeck pitching up and planting his almond hedge? President Jacob Zuma thought so when in January 2015 at the African National Congress's 103rd Anniversary bash he declared that Van Riebeeck's arrival was the start of all South Africa's problems.[22]

It is, of course, a deeply stupid question on so many levels that you would need an elevator to visit them all (sometimes it feels like a paternoster) but as the world is daily subjected to utterances of profound stupidity from those supposedly clever people in academia, the media and government, I'll make an attempt to answer it; no. Firstly, without the establishment of a victualling station at the Cape it is doubtful if contact between East and West could have been carried on, given the existing state of naval technology; so, no spice trade, no ceramic trade, no cultural contact and the triumph of a profound ignorance about the world to the detriment of all. Secondly, at about the same time as Van Riebeeck was pointing his matchlock muskets at the Khoikhoin, Jacob Zuma's Bantu ancestors were sticking assegais into them and booting them off the best grazing land in the area now known as the Transkei, having already so shifted them out of KwaZulu-Natal so one might equally say that the problems of South Africa begin with the arrival of the Bantu rather than the arrival of the Dutch. Zuma is a Zulu but we can't say that the problems started with the Zulus because there were no Zulus until Shaka formed that nation circa 150 years after Van Riebeeck schlepped ashore – so actually, the Dutch have a better claim to ownership of the Cape than any black people. Thirdly, *it happened* and there's no undoing all the historical hares that were set running by the event. Just as it is pointless to cry over spilt milk so is it unproductive to pin the blame for your present problems on something that happened in the deep, dark, distant past. Back

---

[22] http://ewn.co.za/2015/02/19/Zuma-reiterates-SAs-problems-began-with-van-Riebeeck

in the 1980s, the UK Monster Raving Looney Party stood on a platform of 'Repatriate the Normans'; it has about the same intellectual worth as President Zuma's remarks. There is no straight line of development between the Dutch arrival and the present state of South Africa; you can only discern one by looking backwards and tooled up to the teeth with the inestimable benefit of hindsight; in reality, the present is formed by accident, cock-up and the Law of Unintended Consequences as much as it is by deliberate intent. And Van Riebeeck had no such intent. He intended to set up a victualling station; both he and his bosses in Holland would have been horrified at the prospect of embarking on some latter-day anabasis. There were three centuries between the arrival of the Dutch and the establishment of Apartheid and it is just fanciful to imagine that from the fact of a ship bumping the shoreline, it was an inevitable consequence that Nelson Mandela and Jacob Zuma would end up banged up on Robben Island pondering their connection with a fellow convict called Herry who was as different in race, language and culture to them as he was to the Dutch.

Fourthly, I'm writing this bit sitting under bougainvillea on a wine farm outside Paarl, half-cut with an excellent cabernet-shiraz after having arrived in this excellent country on that marvel of modern physics known as a jet plane, then driving here in a chariot powered by the internal combustion engine up a tarmac road lit via a bloody good steak, chips, mushrooms, onion rings with a starter of pork liver pâté, bread and butter, followed by ice cream and liqueur coffee served up by Zimbabwean waiters in a fantastic bar constructed from brick and concrete, lit by electricity and cooled by air-conditioning, with free Wi-Fi, great blues music and paid for by a credit card. None of these good things - excepting some of the labour - derives from indigenous South Africa; even the beef and milk has been improved beyond all recognition by Aberdeen Angus and Louis Pasteur while that great staple of African life, the mealie/maize/Indian corn, is an American import by way of Europe. And the Zimbabweans are only there because Mugabe threw the European farmers out of his country and thereby ruined it. If this seems a bit elitist to you, then I might also refer you to the Fisherman's Bar in St. Lucia up in KwaZulu-Natal; it's the sort of place that probably isn't covered by your travel insurance but it does do fish and chips, chicken and chips, curry and Jaeger bombs and owes just as much to indigenous South Africa as that swanky place in Stellenbosch, i.e., nothing.

Fifthly and finally, without going into a complete repeat of the Monty Python sketch *'What have the Romans ever done for us?'* I might just point out that, if you are a black South African, you wouldn't be reading this had it not been for the arrival of the Europeans because the Bantu had not developed a written language. South Africa, my dear, irritating ex-girlfriend, is a product not of one race or culture, but of *all* of them and it will be immeasurably diminished if one of them is lost; and van Riebeeck deserves credit for his part in making it so.

\*

The Dutch Colony.

It would appear from your letters, that you are about to found and establish a city at the Cape, and to lay yourselves out for the extension of the Colony; but according to the views we entertain here, you may dismiss such ideas out of your minds, and proceed with the garrison and free men whom you now have, without any further increase ; for of what use would a large Colony there be to us if we must always support it from abroad; besides, the men are more useful to us in India, you will therefore, as we have often directed, keep all upon a reduced scale, which will be the most satisfactory to us.

*Extract of a Despatch from Chamber XVII to Commander G. Van Harn and Council. Aug 23rd 1661.*[23]

The Hottentots have always been looked upon as very savage men, without any knowledge, but we greatly suspect this to be a mistake, for, in our opinion, they are very arrogant, equal to our common people in natural understanding and more circumspect...needless disputes with them will be of no service to the Company, for they can do more harm to our inhabitants than we can do to them.

*Governor QuaelBergen to Chamber XVII, 20th Jan 1688.*[24]

I'm accusing the Left of creating a false, politically correct narrative of History so I should explain what this means. I first heard the phrase back in the 1970s but it wasn't until I did my teacher training in Multicultural Education at Reading University at the end of the 1980s that it smacked me in the intellect right proper. The basic principle establishes a set of alternatives which are assumed to be fixed in a permanent relationship of conflict. These alternatives are Black/White, Female/Male, Poor/Rich, Gay/Straight, Disabled/Able-bodied and the assumption is that the alternative to the left of the divide is virtuous, on the side of the Angels and more 'correct' than the alternative on the right-hand side. The academic term for this is 'intersectionality' – if, indeed, this nonsense actually deserves an 'academic' term. So, in a dispute between Black and White, the assumption is that Black is right and White is wrong and so on. That this provides a rich seam of satire is obvious – the Poor, Black, Disabled, Lesbian is something of a trump card in any dispute – just as is the potential for ludicrous contradictions – is Black Male Idi Amin more virtuous than White Female Mother Theresa? Now that 'Black' has morphed into BAME (Black and Minority Ethnic) and gone global, the absurdities have multiplied; BAME make up about 84% of the world's population, yet they are still, apparently a minority.

Another one of the surprising things that I learned in Reading University School of Education, that august abode of intellectual giants, was that despite the fact that I had once been a member of the Anti-Nazi League and had managed to rub along fairly well with acquaintances from backgrounds, races and countries diverse, as a white man I was a racist; even if I didn't think I was and had never given anyone cause to think I was since I mistakenly mistook Tenny Sullivan for a Zulu when I was nine years old (he was West

---

[23] Moodie, *The Record.*
[24] Moodie, *The Record.*

Indian, I think), still I was one; it was imprinted in my culture and, sorry, but there was nothing I could do about it; anything I did, wrote or said was, therefore, tainted by racism and clearly suspect, a load of old tosh (unless of course, I was spouting some old tosh that the Left agreed with) and patently untrue. Remarkable though it is, this sort of attitude is centrally embedded in the tenets of the Left and a real live prism through which they interpret History.

The concept is the bastard child of what Marxists call 'false consciousness'. If you are foolish enough to think that summary executions at the hands of a wealthy psychopathic playboy like Che Guevara, sixty million victims of starvation brought about by a Chinese megalomaniac like Mao or incarceration in one of Stalin's Arctic Gulags is a price that is a bit on the high side for the promise of a socialist Utopia possibly to be achieved sometime in the next few decades hence (ETA tbc) then you are suffering from *false consciousness*. You are, in effect, suffering from a mental illness because you don't agree with the Marxists. Political correctness is the antidote to that illness because it lays out an easy to follow framework for even the dimmest denizen of the Socialist Workers' Re-education Camp. If in any doubt, or in need of any facts – actually, you really don't need facts, assumptions will do – go with the alternative on the left of the equation. So, if the cop shoots the criminal, whether the cop is right to do so depends on whether that cop is White (he's wrong), whether the criminal is poor (he's wrong) or female (he's wrong) much more than whether the criminal is packing a bazooka and carrying a bag over her shoulder clearly marked 'Swag'.

In truth, in African History political correctness is horribly common and in general it means that there is a presumption that Black Africans are always right and White colonists are always wrong; even when *they are not*. That the divide has always been Black and White; *it is not*. That Black Africans are always the victims, even when they are not – *and they are not*; from the diplomatic wheeler-dealing that the Saldanian clan leader Oedisoa engaged in to try to persuade the Dutch to help him against his enemies, right through to the sharp operators of the ANC in exile, Black Africans were active and vigorous actors in this great centuries' long drama. Sometimes they lost and sometimes they won; sometimes they were admirable and sometimes they were not; but poor, helpless victims is the last thing they were. (Just so that you don't get tied up too much in the strangling illogic of this Marxist nonsense, I recommend that you keep Robert Mugabe in mind for the next couple of chapters; OK, he's not South African but he is black and he'll do until we meet absolute bastards like Shaka, Dingane and Mzilikazi. These are not people that you would willingly invite round for dinner). And the manufacture of this victim narrative isn't funny because it builds up an intellectual environment which allows influential media such as the Huffington Post, South Africa, to publish articles entitled *Could it be time to deny white men the vote?*[25] What about Jews while we're at it? My blood pressure has just gone up and if yours hasn't, it should have.

*

---

[25] http://www.huffingtonpost.co.za/shelley-garland/could-it-be-time-to-deny-white-men-the-franchise_a_22036640/ April 13, 2007.

Van Riebeeck's almond hedge was intended to mark off a specific bit of territory for the use of the VOC. It's worth reiterating here that the face of the colony was set firmly seawards rather than gazing avariciously inland and that the priority was always to service the ships going to and from the East. The continent was the unknown, the outback, the bush, an inconvenient if not insignificant fact but one that the VOC fervently hoped might be ignored – 'the soup… was not worth the cabbage'[26] - as long as there was enough trade and food to supply themselves and the fleet and as long as reasonably civil relations with the Khoikhoin clans could be maintained.  Thus, the almond hedge; nothing more than a large cattle enclosure that the Khoikhoin couldn't steal from and not at all a fortified beachhead preparing for a breakout; indeed, the Goringhaiquas were permitted back inside it within a year. The VOC was in business and the last thing it wanted was the expense of conquest and the further expensive responsibilities of government.  Van Riebeeck's successor was expressly warned against any colonial project that went beyond supplying the needs of the ships.[27]

The Company was to be disappointed. Right from the beginning, there were those among the colonists who saw opportunities in the hinterland, even if they underestimated the difficulties that they might face. Runaway slaves were the most likely to head for those distant pumice-blue hills, but the first attempt was made by the hapless Jan Blank and his mates who in September 1652 decided that they had had enough of the Cape and resolved to walk to Mozambique but, upon being chased by a Rhinoceros, thought better of it; he was keelhauled and got two years in irons for desertion; (and on being given remission a year later for good behaviour this criminal mastermind took to stealing the Company's cattle; just how he thought he wouldn't be found out in a community that small beggars belief; the punishment was to be dropped off the yardarm tied to a rope, a process which resulted in certain dislocation of the shoulders – then back in irons). The Freemen, mainly farmers of an independent attitude, saw the fertility of the land just over Table Mountain and reckoned that there was enough there for a hundred families with room left over for the Khoikhoin herds. This was, as we have seen, disputed but the temptations of open land, for most of the year deserted, were too great and it was not unreasonable for the Dutch to claim in justification that their need was great, the country wide and accommodation in this matter eminently possible.

When the word spread to the passing ships that there was an abundance of apparently unoccupied fertile land, the number of Freemen began to increase, encouraged by the Company through the pretty free grant of land on condition that they traded with the Company and the Company alone; all trade was supposed to go through the castle despite this being neither practical, desirable or enforceable. As might be expected, as the number of colonists increased, the number of disputes over Khoikhoin petty theft increased accordingly, leading the Freemen to demand protection from the Company or, if this was not forthcoming, the right to defend themselves; there had already been incidents where they had taken the law into their own hands.

---

[26] Moodie, *The Record*, Joan Maetsuyker to Van Riebeeck, 25 Dec 1655.
[27] Moodie, *The Record*, Chamber XVII to Van Harn, 23rd Aug 1661.

Acutely aware of the need for the food supplies that the Freemen provided and feeling for his fellow colonists, Van Riebeeck early on began to ask for troops to protect them and thus was caught between a boom spiral and a vicious circle; the more that food was abundantly provided, the more ships would call at the Cape and demand would soar – by 1660 already, 1,000 cattle were required annually. More Freemen and more land would then be needed to meet this demand and thus would there be more demand for the necessary functions of government – coinage, justice, property deeds and defence against the depredations of the Khoikhoin. There was also the desire to find out about the country that would lead the VOC to send off various expeditions about the coastlines and into the interior with varying degrees of success; in November 1660, one set out for the mythical city of Monomatapa, accompanied by Doman, eager to make amends for his rebellion. The expedition failed after one of the principals, Jan van Meerhof, was kicked by a quagga. (He seems to have been jinxed. On an expedition in March 1661, his musket exploded just as he was trying to shoot an angry hippo and he counted himself lucky to get off with just a broken thumb, as well he might. Hippos are bloody dangerous; fortunately, like Daleks, they can't climb steps, which was a relief the night they turned up to drink out of the swimming pool at my guesthouse in St. Lucía, I can tell you). Furthermore, the demand for more sheep and cattle made it necessary to go further into the interior and by 1666, trading expeditions were going over what is now Sir Lowry's Pass and into the Caledon area. Two years later, the Company was landing traders at Mossel Bay. On top of that, Freemen hunters were licensed to bring in the game that was plentiful but too sharp to come within musket shot. All these things conspired to pull the colonists into the interior.

By the time that Governor Simon van der Stel arrived in 1679, there was still only speculative knowledge of the coastline beyond present day George and tales of fabulous cities like Monomatapa and Vigiti Magna, deep rivers and great civilisations slavering to trade with the Dutch were still given enough credence to allow expeditions to be sent out in search of them; the Orange River was yet to be discovered, despite having been sailed past on any number of occasions. Northwards, anything beyond the Olifants River, which runs roughly SE from Strandfontein, Clanwilliam and Citrusdal, was something of a mystery too, although the coastline was better known.

There were other developments drawing the colonists outward too. A number of the colonists applied to marry their slaves who, on being emancipated, were duly wed. Families began to arrive with a view to permanent settlement. Eva, who seemed equally at home among the Dutch as among the Khoikhoin (and wasn't above a few of Herry's tricks) married Pieter Van Meerhof, brother to thumb-less Jan. We cannot know how many runaway slaves, Dutch Freemen or other European arrivals married Khoikhoin partners because the records were both scant and progressively worse kept the further away from the Cape one went, but it seems likely that right from the beginning there was some mixing. Also, Khoikhoin were increasingly employed by the Freemen whether or not the Company liked it, while the necessary and inevitable and illegal trade relations created further bonds. Some free Burghers began to assess their interests as being more aligned to the Khoikhoin than with the Company to the extent that the closely guarded secrets of musketry were betrayed to them and aid given to them during the First Frontier War.[28] Others found life as an independent farmer in conditions of drought, Company restrictions, crushing debt and short commons just too onerous and wanted the way out provided by that wide horizon. What was more, the further the Freemen went into the interior, the less control the Company had over them and the more the independent Burghers penetrated inland, the more clans came into contact with them and the opportunities for illegal trade, conflict, theft, retaliation and escalation increased accordingly. Given the weakness of the clan chiefs' authority to restrain Khoikhoin behaviour, a situation of lawlessness was almost guaranteed, especially as war between the different clans seemed to be a frequent and, to the Dutch, a bewildering occurrence.

There was no frenetic land grab or orgy of dispossession however. For a start there weren't enough colonists to do the grabbing; twenty years after the colony was founded there were still less than a hundred settlers and it took them twenty-seven years to get as far as Stellenbosch and another twenty-three to settle Simonstown. Neither of these places are above an hour's drive from the Cape Town waterfront, even in traffic. By 1700, the furthest settlement was at Waveren, now known as Tulbagh and today an hour and a half's drive away up the Berg River; so according to that unimpeachable source, the Tulbagh Tourist Info, when Pieter Potter stumbled through the narrow crack in the mountains by the Little Berg River in 1658, it still took another forty years before the land was settled, another forty before this most religious of people had enough spare pelf to build a church, another fifty after that to build a decent one and all those beautiful Cape Dutch houses weren't built until 1807, extended fifty years after that and then re-built in 1969 after an earthquake. It took until 1734 before claim was laid to Mossel Bay, which gives a rate of expansion of roughly 5 km per year. So much for a land grab; expansion was positively glacial.

Much of the land was purchased not conquered and although it is probable that there was a fair amount of encroachment and sharp practice involved in the process, it isn't fair to assume that the Khoikhoin were always cheated or robbed of their land; when in 1672, Gogosoa's son and recognised overlord of the Cape Khoikhoin, agreed to sell the land already occupied by the settlers, he was in theory paid £800 but in reality, was bilked out of all but a few quid,[29] but this was land that they had already lost by right of conquest and to which Gogosoa's claims were, at best, tenuous. For one thing, we would have to assume the Khoikhoin to be extraordinarily stupid not to spot a bent deal when, if anything, they had proved themselves to be effective traders – the price they got for their cattle increased three-fold in the first five years - and understood the reality that when pasturage went under the plough it was gone forever. The negotiations at the end of the First Frontier War showed that they also understood the Dutch concept of property rights, of ownership by right of conquest and if there was a certain amount of mutual incomprehension (Dutchman: *They trade land for beads and a bit of copper wire? Incredible....* Khoikhoin: *They grow grass in rows and eat it? Madness....*') there can be no doubt that the Khoikhoin knew what they were doing. It is also the case that they still vastly outnumbered the Dutch if it came to another war and the Dutch had no illusions about either of these things. Cape Town should more properly be known as

---

[28] Moodie, *The Record*, Van Riebeeck's Journal, 4th July 1660.
[29] Theal, *History and Ethnography* Vol II, p.200.

'Cape Village' because fifty years after its founding it could still boast fewer than a thousand residents (and was still officially known as the Castle of Good Hope).

Indeed, it's also possible to see these as smiling years; much more Breughel than Bosch at any rate. The first apples, the first cherries, olives, grapes, roses.... The Khoikhoin had early on acquired a liking for bread, cheese and sugar while wine made a welcome change to *dagga*; tobacco was already known but the Dutch were keen to supply plenty of what was then seen as both a medical benefit and a recreational boon. There was work for wages if and when they wanted it (money or in kind, usually tobacco; young girls were sent into domestic service in such numbers that the need for interpreters rapidly diminished), rising prices for their livestock, a ready supply of the metal goods that they prized so highly that it was not unknown for them to steal a boat and burn it just to get at the nails. Provided they did not trample the crops and remained on the thoroughfares, they were welcome to go where they liked with their cattle and as long as they refrained from stealing the colonists' cattle – admittedly something they found difficult to resist – there was little reason for conflict. Becoming subject to the Dutch law, they also benefitted from its protections – in 1672 Willem Willems was arraigned for the murder of of a Khoikhoin promptly escaped custody and then reappeared from Holland with a pardon apparently signed by the Prince of Orange (in the meantime his wife had managed to get pregnant by another man and so he was sent to Robben Island to prevent him doing harm to her); in 1674, Mayke van der Berg was flogged and branded for her second offence of stealing Khoisan cattle (a real criminal mastermind this one; she was also a fence for which she was branded once more); in 1707 Jan Dirks was tortured into confessing to the murder of a Khoikhoin named Lapjie; the Company simply would not tolerate the infliction of routine brutality on valuable workers. There was also the introduction of a basic system for looking after orphans which seemed to be open to anyone and funded by charitable donations and government levy; it was so well-funded that it went into the banking business offering mortgages on land at the very decent interest rate of 6%. The Khoikhoin lost their valuable pasturage in the immediate surrounds of Table Mountain but there was still plenty of it left and their grazing grounds beyond the still impregnable barrier of the enclosing mountains remained intact. Just how little they had lost can be ascertained by the fact that beyond the foot of Table Mountain there were only two tiny outposts, one at Saldanha Bay with its glorious, turquoise lagoon and warm Caribbean-like waters, the other a farm in the area of Hottentots Holland (now Kuils River, just north of the Khayelitsha shanty), and one cattle station at the Tygerberg (now a suburb of Cape Town), plus seven farms beyond the isthmus.

Again, the picture is mixed though; after the death of her husband, Eva seems to have succumbed to the debilitation of alcohol so noticeable in indigenous populations that lack a genetic resistance to the worst of its effects and which is still prevalent in the mixed-race populations of the Cape – drunkenness, foetal alcohol syndrome and all the problems that go with it remains a major problem today. Reprimanded on several occasions for licentious behaviour and bouncing between her Dutch and Khoikhoin relatives, she was sent to dry out on Robben Island on several occasions and deprived of her much-neglected children. Theal thought her case was important because up to that point there was little race discrimination in the colony (Governor van der Stel was the Eurasian son of an Indian slave girl) and the adoption of Christianity was the point at which 'them' became 'us'. This idea is supported by the curious case of the Hottentot girl who committed suicide in 1672 and thus sparked a legal case to decide whether she was a heathen or a Christian and thus subject to Christian practices. The court decided she was Christian because she had been brought up in a Dutch household, lived according to Dutch customs and had taken a number of Dutch lovers; the sentence was for her body to be hanged on a gibbet for the crime of suicide. Eva's example, Theal concluded, led the then Governor, to posit the idea that there was some hereditary resistance to 'civilisation' in the Khoikhoin population and that a longer exposure to that civilisation would be required before they could be expected to fit in with European ways – Eva's daughter married a well-to-do farmer but her son seemed to have inherited her alcoholism. That said, it is still reasonable to describe the Dutch colony as an island of relative peace and prosperity, a refuge for those Khoikhoin fleeing widespread internecine war in the interior in which the necessities (and some luxuries) of life were reasonably certain of attainment and doubly fortunate to avoid being visited by the wars in Europe which for a Dutchman in this period included three Anglo-Dutch wars and the Nine Year's War against France. The face of the colony was still set firmly seawards, work on the castle began and ceased according to politics in Europe rather than the Cape and it was no threat to anyone as long as the Dutch were allowed to service the ships, which makes it all the sadder that the Cochoqua clan leader, Ngonomoa, decided to embark on a second Frontier War.

This second war had been brewing for some time. Ngonomoa had long been identified as an accomplice of Herry's in the theft of the Company's cattle back in 1653 and twenty years later was suspected of the murder of two Burghers out on an expedition to the north. There had also been a spate of muggings and robberies of Burghers by Khoikhoin which resulted in the arrest, flogging, branding and incarceration on Robben Island of five miscreants. On top of this, in 1672 negotiations with Dackgy (aka Captain Cuyper) had resulted in the ceding of much of False Bay and the Hottentots Holland where it was hoped to establish respectively, an alternative anchorage at Simonstown against the NW gales and more arable farms. It is not entirely clear that Dackgy had the authority to do this but with the interior convulsed by a series of internecine wars, there was no-one to stop him. It is also the case that by October 1672, the Company was in contact with Khoisan clans as far inland as Bot River with whom Ngonomoa was at war. This appeared to further heighten Ngonomoa's long-hostile attitude and shortly afterwards a party of hunters were robbed by his men and threatened with murder, which only increased the determination of the Company to settle his hash as soon as the proper opportunity arose. In July 1673, that opportunity arose when Ngonomoa's people killed four soldiers at Saldanha Bay and plundered the Company's goods; a separate party of eight Burghers and a slave were also attacked and killed. The response was swift and a raid on his kraals in the Winterhoek area netted 800 cattle and 900 sheep while the following year, a similar expedition mounted with the aid of 250 Khoikhoin brought in another 800 cattle and 4000 sheep. Ngonomoa attempted to make good his losses in livestock by raiding loyal Khoikhoin kraals in March 1676 but was caught out again in November 1676, only escaping by splitting his clan up into small parties and flying into the mountains.

Like the first war, it can hardly qualify as a 'war of resistance' mainly because most of the local clans fought against Ngonomoa; there had been a subtle shift in the relations between the Company and the Cape clans and more and more, they were working *for* the Company, herding *Company* sheep as well as their own livestock and doing rather well out of it too; within ten years, they were able to supply 500 sheep at the drop of a hat. I find it hard to think of Ngonomoa's war as anything more than short-sighted stupidity; his only musket was repossessed before the war; he had no allies worth the name but plenty of enemies among the Namaquas and the other clans; his only advantage – mobility – had been negated by the Dutch employment of cavalry and he was caught out and defeated in the same place twice. The reality is that he was regarded as a minor nuisance, an inconvenience rather than a threat and by 1676 the Company was looking to find a way to end hostilities, make safe the roads and get the cattle trade going again. In June 1677 a peace was patched up and the Dutch could get on with bringing in cattle from the most important clans who were now to be found in the area now known as Swellendam, beyond the mountain barrier.

This process brought about another subtle shift in the relationship of the Company with the Khoisan. Prompted by the constant petty warfare in the Overberg, Sergeant Visser was despatched in July 1677 on a mission to arbitrate and adjudicate the disputes and so bring about the peace so necessary to the cattle trade. Combined with the declaration of October 1677 that the Berg River was the furthest limit that a Burgher might travel to without permission – effectively the establishment of a border – the increasing willingness to punish Khoisan accused of violence or robbery directly rather than hand them over to their chiefs for justice and, not least, the admission that much robbery was due to hunger and so to provide relief in the form of employment on public works, meant that the Company was beginning to look like an overlord. It was even issuing staffs marked with the Company arms to those chiefs deemed to be in alliance, but in reality, in subordination to it. Within a very few years, it *was* the overlord.

\*

> This place of refreshment for shipping is esteemed of the greatest importance to the Company, and the directors have been induced to construct a new castle, which, after three years hard labour, has been nearly finished.... And as this great castle has been built, it has become highly necessary, now still more than before, and is a matter of course, that a good Dutch colony shall be planted and reared here....
>
> *Extracts of Memorandum for the information of Governor Bax 16$^{th}$ March 1676.* Moodie, *The Record.*

It appears by the account books of this Cape that subsequently to the instructions left here by the present Governor General, Mr. Ryckloff van Goens, in 1657, the Colony has cost the Company an expence—after deduction of all the profits—of $f1,005,207$ 14 10 of which sum the expences of the shipping only constitute $f451,971$ 14 9; but if to this we were to add the materials, and the wages of Company's servants, it would amount to a sum which would almost exceed the bounds of credibility. It naturally follows, from this short statement, that it is now full time to think of the means by which the Company's affairs may be henceforth carried on with the smallest expense, the shipping being still properly supplied, and how the Colony may be, at the same time, extended with greater profit, and with a greater population.

*Memorandum for Commander Simon van der Stell and Council, &c. 16th March 1681.* Moodie, *The Record.*

Simon van der Stel, Governor 1679-99, was the first colonist in the sense that we understand it today. When he arrived at the Cape he came with the idea of turning the tiny settlement into a second Holland rather than simply improving its nature as a way station on the route to India and it seems that from the outset, he intended to live and die there rather than do his time and move on to some other post, preferably in the East, where pickings were somewhat less slim. What motivated him is difficult to say; he might have gleaned some concept of replicating the colonial system of the ancient Greeks from a liberal education, or perhaps his model was the English plantations of Virginia; he might also have been inspired by the remarkable scheme, floated at the time when Louis XIV looked set to conquer the Netherlands, for 200,000 Dutch to be shipped out to Batavia to found an entirely New Holland. Later on, his motivations became increasingly pecuniary as the insecurities of old age began to bite; he had married money but had little of his own. Early on there might also have been something rather more prosaic at work; his sons accompanied him to the Cape, his wife did not, raising the prospect that his real drive emanated from an unhappy home life and a chance to start afresh.

Theal described him as being witty, good company, possessed of bags of good sense, but also intensely and perhaps blindingly patriotic. For him, what was Dutch was good and what wasn't wasn't and van der Stel therefore set out to import Dutch laws, language, customs and institutions wholesale and, after a brief survey of the Company possessions convinced him that the land was suitable for extensive settlement, cultivation and civilisation, promptly put his plans in motion. Eight families were given *carte blanche* to carve out farms as big as they could work anywhere in the Stellenbosch valley (he named it for himself; Simons Bay followed) and given various tax incentives to start growing corn and breeding cattle; freeholds replaced the onerous terms of previous grants that disincentivised farm improvements; Government officers were incentivised to stay in the colony through similarly generous grants; sailors and passengers on board ships that called in were seduced with promises of land on easy terms while marriageable women were requested from Amsterdam 'for the solace of [the] cares' of 'the strong, gallant, and industrious bachelors'.[30] Forty-eight took the bait. Even so, despite free passages, the offer of farms and a discounted return if after a few years of residence in the colony they found it was not for them, only a trickle took up the offer. Nor could very many of the persecuted French Huguenots, penniless often and with no other prospects, be persuaded to accept what was on offer (which was pretty good;

---

[30] Extract of a Despatch from Commander Simon van der Stell and Council to the Chamber XVII, 6th Feb 1685. Moodie p.394.

Drakenstein and Franschoek, perhaps the prettiest valley in Africa fell to them). Those that did come totalled not much more than fifty or sixty families; in truth van der Stel didn't think much of them, being French, and in many cases, the feeling was mutual.

Within three or four years, the experiment in growing grain at Stellenbosch was enough of a success for the colony to start exporting wheat but the fertility of the Cape soil had always been over-estimated and it was quickly realised that more farms and more colonists were needed. In 1687 farms were laid out in the Drakenstein area for the first time and plans were advanced to spread up the Berg River as far as Saldanha Bay, purchasing the land from the increasingly co-opted and absorbed Cape Khoikhoin. They in turn were becoming ever more dependent on the Dutch as the Overberg Khoikhoin became the main suppliers of cattle and their own herds declined with the loss of pasture and the fondness for tobacco and arrack; by 1700, it was the Dutch who decided who should be the clan leaders, the Dutch who dispensed justice as the paramount authority and the Dutch who acted as arbiters in the constant petty warfare both within and without the boundaries of the colony.

Similarly, as the VOC's meat requirements rose steadily to something in the region of 3-4000 sheep annually, the decision was taken to reduce further the reliance on the intermittent Khoikhoin supplies by allowing the Freemen to engage in the cattle trade. Furthermore, under the threat of the war in Europe the VOC had been forced to concede a certain amount of power to the Freemen, now increasingly known as 'Burghers'. In return for agreeing to serve in the militia, the Burghers got a say in the administration of the colony by occupying positions in a *Krysgraad* (Council of War), the High Court, a Heemraad for the settlement of civil disputes, and other administrative bodies. Van der Stel also established a sub-governorship, the *Llandrost,* at Stellenbosch which became the model for the government of the Cape up to and beyond the British occupation a century later. This was important because although the ultimate authority remained with the VOC, the *interests* of the VOC and the Burghers were not always aligned.

Van der Stel was also the first Governor whose primary view was not seaward. His gaze was fixed firmly north and eastwards and in August 1685 he fitted out the most extensive expedition for exploration yet mounted. Gone were any ideas of sending out a few adventurers equipped only with a couple of pack oxen, vague instructions and great expectations; van der Stel's odyssey required twenty-four wagons and carts, several hundred dray and pack oxen, horses, two cannons and a collapsible boat. With him went Burghers, soldiers, mixed race drivers, slaves, Khoikhoin interpreters a little over a hundred strong all told, and his aim was to finally nail the question of whether the great city of Vigiti Magna really did exist up beyond Namaqualand. Luck was with him (considering his terrible Longitudes; 37º would put him in Swaziland rather than Namaqualand) because a long drought had recently ended, the rivers and *vleis* were full and good progress was made beyond the Olifants River and good contacts made among the Namaqualand peoples; Vigiti Magna was finally dismissed as the fairy tale it was, but in honour of the longevity of the fantasy, van der Stel named the river that he found after it. Later the name would morph into the 'Great River' and then finally the name by which it is known today, the Orange, after the colour of the silt it carries as much as the Dutch royal house. (Colonel Gordon named it the 'Orange' in 1779; chances are that this will be renamed the Gariep, or possibly Senqu, or even IGqili, at some time in the near future because 'Orange' is apparently a symbol of colonial subjugation, rather than a convenient and descriptive term understood by all South Africans). By the end of November, the expedition had reached the sea at Hondeklip Bay and then spent the next three weeks attempting to push further northwards but by then the terrible heat of December had dried up the water and return became necessary. What followed was eighteen gruelling days of water shortages, dying oxen and forced night marches before the expedition got back to the Olifants River and the relief of its grass and water.

Van der Stel's expedition had lasted five months and although there was not much to show in the way of material gain, in terms of geography the expedition was a great success. The maps might not have been Ordinance Survey standard but certainly the ones that were produced as a result of the knowledge gained were useful. What was perhaps just as important was that the fictional cities and rivers were removed from the maps and, furthermore, that any further exploration should be directed eastwards beyond the mountain barrier where better trading opportunities existed.

The problem of how to get over that mountain barrier remained; one way was to bypass it by sea and van der Stel kitted out several exploratory voyages that went as far as Delagoa Bay (*Rio de la Goa*) and picked up a number of Europeans sailors variously shipwrecked and fluent in the languages spoken who were then able to give some accounts of the Bantu peoples (*Magoses, Matimbes, Mapontes, Emboas and Makriggas* - a rendition of *amaXhosa, Tembu, mPondo* probably; the last were Bushmen; *Emboas* might be a version of *Tembu* or it might be a location) then inhabiting the lands of what is now KwaZulu-Natal and the Eastern Cape. Other than that, only small parties could hope to get up the steep kloofs of the Berg. That said, in 1689 van der Stel sent out a party of thirty or so in two wagons led by Ensign Schryver to meet up with a Khoikhoin clan known as the Inqua Hottentots, who, it was hoped, might turn out to be the much sought-after inhabitants of Monomatapa. There was no Monomatapa at the end of the journey, but there was a great increase in knowledge for the party made it all the way to (present day) Swellendam, crossed the Langeberg and went through the Karoo to Oudtshoorn and then on as far as (perhaps) Willowmore. There they met a chief called Hykon who, among others, filled them in on the basic state of relations between themselves, the Xhosa and the Bushmen; there was often war between the various Khoikhoin clans and the Xhosa but basically, everyone hunted the Bushmen and killed them on sight for they were great thieves – an analysis that the Europeans quickly experienced when attacked by them and came to agree with.

Even better, as far as the VOC was concerned, the potential for increasing the trade in cattle was there; the party came back with a thousand head. The problem was that of distance. Driving cattle that far would need grazing and water if they were not to arrive exhausted and under-weight and van der Stel was faced with the reality that the only way to get the cattle of the far distant interior was to drive it to the coast and pick it up by sea. Thus, the exploration of the coastline and the survey of Algoa Bay (roughly Port Elizabeth); if the cattle could be brought down the Sundays River – or the *Nukakamma*, the Grassy River as the Khoikhoin called it - grazing and drinking to their hearts' content, then loaded at Algoa Bay, the demands of the VOC for meat would be satisfied.

And thus the elephant trap. Geography determines the History. We are going to see this time and time again in South Africa. The geography of the sea route to India dictated that a victualling station was needed at the Cape for the supply of meat and vegetables. The geography of the Cape dictated that the only way to get those victuals was to establish a vegetable patch in the environs of Table Mountain and trade meat from the locals; when demand for vegetables outstripped supply – by 1700, roughly sixty ships a year was calling - that meant ploughing up the pasture; when demand for meat outstripped supply that meant first taking pasturage from the locals to raise their own and then, when this was still not enough, the ultimate establishment of a second station at Algoa Bay to supply the deficiency. To secure those stations, physical occupation was necessary, if only to prevent the jetty being pilfered and broken up for firewood. Occupation meant a willingness to defend the property. A willingness to defend the property quickly hardened into rule of that property; and in that nutshell is the kernel of colonial advance and ultimately, empire.

*

It's rarely a good sign when the son succeeds the father in office. The Chinese will tell you of the Law of the Third Generation; the First founds it, the Second builds it, the Third - spends it. In Africa, it has to be said, it's rare enough to get past the first generation before the spending starts in earnest and in South Africa itself…well, Mandela, Mbeki, Zuma says it all. (And Zuma was, at the time of writing, trying to install one of his wives as successor – unsuccessfully, thank God. He got his matching orders a couple of months later). So, when the increasingly avaricious Simon van der Stel managed to get his son installed as governor, it is fair to say that the news was met with a certain amount of dismay by the good Burghers of the Cape of Good Hope.

Willem Adriaan van der Stel was as bent as they come and seized on the opportunities presented by the opening up of the meat trade, the expansion of independent farming and the Company's remaining monopoly of shore to ship trade to fill his boots. Thoroughly abusing the Governorship, he managed to buy up by proxy one third of all farms in the Cape, employ Company staff and slaves to work them and then award the VOC supply contracts to farms belonging to himself or his cronies. His first farm, Vergelegen, was obtained by using his official position to grant the lease to an employee and then buying it off him for a song; he planted vines on it and though the farm was later broken up, it still produces rather good wine. This was a scam as corrupt and effective – and remarkably similar to - anything President Zuma pulled off but was finally brought to an end by the outrage of the Burghers, who blew the gaffe to the Court of Directors on this and a whole host of other scams. In September 1706, the farmers of Waveren, Riebeecks Casteel and Groenkloof (round about Malmesbury today) rode into Stellenbosch tooled up and demanding of answers and defied young Willem to arrest them as he had his previous opponents. Van der Stel called in his own troops but this was not enough to avoid being recalled and dismissed in 1707. The result of these proceedings was that many Burghers came to the view that as the government was corrupt, they need not take it seriously; and as the geographical distance between them and the castle increased, the respect accorded to it diminished proportionately; tax evasion was only the most obvious symptom of this loss of faith.

Willem Adriaan van der Stel also went against his father's views that the colonists should be kept within the confines of the Cape and under the watchful eye of the Company by issuing the first grazing licences and grants of farm land in the 'Land van Waveren', a beautiful valley now known as Tulbagh. This was significant because Waveren was too far away over non-existent roads to bring market garden crops for sale in Cape Town so mixed farming was not really a profitable option. Instead, cattle ranching would be the way forward because meat can walk to the slaughterhouse. It was also an attractive option for any new farmer just out from Europe because a large herd could be built up quite quickly from a relatively small outlay – a bull and a couple of heifers was the foundation of a fortune – and it was less labour intensive than arable and so more profitable. What was more, cattle ranching in the interior made the independent Burgher quite a lot more independent because if he chose *not* to take his stock to market, he could still live on the meat, hides and milk that they produced. The motivation at work here was not so much capitalist production for the market but self-sufficiency. Achieving this end would need some adaptation to the Khoikhoin way of life as the Burgher eschewed the settled life of a house and garden and took to his wagon to follow the annual grazing cycle into the Karoo and back but it also meant that, in theory, he might never need to talk to a government official, nor pay a tax ever again. For many, this wild, free, open life on the veldt was an attractive prospect and thus was born the *Trekboer*.

*

> A people of this sort called Obicquas, during last month, took the cattle of a party of Burghers who had gone inland to shoot sea cows, and killed one of the party; this affair absolutely demands revenge, otherwise worse consequences might be looked for. These are a kind of men who live in the mountains, who maintain themselves entirely by robbery, and have nothing to lose by war; they do not hesitate, upon a favorable opportunity, to steal the cattle of their own nation, under whose dominion they live, and therefore the Captains are always looking out for opportunities for revenge.
>
> *Extract of a Despatch from Commander Simon van der Stell to the Chamber XVII. 30th April 1684.* Moodie, *The Record*.

By 1700, the Khoikhoin in the Cape had pretty much been co-opted and absorbed into the local economy as part-time and casual labourers or existed alongside it in the wide spaces still available, and their relationship with the VOC regulated by the appointment of clan chiefs as 'Captains' through which contact could be maintained, negotiations conducted and a certain amount of self-government preserved. This, of course, was an entirely rational choice made by the many who decided that a settled existence with regular food, grog, tobacco and wages was preferable to the uncertainties of the long hard slog of transhumance that their previous existence demanded. Beyond the Cape, Company relations with the Khoikhoin were generally good with a thriving trade, much co-operation in the matter of shipwrecked sailors and a shared attitude to the Bushmen or *Obiquas* - the Khoikhoin word for the Bushmen was 'murderers'. This was important because as the colonists went up the first step of the escarpment towards the interior, they came up against the Bushmen in large numbers for the first time.

For the Bushmen, the expansion of cattle farming in Waveren, Riebeeck Casteel, a solitary mountain twenty miles west of Waveren, and the Groenkloof was something of a poisoned chalice because hunting cows and sheep was a lot easier than chasing the red hartebeest, white-faced bontebok or the zebra; so we might imagine the Obiquas rubbing their hands with glee when the first Burghers arrived at the head of their herds and began grazing those long, wide beautiful plains and valleys which also, conveniently, sat right next to mountain ranges which contained about a million likely hiding places for a band of Bushmen. It was a poisoned chalice because they also knew that retribution would follow, having been stealing Company property for the twenty years past. In March, 1701, the Bushmen struck and struck hard; Captain Kees of the Cochoqua was already under pressure before his watchman was wounded and forty cattle were lifted from his partner, Gerrit Cloeten, at Riebeeck Casteel; in April, a hundred sheep went too; in May, 145 cattle were lifted from the Company's cattle post on the Berg River between Riebeeck Casteel and Waveren.[31] Unfortunately, rustling these animals came at a price and that price was an effective alliance between the independent and semi-independent Khoikhoin clans and the Dutch colonists aimed against them; the Third Frontier War had begun.

Van der Stel sent out what troops he had and established a chain of military posts manned variously by small sections of ten or so mounted men and a series of skirmishes followed. The Burghers, however grateful for the help, preferred to rely on their own resources though. This went for those Khoikhoin Captains who had thrown in their lot with the Dutch too and much against the Company's will, Captain Kees and Gerrit Cloeten, banded their followers together and went after the raiders without waiting for legitimate authority. Bands of colonists, sometimes honest men driven to vigilantism, often the merest bandits, ranged far beyond the frontier retrieving cattle whether they needed retrieving or not. The Bushmen raids went on though and spread westward and northwards across the frontier zone as the Grigriqua clan to the north joined in; in November, Captain Kees lost another 274 cows and in January 1702, Captains Jan Pietersz and Griego were relieved of 89 more; in February Captain Kuyper's five wives and all his children were killed when his 150 cattle were stolen from his kraal on the Berg River. The Company cavalry galloped about, a few Bushmen were killed, a couple of Dutchmen were speared, other clans including parts of the Cochoqua joined in on either side according to interest and the problems continued until a peace was cobbled together in 1705.

---

[31] Nigel Penn, *The Forgotten Frontier* (Cape Town, 2005) p.33.

This Third Frontier War of 1702-5 (again, this moniker seems to have been applied much later; Theal published in 1909 and gave it no such name) was different in nature from the first two wars because it was not about the fundamental conflict between pasture and the plough but rather about the equally fundamental clash between property rights and straightforward theft. It was also an example of how the fundamental interests of the Dutch and Khoikhoin livestock farmers took precedence over any racial or 'national' consciousness. Leftist Historians are quick to highlight the divisions between black and white and yet, as we shall see, examples of Africans joining up with their 'colonial oppressors' to stand shoulder to shoulder in the fighting line are legion. This does not mean that racial and national considerations did not exist – they did – but they were only parts of the picture, not the whole of it. Some colonists undoubtedly did regard the Khoikhoin as 'black, stinking dogs' (we don't know what the Khoikhoin called the Dutch: *cheese-faced grass-combing buggers* perhaps?) but there were plenty who did not: the Company made it expressly clear that this sort of name-calling was unpleasant and unproductive of good relations.[32]

In this particular outbreak of hostilities, a distrust of the government's willingness and competence to defend their flocks and police the frontier was at the root of many of the colonists and Captains' independent actions. This the Company knew and was disturbed by. When Johannes Starrenburg, the Llandrost of Stellenbosch, went over the frontier in 1705 to trade for cattle, he confirmed something else that was just as disturbing; bands of European 'vagabonds' were operating way beyond the colonial boundary, learning to live off the land like the Khoikhoin, behaving in just the same brutal way as the Obiquas and having an equally disruptive effect on the cattle trade. If the Khoikhoin in the Cape were becoming more 'Europeanised' then it is also true that the Europeans on the frontier were becoming more 'Africanised'. As yet though, these groups remained very much in the minority with perhaps no more than twenty-five independent stock farmers on the northern frontier and fewer still along the limit of the Cape's influence, the Breede River. Still, it was indicative of the direction of travel that in 1710 a grant of land was made near present day Caledon, way beyond the mountain barrier, for the purpose of providing accommodation and food to those who visited the hot springs there in hope of a cure for their ailments while the following year saw the Company surveying the forests at Riversonderend to replace the exhausted fuel supplies of the Cape.

This situation was radically altered when the devastating smallpox epidemic of 1713 fell upon the Khoikhoin and virtually wiped them out leaving the Cape and large parts of the interior virtually empty of people and open for settlement by anyone willing to risk life, labour and savings on farming for themselves. Epidemics of European diseases on native populations during the colonial period have often been regarded as a form of bacteriological warfare and there is some evidence – hotly disputed, it has to be said – that Britain's own Lord Amherst attempted to introduce smallpox into the Native American population during Pontiac's rebellion of 1763.[33] I'm not an immunologist, but apart from whether the handing

---

[32] Moodie, *The Record*, Instructions to Ensign Tullekens, 9th May 1662.

[33] Philip Ranlet, *The British, the Indians and Smallpox: What Actually Happened at Fort Pitt in 1763? Pennsylvania History: A Journal of Mid-Atlantic Studies* Vol. 67, No. 3, Crime in Pennsylvania (Summer 2000), pp. 427-441.

out of blankets from infected people would actually do the job (smallpox dies on contact with air), it would seem to be a highly dangerous tactic and as potentially devastating to one's own side as to that of the enemy; you would need the whole army and everyone they came into contact with to be 'salted' or risk having the disease decimate your own ranks; and you would need to find someone confident enough in his immunity willing to do the handing out ('Volunteers? Anyone?').

That said, there can be no doubt that this issue has seen frequent attempts to 'weaponise' the historical record by 'multicultural revisionist' Historians keen to disembowel the pride of white or European heritage people in their past achievements.[34] Perhaps the worst modern example of this was the case of Ward Churchill who between 1993-2003 re-visited the whole 'infected blanket' meme and deliberately fabricated the lie that the US Army had handed out cholera infected blankets to Native Americans in 1837. Churchill, Professor of Ethnic Studies at the University of Colorado had never managed to achieve a Ph.D. and his MA degree was in Communications rather than History, but he had managed to gain his position under a positive discrimination 'diversity' recruitment programme that he just happened to be working for (who'd have thought it?). A serial Left-wing fantasist who claimed he had been radicalised while serving with US Special Forces in Vietnam (he was actually a film projectionist), he also claimed to have taught the radical-chic Weather Underground terrorist group how to make bombs. Finally rumbled for falsifying sources and concealing evidence that actually disproved his allegations, he was censured by the university and in 2007 dismissed. His response to his condemnation was: 'So I glad handed things a bit: *mea culpa.*'[35] That's the attitude of the Left in a nutshell; it's OK to lie if it advances The Cause because ultimately, the end justifies the means.

There isn't any evidence whatsoever to say that the Cape epidemic of 1713-14 was deliberate and it really is a pity that I even have to write this sentence; for a start, some 20% of the European population perished during the outbreak; in 1682, 'fevers' carried off 85 souls from a headcount of 685 colonists as well as an extraordinary number of Khoisan while in 1687 van der Stell noted a 'burning fever' among the Khoisan, the colonists and the Company slaves that 'drags many, young and old, to their graves'.[36] The saner reality is that in the 17th and early 18th Centuries, diseases were considered to be an Act of a mightily displeased God and that until Jenner discovered safe vaccination in 1796, the idea of trying such a thing would probably have brought about a conviction for witchcraft. Vaccination was known about before Jenner but it provoked rioting in colonial America when it was tried in the 1760s. Blaming the Europeans for smallpox, measles and such other daily hazards of 17th Century life is as idiotic as blaming the Black Death of 1348 on the Chinese because that plague originated on the Silk Road. Smallpox hit Cape Town in 1812 and Bubonic plague hit both Kingwilliamstown and Cape Town in 1901.[37] Who shall we blame? Perhaps the slaves who brought it with them in Portuguese ships?[38] No; it is ridiculous.

---

[34] In this case by a chap called Francis Jennings, author of *Empire of Fortune* (New York, 1988).
[35] http://quod.lib.umich.edu/p/plag/5240451.0001.009/--did-the-us-army-distribute-smallpox-blankets-to-indians?rgn=main;view=fulltext
[36] Moodie, p.420.
[37] F. Maurice, *History of the War in South Africa 1899-1902* (London 1906) Vol 4, p. 629
[38] http://dhsouthafrica.leadr.msu.edu/research-papers/prize-negroes-in-cape-town-and-the-atlantic-abolitionism-4/

Right: back to real History. How many Khoikhoin died in the epidemic can't be known given the scant records but we can be certain that they were hit very hard indeed, with mortality rates perhaps as high as 30%. First noticed in the Company slave lodge in April, the disease quickly ran through the Cape and out to the outlying areas, causing a panicked exodus into the interior. Labourers died in their droves and livestock supplies collapsed as the herders succumbed, until by the end of 1714 destitute Khoikhoin survivors were straggling in, reporting their Captains dead, their clans 90% wiped out and their cattle scattered. It was a blow from which the Khoikhoin never recovered and within half a century or so, according to the admirably balanced Graham Parker and Patrick Pfukani (whose *History of Southern Africa* I borrowed from the International School of Choueifat library in 1992 and am still fully intending to return), they disappeared as a distinct people, merging into the melting pot of what would come to be called the 'Cape Coloured' population.[39] Well, perhaps not entirely; turning up at a guesthouse in the one horse dorp of Britstown on the way to Kimberley in 2015, I was pleased to see that the golden skin, slight figure and epicanthic fold was still present in the fine form of the barmaid who popped the top off *een koue* beer for me. Small comfort, perhaps, but still....

The Company response to this unwelcome economic catastrophe was to introduce the Loan Farm, a system of land tenure that was to have enormous repercussions for the development of South Africa. Aware that the Khoikhoin could no longer supply the cattle needed in anything like the required numbers, the Company had little choice but to allow more Burghers to become independent farmers. Being also aware that most of the Burghers simply did not have the means to set themselves up in business by buying Freehold land in the Cape, the decision was taken to allow Burghers to claim farms on payment of a nominal rent of 12 Rixdollars, which was roughly the equivalent of about six months' pay. A first look at this proposition shows it to be rather unattractive; the rent was high and the costs of setting up a Loan Farm, including stock, tools and enough provisions to see the farmer through the lean time before profits might be realised was reckoned to be nearer 330 Rixdollars than 12. The size of the farm allowed for that money was established as being the radius of as far as a man might walk in a half hour – about one and a half miles, which meant 2400 hectares/6000 acres/25 sq. km – huge by European standards but also requiring a great deal of labour to manage.

What the shrewder heads realised though was that not only might a man walk *very* quickly if he was so minded, or even stick one arm over the saddle of a horse and walk *even quicker* but also that in the absence of anything resembling an official land surveyor, a farm of very great proportions indeed might be obtained. Or *two*; one official (declared at the *official* size) and one *unofficial*. And as to the rent…well, that might be late, delayed or not paid at all in the case of *unofficial* farms. In effect, the only real constraint on the size and number of these farms was the ability to maintain effective occupation against the claims of neighbours or the attacks of the Bushmen. As to labour, well, there were plenty of Khoikhoin now bereft of their clans or families who were willing to work for wages as herders or drovers, using their

---

[39] G. Parker and P. Pfukani, *History of Southern Africa* (London 1975), p.43. It's a school textbook and refreshing to read, devoid as it is of political correctness.

skills to maintain a connection to their pastoral lifestyles and perhaps, in time, build up an independent flock of their own. There were also plenty of landless labourers in the Cape who might act as sharecroppers, tenants or *bywoners* and who might also be willing to work for part-payment in kind, *kos and klere* – food and clothing – while out on the frontier there would be runaway slaves, all sorts of criminals, *bergies* and vagabonds who might also be glad of a settled and secure position, as long as too many questions were not asked. Security against the Bushmen might be achieved by neighbourly co-operation with Khoikhoin herders equally preyed upon, or by pooling herds, water, grazing and guns with fellow Europeans in a *trekboer* clan of their own.

Waveren was the gateway because as yet it was difficult to get over the Hottentots Holland mountains that tower straight up 450m from Stellenbosch and the Cape Flats; Sir Lowry's Pass carries the main N2 winding up there now and from the top you can admire the paragliders from above, see the surf along the False Bay strand and the mountains that hem in tiny Franschoek; and then you can have fun working out how to get a team of oxen to pull a wagon up it and through the jagged broken country beyond in the absence of the N2. It was possible but a lot easier going down than up so Waveren provided an easier route. And out there, beyond Waveren going ESE was the Langberg and beyond that the Langkloof, long, long valleys with good water, good pasturage, plenty of game, a benign climate; going SE were the rich, green lands along the Breede River that would become known as Bonnievale and a little south of there, more virgin pasture and corn land than a reasonable man could imagine. Go NE and the Karoo awaited, dusty, harsh desert but for those who knew how, perfectly capable of supporting sheep when the rains turned the baked clay to moorland as good as anything in England. Go north to the Piketberg, Winterhoek, the Cedarberg and there was more land capable of carrying sheep and bearing good crops. Roughly speaking, and fired up by the tales drifting in from the hunters, the travellers, the escapees and the Khoisan themselves, the Dutch knew that for those with the daring, the imagination and the appetite for sheer hard work, there was good land for 800km going East and 300km going North. There was also something more; something far, far more important; for those who had experienced indentured servitude, the rigorous discipline of military service or life at sea, or contracts and regulations that always seemed weighted in favour of the Company; for those who had the courage to be free, there was also the promise of an independent, prosperous life – the dream of the *lekker lewe*.

*

### The Time of the Commandos.

The right of the aborigines to endeavour by every means in their power to retain possession of the territory that had been their ancestors' from remote times was utterly ignored, and indeed it was not possible that it could be respected. It was simply a question: shall the country remain in the occupation of savages in the Palaeolithic stage and without peaceful intercourse with other human beings, or shall it become the home of civilised men having a place in the brotherhood of nations? In this view of the matter, the Bushmen were regarded as marauders, and were constantly so termed. From their point of view, if they could have given expression to their feelings, the Europeans would unquestionably have been considered the marauders and they as patriots defending their country.

> *G.M.Theal, The History and Ethnography of Africa South of the Zambezi p.126.*

The small weak Bushman, so near the beginnings of man's creation, with his hollow back, and his hollow cheeks, and his wrinkled, loose-skinned body, and his bows and arrows and unguents and poison and magic and strange artistic gifts, made his paintings on stones and in caves, and was hunted (as depredating wild beasts are hunted) from the land south of the Orange.

> *Sarah Gertrude Willim, The South Africans, (London, 1926) p.9.*

During the 1870s, a German researcher by the name of Dr Wilhelm Bleek aided by his English wife, Lucy Lloyd, began to collect up specimens of Saan or Bushman folklore from the Bushmen convicts employed on the dock works at Cape Town in an attempt to preserve something of their language and culture. The result was a remarkable collection of stories with such fantastic titles as *The Mantis Assumes the Form of a Hartebeest*, *The Story of the Leopard Tortoise* and *The Children are Sent to Throw the Sleeping Sun into the Sky* which Bleek and Lloyd hoped would allow an insight into Bushman culture. Unfortunately, the stories really lacked any recognisable structure, followed no obvious logical pattern and imparted no intelligible wisdom. Reading them today is a baffling experience and although some interesting nuggets can be discerned – the moon is regarded as a male, is made of leather, and is 'cut away' progressively by the sun (female) until he is forced to beg for mercy, at which point the sun relents and allows him to grow back – the most interesting thing about the stories is indeed the fact that they are unintelligible. This allows us some insight into the mutual incomprehension that formed such a feature of the relations between the Bushmen and the Trekboers. The difference in attitudes to property rights has already been alluded to but it seems to me that the inability of either side to come to some sort of accommodation in the competition for land, grazing rights and water from the appearance of the Trekboers to the virtual extermination of the Bushmen is rooted in deeper soil than mere conquest. Attempts to buy off the Bushmen by turning a blind eye to their depredations or by handing out 'presents' (Dane geld?) of sheep tended to fail. From the Bushmen perspective, self-interest would seem to dictate the negotiation of some form of relationship based on mutual interest or at least subordination; the Trekboers always wanted for labour, the Bushmen were faced with extermination and on these two harshest of facts, some form of arrangement should have been possible, yet it never occurred. The Bushmen were hunted to extinction, their children taken from them and brought up as Trekboer dependents or consigned to the tender mercies of whoever could be found to look after them.

Reading through the accounts of these years, one cannot but be shocked at the relentless and merciless brutality employed against the Bushmen and because we have so little to work with to explain the situation as viewed from the Bushmen side, we have come to the view that the

Trekboer was indeed a merciless, brutal and rapacious figure. Race has usually been used as an explanation for the destruction of Bushman society; conveniently the Bushmen were black and the Trekboers white and so this fitted in quite easily to those notions that held up Apartheid as some naturally occurring feature of white society. Yet we have almost no evidence of Bushman attitudes to confirm this. We have nothing to inform us as to their aims; were they fighting heroically for their land or could they not discern the difference between wild game and farmed livestock? And we should also bear in mind the fact that the Bushmen were cursed and hunted by the Xhosa and the Khoikhoin for exactly the same reasons as the Trekboers hunted them; constant predation on flocks; real hatred for the waste they inflicted when, rather than take one or two beasts for their consumption, they might take hundreds and wantonly slaughter anything that they could not eat. Certainly, they were not the little green pixies depicted in that fine movie *The Gods Must be Crazy* or Africa's equivalent to the thoroughly fraudulent Native American Rainbow Warriors; for a start, murder rates among the Bushmen are about forty times those that you find in London.[40] While it might seem rather harsh to blame the Bushmen for their own demise, it does seem mightily strange that they chose not to adapt to the new realities and come to some arrangement before defeat turned into extinction and rather patronising to assume that they did not have the imagination to put forward some sort of a deal before it was too late.

It really is too late now to come to some proper conclusion that is anything more than speculation. The good Dr Bleek was able to interview only a handful of members of a clan based around Colesberg and nowhere in any of his researches do the Bushmen refer to any of the processes that brought about their destruction.[41] By the time that Laurens van der Post began writing about the Kalahari Bushmen in the 1950s, a gap of centuries and miles of distance had opened up so wide that it would be a brave historian who attempted to bridge it and van der Post was a journalist, not a historian, and being a journalist, perhaps given to invention. Modern academic researches point out that Bushmen narratives have now been over-written by Christianity, literacy and exposure to two centuries of modernity and so obscured as to be little use in writing History. Furthermore, many of the Bushmen groups studied speak languages that are mutually unintelligible so we are faced with a problem similar to trying to interpret the ways of Scotsmen through the language of Sicilians. Great efforts have been made to interpret rock art as a way to understand the Bushmen but even with the best intentions, most of the conclusions that can be drawn about their cosmology, myths and everyday culture from such sources at best fall into the category of informed speculation. The four common themes tell of a ritual circle dance, a shamanic out-of-body experience, the hunting of animals and, perhaps most striking (I saw these in Elands Bay), the placing of handprints which may be a form of signature, an affirmation of life or perhaps a reaching out to the spiritual world. Impressive as they are, they tell us little about their councils, politics or attitudes to the encroaching Europeans and Bantu. All that we can say is that they were relentless predators capable of organizing themselves into groups much larger – sometimes in the hundreds - than the simple picture of small family eco-friendly groups so

---

[40] Patrick West, *The Poverty of Multiculturalism (Civitas, 2005)*.
[41] Penn, *The Forgotten Frontier*, p.5.

often given. So, this is again, one of those things that we just cannot know for sure but we can draw two reasonable conclusions; that the Bushmen were driven to the point of extinction by the Trekboers (among others) is a fact; that this was entirely the responsibility of the Trekboers is not. The Bushmen were exterminated because they fought to the end and would not surrender. For some people this was heroism, for others suicidal madness and it remains a puzzle.

Nigel Penn put forward the idea that the Bushmen world was as much spiritual as physical and that to lose access to certain places was to suffer a vital spiritual loss that could not be replaced and he might well be correct. He also held out the possibility that the Bushmen conceptualized the Boers as a species of lion and as lions are relentless, apex predators it simply isn't possible to surrender and expect mercy. This is an idea that I find attractive; at Brandberg in Namibia, the site of the famous 'White Lady' rock paintings, some of the animals painted there are shown as having back legs that are human and this may (or may not) support the idea that humans were not separate from the 'animal' world but in some way 'animals' themselves. There may well have been other reasons too; neither the Khoikhoin nor the Xhosa rated the Bushman as a useful slave and were as likely to kill those who hoped to gain refuge as to absorb them; the Tswana were particularly hostile and considered it meritorious to exterminate any Bushmen under any circumstances.[42] It seems that all hands were against the Bushman because he was a wild thing, a predator, viewed almost as a species of leopard. He must be killed for the sake of the herd and his women and children must be given the scant mercy of a servants' life; a life that required them to abandon the wild hunt they had known and enter into the way of the pastoralist. Theal's judgement is hard to argue with: 'they could not adapt themselves to their new environment, they tried to live as their ancestors had lived, and therefore they were fated to perish.'[43]

*

The principal institution by which the Bushmen were defeated was the Commando, a formation, often *ad hoc,* of mounted men armed with guns that developed from the European *dragoon* or mounted infantryman. When adapted to the particular characteristics of South African landscape and warfare, what made the Commando different from the more regular dragoon, was that it was made up of *civilians* and only very nominally under the control of the Company. I'm going to spend quite a bit of time looking at this for two main reasons. Firstly, in his admirable study of the conflict between the colonists and the Khoisan in the 18th Century, Nigel Penn came to believe that this institution became not just an instrument of war, but the defining feature of Trekboer society; it formed them and made them different from what they were before. In effect, this was the institution that changed them from being Dutch colonists to *Afrikaaners*, people who had cut off their connection to the homeland and become Africans themselves. Secondly, the Commando became not just an instrument of war but a cultural icon that helped define the Afrikaaner vision in the 20th Century and

---

[42] The Autobiography of the Late Sir Andries Stockenstrom Bt Vol 1 p.188
[43] Theal, *History and Ethnography*, vol II, p. 509.

marked them out as being successful warriors with a claim to superiority, government and land ownership by right of conquest. So, it's quite important, I'd say.

Right from the beginning, the Dutch considered themselves to be a match for the indigenous people in a war because the Khoikhoin had no guns. Even accepting the primitive nature of the matchlock, with its excruciatingly slow rate of fire (one shot per two minutes) and poor accuracy at anything beyond 50m, its superiority over the light bows and spears of the Khoikhoin was obvious. It was powerful enough to drop a lion or a hippopotamus and despite it being quickly noticed by the Khoikhoin that matchlocks and muskets were unreliable in the rain, they were powerfully impressed by its potentialities for warfare. Needless to say, they made attempts to get hold of these new weapons by stealing or by barter, a fact that did not go unnoticed by the Dutch who made great efforts to prevent this particular form of technology transfer – in 1677 it was made a capital offence to sell guns to Africans - but the real difficulty lay in obtaining a sufficient supply of powder and lead, of which the Dutch held the monopoly.

During the First Frontier War 1659, Van Riebeeck had toyed with schemes of fortification, all of which were impractical, or had sent out infantry patrols whose fieldcraft was nowhere nearly as good as that of the Khoikhoin and thus usually unable to get close enough to bring their weapons to bear. Soldiers landed from passing ships were of even less value as their standard of fitness had been so reduced by the long voyage that they could not hope to catch the Khoikhoin. Within a very short time, therefore, van Riebeeck was actively pursuing the formation of a troop of dragoons which would allow him to combine his advantage in firepower with a mobility to match that of the Khoikhoin. His first request for horses from the Company directors was made in March 1658 repeated in January 1659 and March 1659 but it was not until May 1660, after the First Frontier War was over, that a permanent mounted force was established. It soon proved effective in its role of acting as a deterrent to Khoikhoin cattle-lifters.

However, it was not the threat from the Khoikhoin that led the colony to take the decisive step of involving the civilians of the colony in their own defence. Up until this point, this had been the job of professional soldiers sent out for the purpose and supplemented where necessary by troops and sailors landed from passing ships, but with news of the outbreak of war with England reaching the colony in September 1664, it was thought expedient to raise a militia to resist the possibility of an English attack. 'This afternoon,' reported the Governor, 'We reviewed all these Burghers and country farmers, properly armed, and marched them into the Fort, where the senior sergeant, Elbert Diemer, being proposed as Ensign, they were for the first time, presented, in the Company's name, with blue colours, a schiarf and a plume.'[44] No English attack materialized, but the successful formation of this militia led the Company to place more emphasis on it as a cheaper alternative to paying professional soldiers.

---

[44] Moodie, Z. *Wagenaar's Journal*, 2nd October 1664.

So much progress had been made in the training and development of the militia forces that by 1688 Governor Simon van der Stel was able to report that he could put 350 men into the field if necessary. By 1672 the militia, reviewed four times a year, was considered sufficiently effective to be sent out as part of a punitive expedition against Ngonomoa in 1673 and again in 1674. Crucially, though, it was not simply a *Dutch* force; when Ensign Cruse went out to fight Ngonomoa in May 1674, he went with 50 regulars, 50 militia, and 250 Khoikhoin lent by those clan leaders who were in dispute with Ngonomoa. This force, assembled *ad hoc*, established the pattern for successful African warfare combining, as it did, mobility, firepower, flexibility, local knowledge and, by rewarding the participants with the booty of the enemy's plundered livestock, a very strong incentive to act aggressively.

As the Dutch settlements spread out into the hinterland during the 18th Century, the militia forces began to assume an identity separate from those of the Dutch regular forces because they assumed different roles. In effect, regular soldiers were tasked primarily with the garrisoning and defence of Cape Town against the possibility of attack from European forces while the militia forces were more concerned with defending the farmers in the interior from the Bushmen. In the event of serious threats or disturbances there would of course be mutual support given, but the particular nature of the Commando system meant that its ethos and methods developed separately from those of the regular forces.

Regular European forces operated according to a strict hierarchical system of appointed officers and a table of ranks which was expected to function by passing orders down a chain of command and passing information up it. Both the hierarchy and chain of command was enforced by a formal system of coercive powers but also through an informal system of mutual respect. Officers were expected to care for the men under their command and soldiers expected to be treated according to an understood code of behaviour. The final authority which regular forces recognized was usually the national government or, in the case of chartered companies like the Dutch East India Company which held delegated powers from the national government, the Directors of the company.

In the Commandos, this system was only partially replicated. A chain of command existed which ran downwards from Field Commandant, Field Sergeant, Field Corporal to *manschappen* or Private but there was little that could be done to enforce obedience to this hierarchy without the active acquiescence of the *manschappen* themselves. This was, in effect, a democratic body who chose their own leaders and obeyed them only if and when it suited Jannie or Gerrit to do so. It took much persuasion, therefore, to assemble a Commando to attack Bushmen settlements or bands, especially if it meant a farmer leaving his own property undefended at the same time, a fact which the Field Corporals continually railed against. The fact that the Field Corporals themselves tended to be chosen by and from the farmers of a particular area also led to petty jealousies and disputes over who should actually exercise command. Men who had previously held rank as Field Corporals were often unwilling to defer to younger men so appointed and as a result the rank of Field Sergeant was instituted, almost as an honorific, to salve wounded pride. The final authority in the chain of command rested only in theory with the Governor of the Cape and the

Directors of the East India Company. In practice, the men who served in the Commandos were unwilling to accept the authority of anyone further than the Llandrosts – the Company's district administrators - and even this acceptance was conditional.

The effect of this conditional loyalty was to have both military and political effect. Militarily, the conflict with the Bushmen gave the cattle ranchers, the *Trekboers*, an independent identity from the arable farmers, the *Burghers*, nearer the Cape which was reflected in the *de facto* separation of the 'Field' soldiers on the frontier from the 'Militia' soldiers in the Cape made by the Llandrost of Stellenbosch in March 1777.[45] From then on although *de jure* Trekboers still had to do service in the militia by turning up for the annual exercises known as the *wapen schouwing*, in practice they were excused. The political effect was to remove effective day to day control of the Commandos from the Governor and make the Directors almost an irrelevance to their activities. The only real control that the Governor had over them lay in his control of the supply of powder and shot without which their effectiveness was severely restricted. It also meant that a variety of political forces within the Dutch colony now had access to armed force; the Directors controlled the regular forces through the Governor, who in turn controlled the Burgher militia forces through the Llandrosts, who in turn could call upon the Boer Commandos. At each stage of the chain of command, however, obedience was conditional on the acquiescence of the subordinate commander; the Governor decided how, when and where regular forces were deployed and could, if he chose, ignore the advice of the Directors which, necessarily had to be interpreted in the light of local circumstances; the opposition of the Llandrosts to the calling out of the Burgher militias in their own areas would be a decisive factor in determining the strength and commitment of those forces, leaving the Governor to rely on the Cape Town Burghers and what he could raise from Khoikhoin, Cape Malay and slave elements to hand; the Trekboers themselves would decide whether they turned out at the request of either the Llandrosts or their own officers. In short, the decision of the Llandrost of Stellenbosch in 1777 put the Trekboers into a situation of near military autonomy and thus a sort of quasi-political independence. This was illustrated by the unauthorized raising of a Commando in 1780, led by Field Sergeant Josua Joubert and Petrus Hendrick Ferreira, which went out against the Xhosa.[46]

The methods by which the Trekboers operated varied considerably. The word 'commando' simply means 'a command' denoting an ad hoc force of variable size and composition constituted for a short-term defined operation. In the 18th Century struggles this usually meant the retrieval of stolen livestock or an attack upon a Bushman kraal or mountain refuge along the northern border of the colony. By the end of the 18th Century, as the colony expanded and new Llandrosts were appointed to the districts of Stellenbosch, Swellendam, Uitenhage and Graaff-Reinet, the sheer extent of this border, which ran from the mouth of the Buffalo River in the west, along the Hantamberg, Roggeveldberg, the Nieuveldberg and on to the Sneeuberg and Bruntjes Hoogje around Graaff-Reinet in the east – some 800km of mixed

---

[45] Moodie, *Records of a Meeting of the combined Boards of Llandrost and Heemraden, and Llandrost and Militia Officers of Stellenbosch, 28th March 1774.*
[46] Moodie, *Extract Resolution of Van Plettenberg's Council, 25th July 1780.*

mountain, desert, bush and plain - necessarily meant a devolved structure was required. This was especially the case because the Trekboer farms tended to be widely dispersed and herds were constantly on the move to take advantage of the available pasturage. Nor were the Trekboers very numerous – the total number of male colonists was 2300 in 1773, with a further 6200 dependents.[47]

The effectiveness of the Commando system rested at local level on the Field Corporals, of whom there were twenty-one on the northern border in 1774, and who were authorized to call out a Commando to provide a rapid response to cattle lifters. This was a challenge in itself as already noted, and there were numerous cases where the available manpower was not adequate to the task. The Field Corporals were also required to furnish reports on the situation in their districts which were the basis on which larger Commandos might be assembled. Adriaan van Jaarsveld's report from the Sneeuberg in the summer of 1775, one of the areas hardest pressed by the Bushmen in the 1770s, lists a series of livestock losses 'which led everyone to wish that the time were come for the great commando…to take the field.'[48] Above the Field Corporals were the Field Commandants, one for the northern border under the control of Stellenbosch district, and one for the Eastern border, which was under the control of the Llandrost of Swellendam. There was no standard size for such a Commando, nor any standard length of time for it to be in the field. Often the Field Corporal would simply collect whatever handfuls were available in the hope of catching the raiders before the stolen cattle disappeared into the mountains, but twenty armed and mounted men would be the minimum size for an effective force. The upper limit for what was practicable in the 18th Century was probably no more than 250.

Mounting a larger operation required the co-operation of several districts and the logistical support provided by the Llandrosts. Opperman's Commando of 1774 was a large, deliberately planned affair which put 100 Dutch and 150 Khoikhoin men into the field from the 16th August to 7th November 1774 operating in three columns. In practice the duration of large Commando operations was dictated by the weather, either because of the difficulties experienced during the hot season or the needs of the harvest, and as a result the period August-November, after the cold season and before it became too hot, tended to be favoured. Such a Commando operation would be composed of both horse and foot, with all men being armed with a musket, and based around a transport column of wagons drawn by teams of oxen to carry the necessary supplies. Each man would be expected to provide himself with a horse and gun if he could, and the farmers of the area in which the Commando was operating would be expected to supply the transport and oxen. Shortfalls in arms would be made up by the Llandrost, who could request the loan of muskets from the Governor, from where the powder, shot and hand grenades would also be supplied. This could be a considerable amount; Opperman's Commando of 1774 was supplied with 90 muskets, 900lbs gunpowder, 1800lbs lead and 3,000 flints. The Boers would feed themselves either by hunting or from captured livestock, as well as from supplies that they would bring from home. The granaries controlled by the Llandrosts might also be tapped, although this would require the authority

---

[47] Moodie, *General Summary of Population 1769 – 73*. p. 16.
[48] Moodie, *Report of Field Corporal Adriaan van Jaarsveld, 4th September 1775*.

of the Governor and, given the parsimony of the Directors of the Company, would probably have to be done on an unofficial basis.

The Commando would meet at the home of a farm in the centre of the district to be cleared of Bushmen and a muster would be held in which a register of those participating would be kept. Those Trekboers who had been called out but failed to turn up would have their names noted and sent on to the Llandrost, who would be empowered to levy a fine on them. Excuse notes were also checked and those that were deemed flippant or insolent were also forwarded to the Llandrost. Very often, Trekboers who were unwilling to leave their properties undefended to go on Commando would send a Khoikhoin servant in their place, or would arrive with only a proportion of the men and boys – 16 was deemed the age at which boys were liable for Commando service – that they were expected to furnish. A turnout of 50% of those called was probably the reasonable expectation of the Field Commandant, although this figure could be lower – Field Commandant Nicolaas van der Merwe reported an absentee rate of 64 out of 91 in August 1774.

Once started the Commando would move in the general direction of the enemy, establish a base or *laager*, and then send out patrols, often composed of Khoikhoin 'without the assistance of [whom]…no good result is to be expected'[49] to locate Bushman kraals or mountain hideouts. Those left in the laager would rest or cast the bullets from the lead pigs supplied by the Company. When a kraal was sighted, a strong detachment would be sent to surround it and then shoot down the male inhabitants and attempt to capture the women, children and livestock. If the Bushmen had retired to shelter in caves or relatively inaccessible mountain strongholds, then patrols would employ hand grenades to blast them out.

From time to time there were attempts made to bring about a peaceful resolution and batons emblazoned with the Company's arms were given to those rare clan leaders who submitted and gave satisfactory assurances of peace. Field Commandant Gerrit van der Wyk made several failed attempts to persuade cornered Bushmen to surrender when on Commando in September 1774.

> 22 [September], at daybreak Steenkamp's spies perceived fire, they galloped to it; the Bushmen having ensconced themselves behind the fence of the kraal, shot Gerrit Bastert Minie through the hat, therefore shot 8; they would accept no peace…the Commandant…called out to make peace, but instead they shot their arrows, therefore shot 10.[50]

Commando warfare was brutal and bloody, often with no quarter given to male combatants. Bushmen often struck without warning, killing the herdsmen before running off their cattle

---

[49] Moodie, *Records of a combined meeting of the Boards of Llandrost and Heemraden, and Llandrost and Militia Officers of Stellenbosch, 28th December 1773.*
[50] Moodie, *Journal of Commando under the Orders of Gerrit van Wyk, 1774.*

and prisoners were rarely taken. The Dutch did have prison facilities of a kind, at Robben Island, but the Company had objected to the cost of maintaining any large numbers of prisoners. In June 1772, 58 Bushmen were taken by a Commando in the Roggeveld and duly sent to Cape Town only for the Company to advise that the women and children should be put out to local households in service to avoid any charge being made on the finances. Commandos were repeatedly warned 'to do no injury to women and children'[51] and many Boers felt distinctly uncomfortable, by reason of religious feeling, European tradition or simple common humanity, when non-combatants were killed or injured. Inquiries were instituted in several such cases, but it is doubtful if anything came of them due to the unwillingness of witnesses to testify against someone who they might later need to rely on in battle, as well as the sheer weakness of the political and judicial power of the Llandrosts. The practice of putting prisoners out to service with Trekboers or Burghers, whereby captured men, women and children were placed as bonded labourers for, theoretically, a fixed term of years became known as the 'apprentice' system. It began as a pragmatic response to the question of dealing with prisoners of war, but it quickly became open to such abuse that it came to resemble slavery. It was also an incentive for some Trekboers to turn out for Commando service as they might by this means acquire some much-needed extra labour for their farms, although the erratic turnout rates for the Commandos suggest that this was only one reason to do so.

As far as combatant Bushmen males were concerned, however, there were no crocodile tears; many Dutch considered them as 'murderous and rapacious,'[52] '*brutale menschen*'[53] who could not be trusted to keep any lasting agreement and to whom death was only justice. Adriaan van Jaarsveld led a Commando of thirty against a much larger Bushman group in May 1771 and killed 92 of them. Jacob de Klerk, Field Corporal in the Nieuwveld responded to a livestock raid in April, 1772 by calling up a Commando which 'overtook the body of the robbers, and shot fifty one of them, without however, having recovered any of the stolen cattle.'[54] These are extremely high casualty rates and suggest a sustained fusillade maintained for hours, and possibly days, given the limited accuracy and slow rate of fire of muskets. The lack of casualties among the Commandos also suggests that the Bushmen were engaged at long range, possibly from the saddle, as it is unlikely that such heavy casualties could be inflicted in ambush or that the firepower available to small numbers of Boers would be great enough to offset a determined charge. The use of poison arrows by Bushmen warriors was a further incentive to engage beyond the range of their bows – Okkert Schalkwyk was wounded on the 13th September 1774, 'suffered with the wound nine days and died on the 21st'.[55]

\*

---

[51] Moodie, *Instructions to Ensign Cruse, 12th July 1673. Also Instructions to Field Commandant Godlieb Opperman, 19th April 1774.*
[52] Moodie, *Llandrost Faber to van Plettenberg, 23rd May 1772.*
[53] Moodie, *Governor van der Stell to Chamber XVII, 23rd December 1679.*
[54] Moodie, *Llandrost Faber to Acting Governor van Plettenberg, 10th April, 1772.*
[55] Moodie, *Report of Field-Commandant Nicolaas van der Merwe, Sept 1774.*

The Commando system not only enabled the Trekboers to grind down and defeat the Bushmen during the 18th Century, but also gave them a potential for political independence from the government at the Cape. The constant struggle against the Bushmen and the absence of aid from the regular Dutch forces reinforced attitudes that regarded adherence to the restrictions imposed on them by the Company as onerous, feelings that had been present among the colonists right back to the time of Van Riebeeck's governorship and presented an ongoing set of grievances.

The first main source of grievance lay in the colonists' complaints that the Company consistently failed to protect them from the depredations of the Khoikhoin and the Bushmen. At the heart of any relationship between the ruled and their rulers, in the European tradition, is the social contract that the governed shall be protected by the governors from external enemies in return for the payment of taxes, tribute or homage. The constitution of the Dutch East India Company as a 'quango' with a commitment to generating profits for the shareholders necessarily meant that this social contract could only partially be honoured because the cost of soldiers, and still more so, war, would eat into those profits. In the choice between maintaining a profitable trade and ensuring the personal security of its employees, the Directors had no hesitation or doubt in putting profitability first. The supply of fresh vegetables and meat to the Company ships 'our chief object in forming the establishment…must of necessity be first attained' and as far as the Directors were concerned 'the ill-will of the Hottentoos must in some measure be overlooked.'[56] There were limits to this forbearance and the Company did approve the use of retaliatory measures, but as far as the colonists were concerned these limits were far too liberal especially when

> …we daily suffer great annoyance from this set of people [the Khoikhoin], as they never meet anyone incapable of defending himself, but they plunder him bare, threatening those who resist with murder, by placing their hassegays against their breasts.[57]

The failure of van Riebeeck to take any effective action against Herry's numerous transgressions severely dented the Company's credibility from the beginning, especially as the colonists were then expressly forbidden from taking reprisals of their own on pain of a flogging.[58] Ideally, the Company wanted to keep the colonists and the Africans separated, in part to prevent incidents of petty theft and robbery on both sides, and the various schemes of fortification proposed by van Riebeeck, as well as the planting of his famous almond hedge had this as one of their main aims. As the colony expanded there were some attempts to provide soldiers to protect those farmers further afield; in 1726, soldiers had been despatched at the request of the Khoikhoin to protect them from both Bushmen and vagabond Europeans and a few years later similar posts were established at St Helena Bay on the west coast and near Swellendam on the south, but the distances involved and the tactical problems of protecting wide, sparsely populated areas were too great to be overcome in this manner. Those parties of elephant hunters who by the 1730s were beginning to range as far as Natal

---

[56] Moodie, *Chamber XVII to Van Riebeeck, 2nd September 1658.*
[57] Moodie, *Van Riebeeck's Journal, 24th January 1654.*
[58] Moodie, *Van Riebeeck's Journal, 18th October 1653, June 23rd 1654.*

could expect no protection at all from the Company. By the end of the 17th Century the Company had effectually delegated the protection of the Burghers and Trekboers beyond Stellenbosch to the Llandrosts and the militia. By the last quarter of the 18th Century, the expansion of the Trekboers into ever more remote areas had replicated the problem and the Commando system had only partially alleviated it. 'The fury of the Bushmen still continues,' complained one group of farmers appealing for a Commando. 'We have been consumed by the land-ruining Bushmen...some of us are already flying to save our lives...so that there is scarce any hope of recovery.'[59]

The strain put upon the social contract between the Trekboers in the remote areas and the Government at the Cape was so great as to break it almost entirely. Individual trekboers out on the frontier whose houses were 'shot...full of arrows and stolen from him 900 sheep' were unlikely to spend much time waiting for permission to retaliate from either Cape Town or the Llandrosts at Stellenbosch or Swellendam, but would be more likely to look for mutual support from those who might be in a position to give it, i.e., their immediate neighbours. This fragmentation of political unity manifested itself in the increasing reluctance of the Trekboers to turn out for Commando service – in August 1780, Field Corporal A.P. Burgher ordered a Commando 'but got only 7 men and 10 Hottentots, so that he dared not go out with so few.'[60] Isaac van der Merwe was even less fortunate, getting not a single man, while Field Corporal Cornelius Botman on the eastern frontier reported that whenever he called out a Commando, those called decamped to the neighbouring district of Swellendam where he had no authority. The extent to which the Trekboers might now accept allegiance to the Company was open to very serious question and more likely to be based on kinship or sentimental links with the Burghers of Stellenbosch and Cape Town, rather than any corporate or national loyalty.

At the extreme end of the scale, certain groups of Trekboers were beginning to resemble independent clans on the verge of rejecting all superior allegiance or authority. This appeared to be the case with the Prinsloo family who were engaging in active hostilities against the Xhosa on the eastern frontier, and whom the authorities recognized as 'mischievous inhabitants...who cause disquiet and will not fail to do all that is possible to have the Kafirs removed...in order to enlarge the extent of their own farms.'[61] Willem Prinsloo had settled beyond the colonial boundary against the express orders of the Company, raided cattle from the Xhosa, and set the Llandrost of Stellenbosch at defiance over attempts to get his family to move back into the colony. To all intents and purposes this was a declaration of independence.

The second main grievance against the Company was an old one too and it concerned the right to trade freely with passing ships and the Africans. One of the first acts of van Riebeeck was to establish a monopoly over all trade within the colony. Only the Company could trade with Africans, with passing ships, with Europe, Batavia or anywhere else. Company servants

---

[59] Moodie, *Letter from nine Inhabitants of Sneeuwberg to Commandant Opperman, 18th March 1776*.
[60] Moodie, *H. van der Merwe, Sneeuwberg to the Llandrost of Stellenbosch, 20th August 1780*.
[61] Moodie, *Llandrost of Stellenbosch to Governor van Plettenberg 13th March 1780*.

and free colonists alike were initially required to direct all their business to and through the Company, but this was quickly subverted and the restriction was limited to the cattle trade with the Africans and with passing ships. In theory, the Company set a fixed price for bartering cattle from the Khoikhoin which was not to be exceeded by the colonists, but this too was found to be onerous and unworkable as the free colonists found ways to get around the system. Attempts to prevent this illicit trade were repeatedly made and just as repeatedly ignored. The Company had tried to enforce the laws against illicit trade through its own courts and malefactors were harshly treated, but the trade was so vital that most people continued to ignore these strictures, especially when, in an expanding colony, the arm of the Judiciary began to have difficulty reaching out to the more remote areas. In 1739, an attempt was made by the Company to stamp its authority on these outlying areas when ten Trekboers living near the Piketberg in the north of the colony bartered a herd of cattle from the Namaquas on the Orange River, but whose servants then stole some on their own account. The Namaquas duly complained to the Governor at Cape Town who in response ordered that the whole stock of those Trekboers be impounded and, suspecting others of being complicit in the trade, impounded the stock of those against whom no actual complaint had been made. This heavy-handed response was met by open rebellion on the part of the Trekboers of the district, who refused to respond to the court summons and leveled accusations of tyranny against Governor van den Henghel, a situation which was only resolved when a Bushmen raid necessitated the accused being required for Commando service. Those who answered were pardoned and only the ring leader, Estienne Barbier, was caught, tried and hanged. Such a compromise did nothing to strengthen the respect for law among the Trekboers and by the 1770s such large-scale expeditions to barter cattle were common. In 1777, the Prinsloo clan, in the company of their neighbours, the Feirreras – among whom were the leaders of the unauthorized commando of 1780 - were bartering cattle from the Xhosa and keeping them away from the Company by pasturing them on the far side of the Fish River i.e., on Xhosa land.

The third ancient grievance lay in the perennial issue of theft. In essence, the Dutch tended to interpret theft by individual Dutch people as an individual act, while seeing theft by Africans as, generally, an act licensed by clan leaders and thus, almost, an act of war. This led to a rift between the Dutch colonists and the Company because successive governors were unwilling to respond officially to acts of theft as this would necessarily mean an official act of retribution which could bring on an armed conflict and so disrupt trade. To the colonists this looked like the Africans were being given *carte blanche* to rob them at will. Van Riebeeck had sympathy with their plight and considered enslaving the Khoikhoin as a reprisal, but the Company insisted on leniency and he, as the official embodiment of the Directors in far away Holland, had to implement their policy whether he liked it or not.[62] When the patience of the Company did run out and punitive expeditions or Commandos were ordered, they were often seen as shutting the stable door after the horse had bolted.

---

[62] Moodie, *Van Riebeeck's Journal, 24th January 1654.*

Dissatisfaction with this diplomatic approach to theft by Africans was exacerbated by the very severe sentencing regime to which Dutch thieves were subject; in October 1659, H.J. van Schank received 100 lashes and 16 years in chains for stealing sheep from the Company,[63] while in 1666 Anthony Jans and his accomplice, Anthony Arents, were flogged and sentenced to three years on Robben Island for stealing a cabbage. It is likely that some colonists might well have drawn the conclusion that Africans enjoyed a privileged position vis-à-vis the offence of theft, in the same way that British soldiers in 19th Century India regarded the Sepoys as unreasonably privileged by their exemption from flogging. Out on the veldt, the urging of restraint by the Company sounded hollow to those Trekboers in conflict with the Bushmen. The temptation to retreat into a siege mentality, to shoot first and ask questions later, was very real and quickly degenerated into what T.E. Lawrence called 'race hesitation'. By the time that the Prinsloos and their allies were coming into conflict with the Xhosa – who were also in conflict with the Bushmen - these calls for restraint were simply ignored.

\*

Here then is the product of the Commando system, the Trekboer; economically independent by dint of his herds, believing that a Loan Farm is his birthright and scathing of the idea that he owes anything at all to the government, he is quick to take up arms in defence of his interests. Pragmatic in his approach to Bushmen, Khoisan or anyone else, he believes in *live and let live* but would not shrink from defending his property or enforcing his claims to the land, grazing and water on which his herds depend. If you fight him, he will kill you, and your children and women will be absorbed into his clan, but for those with eyes to see, he is not invincible. Neither does he think much of the concept of the Rule of Law for experience has taught him that here, out on the frontier two hundred hours by ox wagon from the Cape, the rule of law has been supplanted by the rule of the assegai, the poisoned arrow and the gun. His language, *die Taal*, is becoming distinct from the original Dutch as his bonds with the old continent slip and his formal education is virtually nil because he has far outrun the reach of the schoolmaster and the beadle. Beyond an acquaintance with the family Bible, there is nothing of literature and no new ideas. The intellectual revolution of the Enlightenment has passed him by entirely, so he never questions the legitimacy of slavery, knows nothing of the scientific method and clings firmly to the stern wisdom of the Old Testament. He regards himself as Abraham, the patriarch of his clan, Moses escaping from the Egyptian bondage of the Company and Joshua conquering the Promised Land, all rolled into one. He is also the inheritor of the Calvinist tradition; he is one of the 'Elect', whom God has blessed and though not all those who surround him are to be despised, nor are they the chosen of God. He is that strange hybrid of European and African; he is no longer Dutch as a Dutchman would recognize him; he has become the *Afrikaaner*.

\*

---

[63] Moodie, *Abstract of Criminal Convictions before the Court of Justice, Cape of Good Hope, No.39*.

In the new South Africa, there were other groups more able to adapt to the disruptive realities of an exploding frontier and the arrival of a new order than the Bushmen. These were the mixed-race people. As we have seen, intermarriage between Europeans, slaves and Khoikhoin was a feature of Cape life right from the outset and their offspring were accorded status according to whether their parents possessed a status strong enough to assert it. Some were known as 'Gedoopte Baastards' or 'adopted bastards' and were generally baptized but many were not; whether the term 'baastard' carried abusive connotations in the 17th Century is a moot point but what is certain is that Baastards were part and parcel of the Trekboer way of life, whether working as herdsmen, being treated as servants or accepted as part of the family. Many others became *drosters*, 'fugitives' slipping out of servitude to take their chances over the frontier with other whites where they in turn married Khoikhoin wives and produced their own children. Within the Cape, vagrancy laws were beginning to impinge on the liberties of many Baastards who were not attached to a particular employer or 'master'; this was not evidence of early racism, but a common response to a problem that had been known in Europe since the Tudor Poor Law; (Pass Laws were enacted in 17th Century England to separate out the deserving from the undeserving poor).[64] Loan Farms were harder to get as the 17th Century went on and this drove more Baastards towards more marginal land, while at the same time the demands for Commando service encouraged others to push further out. This was especially the case along the Orange River and in Namaqualand where the geographical and cultural distance from Cape Town afforded greater independence than even colonial society allowed. Here the Baastards became independent pastoralists, hunters and traders, known as *Oorlams*, fighting the Bushmen, jostling for space, avoiding the government and generally developing in much the same way as the Trekboers to the East and South.

The issue of race here is irrelevant; people of all skin tones adapted in similar ways because the landscape and Bushmen resistance exerted similar evolutionary and existential pressures on all. Indeed, many Baastards were neighbours of Trekboer farmers, working and fighting with, for or alongside of them as in many cases their interests coincided. The most famous of these groups were the Griqua, led by Adam Kok, a manumitted slave who began farming in the Piketberg in the 1770s before heading up to Namaqualand to establish himself in the ivory trade (the name was possibly adopted from the *Grigriqua* earlier established there). By the time of his death in 1795, Adam Kok and his clan were major farmers, cattle traders and ivory magnates whose influence could be felt as far eastwards as present-day Kimberley. Claas and Piet Barends were of slave/Khoikhoin origin and achieved a similar degree of success and independence as cattle traders and hunters up on the Orange River during the same period.

Inevitably, some of these drosters, Griquas and Khoikhoin found the arduous, patient life of the pastoralist unsuited to their particular persuasions and turned criminal, forming themselves into parasitic bandit groups 'desperate, armed and ravenous.'[65] These bandit groups gradually began to coalesce into larger, more stable societies still composed of the

---

[64] https://www.londonlives.org/static/Vagrancy.jsp
[65] Penn, *The Forgotten Frontier*, p.166.

same motley collection of drosters, criminals and deserters but possessing the essential advantages of knowledge of horse, gun and the management of a Commando so that by the 1770s complaints began to flood in to the Llandrosts of attacks by 'Bushmen-Hottentots' and Baastards in Namaqualand. Klaas Afrikaaner was of mixed slave/Griqua origins and first came to the attention of the authorities when he attempted to murder Adam Kok and was duly dispatched to Robben Island but there were plenty of willing replacements so that by 1786, the Orange River was pretty much off-limits to any kind of peaceful settlement. Instead, it was a frontier of constant theft, raid, predation and utter lawlessness in which different Oorlam, Saan, Griqua, Khoikhoin, Trekboer and Namaqua groups in kaleidoscopic combinations preyed on each other while the Llandrost of Stellenbosch, 700km and three weeks travel by ox wagon away to the South, struggled to comprehend, never mind control, the situation. If a state cannot settle disputes and enforce its decisions, to all intents and purposes it is no longer in charge. By 1780, this was exactly the future facing the VOC.

*

### Meanwhile, Back at the Cape.

The emergence of the Trekboer as a distinct figure was a remarkable and dramatic feature of these years, yet it should not blind us to the more prosaic and ultimately more important development of the Cape Farmer, for it was they who provided the solidity to the European colonization of the Cape. Gradually, gradually, with many setbacks of drought, rust and plagues of locusts in between, they learned which crops worked and where, expanded wheat production northwards into the Swartland, persuaded the Indies to buy their execrable wine and began to export ivory, hides and ostrich feathers in small quantities over and above their usual task of victualling the weekly (on average) ship. By trial and error, they learned that free trade was better than Company control and learned how to bring pressure on the administration to erode the VOC monopoly. Slave labour allowed them to bring more areas under the plough and though they could not be described as wealthy in monetary terms, they were increasingly achieving self-sufficiency and producing a surplus for sale. By 1750, the population of the colony was reckoned at around 10,000 divided more or less evenly between Europeans and slaves and it is fair to say that the Europeans were beginning to resemble the sturdy yeoman farmers and staid but steady country gentleman that made up the ideal Dutchman, who knew his rights and expected government to be predictable, reasonably efficient and respectful of those rights.

The petty, traditional and expected perquisites and *cappabar*, levied by government officials were acceptable as long as they were kept within reasonable limits but by the 1740s, as corruption became a growing problem within the VOC, this was beginning to provoke a reaction. Payments for licences, stamp duties of one kind or another continually increased; a farmer who sold a legger (516 litres) of wine to the Company signed a receipt for £8, but walked out of the office with just over a Fiver in his pocket; weights, measures and exchange rates were manipulated all to the Company's advantage so that a farmer paid his taxes in Rixdollars valued at 4% more than the Rixdollars he received in payment for anything he sold to the Company. As with the Trekboers, this had the effect of eroding the legitimacy of the VOC in the eyes of the farmers and as the destruction of the Khoikhoin by smallpox (a second epidemic hit them in 1755-6; two thousand slaves and colonists also bought it) had left seemingly endless tracts of land open for the taking, there was always an option for a man who felt himself bilked. So many of them were taking this option that in 1745 the Company established a third Drostdy to add to those of the Cape and Stellenbosch, named for Governor Swellengrabel's missus, at Swellendam (the *grabel* was possibly just a bit too much of a mouthful and so dropped), where the route from Waveren came down the Breede River and opened out onto the rich, fertile soils that lie southwards, all the way to Cape Agulhas and Mossel Bay.

The Governor's aim in doing this was to control and *limit* the ongoing expansion rather than facilitate it; no one was supposed to go beyond the Great Brak River just east of Mossel Bay but already there were parties of elephant hunters, vagabonds, bandits, cattle traders and escaped slaves ranging far and wide and few of them were much bothered by the thoughts of the Company so the Governor was very largely ignored; by 1750, the Trekboers on the coast were well past the Gamtoos River. Twenty years later, a commission found a thriving illegal trade between Trekboers and the Xhosa on the Fish River that had gone completely unnoticed up until then; the main give-away was the presence of a well-used road heading eastwards out of Swellendam. In 1770, the border was shifted to the Gamtoos and all beyond it were ordered to move back - with the same success as before. In 1775, it was an elephant hunter by the name of Prinsloo who told the Company where to stick their restrictions and so the jurisdiction was extended to the Fish River.

Perhaps the main reason why the farmers beyond Mossel Bay had gone unnoticed was the fact that travel by land eastwards was extremely difficult. Now, it's a question of scooting down the N2 all the way along the delights of the Garden Route, stopping off perhaps at Wilderness, Knysna and Plett but this route only really became practicable during the 1860s when the Seven Passes Road was thrown across the deep gorges, thick forest and swamp. During the 1750s, the route lay up what is now known as the Montagu Pass, an eye-wateringly steep drive for a saloon car today. Even the modern motorway that goes up from George means second gear for most of the way; in 1750, it was a three-day haul involving block and tackle and rope work to get a wagon up. After that, the road ran down the wide and beautiful Langkloof Valley – the R62 is a spectacular road trip – which came out at Algoa Bay. To all intents and purposes, once a Trekboer had gone up the Montagu Pass, he was on his own, unknown to government and entirely dependent upon his own resources.

Those who chose not to head east grew increasingly discontented at the restrictions of government and when, under Governor Plettenberg, government corruption began to go further than was expected or reasonable, dark mutterings came increasingly to the fore. From America and France talk of rights and liberties and revolution began to filter into the colonists' consciousness and for many, no doubt, the Castle of Good Hope began to resemble the Bastille. This all came to a head in 1779 when a brutal, drunken scoundrel of a fellow by the name of Buitendag, but also the black sheep of a respectable family, was deported from the colony. This was in accordance with the wishes of his neighbours and even his wife but somehow, during the three weeks delay between request and enactment, Mrs. Buitendag and the neighbours had had a change of heart and applied for a stay in the law. What they had objected to was his arrest by the slave catchers – a generally disreputable bunch, all things considered – and the fact that he had been deported without trial. From this came a demand that some representatives of the Burghers should be *elected* to sit in the government and protect the liberties that they felt they were owed as free Dutchmen as well as to sort out the now rampant corruption. Four of them headed off to Amsterdam to make their claims and a commission was duly constituted to look into the matter. How bad relations were between the Burghers and the Cape government can be ascertained from the memorial that Governor Plettenberg fired off, accusing the representatives of being entirely *unrepresentative*, their moaning unjustified and self-serving, and finally, that if the Company did not believe him, they could shove their job.

It took four years (there was a war in Europe) before the Directors of the Company made a few trifling concessions to the Burghers but dismissed the substance of their demands and during that time the grievances of the Burghers had grown rather than diminished, largely because the war had brought a large contingent of French troops to garrison the Cape against the English. This had alerted them to the weakness of the Company and the increased potential for trade free of Company restrictions. They also grew in moral status because they had loyally turned out for militia service as required.

*

### The End of the Dutch Colony.

The root of the Company's problems lay in the decline of Dutch power relative to that of Britain and France. Her apogee in the 17$^{th}$ Century was followed by rapid decline in the 18$^{th}$ Century; between 1652-74, she had beaten England at sea; by 1782, she was dependent upon the French to secure her from the English. The VOC too had steadily declined and its Cape station had always struggled to pay its way – its wines were undrinkable, its wool unsellable, the income from loan farms was often uncollected and the expenses of government seemingly never ending. By 1779 the colonists were increasingly rejecting its legitimacy and demanding a say in their own government; the Company paid its last dividend in 1782; in 1783, it began to issue paper money, attempted to bring in new taxes, cut back on defence expenditures all of which measures did nothing to alleviate the growing disillusionment. Petty quarrels brought officialdom into disrepute; during a sermon in 1790, the Reverend Seurier made a pointed reference to Jezebel while the Governor's wife was in the congregation to which the Governor responded by having the street on which the good Reverend lived renamed Venus Street and affixing the street sign over his residence. This no doubt gave everyone a good laugh but did nothing for the Company's good standing. Corruption got out of hand too when the Company cut the salaries and perks of its employees in the hope of restoring some semblance of profitability to the Balance Sheet; Governor van der Graaff's son achieved notoriety in this respect by running the Company stables as if he owned them himself. Powder, muskets and shot were the only thing that the Trekboers really required from the Company and although they were prepared to make a show of allegiance to the Llandrosts for the legal cover this gave them in the matter of land titles and war, taxes were anathema and paper money, or 'cartoon' money as Theal called it, regarded as worthless; only gold and silver coins were valued. When in 1792, the Company tried to introduce an inheritance tax to recoup some of the losses it was making in the colony, the Burghers pointed out that the losses of the Company belonged to the Company and as they had had no say in the running of the Company, they did not see why they should have to stump up to cover them; in short, *No Taxation Without Representation*. When revolution in France was followed by war in 1793, the Company moved its Cape headquarters to Java - its heart was always out East, an obvious conclusion when one compares the paltry little fort at the Cape with the massive fortress at Galle in Sri Lanka; the following year it declared itself bankrupt.

During the 1770s, the Bushman resistance brought crisis piling in upon crisis. The battles fought along the line of the escarpment that marks the barrier between the coast and the interior pushed the Trekboers south eastwards off it, towards the Zuurveld where a new competitor, the Xhosa, barred their way. The Northern frontier was now reckoned to run from the West coast at the Buffalo River, then South Eastwards to the escarpment and along it following the northern edge of the Great Karoo, to Graaff-Reinet and hence South Eastwards to the sea. This Eastern frontier was anchored on the high country of Bruintjies Hoogte, today marked by the towns of Cradock and Somerset East, and ran down across the Zuurveld between the Sundays River and the Fish River to Algoa bay. Everything west and south of these lines were now Dutch or Afrikaaner Trekboer territory; north and east of them were still disputed.

The potential for further unwelcome conflict resulted in Governor Van Plettenberg's tour of the frontier in 1778 in which he made two quite momentous decisions. Shocked at the extent of the advance of the Trekboers, he attempted to halt it in its tracks by negotiating a treaty with the Xhosa that fixed the Fish River as the boundary between the two and then authorized the frontier authorities to raise Commandos to ensure that the Xhosa would keep to their side of it. In doing so, he effectively drew the line on expansion but at the same time hardened up the meaning of occupation; this area was now Company land, Dutch land, Trekboer land and though the river marked the final extent of the expansion of the colony, it was also intended to stop the Xhosa from pushing any further westwards. He also put a stone beacon high up on the heights above the Karoo near present day Colesberg to mark the furthest extent of any northward expansion that might be contemplated by any Trekboer; no mean feat in itself - I've been up that road from Graaff-Reinet to Colesberg and to do it in an ox wagon must have taken some real endurance. Beyond that beacon the Trekboer was forbidden to go. Plettenberg's efforts were wasted; both the Xhosa and the Trekboers were going to ignore any restrictions on their movements.

At long last and way too late, a new Llandrostdy had been established at Graaff-Reinet in 1786 to try to bring some sort of order to the new frontier, and into it was placed Honoratus Maynier, a humane, idealistic man whom Theal damned as:

'...deeply read in the works of the French philosophers of the day, and, in defiance of what observation should have taught [him], professed to believe that simplicity and innocence are virtues of barbarian life.'[66]

Although not the actual Llandrost – that honour went to Llandrost Woeke but as he was too drunk and quarrelsome to function, Honoratus got the honour – Maynier was the driving force and his greatest desire was to assert Company authority, bring peace to the frontier, end illegal trading and raiding across the frontier and establish the rule of law. He might as well have asked for the moon because Trekboer clan leaders like Conrad de Buys, seven feet tall, living a life almost indistinguishable from any Xhosa clan leader, right down to black wives and concubines, had little time for any idea of law other than an eye for an eye and had no intention of letting anyone interfere in their business. As far as they were concerned, the answer to cattle theft was retaliation swift and when the Xhosa clans busy colonizing the western side of the river refused to move back over to the eastern side, trouble came to a head.

In 1789, when the Xhosa carried out a large cattle raid across the Fish River and the ensuing Commando caught them hard up against a river in flood and prepared to launch into them, Maynier refused to authorize the attack, believing that reason and appeasement were better guarantees for future peace than a general retaliation. The Commando held its fire and the Xhosa escaped with their loot intact leaving the trekboers understandably mutinous. When the Xhosa came across again in 1793, sweeping up 65,000 cattle, plundering farms and murdering their occupants, Maynier refused to call out a Commando again, so the Trekboers called one out anyway; Maynier belatedly led it, against the wishes of the Trekboers, and achieved little before the usual insincere peace was patched up. Maynier, true to his philosophical stance, sent in a report blaming everything on the Trekboers, thus marking him out as one of the earliest of those idealists in South African History for whom facts – what *is* - are secondary to what they *should* be. By this time, however, the Trekboers had had their fill of the VOC and, given the scanty but alarming news of war and revolution in Europe, were coming to the conclusion that independence from the Company would be an option worth considering. They did not spend much time considering it either.

The following year, in 1794 a number of Trekboers, headed by Martinus Prinsloo, Willem de Klerk and Frans Kruger, refused to take the oath of allegiance to the Company's new Governor Sluysken. Their ire was taken out on poor Maynier, in whom they had no confidence and who they forcibly deposed from office in February 1795 with a Commando led by Adriaan van Jaarsveld, the much-respected Field-Commandant of the district. Maynier was a member of the Orange party, committed to upholding the authority of the Stadtholder in Holland against the revolutionary Patriots, and as a reaction to this, rather than any deep-rooted commitment to the ideals of the French Revolution, van Jaarsveld and the Prinsloos donned the tricolour cockade as their badge and named themselves 'Nationals' or 'Patriots'. Sluysken sent a deputation to Graaff-Reinet to try to calm the situation as he could not afford such disruption at a time when an invasion by either the British or French was

---

[66] Theal, *History and Ethnography*, Vol III, p. 178.

daily expected. On the 12th June, the British fleet arrived off the Cape; on the 14th the Patriots put Sluysken's commissioners out of the drostdy at gun point. On the 18th a further party of Patriots carried out a coup on the drostdy at Swellendam which replaced the Llandrost and styled itself as a National Assembly. The French Revolution had come to South Africa, it seemed.

Superficially; there was still a community of interest between the Company and the Patriots in that both had an interest in resisting the British; Sluysken had his duty while the Patriots felt themselves unlikely to get a sympathetic hearing from British officers already engaged in a war against the Tricolour. As a result, Sluysken was able to call out the Commandos from Swellendam and Graaff-Reinet to defend the Cape without actually being their commander but it was to no avail. In June 1795, Admiral Elphinstone sailed into False Bay at the head of the Royal Navy, informed the Cape authorities that the colony had been placed under British protection by the Prince of Orange and that he was going to land General Craig's troops to take possession. There was a bit of a skirmish at Muizenberg close to the place where all those photographs of brightly painted beach huts are taken; at the time it was a swamp, the *Sandvlei*, and some sailors got shot at when they were up to their chests in it; shortly afterwards it was reclaimed by filling it up with horse shit and waste straw from the stables; now it's a golf course; apparently the greens are magnificent. The fight wasn't anything to write home about and within a day or so, the Cape was secured. In response, the Patriots, disgusted at the poor performance of the Company army and the impending surrender of Sluysken, decided on the 27th August to appoint Adriaan van Jaarsveldt as President of a Council of War of what was, to all intents and purposes, an independent republic based at Graaff-Reinet. This is where the colony of Van Riebeeck and the Dutch East India Company came to an end.

*

What can we say of the colony of the VOC? In terms of its own aims, it can be said to have been a qualified success in that it did fulfil its primary purpose of being a victualling station for ships on their way to and from the East but it never fulfilled the hopes of big, easy profits that were expressed from time to time. Certainly, it proved a disappointment in terms of profitability; for the last ten years of its existence – and these were its most profitable times – the income from taxes, licences, rents still left a deficit of £92,000pa after expenditure on government salaries, administration and defence. This is one of the stark facts of imperialism in Africa; it never paid its way for anyone, Dutch, British, French, German, Italian or Belgian, because the costs of conquest and administration were always way higher than the value of the revenues generated. So much for Lenin's assertion that imperialism was the highest form of capitalism.

In terms of the effect of the VOC, we can say that the century and a half of the Company's occupation were indeed momentous but mainly as a result of the Law of Unintended Consequences. The emergence of the independent Trekboer was never envisaged by the Company and it is fair to say that this was an unwanted development as far as they were concerned. For them, the limit of occupation to the Cape peninsular would have been much more preferable as it would then absolve them of the expense of governing the interior. The destruction of the Khoikhoin by smallpox was also momentous and this too was an unintended consequence of occupation; disease benefitted no-one for it diminished the cattle trade and killed off the labour force and we can assign no blame to the Company or colonists for this terrible scourge. Similarly, the Company cannot be held responsible for the grinding down of the Bushmen; rather the key factor in their end was the inability of the Bushmen, for whatever reasons, to adapt to the intrusion of both Dutch and Xhosa colonist and come to some political settlement. What we can say, and it seems indisputable, is that the Company had profoundly changed Southern Africa without ever really intending to and had unwittingly created situations, problems and opportunities in the interior that they were ill-equipped and largely unwilling to deal with. When the Company folded, it handed on these problems intact and unresolved to the British inheritors of the colony and disappeared, as if in a puff of smoke.

What the Company had not done, however, was to fix the future. They had not determined that South Africa would become Apartheid South Africa. South Africa could have developed in many other ways. There is no chain that Van Riebeeck and his successors could forge that could bind the future. It is only Historians who forge the chains intended to bind the past to their particular politics and so try to fix the future – for a while, anyway.

*

### The Arrival of the Xhosa; the British and the Batavian Interlude

The Xhosa resembled their future countrymen, the Afrikaaners, more than those on either side of the Apartheid struggle cared to admit. We know quite a lot about the Xhosa because there had been quite a lot of contact with them recorded in both official records from Ensign Beutler's expedition to them in 1752, the accounts of sailors who had been shipwrecked on the Natal and Transkei coasts and who had walked back along the beach to the Cape (an experience that was undoubtedly less pleasant than it sounds) and from various eccentric travellers. Theal studied, interviewed and wrote about them too. On top of this, J.B. Peires did a lot of work on the oral History of the Xhosa which, being checkable against written records, was a much more reliable form of evidence and from which he was able to piece together some convincing accounts of the Xhosa in the 18th Century. We have met Noel Mostert, of course, who drew a lot of accounts together, loaded them into a blunderbuss of a book called *Frontiers* and sprayed the landscape with a selection of historical shrapnel that to me at least, still managed to miss the barn door of fairness.

Who were they? They were pastoralists living in clan groups loosely under the control of a chief or paramount chief, with a thirst for good land, a willingness to compete for water and grazing, an effective military system and a willingness to give both the Khoikhoin and the Bushmen short shrift. They were expansionist colonisers, much as this description will cause Leftists to shudder, who differed from the Trekboers more in their daily culture and religion than in their vital interests. In some respects, even these were not so different; the Trekboers might prefer a wagon and a shack to a reed mat and a hut, but both ate their own milk, beef and mealies, clothed themselves in the hides of their own animals, and suffered from the same vagaries of drought, flood, locust, cattle sickness and finding dowries/*lobola* for their daughters. Both of them acquired their land from the Khoikhoin using a combination of conquest and purchase, the Xhosa defeating them around 1700 in order to take the Transkei.[67] The material culture of the Xhosa was somewhat less than that of the Boers; they knew little of textiles, had only the basics of metal work and had yet to find a use for the wheel but they produced enough for their needs. Religion provided another difference but this was less important than most other things; the Trekboers were Christians of a sort, the Xhosa practiced ancestor worship and animism of a sort. There was also what my old sociology teacher (bless his cotton socks) called 'sex-role sterotypation' whereby men looked after the cattle, women looked after the crops and domestic chores while the kids just got in the way as usual; probably a stricter division of labour to that common among the Trekboers, but one that was still recognizably similar. Like the Trekboers, they were suspicious of authority and evolved a series of customs and practices which did much to prevent autocratic tendencies emerging in a chief. The most important of these was the idea that the heir to the chiefdom should come from among the youngest children rather than the firstborn in order to guarantee that the rule of a young chief was tempered and informed by the wisdom and advice of elderly councilors. That was the theory anyway; perhaps the defining characteristic of the Xhosa leadership was the dire shortage of leaders worthy of bearing the name and a distinct shortage of anything in the way of political wisdom. Perhaps the biggest difference lay in the institution of the *amaButho* system; in common with many other Bantu, Xhosa boys were organized into age-sets, became men on circumcision and from that point on were expected to fight or work for the Chief whenever his age-set/regiment was called upon. Nothing comparable existed among the Trekboers.

Only in the matter of *amatakati* were the Xhosa startlingly different from the Trekboers. The Xhosa believed that any particular bad luck or calamity was due to the spells of a sorcerer and that when this happened a witchdoctor, a *sangoma*, was required to 'smell out' the *amatakati* who would then be 'eaten up' or put to death in any number of horrible ways. Against an accusation there was no defence and the only option was to flee the moment one got wind it was coming. Very often, accusations were made out of jealousy, spite, to dispossess a rival of his cattle or dispose of an enemy and there is about as much justification for this practice as there is for a secret police purge or a Twitterstorm. That hasn't stopped some people from attempting to excuse it; one writer described it as a means of balancing society by 'the elimination of blatant acquisitiveness, restraint upon individual influence [and] those seeking to disturb the body politic'. I dare say that would be a fitting motto hung over the doors of a Gulag.

As to the Xhosa views of white people, one can only say that they were puzzled about the ships that could be seen floating past the coastline out there on the horizon and the ragged individuals who from time to time seemed to come washing up on the beach out of them. They believed that white people originated from somewhere at the bottom of the ocean and

---

[67] Theal, *History and Ethnography* Vol.3 p.81.

that they floated up on sea shells, which the sails of a ship resembled. Perhaps; they extended hospitality or displayed hostility as seemed most advisable at the time until they began to come into more regular contact with the Trekboers along the Fish River in the late 18th Century. By the 1780s, some of them had chosen to find work on the farms of the Cape.

In terms of political organization, the Xhosa were in some disarray at this time. This was a consequence of Chief Phalo's decision c.1730 to violate the custom of not taking a Great Wife (who would produce an heir) until he was older while still having children by his Right-Hand Wife (the first or 'wife of his youth'). Thus, two sons, Gcaleka and Rarabe (pronounced *Khakhabaye;* 'r' in Nguni orthography is pronounced 'kga'), grew up in a rivalry which resulted in the division of the tribe into two virtually separate clans, the paramount Gcaleka and the nominally subordinate Rarabe. Death by natural causes and battle reduced the ruling family further so that by 1782, the paramount chief was the three-year old Gcaleka, Ngqika, watched over by his uncle, Ndlambe of the Rarabe.

Already intermingled with the Trekboers at the time of Plettenberg's arrival on the Fish River in 1778, the Xhosa clans that the Governor served notice on to retreat to the eastern side of the river were reluctant to obey. This was because the clans that had crossed the river had done so to get away from the Rarabe who were waging war there. Unwittingly, Plettenberg had added two active ingredients to what with competition for grazing, the endless theft and counter-theft of cattle, mutual ignorance of aims and situation, was already a recipe for disaster. The first of these ingredients was that Plettenberg believed he had got an agreement with the Xhosa in general rather than with just a couple of clans; this would be a mistake repeated many times because Xhosa Chiefs were not like Henry VIII or Louis XIV but wielded much less power and influence.

The second active ingredient was his belief that he had the power to compel the Trekboers. He did not; the Prinsloo clan regarded the Company with the usual contempt. Demanding that the Xhosa clans decamp was therefore, the spark to the tinder. The inevitable hostilities began in the Bruintjies Hoogte area in 1778, Commandant Adriaan van Jaarsfield was authorized to take a Commando into the field against the Bushmen and, if the Xhosa would not go back across the Fish River peacefully, attack them too. They would not.

The first war between the Dutch and the Xhosa that followed consisted mainly of cattle raiding and then the shifting of the Xhosa clans in the Bruintjie's Hoogte area back over the Fish River. Down in the Zuurveld they stayed put but it was not a *Xhosa War of Resistance* by any means. (We are back to the significance of names here again; *resistance* implies that the Xhosa were being dispossessed or occupied when in reality this was a conflict between two competing groups of colonists). For a start, the Rarabe hoped for an alliance with van Jaarsfield because they hoped to extend their control over those clans on the western side of the river. In the Zuurveld, the Rarabe were also interested in bringing the Mbalu and Gqunukhwebe clans into their orbit especially as they were also fighting against each other over the grazing. The second war of 1793 was pretty much the same, beginning with a large Xhosa raid on the Trekboers' cattle and ending (as we have seen) when Maynier's attempts to prevent the Commandos going out resulted in the final revolt of the Trekboers against the authority of the VOC.

What's in a name? These wars were the start of nine 'Frontier' wars between the Cape Colony and the Xhosa, yet as we have seen, that term has already been used for the war between Van Riebeeck and the Khoikhoin in 1659. Parker and Pfukani preferred to call the 1659 war, the *First Hottentot War* and the 1781 war the *First Xhosa War of Resistance* which was rich; it could hardly be called a war of *resistance*, given that they argued that the Xhosa started the war. During the 19th and much of the 20th Century, these wars were known as *Kaffir* wars but as that initially innocent term, picked up from the Arabic for *infidel*, came to acquire an insulting meaning – it is illegal to use it in several southern African countries – alternatives were sought. This in its turn led to a fair amount of strife; the Left believe that if the language can be hijacked then the political programme will be enabled and so pushed *War of Resistance*. Think back to 1982, if you're old enough, and consider the effort the British Left put into pushing *Las Malvinas* instead of *The Falkland Islands* in the hope that if the term was accepted, Britain would lose the war (against a Fascist colonial regime indeed; I know, amazing, but the hypocrisy of the Left knows no limits). At the same time, the usual suspects began to push for the *First Indian War of Independence* to supercede the astonishingly accurate and perfectly descriptive *1857 Indian Mutiny;* not even those Indians who were busy changing the names of Calcutta and Bombay to *Kolkata* and *Mumbai* were interested in that one. So, *War of Resistance* became popular for a while until the more sensible and accurate *Frontier War* was settled on, which is heartening.

Even so *frontier* itself has a particular and distinctive meaning for Historians of South Africa (and the American West especially) and unless you are careful, you end up using a loaded term; fortunately, this nuance escapes most people so it's relatively harmless. In essence, the *frontier* is not a line on a map but a 'zone of penetration' which 'opens' when two distinct societies collide and 'closes' when one of those societies achieves a dominant position. Now this is a useful idea as far as it goes but, and this is the big BUT, into this idea was smuggled a right little bugger of a bad idea and that little bugger of a bad idea was that one of these societies was 'indigenous' to the region while the other was 'intrusive'. There are absolutely no coconuts for guessing who got labelled with being 'intrusive' when in reality, both the Boers and the Xhosa were 'intrusive' and neither had a claim to being 'indigenous' to the area around the Fish River; the 'indigenous' title goes to the Khoikhoin and the Bushmen, both of whom were disposed of by the 'intruders'. So, from being a useful idea, the concept of the 'frontier' suddenly became a stick with which to beat first the Boers, then the British and finally, white people in general. You have to pay attention when dealing with Leftists and Historians of South Africa; and just because you think you might be a bit paranoid about all this doesn't prove that the bastards aren't out to get you. They are.

When the facts at the historian's disposal are deliberately obscured, deliberately manipulated, routinely skewed and worse, ignored, in order to establish a History that is fixed (in both senses of the word) in order to support a single interpretation that is in turn intended to endorse, support and advance a particular political programme, then there is a very big problem. This is effectively what happened from the 1960s onwards as Historians began to drift leftwards politically, a drift that in the 1980s increasingly became such a stampede that by the time I started off in academia in 1998 Historians of the Right began to look increasingly like an endangered species. The conservative philosopher Roger Scruton noted the disturbing tendency for Left-leaning professors to appoint only other Leftists to academic positions while he was at Birkbeck in the 1970s. Hardly surprising considering the old fraud Eric Hobsbawm was there, a man who supported the Nazi-Soviet pact, never relinquished his Communist Party membership until 1991 and up to the point of his death in 2012 believed that the mass murder, starvation and brutal oppression of Stalin's Russia was really a noble experiment and the millions of deaths would have been worth it if Communism had actually worked, a view that begs the question of whether it would have been better to be experimented on by Dr Mengele than Dr Hobsbawm; needless to say, he never took the opportunity of living in a socialist paradise, preferring to stay in the leafy suburbs of the bourgeois, capitalist West he so despised.

Inspired by the ideas of the Italian Marxist Gramsci, the more rabid Leftist academics believed themselves to be engaged in 'the long march through the institutions' whereby the organs of society would be gradually taken over by the Left and so become tools to usher in their grand vision of socialism. The stranglehold they established was great; if you weren't a fellow traveller, you didn't get published, and you didn't get the jobs. When I was studying at the University of East Anglia, one of my fellow doctoral students, a scion of one of the wealthiest families in Britain who hoped for a career as a professional historian, considered it wiser to sport a copy of *The Guardian* about the department rather than be seen with *The Daily Telegraph* – and this department was run by a Conservative. According to the *Washington Post*, by 2014, the number of US academics who self-identified as being of the Left was over 60% while those who self-identified as being of the Right was down below 15%; in the fields of Humanities and Social Sciences, those figures were probably more than 90% and less than 10% respectively[68] and I would make a wild guess that those figures were replicated in the UK too (and replicated in journalism too; try being a Tory at the BBC and see how long it takes you to get off the 'Granny's cat stuck up a tree' desk; Channel Four is a lost cause completely).[69] The clear fact is that in the last fifty years, just about anyone who wanted an academic career needed to buff up their Leftist credentials, write essays that would please the Leftist gatekeepers to those prized plums of position and tenure and then ensure that their students did the same.

The result was seen very quickly in most fields of historical study. 'Facts' became Humpty Dumpty facts; ('When *I* use a word,' Humpty Dumpty said, in a rather scornful tone, 'it means just what I choose it to mean – neither more nor less.') So, the facts would mean whatever they were intended to mean and in Imperial and South African History, they were intended to mean that the idea of imperialism was an unmitigated evil, the British Empire the embodiment of that evil and, crucially, that it was responsible for many, if not all, of the evils

---

[68] https://www.washingtonpost.com/news/wonk/wp/2016/01/11/the-dramatic-shift-among-college-professors-thats-hurting-students-education/?utm_term=.b6476cba0a5f
[69] http://www.telegraph.co.uk/news/2017/11/07/cosmopolitan-elite-must-learn-humility-else-fury-english-will/

of the Third World of which the biggest was Apartheid. This was a dishonest travesty of anything recognisable as even an approximation to the truth, a generalisation that admitted of no nuance or exception and was all the more heinous for being premeditated and deliberate. Even those who were more moderate imbued the view that the more Left-wing influences there were in society the better so that by 1980, saying something nice about the British Empire was like letting off a fart at the funeral of a much-loved auntie. 'Who controls the past controls the future,' said George Orwell. 'Who controls the present controls the past.' Never was a truer word spoken.

And it's getting worse. In October 2017, an article that dared to suggest that perhaps colonial rule might have had some positive aspects provoked the resignation of half the editorial board of the journal it was published in (that rip-roaring, fly-off-the-shelf journal of genius *The Third World Quarterly*). Forty other academics wrote a letter to the *Times Higher Education Supplement* protesting that it should never have been published at all as colonialism was a 'crime against humanity'. Even worse, the publishers, Taylor and Francis, agreed to withdraw the article because of 'serious and credible' threats of violence directed at the editors.[70] This was followed in December 2017 by sixty Oxford academics objecting publicly to *even* the study of empire, which is, as anyone of sound mind would agree, grotesque; a university *objecting* to study.[71]

The skewing of facts to fit the theory by Leftist Historians is something that I've come across time and time again in studying South African History but just so you know I'm in earnest about this and not just grinding an axe, I'll provide you with just one of the worst examples of this. It comes from the Professor of Commonwealth History, Director of Commonwealth Studies at the School of Oriental and African History and who has a fair claim to be the absolute doyen of South African Marxists, and it was published in no less an august work of apparently impeccable and impartial scholarship than *The Cambridge History of Africa*. The offending passage is concerned with the Anglo-Zulu War of 1879. When I have an idle moment in the bath or out on a walk I sometimes amuse myself by picking it apart word by word, phrase by phrase and sentence by sentence but as we are going to deal with the Zulus later on, it would only bore the pants off you if I did it here. Needless to say, I did pick it apart when I was studying for my Master's degree under one of the Professor's protégés, much to his ashen-faced chagrin; to be fair to the old chap though, he did have the good grace to admit that I had a point, once I had bludgeoned him with enough footnotes.

Anyway, here the good Professor makes a statement that any reasonable person might mistake for a straight-faced, bare-faced, jaw-dropping attempt to misrepresent the actual facts on a gargantuan scale;

> *On 11<sup>th</sup> January 1879, Lord Chelmsford entered Zululand with a body of British troops. Eleven days later, they had been disastrously defeated by the Zulu at Isandhlwana. Even with reinforcements, Chelmsford was unable to retrieve the*

---

[70] Bruce Gilley (2017): The case for colonialism, Third World Quarterly.
[71] http://www.bbc.com/news/uk-england-oxfordshire-42423269

situation: *further defeats at Rorke's Drift, Eshowe and Hlobane were only partly avenged by the British victory at Ulundi six months later. Although Ulundi was elevated into a spectacular military victory, after which Chelmsford could honourably resign the command to Sir Garnet Wolseley, it signalled the exhaustion of both sides rather than the destruction of the kingdom.*[72]

*The Battle of Rorke's Drift was a British defeat.* Yup. You'll be familiar with the battle of Rorke's Drift because that's the one depicted by Michael Caine and Stanley Baker in the movie *Zulu* that comes on the TV every Bank Holiday. It's the one where a garrison of a hundred or so pith helmeted and red-coated stiff upper lipped Welshmen see off four thousand Zulus while singing *Men of Harlech*. (I'm writing this on 22nd January, 2018, the 139th anniversary of the battle, which is serendipitous, I feel).

Now shot full of holes as far as strict accuracy is concerned, the movie is right in quite a few of the essentials, including the essential fact that it was a *British victory*. It's a battle that even the Zulus admit was a defeat. It's the one that Ian Knight, the foremost historian of the Zulu war and a bit of a Leftie himself admits was a British victory. Honestly, I can hear Lieutenants Bromhead and Chard along with the other nine VC winners spinning in their graves as I write. Chief Buthelezi, who starred in the film as the Zulu King Cetshwayo, also thought the idea that his mob won the battle was garbage, as indeed it is. I know; I asked him myself.

Now note also that she uses the term 'a body of British troops' which, given the prevailing demographics of the day, might be interpreted as 'white' troops; she left out the fact that there were large bodies of Africans in that army. Note also the claim that 'Chelmsford was unable to retrieve the situation'; *he won the bloody war* and if that isn't retrieving the situation, I don't know what is. This wasn't the end of it though; while taking care to reel off all the *British* defeats, she left out all the *Zulu* defeats bar the last, final one at Ulundi – Khambula was the big one. And on top of that, she claimed that the British Empire was *exhausted*; this is not something that can be defended on any measure of power, military, industrial, naval or financial that I can think of. Now, you might say that this is just a historian making a selection of the relevant facts as per normal but I would argue that if this is an attempt at a fair selection then it rates as an epic Fail. Go to the bottom of the class.

Now baiting Lefties is a fine pastime and I'll be doing plenty of it in the pages that follow but in order to be fair, I should point out that much of the false narrative they created - that British imperialism was an unmitigated evil and responsible for Apartheid - was intended to undermine the Apartheid system then in operation and for this they may be excused litter-picking punishment in the playground for one lunchtime only. In some cases, such as Jeff Guy and most of the academics in South African universities under that ludicrous system, they might even be given praise but this should not detract from the deleterious effects that the construction of this false narrative has had.

[72] Fage J.D. Oliver R. The Cambridge History of Africa Vol 6. 1870 – 1905. (CUP 1985). Marks S. *Southern Africa, 1867 – 1886, p392 – 393.*

*

On with the show. Establishing itself in 1795, the new British authority was anxious to be as conciliatory as possible to all elements within the colony as the last thing it wanted was to face any internal threats at a time when powerful French forces might appear from Europe or their base at Mauritius to contest their control of the Cape. To this end, a generous deal was offered; as long as the inhabitants accepted 'Orange' party Llandrosts (those loyal to the House of Orange), they were promised redress for many of their grievances, a regeneration of the economy through the resumption of trade and a restored metal coinage, and a supply of ammunition should they require a Commando. However, neither van Jaarsveld nor Prinsloo and the rest of the Patriots blethering on about independence and republics out at the one horse dorp of Graaff-Reinet were prepared to accept this and would only go so far as to offer free trade and neutrality in return for the right to run their own government.

This was naive in the extreme; the British government was not the bankrupt Company, nor were its armies ramshackle mercenaries or amateurs. Indeed, this was the first but not the last time that the Boers misunderstood the British character. Normally, the British are like hobbits; peaceable, more interested in golf, gardening and football than fighting but once committed to a war they become relentless, determined enemies able to harness anything and everything to the pursuit of victory. These are the people who sent a contemptible little army to fight the Kaiser's masses in 1914 and two years later broke the Germans' back on the Somme; most people associate modern *Blitzkrieg* warfare with the Germans but the truth is that most of the techniques and concepts associated with combined armed operations – indirect fire artillery, aircraft, tanks, tooled up infantry carrying out fire and manoeuvre – were invented by the British army. In the period in question, it was also Wellington's Peninsular veterans who opened up the 'Spanish ulcer' in Napoleon's stomach and who broke the best unit in the French army – the Imperial Guard – at Waterloo. And then, as is the British way, they (we) all went back to golf, gardening and football. In Afrikaaner mythology, the Commandos always ran rings around the British but the reality is that bar the 1881 First Anglo-Boer War and despite the initial victories of 1899 and a few odd skirmishes later on, the Afrikaaners always lost when they took on the British. (Cue: screams of protest from ornery old Boers; but as a particularly ornery old Boer once said: 'the harder the blows struck by the enemy the more resolute and the more determined this people will be to see this business through'. His name was Jan Christian Smuts[73]).

So, it was that when the Boers up in Graaff-Reinet sent in their demands, in March 1796 Major-General Craig dispatched 300 men to Stellenbosch as a warning, raised a regiment of Khoisan soldiers and cut off the vital ammunition supply to the interior. The capture of a Dutch fleet sent to re-take the Cape in August 1796 at Saldana Bay was a severe blow to the Patriots, while the rapid deployment of 2500 troops and eleven guns to that same Saldana Bay, the quartering of dragoons on recalcitrant Burghers at Cape Town, and proclamations to the effect that any help given to the said fleet would result in death, convinced many Patriots that the British would apply decisive force if they were not minded to accept the milder

---

[73] Sarah Gertrude Millin, *General Smuts* Vol.II (London, 1936) p.153

measures that advertised the benefits of British occupation. By December 1796 the Patriot party had accepted the realities of the situation and submitted but not without dispatching Jan Pieter Woyer to Batavia in a Danish ship in the hope of gaining assistance. In the event, he succeeded in persuading the authorities at Batavia to dispatch the *Haasje*, carrying 16,000 kgs of gunpowder and eight field guns, only to see it attacked and her cargo captured by an English whaler assisted by a Portuguese ship when forced to put into Delagoa Bay to make repairs in August 1797.

The iron fist having been displayed, the British went back to advertising the milder measures of the velvet glove which they much preferred and which were usually more effective. Free Trade was their first offer and it was eagerly accepted. At first glance this doesn't look like much but it was a momentous shift after a century and a half of the badly maintained VOC monopoly. The prevailing orthodoxy in van Riebeeck's time and for long after was that the wealth of the world was fixed and that in order for a state to gain a bigger slice of the pie, it was necessary to deprive someone else of their share. They also thought that foreign trade ought to be a state monopoly while at home personal thrift and saving were virtues to be encouraged and excessive consumption curbed through sumptuary laws (parasols were once banned by the Cape authorities as encouraging idleness and a tendency to luxury) and price controls on everything from wagon wheels to elephants' teeth. This was called 'Mercantilism' and though I doubt very much if many Lefties know the term, I've certainly come across very many of them who agree with the basic tenets.

Mercantilism was the reason why the VOC made such continual efforts to control trade within the colony and why these efforts caused such resentment among the colonists, both Burghers and Trekboers. Trekboers were not educated and so could not understand economic theory and so could not see anything wrong with buying a cow off a Khoikhoin or a Xhosa on the principle of 'willing seller, willing buyer' and then selling it on to someone else for a profit. When the British arrived with their new-fangled notions of *Laissez-faire*, of letting people go about their business with as little interference or regulation as possible within an established legal framework of enforceable contracts and minimal taxation, just about everyone who wasn't on the VOC payroll breathed a sigh of relief; especially as the British also abolished torture and 'barbarous methods of execution'. The Burghers could now look forward to growing their profits, expanding their businesses, employing more people, demanding and creating a wider range of goods and services, in the way that seemed best to them, following the 'hidden hand' of the market rather than busting a gut to stay on the right side of laws that being both illogical and unenforceable favoured the corrupt and the criminal over the honest trader. In short, the British ripped up regulations and freed up enterprise to create more and more wealth in the only way possible if people wish to enjoy any sort of standard of living beyond the level of the merest subsistence. It's called 'Capitalism'. What the British and anyone not on the VOC payroll understood instinctively was that the percentage size of your slice of the pie wasn't as important as the overall size of the pie and if you could make the pie bigger, everyone got a bigger slice. This is the difference between mercantilism and capitalism; the former assumed that the wealth of the world was fixed, the latter knew that it wasn't and could be very quickly grown, once the government got out of the way.

The second of these milder measures was an invitation to dinner with Lady Anne Barnard who arrived as official hostess to Earl Macartney, the Viceroy. Macartney himself was an experienced diplomat having led missions to Russia and China and held Governorships in India and the West Indies but whereas few people remember his name today, Lady Anne Barnard is remembered with great affection by even the most hard-bitten, *rooinek*-hating, Afrikaaner tour guide. Witty, intelligent, peaches and cream handsome, she was a feature of London society with a reputation as a coquette, turning down eleven offers of marriage before, at the age of 42, finally accepting the unknown Andrew, twelve years her junior, with whom she did actually fall in love. It did her social life no good at all and if it hadn't been for her working her contacts, it is doubtful if Andrew would have got the appointment as Macartney's secretary. At the Cape, eager to keep up her contacts with Sir Henry Dundas, Secretary of State for War (and rejected suitor), she sent him a stream of amusing letters detailing the goings-on of the colonists, her adventures in the interior and the life of the Cape Dutch. A quick squizz through her Journals leaves one in no doubt that she enjoyed her time in South Africa, climbing up Table Mountain, (which is some going – I've successfully avoided attempting it on many occasions) charming all and sundry, gossiping relentlessly and living in a state of bliss with her new husband in a cottage called 'Paradise'. She seems to have caught the particular bug that everyone gets when, for the first time, they drink in the fresh air of Cape Town, take in the golden light of the oaks around the white swirling gables of the Cape Dutch architecture and marvel at the clear blue of the sky over the combed red earth of the lime green vineyards. She had the kind of enthusiasm that was infectious and a dismissive attitude to any sort of privation or difficulty. With the locals, she was a hit, holding dinners that were meant to break down barriers and largely succeeding, providing a meeting place where the British and the Dutch could mingle and learn a little about each other and so encourage the personal relations with influential people that British diplomats have always sought to cultivate.

The fine picture of the Cape given to us by her Journals has been the main reason why she is held in such affectionate regard – there is a room in the castle named after her and you can stay at her country pile, now the Vineyard Hotel in Newlands - but beneath the fluff, Lady Anne Barnard was a pretty astute observer and quickly picked up on the essentials of many of the problems the British would encounter in the coming century. From the beginning, she reported, there were doubts among the Cape Dutch that the British were serious about a long-term occupation, and doubts among the British that the Cape was really much of an acquisition at all.[74] She expressed a suspicion that too much importance was placed on the necessity of conciliating Cape Dutch opinion and roundly condemned the turning of a blind eye to the violation of British anti-slavery legislation[75] which was part of it. Even though she showed a marked ambivalence to the institution itself, she did not agree that laws should be flouted and was influential in having Sir George Yonge, one of Macartney's successors,

---

[74] Lady Barnard to Dundas, 10 July 1797. Reproduced in H.J. Anderson (ed), South Africa a Century Ago (1797 – 1801): Letters written from the Cape of Good Hope and Extracts from a Journal by The Lady Anne Barnard, (Cape Town, 1901?).
[75] Lady Barnard to Dundas, 10 July 1797.

removed as Viceroy for accepting a large bribe from a slave trader landing slaves illegally at the Cape. She reported the opinion of the senior naval officer at the Cape, Admiral Pringle, that the place was undefendable and that any development of the colony would probably turn it into another United States of America, more likely to rob Britain of India than secure the imperial jugular, and that 'no pains should be taken with the interior of the country' beyond ensuring that the immediate area should produce enough for the re-victualling of passing Indiamen. Neither could she say much that was complimentary about the economy, but noted that apart from wine, bread and meat, everything else was extraordinarily expensive and in short supply.[76] There were plenty of hopes about the possibilities of gold mines and unicorns[77] and she hoped that settled government and the presence of British forces would stimulate trade, agriculture and industry, but success in this would all lie very much in the future. In the interior, 700km away at Graaff-Reinet, she reported an ominous gathering of Boer Malcontents who were determined not to accept any rule but their own.

This was accurate forecasting; there *was* always an ambivalence in the British assessment of the value of the Cape and a doubt among the Cape Dutch as to whether the British would not suddenly up sticks and leave – to this day, South African Englishmen are known as *Soutpiels*, people who have one foot in the Cape, one foot in London and stand with their pride and joy dangling in the Atlantic; 'salt dicks'. The question of how far to push the anti-slavery issue at the cost of alienating the Cape Dutch and the Trekboers was one that would have repercussions right up until the present day. The question of how far the Cape could be isolated from the interior in terms of defence was one that had plagued the VOC and would plague the British in very similar ways. Ditto the economy; South Africa has always looked richer to European eyes than it actually is and the dreams of gold and unicorns were for the most part just that – dreams. And as for Boer Malcontents, well, she was spot on there too.

Where she was not so observant was in the matter of her husband. He lacked both her social status and her social skills and he was unable to form working relationships with either of Macartney's successors. After they were recalled in 1802, he struggled to find work until he was sent back to the Cape in 1806, much against Lady Anne's wishes as she feared for his health, and he died there in 1807. The news reached Lady Anne in England along with the revelation that Andrew had an illegitimate child, Christine, a daughter by a slave girl, who was conceived back in 1802. To her credit, Anne refused to abandon the child, brought her up in the Berkeley Square house and made her the amanuensis for the memoirs that she wrote in her sixties. She died in 1825 and her Journal was published in 1901.

*

In 1799, the Third Xhosa/Frontier War broke out and although you can read a History of South Africa and skip over it without really noticing such a minor interlude, I'm not going to let you off so easily because this war is a great episode for testing out that idea of the 'frontier'. As well as that, it contains such bizarre and colourful episodes that I really can't pass over it. The main amphitheatre of the action was an area of land called the Zuurveldt

---

[76] Lady Barnard to Dundas, 10 July 1797.
[77] Lady Barnard to Dundas, 10 August 1797.

which lay between the Fish River (now known as the Great Fish River) and the Sundays River. Roughly speaking, the Sundays River today runs down from Graaff-Reinet in a SSE direction and empties into the Indian Ocean at Port Elizabeth (actually Colchester) in Algoa Bay. At the top end is the dusty, arid Karoo which gives way around Jansenville to the long steep ridges of the Zuurberg mountains and thick bush of the Addo Elephant Park after which the land becomes increasingly fertile; the last time I was there in 2017 all the talk was of growing avocados but in 1799, grass would have been the main topic of conversation (that, and the fact that there was no booze to be had *at all* in Graaff-Reinet). The Fish River also runs down from the area of Graaff-Reinet but further eastwards until it cuts through to the rich, rich grasslands around Cradock – after coming down from the Karoo, it is impossible to not be struck by the lushness of this area and you don't need to spend much time driving through Cradock (blink of an eye really: and the sausages in the Wimpy there are the smallest I've ever seen) to see that this is good farmland; in the early morning, the rocks of the mountains are golden and the grass is an intense lime green. From Cradock the river meanders down the escarpment to empty into the Indian Ocean at Seafield; importantly, in a country where rivers can be seasonal or, like the Sundays River, brackish, this one flows all year round. So, the Zuurveldt is a belt of land lying NW-SE enclosed by the Sundays and Fish Rivers, about 200km wide, very fertile and, just as importantly, connected to the Cape market through the rudimentary port at Algoa Bay.

The disturbances began when the general consternation produced by Bonaparte's expedition to Egypt in 1798 fanned the Patriot cause into revolt again. The withdrawal of experienced British regiments from the Cape garrison coupled with a disastrous fire which destroyed most of the commissariat stores and killed 130 horses belonging to the dragoons led many to suppose that the British at the Cape were vulnerable and so communications were opened with the French at Mauritius.[78] At the same time Adriaan van Jaarsveld was arrested on a financial irregularity, which prompted Marthinus Prinsloo to call out a Commando and, in January 1799, release him from the custody of the three (a whole three!) dragoons sent to escort him to Cape Town. Beneath this attachment to this highly regarded, tough as old boots, biltong-and-bullets, elderly Commando leader were the usual complaints about grazing, the occupation of the Zuurveldt by Xhosa clans who were supposed to have gone back over the Fish River and the ban on Boers crossing that same river to graze on the other side. There was also an undercurrent of feeling among some of the wilder souls like Conrad de Buys, at that moment living at Ngqika's 'Great Place' or main kraal, that an alliance between the Patriots and the Rarabe might serve to clear the Zuurveldt of both the Xhosa clans *and* the British.

The insurgents met with little success and the rapid and decisive response of the British snuffed out the rebellion. General Vandeleur's dragoons (8th and/or 28th Light Dragoons) immediately galloped through Swellendam and along the coast to meet up with two companies of the 91st Foot and the Khoisan Regiment then landing at Algoa Bay. The whole force then marched on Graaff-Reinet arriving there on the 18th March 1799 and putting an

---

[78] G.M.Theal, *History of South Africa from 1795 to 1872* Vol. I, (London, 1915), p. 50.

end to Prinsloo's capers. Such a demonstration of force had effects other than to overawe Prinsloo's rebellion and bring him to submission. Combined with the policy of conciliation, of confirming Dutch officials and civil servants in their posts, the presence of British forces held out the possibility, especially to those Boers on the northern frontier, that their security needs might be catered for more effectively than previously and fifty-three Boers from the Sneeuberg correspondingly turned out in a Commando *in support* of Vandeleur. The presence of the Khoisan Regiment also brought about a general desertion of Boer farmsteads by Khoisan servants and apprentices in the belief that the British presence meant liberation from what was effectively bonded labour. One hundred immediately joined the regiment at Graaff-Reinet, while some hundreds of others joined the camp. This was a severe blow to the Boers of the area as it demonstrated that the British could, almost at a stroke, undermine the viability of their farms by removing their labourers and, if they so chose, to dispossess them altogether. Only by submission could they expect to hang on to their livelihoods, and this bitter pill fragmented the Dutch polity even further. Those who could not swallow it disappeared into the Xhosa country, among them men with such names as Frans Kruger and Coenraad Bezuidenhout. Van Jaarsveldt, along with Marthinus Prinsloo, was re-arrested and eighteen of the insurgents were incarcerated in the castle at Cape Town in June 1799. Any hope of French assistance evaporated with the capture of the *Prudente*, carrying ammunition and volunteers from Mauritius in February 1799, and the repulse of the frigate *Preneuse* from Algoa Bay in September 1799.

The priority of maintaining the security of the naval base at Cape Town necessarily meant conciliating the Dutch, but the fragmentation of the Dutch polity allowed the British considerable discretion in choosing which sections of that polity to conciliate and in what measure. Influential opinion in Cape Town and the food producing areas of Stellenbosch were obvious candidates for a bit of soft soap from the government and a good dinner from Lady Anne Barnard and, of course, the British would sooner be on good terms with the Boers of the interior than not, but there were limits. In particular, those limits did not include being sucked into the intractable problems of a volatile frontier and, beyond the provision of some powder and shot for the occasional Commando where necessary, the British had no desire to take the side of clans like the Prinsloos in their conflicts with the Xhosa. Neither had they any desire to intervene in the civil war that broke out among the Rarabe when the regency of Ndlambe was ended. Plainly stated, British troops were there to defend Cape Town, and not the Boers. This was demonstrated when, in the middle of dealing with the Boer malcontents in Graaff-Reinet, there was a major outbreak of disorder in the Zuurveldt in February 1799 – the Third Xhosa War.

The British had hoped to conduct their relations with the Xhosa on the same principles as had the Dutch East India Company; that both sides should recognize the Fish river as the border between their respective domains and pull back their respective peoples to their respective sides of it, and that contact between the Boer and Xhosa colonists should be prevented in order to rule out the possibility of theft or injury to either party. In 1797, Governor Macartney sent Secretary John Barrow (smart, yes, but only twenty years old) on a visit to the Xhosa to negotiate these terms and he returned satisfied that Ngqika had agreed to them.

However, just like Plettenberg, Barrow made the mistake of assuming that Ngqika was the chief of all the Xhosa clans, rather than just the Rarabe, and failed to realize that although Ngqika had some influence over those clans who had drifted across the Fish River into the Zuurveldt, this was by no means a sovereign power. The Mbalu and the Gqunukhwebe clans refused to discuss withdrawal with Ngqika, while Ndlambe's clan had fled there to *escape* from Ngqika. Thus, when Vandeleur, in the company of Barrow, ordered Chungwa, leader of the Gqunukhwebe, to leave the Zuurveldt in May 1799, he was surprised to find his orders refused, his camp attacked and an isolated patrol of the 91$^{st}$ slaughtered in an ambush. If this was not enough, the Khoisan clans, led by Klaas Sturmann, who had initially sought British protection, now interpreted the situation as one in which they might exploit the discomfiture of the Boers and their estrangement from their source of ammunition supply, by plundering the district themselves. The whole of the frontier exploded, farms went up in smoke and the Xhosa clans in the Zuurveldt teamed up with roving bands of Khoisan to lift as many cattle as they could. The Boers went into laager and Vandeleur retired on Algoa Bay.

Ignoring the fact that a large number of Khoisan had sought the protection of John Barrow and that others were serving both in Vandeleur's command and in Boer Commandos, some writers have been tempted to declare that this was the beginning of a race war. In South African History this is a recurring meme; if white soldiers and black soldiers are fighting then it is assumed they must be fighting each other and this must be about race, yes? No; very often they were fighting on the *same* side but in almost every case the role of black soldiers fighting *alongside* their white comrades is played down, airbrushed out or just ignored. The other recurring meme is that the British Army blunders hopelessly about while their nimble opponents run rings round them and their cowardly and incompetent officers scratch their heads and skulk. If this was the case then it's a wonder the Empire was ever built at all. The one question that just about all Historians of South Africa never really feel comfortable in answering is the most obvious; if the British were so hopeless, how come they kept on winning?

Let's take Mostert's accusation that General Vandeleur was 'baffled'[79] by the situation and afraid for his reputation to the point of cowardice.[80] *Cowardice*? That is about the most serious charge you can make against a soldier and if Mostert made it to his face he would instantly have been presented with a choice of swords or pistols and the opportunity to put to the test the theory that the pen is indeed mightier than the sword. This is Vandeleur's record; on active service against the French in Flanders 1794-6; led three devastatingly successful charges during the Second Maratha war in India 1804-6; commanded an infantry Brigade of the Light Division in the Peninsula and led the assault into the breach at Ciudad Rodrigo suffering a severe wounding; saw action at the Battles of Salamanca, Vittoria and the Nive; chosen by Wellington, the greatest soldier of the age, to be second-in-command of the whole British cavalry at Waterloo, he assumed complete command after Lord Uxbridge had his leg blown off. Now, even given that the Frontier War happened early on in his career, is it

---

[79] N.Mostert, *Frontiers,* (London, 1992), p. 292.
[80] N.Mostert, *Frontiers,* (London, 1992), p. 293.

reasonable to suppose that such a man, a veteran already, was a cowardly incompetent? No, it isn't.

In reality, Vandeleur's retirement on Algoa Bay was consistent both with military orthodoxy and good strategy in that he correctly identified it as the vital ground in any conflict on the eastern frontier. This was the gateway through which supplies and reinforcements would come for any campaign in the area, as well as being the port most likely to be used by the French to intervene on the side of the Boers. The orders which he then received from the Acting Governor, Major-General Dundas (Sir Henry's nephew), reflected the strategic priorities which the British held; he was to recruit Boer Commandos to push the Xhosa over the Fish river and then to conclude a peace.[81] The last thing Dundas wanted was a war with the Xhosa that might coincide with a French attack, but the threat of a Boer outbreak if the Xhosa were not resisted also needed to be taken into account.

The scale of the outbreak and the disruption of communications, coupled with the fragmentation of the Boer polity in the frontier districts and Vandeleur's withdrawal, allowed the Xhosa and Khoisan insurgents a greater freedom of manoeuvre than they might otherwise have had and armed bands penetrated down the Langkloof valley during July 1799 as far as George – further than the Xhosa had ever been before and far beyond what they accepted as any legitimate claim to ownership. Graaff-Reinet was isolated and the Boers of each particular district were forced into laagers that camped wherever there was pasture for what cattle they were able to keep out of the hands of the Xhosa and Khoisan. On 10th August a mixed force of Xhosa and Khoisan attacked Vandeleur's camp in an attempt to run off the commissariat cattle but without success, and when Dundas appeared in September with Commandos called out from Swellendam and Stellenbosch, along with some Companies of the 61st and 81st Foot and fifty Dragoons, the British were ready to retake the initiative. This took the form of a large military movement designed to persuade those armed bands within the colony to withdraw while at the same time sending the pleasant but deeply unpopular Maynier on a mission to the Xhosa to negotiate a peace which left the Xhosa, under Ndlambe, in possession of the Zuurveldt and most of the Boer cattle. The settlement was accepted on 16th October 1799, the Commandos sent home and Maynier established as Resident Commissioner for Graaff-Reinet and Swellendam. It was an unequivocal victory for the Xhosa – who had also lifted most of the cattle stolen by the Khoisan clans. How the Boers felt about the settlement may be gauged by the heavy irony of G.M. Theal writing in 1915.

> 'Some white men, they [the Boers] said, had risen in rebellion [at Graaff-Reinet], and though they had not shed a drop of blood nor forcibly deprived an individual of a shilling's worth of property, they had been pursued, disarmed, and fined, and at that moment eighteen of them were in a distant prison awaiting trial for treason. Some Hottentots had risen in arms, and though they had murdered men, women, and children, and had pillaged farms and burned houses, they had not been pursued, nor was their plunder taken from them, nor one of their number made prisoner. If the

---

[81] Theal, *History of South Africa from 1795 to 1872*, Vol. I, p. 59.

government regarded this as justice, nothing but the direst necessity should make them [the Boers] obedient subjects. And then in their ruined state, the man whom of all in the world they disliked most was placed over them with nearly unbounded authority.'[82]

That the British policy of avoiding wars in the interior by some measure of appeasement of African polities at the expense of the Boers was not simply a local expedient can be seen by its repetition on both the north-eastern and northern frontiers in the case of the Bushmen during each of the governorships of Macartney, Dundas, and Sir George Yonge. Macartney had instructed the Field cornets Visser and Louw in 1798 to negotiate a settlement with the Bushmen clans across the northern frontier on the basis of the occasional provision of livestock by the Boers in return for cessation of raiding. Visser had long been an advocate of peace with the Bushmen achieved on the basis of goodwill, presents, the appointment of Captains to bring them into a relationship with the government similar to that enjoyed by the Khoikhoin and recognition of exclusive use of tracts of land across the Sak River. Influenced by John Barrow's disgust at the treatment of Bushmen as virtual animals, Visser was also a Christian. Jacobus Louw had, on his own initiative, managed to keep the peace in the Onder Bokkeveld for fifteen years. Despite early success, the settlement broke down, as all others had broken down because there was no central Bushman authority and only those personally consulted acquiesced.[83] Similarly, in November 1800, Yonge offered an amnesty and a farm to the Oorlams leader, Jonker Afrikaaner, if he would give up living by robbery of both Boers and other Bushmen clans in the Hantam area and along the Orange River. He refused.[84]

What does all this tell us about the 'zone of penetration' and the attitudes of those who were doing the penetrating? The first thing that strikes a fair-minded reader is that British policy was remarkably clear, firm and accommodating. Much of it involved the use of expedients in a volatile situation and much of it was pretty *ad hoc* but in general it was consistent to its aims and showed no particular favour to one side or another. In the matter of territory, the British showed no desire to possess land for the sake of it, nor cared whether this suited the Boers or not. If the Xhosa were prepared to stop at the Zuurveldt then this would be as acceptable a boundary between the colony and the Xhosa as the Fish or Sunday's Rivers – as long as it *remained* the boundary.

The second conclusion we can draw is that race was still a notion of only secondary importance but one which was far more complicated than a simple black/white division. Conrad de Buys, the seven-foot-tall Trekboer malcontent who had adopted a lifestyle more Xhosa than Dutch, was in a sexual relationship with Ngqika's hugely fat and powerful mother and had offered the hand of his fifteen-year-old mixed-race daughter to Ngqika. He, along with many other malcontents, thought nothing of allying with the Xhosa against the British, a fact that rather punches an iceberg shaped hole in the titanic efforts to project Apartheid attitudes back a century and a half. It is true that John Barrow was appalled at

---

[82] Theal, *History of South Africa from 1795 to 1872*, Vol. I, p. 63. Adriaan van Jaarsveldt died in jail. The rest were set free by the Batavian government.
[83] Theal, *History of South Africa from 1795 to 1872*, Vol. I, p. 67.
[84] Theal, *History of South Africa from 1795 to 1872*, Vol. I, p. 66.

what he saw as the indiscriminate slaughter of the Bushmen by the Boers but, as we have seen, the explanations for this are rooted more in mutual incomprehension than in notions of race. Similarly, Barrow was appalled at the treatment meted out to Khoikhoin servants by the Boers, comparing it to the worst abuses of slavery but (and we'll look at the whole slavery issue when we get to the abolition) their treatment at the hands of the Rarabe was scarcely better. Among the Gqunukhwebe, intermarriage with the Khoikhoin was common and, of course, even those Trekboers who maintained more of a 'Dutch' lifestyle than Conrad de Buys were apt to take black or mixed-race women as wives or concubines.

The third conclusion we can draw is that just as Ngqika quickly realised that not all white people belonged to the same clan, the Boers realised that the British could not be relied upon simply because they were European. Nor indeed, could they automatically rely on the Cape Dutch who, if anything, were rather closer to the British than the Trekboers in their outlook, lifestyle and business interests. So, this idea of the frontier being a 'zone of penetration' does have some legs after all as long as we jettison the twaddly bits about the 'indigenous' and 'intruder' people.

*

Under the terms of the Peace of Amiens between Britain and Revolutionary France in 1802, the colony at the Cape was handed back to Holland – now under French control and known as the Batavian Republic – and a new government arrived. Both Commissioner-General Abraham de Mist (Feb 1803 to Sept 1804) and Governor Jan Willem Janssens (March 1803 to January 1806) were loyal to the republican government but they were more inclined to the royalist Orange party than to any Patriot cause. Within the Cape colony therefore, the Batavian authorities were anxious to reassert control over the rebellious Boer clans on the frontier while at the same time fulfilling their primary mission of maintaining the Cape as a base on the route to the much more valuable possessions in the East Indies, ready for when the House of Orange might return. This in turn meant that the Burghers would need to be conciliated and both De Mist and Janssens tried to steer a middle path between the pro-French 'Jacobins' or 'Patriots' and the pro-British and anti-revolutionary 'Orange' bodies of opinion. In effect, there was little difference to the policies adopted by the British.

In April 1803, Janssens left for a tour of the eastern districts. The destitute state of the frontier Boers put him in a strong position to bring them to heel and attempt to make a settlement on the eastern frontier. Thomas Ferreira and Jan Arend Rens, leaders of two of the more refractory Boer families, were removed from the frontier and given enforced residence at Swellendam. Khoisan servants, many of whom were without visible means of support after having had fled their masters, were given 14,000 acres at Bethelsdorp to settle on under the supervision of Dr. Van der Kemp and the London Missionary Society. Those who chose to go back to their former masters were assured that proper contracts would be drawn up and enforced, while negotiations were opened up with Klaas Stuurman which led to a cessation of hostilities and the allocation of a tract of land to him on the Gamtoos River. During May and June negotiations took place with the Xhosa clans on both sides of the Fish River which confirmed the status quo on the Zuurveldt, forbade the employment of Xhosa by Boers, and yielded up a number of malcontents from the Xhosa country, including Conrad de Buys, who were thereby removed from the frontier. In April 1804, a new district, Uitenhage, was created on the eastern frontier by taking responsibilities from Swellendam and Graaff-Reinet, which had the effect of dividing the frontier Boers of Graaff-Reinet into two different magistracies and thus reducing their collective strength, and a military officer was appointed Llandrost. In July, this process was repeated with the separation of the northern frontier districts from Stellenbosch to form the new magistracy of Tulbagh and a reform of both the Commando system and the local government was carried out.

All in all, the Batavians were good bureaucrats, unspectacular but effective, and it is to them we owe the Census of 1805 which revealed that the Cape contained 25,757 Europeans exclusive of soldiers, 29,545 slaves and 20,006 Khoisan or Baastard servants. Cape Town had 1258 houses and buildings exclusive of public buildings, 6273 Europeans, 1130 'free blacks', 9129 slaves and 452 Khoisan[85] and so now we can properly call it Cape Town rather than Cape Village. That these reforms were carried out at all was remarkable because from the moment the Peace of Amiens fell apart in 1803, no one was under any illusions that the British would not be back and preparations were made accordingly.

In February, 1804, all British nationals were ordered to leave the colony but as the government had no way to enforce such a declaration, the proclamation was modified to an enforced residence in Stellenbosch, and then further modified to expecting a general promise from Britons that they would do nothing hostile. Lt-General Janssens, took over the effective running of the government from the civilian M. de Mist, who by his own admission, knew nothing of military affairs, raised a corps of gunners from the Asians in the colony which became known as the Malay artillery and equipped them with field guns as well as training them to man the garrison artillery emplaced in the castle. They were integrated into units with Dutch gunners and Mozambican slaves. The six hundred strong 'Hottentot' infantry regiment was put through a training programme designed to bring it to a peak of efficiency and an attempt was made to raise mounted forces from the Cape Dutch Burghers. In addition to these forces, Janssens had the Waldeck battalion, a four hundred strong German mercenary unit, the 22nd Line infantry regiment (350 regular Dutch infantry), the 9th Jaeger battalion (200 Regular Light infantry, composed of many different European nationalities), and 130 Dragoons (mainly Dutch Regular cavalry). When the British invasion took place, Janssens was also able to rely on the crews of two French ships, the *Atalante* and *Napoleon* which had been wrecked or run ashore on the Cape peninsular. It did no good.

The British arrived in Table Bay on the evening of 4th January 1806. Packed on board the East India Company transports were 6,600 men of the 24th, 38th, 59th, 71st, 72nd, 83rd and 93rd Foot and the 20th Light Dragoons. They were accompanied by a powerful fleet of three 64-gun ships, one 50-gun ship, two 30-gun frigates and three brigs (usually carrying 18 guns each). Janssens had first been warned of the fleet's approach on the morning of the 4th but because of a gale and heavy surf the British were unable to disembark until the 8th, thus

---

[85] Theal, *History of South Africa from 1795 to 1872* Vol.I, p. 188-9.

giving him the chance to call out the Burghers and concentrate what forces he had to resist the British advance.

In reality, however, Janssens chances of mounting anything more than a token resistance to this force were slim. His main artillery strength was concentrated in the batteries that protected the port of Cape Town, the Amsterdam, Chavonnes, Great Mouille and Little Mouille, but there was little reason for the British to risk landing under them when they could land anywhere in Table Bay and march up to Cape Town under the protection of their own naval gunfire support and take them from the landward side. The mobility afforded by the fleet transports meant that the British could land wherever they felt was most advantageous to them and expect to get ashore before Janssens could march his troops up to oppose them. As it was, Commodore Sir Hope Popham and General David Baird put their redcoats down on the bone white sand of Losperd's Bay, about twenty miles north of Cape Town (the name is unknown now, except in the form of Losperd's Crescent just off Napoleon Avenue in Melkbosstrand, which is indeed twenty miles or so north of Cape Town) but they also landed troops about half way between Losperd's Bay and Cape town, and at Saldhana Bay, approximately 100 miles north of Cape Town. Even had Janssens been able to get his troops on to the landing grounds it would have done him no good as the guns of the fleet could put down a weight of fire that would have forced him to retreat. Popham's fleet had 360 guns firing balls of from 9 – 68lb in weight, which, by way of comparison, was more artillery than Napoleon fielded at Waterloo.

Still, Janssens hoped to occupy a ridge of higher ground, the Blauberg (it's the place where all those postcard pictures of Cape Town and Table Mountain are taken from), which the British would have to scale and thus oppose their advance from a position which would put him above the elevation of Popham's guns and thus shorten the odds somewhat. However, the distance was too great and he was forced to meet the British forces as they came down off the Blauberg 4,600 strong in the early morning of 8th January 1806.

The resulting Battle of Blaubergstrand was as bloody an affair as either side could wish for; the British lost fifteen dead and 190 wounded while the Dutch roll call showed a total of 337 dead, wounded or missing. This was a proper, toe to toe slugging war, not the glorified skirmishing that had characterised South African warfare to date. The raw numbers do not tell the whole story, however. The fact that the Waldeck battalion deserted at almost the first opportunity – they being mercenaries and not much disposed to dying in a forlorn hope – meant that the Dutch lost 337 out of 1600 men, a casualty rate of almost 25% in comparison to the British loss of under 5%. The high wounded count for the British might be explained by the fact that they attacked in column and thus presented a compact target for the Malay gunners. The prospects for those who were wounded were not good either, given the primitive state of medical knowledge.

Although the British were left in possession of the field, Janssen was still able to retire in good order and as the British cavalry had been among the forces landed at Saldana bay, unpursued. His immediate plan was to retire inland and abandon Cape Town to make whatever terms it could and thus marched to the Hottentots-Holland pass in the hope of raising Burgher forces from the hinterland. The arrival of the British had coincided with the harvest and although the muster had been called, too few to be decisive had actually arrived and Janssen had left most of them in Cape Town to defend it against an attack from either the sea or from Saldana bay. The rapid advance of the British to Cape Town, which fell on the 11th, and then Stellenbosch on the 13th, with a further plan to send a regiment by sea to Mossel Bay to cut off his rear, made any hope of holding out in the interior until a French expedition might reverse the situation unrealistic. Most of his forces came from Cape Town or Stellenbosch and the British proclamation that they should forfeit their lands and possessions if they continued to resist meant a simple choice between a desperate guerrilla campaign of indeterminate length and no guarantee of success or a mild occupation. Janssen did the sensible thing, released his Burghers to their farms and surrendered his regular forces on the 18th January.

There are a number of lessons to be drawn from this campaign. Firstly, was the inescapable fact that Cape Town would fall to any reasonably sized expedition that made it to Table Bay. The fort and batteries there were completely inadequate to defend the town and only by intercepting the expedition and sinking it at sea could the security of this possession be guaranteed. Turning Cape Town into a fortress like Gibraltar was impossible without enormous expense because any circumvallation would need to cover Simonstown as well as Cape Town. Simon's Town had to be included in the scheme because it was necessary to have an alternative sheltered and secure anchorage to cope with the differing seasonal winds. Even were such defences to be built, there would never be a powerful enough regular or militia force to man the walls when the population of Cape Town was so small and divided into Cape Dutch, Boer, African, Slave and British identities. Any defence force organised would also have to cut across these racial or cultural identities, if sufficient manpower was to be mustered. Furthermore, Gibraltar was such a strong point because it could always be re-supplied by a powerful Royal Navy only a week's sailing away, while Cape Town would have to be capable of withstanding a siege of a minimum of twelve weeks – the absolute quickest time it took to get from Cape Town to England and back – and probably longer.

The second reality was the result of Janssen's retirement into the interior. Although short lived and unsuccessful, it meant that however much the British wanted to avoid contact with the interior of the continent, they could not ignore it if they wished to prevent the sudden descent on Cape Town of a force determined to end the British presence there. From the beginning, therefore, the hope of isolating Cape Town from the interior, as Gibraltar was isolated from Spain, was a forlorn one.

The third reality was that the very isolation and vulnerability of Cape Town meant that the British would need to seek local allies if they were to minimise the threat of a local challenge to their supremacy. Simply relying on an oppressive military repression and a strong garrison would lead in the long run to the growth of anti-British feeling and so some conciliation of the local population was necessary, especially as the Cape would retain its importance for the routes to the East whether Britain retained it or lost it during the negotiations that would end the war sooner or later. Good relations with the local population were essential if supplies were to be forthcoming to both passing ships and the garrison itself.

*

## Permanent Occupation

In reality, the chances that Britain would give up the Cape a second time were nil and from the outset they ruled as though the occupation was permanent. However, until the war against Napoleon was over, the British would place a high premium on internal peace. The victory at Trafalgar in 1805 did not sweep the French navy off the world's oceans and they retained important naval bases around the world, especially at Mauritius, retained the capability to send substantial expeditions to distant quarters, while the British blockade was frequently evaded. The French expedition to the West Indies in April 1809 might just as easily have been destined for the Cape (and might well have got there had it not been for the dithering of the French admiral)[86] while the powerful squadrons which were dispatched to raid commerce[87] could also be used to carry troops. This meant that the occupation would be mild and conciliation actively sought.

There would be changes, of course, and perhaps the first and most obvious one was the arrival of so many more British people that Cape Town began to feel more and more of a British town rather than straightforwardly Dutch. For a start, between 1795 and 1819, no fewer than thirty-three British Regiments served at the Cape for shorter or longer periods of time. This meant that accents from Ireland, Wales, Cheshire, Lancashire, Dorset and Ulster would all be heard on the streets of Cape Town and Simonstown in addition to the more usual seafaring twangs of Europe and the East Indies. There would also be a branch of the Turf Club formed, plus hounds for hunting, cricket, billiards, a steady stream of sportsmen out to shoot the abundant game and that particularly British form of torture known as 'Amateur theatricals'.

At this point we should pause and pay tribute to one of the unsung heroes of South African History. His name is Peter Philip who I confess I had never heard of until in 2018 the owner of a guest house in Montagu gave me a copy of his *British Residents at The Cape 1795-1819*. In this huge work of what must have been the most tedious and painstaking amalgamation and cross-checking of obscure records, Philip produced a list of four thousand eight hundred British people who passed through the Cape Colony during this period along with brief biographical details of each. It is a marvellous work of reference which allows us an insight into the lives of those extraordinary 'ordinary' people who came to make a life at the Cape.

Many of them were discharged soldiers who chose to take their chances at the Cape at the end of the Napoleonic War rather than face unemployment in the depression of post-war Britain. Twenty-five-year old William Chadwick arrived in 1818 courtesy of the London 'Refuge for the Destitute' while a fair few others took jobs as *knechts*, agricultural labourers

---

[86] D. Thomas, *Cochrane*, (London, 1978), p. 146.
[87] P. Kennedy, *The Rise and Fall of British Naval Mastery*, (London, 1983), pp. 151-3.

with a status not far removed from the Boer *bywoner* or the Hottentot 'servant'. Some came for a longer or shorter time before going on to Canada, India or back to England. Some were missionaries, some less concerned with the after-life and more interested in the tavern; Sergeant Barraclough, late of the 21st Light Dragoons, seemed to have fought a running battle with the authorities over his habit of both staying open late and serving the amber nectar during Divine service. There were plenty of the shopkeepers, artisans and small-time professionals so despised by both Bonaparte and Marx (who regularly cheated tradesmen); Miss Sydney Barralet arrived in 1819 to set up a millinery shop; Thomas Buckle arrived in 1799 as part of a government sponsored scheme to improve agricultural techniques, stayed right through the Batavian occupation and ended up farming at Saldanha Bay and Groenkloof where by 1813, he had amassed a fortune of 58 oxen, 1 pig, 9 horses and 2 wagons and a clan of two sons, one daughter, two hottentots and two slaves; William Caldwell arrived in 1796 and was by turns, an hotelier, auctioneer, retailer, hotelier (again), postmaster and wine taster; Thomas Carr made stinkwood furniture at Groot Vaders Bosch (how I wish that was *Darth*); Some prospered, others did not; W. Banks of the 21st Light Dragoons was found dead in a ditch, believed murdered, while William Banyard, a schoolmaster was similarly unlucky, succumbing to some untreatable ailment in 1820 before his thirtieth birthday and in serious arrears of his taxes; James Onslow Williams, farming up in the Groen Kloof, lost the greater part of his stock and was bankrupted by the severe winter of 1815 while Lt Donovan and the Reverend Cowan were murdered in 1808 as they explored the interior. Mr Anguish committed suicide (no, honestly), while in 1798 Mortlock and Brooks were unmasked as Spanish spies and sent off to London to await their fate.

Perhaps the most famous arrivals were Benjamin Moodie's two hundred Scottish artisans who came to the Cape in an organised party of indentured labourers; they were snapped up by the Government immediately for public works. (Indenture was an arrangement whereby a worker agreed to work exclusively for one employer for a specific period of time in return for passage out and agreed wages; it has since acquired sinister overtones but actually it is still widely practiced – most Ex-pats are effectively indentured; I was one for six years in the Middle East). Several boat loads of 'Prize Negroes', slaves liberated on the high seas by the Royal Navy's anti-slaving campaign also added to the mix; to prevent their destitution, it being impossible to repatriate them for fear of them being enslaved once more, they were generally indentured before being granted full freedom and usually employed on public works. Despite the attempt to paint this as quasi-slavery by the usual suspects, it was no such thing, just the usual pragmatic response to a new and complex problem. A slave does not own his or her own body; indentures were bought and sold, but the sale did not negate the conditions of the indenture and brave would be the person who attempted to raffle off a British mechanic, as was done to a slave girl by the Paymaster of the 81st Foot in 1802. Complaints about ill-treatment were made and acted upon; one indentured Prize Negro by the name of Jean Elle took Charles Blair, the corrupt official responsible for allocating indentured servants, to court and won his case; it's a funny kind of slavery that allows that to happen. (And the usual suspects also claim that Britain removing the Portuguese exemption from anti-slavery actions in 1839 was just an excuse to get more Prize Negroes into indentured servitude – which is just bollocks).[88] By name, there were fifty-eight Smiths, thirty Browns, thirty-eight Campbells, twenty-three MacDonalds, eighteen Murrays, sixteen Clark(e)s, eleven Hughes, seven Munros, three Murphys, a Bromhead, a Kekewich, two Patons, two Chamberlains, two Durnfords, six Woods, one Buller, one John Locke, J. Smuts (a Dutch resident), one Rhodes, two Kimberleys, Fletcher Christian's cousin Ewan, a Thomas Packenham Vandeleur and, for the technically-minded, one Gubbins. There was a Thatcher, a Cameron, two Blairs - a whipper-in of foxhounds and a corrupt official (no further comment required) - and a flageolet player called Brown; a flageolet is a kind of flute that allowed for a drone and a counter-melody to be played at the same time, a fact that has a certain serendipity to it, I feel. Another conman was the Reverend Halloran who had been present at Trafalgar, was subsequently appointed as Chaplain to HM forces at the Cape and then Headmaster of the English Grammar School; all would have been well if he had not been such a fractious fellow given to writing scurrilous letters to various officials, but the enemies he made discovered that his letters of ordination were forged and he was quickly deported. Alexander Munro, originally from John O'Groates decided that Lands End wasn't far enough and ended up in George; he drowned in False Bay.

Among the wilder spirits was the deserter, Thomas Bentley, who in 1803 ran off to live with the Xhosa; John Cane, who arrived in 1813, became a Zulu chief, interpreted for Piet Retief and was killed fighting in the Zulu civil war of 1838; Sarah Bradbury, who was so smitten by Henry Batt that she broke her contract of service to marry him, was deported back to England as a result but then returned a year later where the happy couple, now reunited, set up a liquor store in Longmarket Street. Open this marvellous book at any page and a life is revealed; Alexander Lillie, one of Moodie's indentured servants, was drowned in Herold's Bay while attempting to rescue a young boy in difficulties. The shoemaker, John Hogg, arrived in the Cape in 1818 but had to wait until 1842 for his moment of fame when he was captured by the Boers at Durban. Master Mariner James Callander spent the five years after 1798 exploring the Knysna area at the behest of the government before being charged with harbouring runaway slaves and being fined for libelling government officials; he also had two illegitimate children to add to his three legitimate offspring and supported two Malay apprentices who we might speculate were also on the distaff side – he was a seaman after all. Samson Dyer, another seaman, was a black American who married Margarethe Engels and worked as a harpooner in the False Bay whale fishery. 'Tiger' Green from Wexford got his name by killing a leopard with his bare hands; no mean feat but the fever at Delagoa Bay got him in the end. Eva van Carvel, 'a free native of the Cape' did her bit to expand the mixed-race population by giving birth to William in November 1812 and thus adding one more son of a gun to the colony – in this case the 93$^{rd}$ Highlander Lt. Gunn's distaff offspring (he wasn't the only 93$^{rd}$ Highlander with a taste for the wild side; Quartermaster M'Kay had two children by a similarly situated lady). That said, Sally Hare virtually populated the colony on her own, churning out sixteen children as the second wife of Captain Joseph Hare, whose duties in the Dragoons or as a Wine Taster clearly did not keep him busy enough. Ann Lovett had bet her fortune on the patent mangle that she brought with her from London while the mysterious Joseph McCabe was born in Cape Town in 1818 - of a father who was not

---

[88] http://dhsouthafrica.leadr.msu.edu/research-papers/prize-negroes-in-cape-town-and-the-atlantic-abolitionism-4/

only unmarried but also had never been in the colony. John Macintosh opened up a brewery in Castle Street – where else?

The immigrants came from all walks of life too; cabinet-makers, apothecaries, accoucheurs, builders, blacksmiths, cooks, teachers, farmers, shopkeepers (including one John Lewis), hairdressers, Lloyds agents and insurance brokers, whalers, actresses – even a professional whistler. What makes it a marvellous book is that it reveals that those early colonists were people adrift on the winds of History but also the sort of people who were willing to take a risk, to save up and venture their small capital on building a business and a life for themselves. They were not the sort to sit and moan or look for a government hand-out when times were hard; they were not Luddites or Blanketeers railing against the realities of a changing world; rather they were people with a zest for life, with one eye on the future and the other on the horizon; they were another grand set of examples of people who had the courage to be free.

The picture of Cape Town and the Cape Colony that emerges from these pages is also one of life and vigour. No metropolis by a very long chalk, it was still a sleepy way station but one that was beginning to toss and turn prior to waking up. It could be a pretty rumbuctious place at times with its fair share of early deaths - fifty was a good age to draw stumps, it seems - illegitimate births, tragic infant mortalities, petty disputes, punch-ups, burglaries, business rivalries, bankruptcies, burgeoning commercial activity, frontier town ingenuity and 'can-do' attitude. The beginnings of civil society are evident in its education and religious subscription societies, its commercial exchange, and the beginnings of government in its appointments of Tide waiters – customs officers – forestry commissioners, Agricultural Boards and postmasters. This isn't the Wild West though; throughout the accounts runs the thread of Admiralty Courts, civil and criminal justice, records, licences, permissions, property rights and land transfers – law and legal order; the very marrow of the *Pax Britannica*.

\*

In terms of external affairs, both Acting Governors Baird and Grey (1806-7) and the Earl of Caledon (1807-11) were keen not to provoke the Xhosa in any way and hoped that the settlement arranged by the Batavians would suffice. This was a false hope, however, because the Xhosa themselves were involved in yet another period of convulsion as Ndlambe and the increasingly tyrannical Ngqika continued to struggle for power within the Rarabe, a struggle that eventually resulted in a split. Talking to the Xhosa therefore became ever more difficult as there were now four distinct groups; the minor clans in the Zuurveldt such as the Gqunukwebe, the Rarabe-Ndlambe also in the Zuurveldt, the Rarabe-Ngqika on the eastern side of the Fish River and of course the Gcaleka beyond them. In pursuit of maintaining something resembling a settled frontier therefore, in 1808, Colonel Collins was sent on another tour of inspection similar in aims and intent to that of John Barrow's.

Collins' route took him along the Orange River and on to Graaff-Reinet where he engaged the sixteen-year old son of the Llandrost, a boy by the name of Andries Stockenstrom, to act as his interpreter and who would rise to be a huge influence on the frontier in the coming years. Visiting first with Hintsa, Chief of the Gcaleka, he was impressed with the park like grasslands and densely populated area known today as the Transkei and left in no doubt as to who the paramount chief of the Xhosa was; it was Hintsa. Travelling on to Ngqika, whom he found to be impoverished, defeated in war by Ndlambe, friendless, despised by Hintsa and well on his way to becoming a stumbling alcoholic, Collins realised that this branch of the Xhosa was in almost terminal decline and deluded about its prospects of return. Heading back over the Fish River, he then met with Ndlambe at a moonlight meeting, which was supposed to intimidate him but didn't, and then Chungwa of the Gqunukwebe who revealed that he was as afraid of Ndlambe as he was of the Boers. All in all, Collins surmised, the Xhosa were weak, divided, and as Hintsa had no interest in fighting at all, incapable of putting more than 4-6000 men into the field. He had hoped to be able to persuade the Xhosa to leave the Zuurveldt, but as this seemed unlikely, he recommended that they be removed by force. Caledon ignored the advice[89] and resisted all calls for a Commando despite the constant reports of raids by Ndlambe's Xhosa and the resultant abandonment of Boer farms in the Zuurveldt. As far as Caledon was concerned, even a rocky peace out on this part of an impoverished and economically unattractive frontier populated by troublesome Trekboers was better than a war. Indeed, by the time that action was taken, some Xhosa clans had penetrated as far west as the Langkloof, all but one of the farms east of Uitenhage had been abandoned, and the coloniser Ndlambe was laying claim to the whole of the Algoa Bay area. What gave Caledon's successor, Governor Cradock, a much greater freedom of action was the capture of Mauritius from the French in 1810, which effectively removed the greatest external threat to the British control of the colony. Collins' report was taken out and dusted off.

This report was an important policy document written by a professional soldier whose main aim was to provide a series of practical recommendations for the stabilization of the frontier and the establishment of effective British control of the area. He had no long-term interests in the colony, fully expected to move on with his regiment and therefore had no particular axe to grind. The recommendation that the Xhosa be pushed back over the Fish River was motivated by strategic considerations; Chungwa and Ndlambe could not be allowed to remain west of the Fish River because this would give them control of Algoa Bay, and thus the swiftest route for the British to the Boers at Graaff-Reinet. His recommendation that the Batavian policy of forbidding contact between the Boers and the Xhosa should be maintained was designed to reduce the incidence of petty theft and cattle raiding, whose costs were unlikely to be outweighed by the benefits of trade, and so remove a cause of conflict. The area, once cleared of the Xhosa, would be policed by Dragoons and light infantry, 'sufficient to control the farmers'[90] based on a drostdy situated nearer to the frontier than Uitenhage, while the Xhosa convinced 'of the superiority of our power'[91] would receive 'annual presents to their chiefs'.[92] Should the Xhosa decide to fight then Collins argued that the frontier would be defended in the first instance by the Commandos, a large contingent of the Cape Regiment, with detachments of Regular troops where available. In addition, Collins wanted

---

[89] Theal, *History of South Africa* Vol. I, p. 234.
[90] Moodie, *Collins to Earl of Caledon, 6th August 1809*.
[91] Collins to Earl of Caledon, 6th August 1809.
[92] Collins to Earl of Caledon, 6th August 1809.

the Zuurveldt to remain empty as a buffer zone, while recognizing it as Xhosa territory (to stop Trekboers moving in to it). Real security would come, he argued, only when the practice of giving out large loan farms was discontinued and the density of the population increased by an influx of 6,000 colonists, of whom 1,000 would come from Europe, 1,000 from within the colony and, by implication, 4,000 Khoisan, Cape Malay, Bastaard or Free Blacks.

Cradock concurred and called out the Commandos from Swellendam, George, Uitenhage and Graaff-Reinet in October 1811 and reinforced them with the Cape Regiment (594 Khoisan), the 21st Light Dragoons (166) and two companies of the 83rd Foot (221 men). The campaign began on Christmas day and by the middle of January the Xhosa had retired across the Fish River. There was very little large-scale fighting and most of the casualties on the colonial side came from Xhosa attempts to ambush parties sent in to parley with them. The combination of Boer irregulars, Khoisan and British regulars was more than enough to flush out the Xhosa from their places of refuge in the thick bush. Lt-Colonel Graham, in overall command of the operation, sent three columns in to the Zuurveldt. In the north, Stockenstrom senior led a Commando down from Bruntjes Hoogte (and was killed while parleying with Kasa of the Imidange clan), while Major Cuyler, Llandrost of Uitenhage, led his force across the Sundays river in the south to attack (and eventually, kill) Chungwa and the Gqunukhwebe, who was supported by Ndlambe. Graham led the centre column into the area south of Addo, sweeping up the cattle as the Xhosa retired across the Fish River. To ensure that the Xhosa did not think of returning, Graham had their crops razed, but forwarded supplies of corn and cattle across the Fish River, while retaining a sufficient herd as a guarantee of good behaviour; the cattle would be returned if the Xhosa stayed on their side of the river.

It had all been very easy; the Xhosa had no answer to the firearms of the British-led forces and the deep thickets that they hid in were penetrated by Boers and Khoisan who knew the country as well as they did. They were divided among themselves, with Ndlambe abandoning Chungwa, Ngqika refusing them aid, and the minor clan leaders shifting for themselves, while their warriors were really little more than an untrained militia, however picturesque in their blue crane feather head-dresses. A colonial force of under 2000 men were able to defeat over three times their own number on ground that the Xhosa chose to defend. The Xhosa had shown themselves capable of sustained low-level frontier warfare in the past; this campaign had shown that the British were capable of decisive force on the frontier now, and for the future.

*

Lt-Col Graham assumed that those farms that lay in the Zuurveldt would now be re-occupied by their previous owners but Cradock disagreed. He wanted to discontinue the Dutch system of assigning enormous loan farms to anyone who cared to pay the trifling rent on them and replace it with secure land tenures which would give smaller farms, a denser population and economic rents. As yet there were no new settlers to take up these farms in the Zuurveldt (even though proposals to bring in Dutch and Scots were made), but Cradock saw land tenure reform as an important tool not just for ensuring the adequate defence of the frontier, but also as a means to prevent the encroachment by Trekboers and assorted freebooters on land outside the declared boundary of the colony. The loan farm system prevented farms from being subdivided or inherited and thus encouraged those who wanted a farm of their own to seek out unoccupied land, often outside the colonial boundary, and often unregistered with the Llandrosts. The Xhosa occupation of the Zuurveldt had been keenly felt by many Boer clans, among them the Prinsloos and Bezuidenhouts, whose young men were thereby prevented from staking out new claims and thus faced with being reduced to the status of landless agricultural servants. This land reform as a means to rein in the Boers was a radical proposal indeed for it threatened to end the whole concept of the sturdy, independent Trekboer striding out into an empty interior. If the reform went through, he would have to adopt a more settled lifestyle, registering his land, paying taxes and staying within the colonial border. Life would still be *lekker* but in order to maintain it, he would have to accept the unwelcome imposition of government.

And government was coming. No more the corrupt neglect of the VOC. Cradock wanted to increase the government's control of the frontier area by appointing deputy Llandrosts at Graaff-Reinet (Ensign Andries Stockenstrom, Cape Regiment, based at Cradock) and Uitenhage (Captain George Frasier, Cape Regiment) and stationing a permanent force of regular troops at Grahamstown to patrol a series of frontier forts garrisoned by Commandos. This was all to be paid for by taxing the Burghers nearer the Cape in return for releasing them from their militia obligations.[93]

Government was coming to the Khoikhoin too. Under the VOC, they had been left under the control of their own clan leaders but as these clans gradually collapsed under the strain of disease, the advance of the Trekboers and desertion, so the never very strong authority of the clan leaders or 'Captains' collapsed too. Leaderless and literally 'lawless' (without government) many of them drifted in and out of service with farmers, headed off to join the Oorlams of the frontier or melted into the Xhosa clans on the Zuurveldt while others simply took to living as vagrants and stock thieves. In Boer, British and Bantu eyes this was not a situation that could be tolerated. All three societies believed that a man must have a place in society, be governed according to law and custom and should respect the property of others (the Eleventh Commandment notwithstanding). When the Earl of Caledon, the first non-military governor arrived at the Cape in 1807, he therefore set about remedying the situation and what emerged was the Hottentot Ordinance of 1809.

This is one of those actions that get the Left really hot under the collar and it has been characterised as inflicting 'forced labour' and '*de facto* subjugation'[94] on the Khoikhoin in order to supply cheap labour to the Boers. In reality, it was nothing of the sort. Rather it was a pragmatic answer to a particularly difficult problem based on established custom and practice informed by the realities on the ground. The Ordinance first brought the Khoikhoin under the law of the colony and thereby extended the protection of the law to them. Cruel

---

[93] Theal, *History of South Africa from 1795 to 1872*, p. 257.
[94] Penn, *The Forgotten Frontier* pp. 268-269.

and arbitrary treatment of them by the farmers was made illegal, and all employment had to be accompanied by a proper contract drawn up in the presence of the authorities. A man could not be detained at the end of his contract if he was indebted to the farmer but rather the farmer must press his case in court. To ensure that the Khoikhoin understood their rights, one Khoikhoin man from each farm or household was to appear before an official to have the Ordinance explained to him and make sure that he understood it. So far so good; in some circles it became known as the 'Magna Carta of the Hottentots'.[95] What the Left really objected to was the fact that from this point on all Khoikhoin were to have a fixed place of abode and were not allowed to move from one place to another without a pass. To them, this looked like the forerunner of the Apartheid era Pass Laws but in reality, this was nothing more than the application of a very common principle of British vagrancy law; it was applied to British settlers in Cape Town during the early years of the British occupation.[96] Fixing Khoikhoin families in one place, preferably working on a farm, gave them the ability to support themselves, kept them from crime, disorder and rebellion and ensured a basic level of social security for those unable to fend for themselves. And there was a real need for this. The colony was not rich and destitution among the Khoikhoin (and the landless Boers) was a real problem. They had no money to set up as independent farmers and as the banks were in a state of collapse there was little chance of borrowing it. Even with modern farming methods, agriculture in South Africa is a precarious business and it is possible today to see stretches of barren land hard by more productive stretches even in the fertile zones. Everything depended on water and without the capital to build dams to catch the uneven and sometimes scarce rainfall, the chances of setting up a successful farm were slim; and there was a three-year drought at this time (just like now; in January 2018, Cape Town was set to run out of water by April if the rains don't come).

This was a paternalist system in keeping with the times. The ruling British Tories were not interested in revolutionary or democratic ideas; as far as they were concerned, such nonsense had given the world Robespierre, the Terror and then twenty years of war. What was wanted was a secure place for everyone, employment under sturdy country gentlemen farmers and no charge on the government. Such laws would not be accepted today (except for China, where strict residency laws are maintained to prevent the coastal cities being overcrowded by peasants from the interior heading for the bright lights and a better life) but by the standards of the time the Ordinance was remarkably liberal and enlightened; for a start, there were no criminal sanctions for breach of contract; as late as 1875, contract law between employer and employee in Britain was governed by the 'Master and Servant' Acts, a title that would certainly be regarded as patronising today, and which included criminal sanctions for 'servants' who broke the terms of their contract (it took the Tories to change that with the Employers and Workmen Act of 1875 which removed criminal sanctions and put both sides on an equal legal footing: note also the change in terminology). In 1812, a further Ordnance was promulgated which allowed the farmer to 'apprentice' any child born to his servants from the age of eight for the next ten years, as long as he bore the expense of feeding and clothing the child from birth. Again, this has been criticised as effectively fixing the

---

[95] Penn, *The Forgotten Frontier* p. 269.
[96] P. Philip, *British Residents at the Cape*, p.148.

Khoikhoin in a sort of penal servitude; some particularly mean-spirited Historians claim that the Hottentot Ordinance was meant to make up for the loss of labour consequent on the 1807 Abolition of the Slave Trade (perish the thought that the evil, top-hatted British capitalists could do anything decent without a vile, ulterior motive) but if you ask what the alternative is then all you will get is a blank stare; should the farmers pay for an employee's children without getting anything in return? If so, how many? For how long? For even the most generous of souls, there are necessary and inevitable limits to charity. Again, the reality is that there is nothing sinister here, just a pragmatic and paternalistic response to a very real problem. It was certainly not a condition worse than slavery as the LMS claimed.[97]

These Ordinances, alongside Cradock's proposed land reforms, were necessarily dependent on the effectiveness of the judicial system, the deficiencies of which the British were also aware of. And some of these deficiencies were glaring, as good old Theal pointed out; one of the several penalties for murder was, for example, to have a sword waved over your head before being banished from the colony, a punishment that no doubt raised as many eyebrows among the Khoisan as it did among the British; death or hanging was both more logical and much more acceptable. For beating to death a slave, one farmer got three months on the grounds that a more severe punishment would bring disgrace on the rest of his family (the rest of his slaves were sold; I doubt that made them feel that justice had been done).[98] Under the terms of the 1806 surrender, the Cape was allowed to maintain its own laws and system of government but this did not mean that those laws and that system might not be tinkered with to the advance of efficiency and a greater control of the population.

The routine administration of justice in the colony at this time was carried out on three different levels. The Veldtcornets (essentially the Commando leaders) were empowered to solve petty disputes within their wards while more serious matters would be settled by the Llandrosts; the most serious cases would then be dealt with by the High Court in Cape Town. This necessarily meant that there were irregularities and anomalies in the way that justice was applied and that access to justice was patchy at best in the more remote districts. A farmer would have few checks on his behaviour towards his servants and there was much sharp practice in regard to the enforcement of contracts. Both Caledon and Cradock were eager to see this situation remedied and Caledon instituted a circuit court made up of high court judges in 1811, whose function was to try cases and to report on the performance of the Llandrosts in each district. This was an important tool in strengthening the control of the government over frontier areas as it reminded Llandrosts where their loyalties lay and limited the influence that the frontier Boers had over them. The first Circuit took place between October 1811 and February 1812, passed off without incident and appeared to gain the confidence of all involved (I say that with ease; the journey out to Graff-Reinet and back via Addo, Uitenhage and George in ox waggons and on horseback would test the endurance of any present day outdoor type; those judges had hard arses). English law held all men equal before it and, flawed though its operation could often be, it held out a reasonable prospect

---

[97] R. Lovett, *The History of the London Missionary Society 1795-1895* (Oxford, 1899) Vol 1, p.545.
[98] G.M.Theal, *Records of the Cape Colony* Vol. X. Letter from Sir John Craddock to Lord Bathurst, April 15th 1814.

that for the first time 'equal justice and equal protection'[99] might be made available to all, given time.

\*

## God Comes to the Cape.

When I was at school in the pre-computer age, very hard sums that involved multiplication and more fingers and toes than I had to count on were resolved by using a thing called a Log Table. This was a book of numbers which when used correctly allowed complicated multiplication and division to be done by simple addition or subtraction, for what reason I am not entirely sure. On my particular copy, handed down by some revolting Molesworth in the Fifth Form, the title had been twisted and abused by means of ink and a vicious imagination from its original *Bishop Colenso's Logarithmic Tables for Schools* to the much less high-minded *Brothel Fables for Rooters*. From that day, I always felt sorry for Bishop Colenso in that assembling a lot of very tedious numbers into a very tedious book must have been very tedious work indeed and to have it so mutilated by some low-browed recidivist in a second-rate grammar school in Bolton was poor reward for such efforts. I always thought that his time would have been better spent doing something more interesting, like being a missionary in Africa, or something. Years later, I found out that he *had* been a missionary in Africa but on looking into his career I was forced to come to the conclusion that perhaps fiddling about with unintelligible numbers to plague schoolboys in Bolton was probably his true vocation; when he went to convert the Zulus, *they converted him* and thus was he sacked for heresy. I'm telling you this because Bishop John Colenso was only one in a long line of unsuccessful and, frankly, very irritating missionaries to descend on South Africa in the 19th Century in the hope that by converting Africans to Christianity, they could persuade them from some of their more irritating habits.

The breakdown in the various peace settlements that poor, isolated Veldkornet Visser had negotiated with the Bushmen along the northern frontier in 1798-99 meant a return to the old story of raid, cattle theft, retaliation and Commando. While individual Boers tried to keep the local Bushmen clans happy with gifts of livestock or tobacco, employing those increasing number of Bushmen who saw which way the wind was blowing and trying to build relationships that might ensure a local peace, many others reverted to seeing them as incorrigible predators to be shot on sight. For both the British and Batavian governments this was intolerable simply because if they wished to retain any control at all over the farmers on the frontier then they had to demonstrate their ability to fulfil the first and most basic function of government - the protection of the lives and property of those they governed. Aware that the basis of this conflict was the conflict between the Bushmen lifestyle and the culture of the colonists, it therefore occurred to the government that perhaps the Bushmen might be persuaded to give up their 'noble savage' existence and adopt a pastoral culture just as the Khoikhoin had done; perhaps they could become 'civilised' before they were wiped out.

---

[99] Cradock's instructions to Llandrosts, April 1812. Quoted in Stockenstrom Vol 1 p.76.

In 1794, Sir Henry Dundas had requested that this sort of job be taken on by the successful Moravian mission at Baviaans Kloof (present day Genadendal in the Western Cape. Modern day Baviaanskloof is 500km away to the east close to the picturesque town of Steytlerville, a place untroubled by cell phone coverage, petrol stations or signage indicating that you are still on the R329 rather than heading down a dirt road to God Knows Where. Having said that, it does have a gay German cabaret; welcome to the Rainbow Nation). Fortunately for the Moravians, they were unable to meet this request and two men from the London Missionary Society went northwards in their place.

The two lucky candidates for the job were a Dutchman, Johannes Kicherer, and an Englishman named William Edwards and in 1799 they set off for the frontier in the company of Visser, six wagons, 60 oxen and 200 sheep. Finding what they thought was a suitable spot for a mission a day's journey north of the Sak River in the stony ground of the Karoo, they outspanned and prepared to convert the Bushmen. They failed miserably. Apart from the language issue (though by now Dutch was pretty widely understood), the Bushmen seemed to have regarded the word of God as simply another set of stories to add to their existing collection and though they were quite prepared to pay lip service to the missionaries, it soon became clear that this would continue only as long as the handouts of tobacco, sheep and cooked food kept coming. A vegetable garden was begun but the Bushmen had little time for its products and when the leader of the local clan tried to take a sheep without permission, knives were drawn and relations broke down. The mission withdrew to a new site and Kicherer and Edwards took up more congenial projects, first in Cape Town and then in spreading the word to the Oorlams groups up on the Orange River. There were some further efforts to convert the Bushmen to Christianity and a settled existence under the Batavians but by the time that Colonel Collins carried out his tour of the frontier in 1809, it was clear that this was a horse that wouldn't run; the conversion of Khoikhoin reaped far greater rewards and so the effort inevitably became directed towards them. The Bushmen would not give up their way of life, continued to raid and steal, were attacked by Commandos in their turn and although Collins was generally in favour of establishing mission stations as a way to build on such local peace settlements as continued to exist, the fact was that there was very little that could be done if the Bushmen wouldn't sit down and talk.

The moment that Sak River mission station packed up and left marks the point at which the Bushmen leave our narrative; they are doomed. For the next sixty years, the Bushmen were regarded as an occupational hazard of farming and hunted down as any other threat to livestock was. Those captured were 'apprenticed' or convicted and put to work on the breakwater at Cape Town, where Dr Bleek found them, others drifted into service on the farms or joined with the Khoikhoin pastoralists who were also trekking into their hunting grounds. Today, those groups of Bushmen who do linger on, far away in the Kalahari make their living more by tourism than by hunting and are often dependent on social security. Up in the Sani Pass in KwaZulu-Natal in 2003, I saw the Bushman paintings depict what happened to so many of them in the end; flinging their spears and firing their poisoned arrows from behind a rock sangar, they were killed in battle. The paintings done in the ochre of dried blood showed the spirits of men shifting into the otherworld where the great, wild herds lived, but also the livestock that was too much of a temptation for them, and the men with guns that came to finish them off. They really had no chance of survival unless they adapted to the changing realities of the modern world. Sooner or later, population pressure alone would kill off the Bushmen, even had they been peaceful neighbours willing to leave the farmers' flocks alone. Laurens van der Post saw in this a great defiance, a heroic resistance; to me, sadly, it looks like suicide.

*

The arrival of the London Missionary Society has been portrayed by the usual suspects as a colonial plot to subjugate the indigenes under the weight of not just 'imperialism' but *cultural imperialism* which, being a concept impossible to actually define, let alone identify as something concrete makes it so very useful to those Leftists who push the Marxist idea that race/class/gender are the real issues in History and black/poor/females etc are its victims (and Marx wasn't actually born until 1814, we might recall; these Marxists are applying Marx to a time before Marx had invented Marxism). So, for example, take *Blood Ground: Colonialism, Missions, and the Contest for Christianity in the Cape Colony and Britain, 1799-1853* by Elizabeth Elbourne. Now I admit I'm on dodgy ground here because I haven't read the full book, but having been dealing with this stuff for a long time, I'm going to rely on my nose and say that it's probably not strictly necessary to go beyond the blurb to get the gist of her argument. Here it is:

> Elbourne traces the transition from religion to race as the basis for policing the boundaries of the "white" community. Emphasizing Christianity's status as a religion of world empire, she explores how Christianity provided opportunities for locals but also contributed to their subjugation through ideological justification of imperial expansion.

Now, it's a point of view, admittedly but let's just think about it for a minute. Let's just, for the sake of argument, agree that it isn't just the sort of garbage that's going to get her a pat on the back from her Right On colleagues but an idea that's worth thinking about for more than a bare three seconds. Let's say that Christianity was absolutely a 'religion of world empire' aiming at 'subjugation through ideological justification of imperial expansion'. Yup. OK. I'm going with it.

So, I've got my evil, British, colonialist, capitalist, white, racist bastard hat on and I'm out to subjugate the Bushmen who for a century and a half have been giving hell to the colonialist bastard Trekboers. So, as the leading naval and economic power in the world I decide not to mobilise some of the power of that navy and economy and send the British Army – that's the one that is currently beating the shit out of the powerful kingdoms of India and giving Napoleon pause for thought – to reinforce the evil, bloodthirsty Commandos and the equally cheesed off Khoikhoin clans to *really* sort the Bushmen out. Instead, I send two sky pilots up to the Sak River armed with nothing more than a couple of Bibles and a heap of tobacco.

I mean, *come on.*

Now if this doesn't make the point, it's time to introduce the blokes sent to the Eastern frontier to convert the Xhosa. Step forward Johannes Van der Kemp, the Reverend Edmonds and John Read. If your aim was the 'subjugation through ideological justification of imperial expansion' of the Xhosa, a more eccentric and ineffective set of men you could not find to do it. (And I really am struggling not to think of them as Larry, Curly and Moe).

Johannes Van der Kemp was a man whose experience of life had filled him with 'wild demons of the inner soul.'[100] At various times a philosopher, medical man, cavalry officer, rake and heretic, he was an expert linguist and an aristocrat who married a mill girl. His conversion to Christianity came when his wife and child were drowned in a storm and from that point on, it is fair to say, the poor man became unhinged. With the good wishes of the government, he headed off in May 1799 to the Zuurveldt in the middle of the war raging there, intending to find Ngqika and convert him. The Boers at Graaff-Reinet, not unreasonably, considered him to be mad, a conviction that Brother Edmonds increasingly came to share; when they were attacked by Xhosa and forced to shelter in a Boer laager, Van der Kemp loaded up his musket but refused to fight, an action that did nothing to lessen his reputation for eccentricity. To everyone's surprise, he managed to make it to Ngqika's Great Place in September 1799 but to no-one's surprise, failed to convince the Xhosa to see the light. The nearest he came to making progress was when he managed to forecast the rain correctly and claimed that it was Divine intervention; Ngqika thought he might be useful as a rain-maker but dithered as to whether he should just kill him or not. In the end, Van der Kemp gave up and went back to Graaff-Reinet (and was attacked on the way back by Bushmen) having achieved the grand total of five converts, all women, all Khoikhoin. Edmonds went to Bengal. So much for the religion of world empire.

Gathering up James Read as a replacement, Van der Kemp also gathered up a large following of displaced Khoikhoin and led them off to found a new mission station at Bethelsdorp but it soon became evident that any real administrative capacity was beyond him. When the Batavian authorities arrived, they visited the mission station and gave it a very poor report. Willem Paravinci, who had been at university with Van der Kemp, considered that he had developed a 'strong tendency towards fanaticism' and that the whole community was simply 'indolent';[101] this was something that even Van der Kemp admitted; 'Laziness,' he wrote. 'Is the most prevalent evil among our people,'[102] yet he refused to encourage his flock to take advantage of the plentiful work available on the farms. The missionaries were ordered to return to Cape Town.

Unfortunately, the Bethelsdorp mission was saved by the arrival of the British, a decision that they quickly came to regret; when in 1809 Van der Kemp floated the idea of moving his mission to Madagascar, Colonel Collins almost fell over himself to accept the offer. Meanwhile, Van der Kemp and Read went back to their calling of spreading the word, teaching the Khoikhoin to read and write, trying to build the New Jerusalem but failing

---

[100] N. Mostert, *Frontiers*, (London, 1992), p. 287.
[101] Quoted in Mostert, *Frontiers*, p.336.
[102] Van der Kemp's Journal, quoted in R. Lovett, *The History of the London Missionary Society 1795-1895* Vol 1, p.503.

miserably. The place was desolation itself, as even well-wishers noted, and quickly became a by-word in the colony for inefficiency, waste and sloth.[103] The 1812 Circuit Court visited it and declared it to be a dump.[104] Both Van der Kemp and Read rapidly became controversial figures through the allegations of misconduct that they levelled in intemperate language at the Boers, through their relations with the Khoisan at the mission – Read married a 19 year old manumitted slave girl who was 41 years his junior and had an affair with another while Van der Kemp bought a slave girl and married her too – and through their refusal to accept the authority of the Llandrost of Uitenhage, an American loyalist by the name of Major Jacob Cuyler, against whom they also used intemperate language. Refusing also to accept Caledon's Hottentot Ordinance, they sent a stream of reports to London which, through influential evangelical connections, found their way into the Department for War and the Colonies. In January 1811, Read claimed in a letter to Lord Liverpool, Secretary of State for the Colonies, that 'upwards of a hundred murders' had been committed by Boers on their Khoisan servants, and that Major Cuyler had refused to investigate them.[105] Liverpool ordered the Cape authorities to look into the abuses and Cradock ordered the Circuit Court out in September 1812. If the British intention was to use missionaries to subjugate the Khoikhoin 'through ideological justification of imperial expansion', then it would be more than fair to say that a pretty poor job had been done of it so far. In 1899, the view of the London Missionary Society was that Van der Kemp and Read had made themselves so unpopular because they 'believed in equal rights for black and white, for Kafir and Boer, for Hottentot and colonist'[106] and that successive Governors in South Africa did more to hinder them than help.[107] Indeed, for very many out and out imperialists, missionaries were a hindrance to be avoided almost at all costs; as Chief Commissioner of Sind in India, Sir Bartle Frere would have absolutely nothing to do with them on the grounds that the locals already had a perfectly serviceable religion in Islam.

Van der Kemp died in December 1811, but neither he nor Read were convincing advocates or competent campaigners once the Circuit Court assembled. Even when Cuyler demanded, as a matter of honour, that a professional lawyer be provided to put the Khoisan cases before the court, and even with the calling of over a thousand witnesses and the arraignment of over fifty Boer men and women, Read could not make his case. The judges concluded that although there were individual cases of ill-treatment of servants, Read and Van der Kemp's accusations of systematic enslavement and oppression of the Khoisan were groundless;[108] 'existing in imagination only' were the exact words.[109]

What the missionaries did succeed in doing, however, was to destroy any faith that the frontier Boers had in the Circuit Courts – this particular episode entered Boer mythology as the 'Black Circuit'. The fact is that these two zealots were in the direct lineage of the

---

[103] Theal, *Records of the Cape Colony* Vol X p.405. N. Mostert, *Frontiers*, pp. 346-8 also pp. 356-8.
[104] Theal, *Records of Cape Colony*, Vol X p.91.
[105] Read to William Wilberforce, quoted in N. Mostert, *Frontiers*, p. 352.
[106] R. Lovett, *The History of the London Missionary Society 1795-1895* Vol 1, p.513
[107] R. Lovett, *The History of the London Missionary Society 1795-1895* Vol 1, p.534
[108] N. Mostert, *Frontiers*, p. 353.
[109] Judges report to the Governor, quoted in Theal, *History of South Africa, Vol. 1,* p. 263.

Witchfinder-General, the KGB inquisitors and the Twitterstorm Trots; they saw the law as a means to push their aims, to convict regardless of innocence and to bring down their just critics by means of mere accusation. As far as the Boers were concerned, they felt with some justification that they had been hauled through the courts on the flimsiest pretexts and subjected to a sterner level of inquiry than their own complaints against either the missionaries or their servants had ever produced; and if you think that a brush with the law is a neutral act I would point you in the direction of the church gardens outside Chelmsford Magistrates Court to watch the defendants ponder their fate in the great lottery of the legal system; British Justice is better than any other but you would still be a fool to go anywhere near it. Cradock had intended that such detailed scrutiny would silence the missionaries and reassure the colonists but instead it produced an opposite reaction. Instead of the frontier being stabilized by the law, the rejection of it by the Boers would now destabilize it.

*

It's not far out of Cradock heading south beyond Cookhouse that you come across it. Blink and you'll miss it, but on the left is a sort of obelisk on a plinth, surrounded by a little iron fence where the litter, rusty cans and broken bottles catch. There's a lay by and a couple of trees there but it isn't much to detain the casual visitor; it's not like the Menin Gate or anything, but this is Slachter's Nek and it plays a major part in Afrikaaner mythology. There are those who say that this monument marks the moment when any sort of trust between the Boers and the British was broken, but this is just not true. Certainly, it broke what little trust there was between the frontier Trekboers and the British but, frankly speaking, there wasn't much of a tie there in the first place and it certainly did not break the growing bond between the Burghers and the British. Afrikaaner nationalist History holds that there is a direct line between the events at Slachter's Nek and the Great Trek and in this they do have a point but the reality is that very little significance was accorded to this episode until the 1880s when the prospect of a British Confederation of South Africa threatened to end the independence of the Boer Republics that the Great Trek had produced. There was a lot of talk about it after the failure of the Jameson Raid in 1896 but no-one put a monument up on that lonely road until 1916 when nascent Afrikaaner nationalist feeling began to sense the possibility of a great resurgence. The chap who unveiled it was D.F. Malan, later to become the first Prime Minister of the Apartheid state. Leftists are not the only ones who understand that an adroit manipulation of the past can lay the foundations of the future. What happened here?

The Black Circuit, Cradock's land reforms and the presence of the Cape Regiment in the frontier districts were all sources of threat to Trekboer independence. Regular troops on the frontier could enforce strictures about contact with the Xhosa as well as bring an end to the practice of maintaining unregistered farms outside the colonial boundaries. Taxes and courts placed equally unwelcome restrictions on their pockets and their sharp practice towards their servants. To the frontier clans like the Prinsloos and the Bezuidenhouts, it appeared that their unrestricted liberties were being systematically removed and their future prospects of large, cheap landholdings denied.

The spark to this particular tinder came when in 1813 a Khoikhoi servant named Booy complained to Llandrost Stockenstrom of mistreatment at the hands of Cornelius Bezuidenhout. Stockenstrom attempted to mediate but for over two years Bezuidenhout refused to answer summons to appear or even faintly to recognize Stockenstrom's authority. Finally, Stockenstrom sentenced him to a month in jail *in absentia* and sent a detachment of the Cape Regiment to arrest him. Bezuidenhout fired on them and was himself killed. The rest of the Bezuidenhout clan, along with the Prinsloos, revolted in protest.

The orneriest of the frontier Trekboer clans really had no conception of the reality of British power and massively overestimated their own influence in the Graaff-Reinet and Uitenhage districts; most of the frontier Boers understood very well that Stockenstrom had justice on his side and supported him. This also went for their projected alliance with Ngqika; a piece of pure fantasy that was quickly betrayed to the authorities before it was properly afoot. Cuyler brought the Cape Regiment against the rebellious faction, while the Commandos rejected attempts to suborn them and Major Fraser brought a troop of Dragoons. Most of the insurgents – under a hundred all told – surrendered, but Hendrik Prinsloo was arrested and Johannes Bezuidenhout was killed in a skirmish as he tried to escape across the Fish River.

The judicial verdict reflected the aims of the government. The new Governor, Lord Charles Somerset, wanted to make examples of the ringleaders and remove others from the frontier. Marthinus Prinsloo, who had been involved in the 1799 revolt but not this one, was ordered out of the frontier district; of the thirty-nine arrested seven, including two more Prinsloos, were also forbidden to live in the frontier districts, while the rest were given token fines of between two and five pounds Sterling (roughly, a year's pay or farm rent) and ordered to witness the punishment of the five leading conspirators who were to be hanged.

There was reason to believe that hangings would be commuted in the same way that those of the Graaff-Reinet rebels of 1799 had been, but this time the government was determined to impress upon the frontier that insurrection simply would not be tolerated. The hangings would take place. Unfortunately, Cuyler and Stockenstrom bungled the execution in front of a large and distressed crowd; when the trap was opened four of the five ropes snapped, and the crowd demanded that such luck should be seen as an act of God and clemency given. Cuyler had 300 dragoons with him, however, and after a couple of hours' search for more rope carried out the sentence. The sheer relentlessness, ruthlessness and apparent inhumanity of the law obscured the very real justice of the sentences and created a real sense of unease among the frontier Boers about the new order that the British had so determinedly established. This was the 1815 'Massacre of Slachter's Nek' and the obelisk on the N10 outside Cookhouse was put up there by Malan and his Apartheid party to commemorate just how evil and unjustly colour-blind British justice was. Not commemorated however, or even commented upon by any Leftist historian I have ever come across, is Stockenstrom's firm conviction that most Boers of the district were *not* opposed to equal justice regardless of skin colour. A few years later, a popular Burgher murdered a 'poor miserable Hottentot'; he was arrested by Boers, tried by Boers, found guilty by Boers and shot by Boers.[110] The reason for

---

[110] Stockenstrom Vol 1, p.93.

this omission? It provides strong evidence that very many Boers were inclined to be colour blind too but that doesn't fit the narrative the Left wish to impose.

*

Somerset.

In 1814, the Cape became officially and legally British by treaty and Lord Charles Somerset, a well-connected aristocrat but undistinguished by dint of fall from a horse which rendered him unfit for military service, was sent out to govern it, which he did for the twelve years from 1814-26. The most pressing problem that faced Britain at the Cape was, for the first time, not the possibility of an attack wresting control of the Cape peninsular away from it but the still unsettled state of her borders. The Northern frontier was in a horribly disturbed state. Oorlams, Bushmen, bandits, Khoisan, Baastard – now officially known as Griqua and based in the region of present day Kimberley – plus Trekboer groups, fugitives, wanderers, escaped slaves and deserters were all up on and beyond the Orange River, engaged in war, commando, robbery and stock theft in an environment of apparent anarchy. As far as the British were concerned this was made palatable by distance; the Orange River was a long way north of the inhabited parts of the colony and as long as the inhabitants stayed there then they could afford to ignore them. This was not the case with the Eastern border however. The region of the Zuurveldt and the land beyond the Fish River was plagued by malcontent Trekboers, a Xhosa polity that had fractured into at least three factions – Ndlambe, Ngqika and Hintsa – large numbers of Khoisan dissatisfied at the onerous conditions of the Hottentot Ordinance, landless Boers, endemic cattle theft and an agricultural system that was yet to come to terms with the practical workings of the Freehold land reforms and the employment contracts of Khoisan labourers. There was also a drought. This frontier could not be ignored because the Xhosa were hard up against the Boers and pressure on grazing meant that any gain by one side was a loss to the other. Nor was it likely that a simple demarcation could succeed because farms were largely unfenced, cattle tended to wander and the border was unpoliced; it was just too easy to graze on the other side of that river, or lift cattle from the bush and in a time of drought, just too tempting not to.

Somerset was determined to impose order on this side of the border and strung up the 1815 Boer rebels at Slachter's Nek to make sure everyone understood this. What he could not do, however, was to control what was happening on the other side of the border. Cradock's recapture of the Zuurveldt in 1812 and his establishment of a chain of forts to defend it was meant to stabilise the frontier but it did no such thing. No sooner had that war ended than Xhosa cattle raids began again. Thousands of cattle were lifted and farm servants murdered on a regular basis and by November 1813 the clamour for action to 'prove to the savages and unceasing robbers that His Majesty's government would no longer be trifled with or suffer the property of the colonists to be destroyed'[111] led Cradock to authorize another expedition. This one would, however, be different in aim from previous ones; most previous commandos against the Xhosa had been reactive in the sense that they aimed to recover stolen cattle or re-

---

[111] Cradock to Lt Colonel Vicars quoted in Theal, *History of South Africa*, p. 321.

assert control of land, but Cradock was determined that this one was to be punitive. Recovering cattle was to be secondary to impressing on the Xhosa that the cost of trespass on colonial territory would be disproportionate to any benefit gained from cattle rustling. However, when Captain Fraser led the Cape Regiment and a Commando of 500 Boers over the Fish River in December 1813 he behaved with such careful restraint that he failed to make the required impression. Instead of sweeping up the Xhosa cattle he took only those with colonial brands and thus recovered only 140 head; the kraals were not fired and nor were crops ploughed up or destroyed. As a result, no deterrent effect was achieved and by 1817 farms were once again being abandoned in the Zuurveldt as a result of the economic devastation brought about by Xhosa theft. What was particularly frustrating to both the British and the Boers was the apparently cavalier way in which agreements with Xhosa clan leaders were disregarded by their subordinates and colluded in by those same chiefs.

Lord Somerset interpreted this problem as being caused by the lack of effective, legitimate authority within the Xhosa polity and saw the solution as being the strengthening of that authority. Somerset had no interest in seeing the disintegration of the Xhosa as an effective entity – such an outcome would only encourage instability and freebooterism – and hoped that by strengthening Ngqika's position as paramount chief he would be able to negotiate more lasting agreements with a leader who could enforce compliance with them. This policy would be effected by meeting with all the major clan leaders in person and making a public show of support for Ngqika which was meant to be interpreted as a clear statement that Ngqika's orders to desist from theft or harbouring freebooters or runaways from the colony could, if necessary, be enforced by colonial military power.

Unfortunately, both Somerset's analysis and the conclusions he drew from them were faulty. Ngqika was indeed the 'king' of the Xhosa but unlike European models of royalty, his power and status was always more conditional than his European counterparts. If a crude comparison may be drawn, Ngqika's position was more akin to King John and his barons rather than Louis XIV's absolutism but we should be wary of pushing this analogy very far. It was a common misconception then as well as now that African chiefs are feudal in nature, but they are not; feudalism was so successful in Europe and lasted for hundreds of years because it involved a social contract whereby the rulers performed certain services – leadership in war, dispensing justice etc - in return for status, services and taxes from those of lesser status. If you think this is bollocks then I would refer you to the arrow taken out of Henry V's face after the Battle of Shrewsbury, the dent in his helmet received at Agincourt (along with the death of his brother, the Duke of York, killed fighting in the front line) and Richard III leading the charge at Bosworth field despite his dreadful scoliosis (which turned out not to be Lancastrian propaganda after all; the Yorkshire tyke really was 'Crooked back Dick'). African chiefs demand the rewards but have no conception that they are in any way obliged to their people; finding one on the battlefield facing the Boers or the Brits is a rarity; this lack of feelings of obligation – *noblesse obligé* - is one of the main reasons why African leadership remains in a woeful state today.

This meant that Ngqika simply did not have the necessary power to enforce his will on the other clan leaders, as he himself pointed out,[112] and that accepting support from the colony might well do more to undermine his status and legitimacy than to strengthen it. Furthermore, the extent of Xhosa royal authority also depended much more on the personal qualities of the individual enthroned than in Europe, where extensive institutions existed to mitigate personal shortcomings, and Ngqika seemed to lack the required qualities for effective kingship. Thus, when Somerset met with Ngqika, Ndlambe and several less powerful clan leaders on the Kat river in April, 1817 the agreements he secured regarding the integrity of the frontier and the respect for Boer cattle were worthless as none of the clan leaders were prepared to accept that Ngqika's word necessarily bound them too. The thieving continued unabated.

Somerset compounded this mistake by accepting Xhosa custom in the matter of making good cattle theft in what became known as the 'Spoor Law'. Under this system, when stolen cattle were chased or tracked to a particular kraal then that family or clan would be responsible for making good any loss, whether they had been guilty of the theft or not. This was a collective punishment rather than an individual one and thus had all the disadvantages associated with the inevitable injustices that would result from it. It also accepted *de facto* if not *de jure* that frontier farmers would be permitted 'hot pursuit' across the border, a state of affairs which was bound to result in a resumption of the cycle of petty theft and revenge which was so detrimental to border peace and stability.

Two factors outside his control then combined to undermine Somerset's policy further. The first was the weather; a long drought impacted on Xhosa food supplies and thus increased the incidence of cattle rustling. The second was the reduction in the forces available to him as part of the general disarmament brought on by the end of the war in Europe. In April, 1817 Somerset had at his call the 21st Light Dragoons (1,000 strong), the 83rd Foot (900), 1/60th Foot (1000), 1/72nd Foot and the Cape Regiment (800), plus artillery. In June 1817 the Dragoons were sent to India, in July most of the artillery was withdrawn, and in September the 83rd were sent to Ceylon and the Cape Regiment disbanded on the grounds of cost. All that replaced them were the poor quality Royal African Corps (400) and a Cape Corps of mixed infantry and cavalry (78 horse, 169 foot) drawn from the disbanded Cape Regiment. This reduction of force – especially the denuding of the frontier of cavalry – was of course noted by the Xhosa and Somerset was again compelled to send out a Commando in early 1818, which in making no distinction (possibly because Captain Fraser did not want to make the same mistake of being too lenient twice) between Ngqika and Ndlambe's kraals further lowered Ngqika's authority. Subsequently Ngqika's authority was almost brought to an end by warfare within the Xhosa polity when, in October 1818, Ndlambe aided by a recently acquired but decidedly bizarre protégé and prophet, Nxele-Makana, defeated his forces at the Battle of Amalinde and reduced him to dependence on food supplies from the colony.

Somerset assessed the situation and decided that the correct course of action was to march to Ngqika's aid and began assembling a force to attack Ndlambe. Lt. Colonel Brereton of the

---

[112] N. Mostert, *Frontiers*, p. 450.

Royal African Corps (now reformed through the drafting of men from the 60th and the discharge of some of the least reliable elements) was placed in command and led his regiment, along with the newly arrived 38th Foot, a Boer Commando under Stockenstrom, the Cape Corps and what was left of Ngqika's warriors over the Fish river. Ndlambe's 18,000 warriors took refuge in the bush in the belief that the colonial forces could not follow them there. This was a mistaken assumption and Brereton routed them and swept up some 23,000 cattle which were then divided up between Ngqika, the colonists who had lost cattle and the government, who sold them to defray expenses.[113]

The decisive settlement which Somerset wanted still eluded him, this time because the Xhosa now had no other means of subsistence than to raid the colonial cattle, as Stockenstrom had warned,[114] and attacks on both Ngqika and the Zuurveldt farms began again at Christmas 1818. By January 1819, large numbers of Xhosa were operating in the Zuurveldt and the Boers began once more to abandon their farms for the security on offer at the military post of Grahamstown. By the beginning of February 1819, Brereton was calling for reinforcements from Cape Town, which duly began to arrive by sea at Algoa bay by the end of the month. Somerset, advised by Stockenstrom, therefore began to formulate a further plan to settle the frontier based on a decisive defeat of Ndlambe and the expulsion of the Xhosa from the land between the Fish and Keiskamma rivers, which would then provide a neutral *glacis* between Xhosa and colonist patrolled by troops to effectively prevent cattle raiding. When Brereton was posted, the man chosen to put this plan into operation was the Peninsular veteran, Lt.Colonel Willshire of the 38th Foot and he was expected to begin operations in May 1819. Nxele-Makana and Ndlambe forestalled him however by making a direct attack on Grahamstown on 22nd April 1819.

\*

We ought to pause at this point and make a quick assessment. Remember old J.K. Galbraith and his *Reluctant Empire*? This is a direct challenge to the 'smash and grab' theory of imperialism that has been foisted on to the world by the Left and it is hard not to admit that Cradock and Somerset are covered by it. I'm going to say it again but the importance to Britain was the Cape as a naval station guarding the trade routes to the East and not because she wanted to gobble up huge chunks of the continent. That over-riding aim required a settled and fixed border – a *limit* to imperial expansion. In order to achieve this, the Trekboers had to be brought to order and a deal done with those on the other side of that border such as the Bushmen, the Oorlams and the Xhosa. Certainly, efforts were made to achieve such a deal – and you can almost hear the sound of British hair being ripped out by the roots in frustration at the inability of the Xhosa and Bushmen to sit down and do one. Internally, the British wanted peace and security; happy prosperous farmers producing meat and veg for sale to the passing ships and taxes to support the very minimal government that the Tories believed in. The biggest item of expenditure was on the military and a habitually parsimonious – to the point of utter stupidity - government in London was very firmly and

---

[113] Theal, *History of South Africa* Vol.I, p.334.
[114] N. Mostert, *Frontiers*, p. 470.

repeatedly of the opinion that, apart from the defence of the Cape peninsula, the colony should be self-supporting in this regard. If a colony wished to avoid paying the taxes necessary to support a large military expenditure, so the argument went, then the colonists ought to find some way to live on peaceful terms with their neighbours and not expect the tax payers of Britain to shell out for them. This is what was meant by 'reluctant empire'; Britain really did not want the expense of conquering or governing Africa. It just wasn't worth it. And yet, here they were about to fight a battle over a place they did not want against an enemy that they did not want to fight and which could very simply have been avoided if the Xhosa had kept to the far side of the Fish River and not attempted to continue their colonial land grab westwards. The British had showed they could keep the Trekboers in line, in the last analysis, by stringing them up at Slachter's Nek. If only Ndlambe, Ngqika and Hintsa had shown the same determination to control their own people! A lot of men were now about to die at Grahamstown because they could not or would not. And the fact of their skin colour had nothing whatsoever to do with it.

\*

I once had a review of a book called *Seven Battles That Shaped South Africa* spiked because I pointed out that the authors had missed out the Battle of Grahamstown. Such is life. At the time, the town wasn't much more than a barracks situated among the rolling hills and aloes of the Zuurveldt. Named after Colonel Graham (van Rensburg, properly), today it is home to Rhodes University and in 2003 was home to several schools at which white ankle socks, straw boaters and powerful prefects were the order of the day. It has the look of Dartmoor or Cornwall about it but the weather is usually better, although in April winter is coming on and the winds are bitter.

During that April of 1819, Ndlambe concentrated around 10,000 warriors outside the town and, by suborning one of the official interpreters, was able to decoy one Company of the 38th Foot out on a wild goose chase and thus gained complete tactical surprise. Such an advantage was quickly thrown away when the prophet Nxele-Makana, in a fit of messianic overconfidence, sent a messenger in to Grahamstown to inform Willshire that he intended to sack it the next day. Willshire was out inspecting the mounted section of the Cape Corps when he was informed by a Khoisan clan leader, the elephant hunter Boesak, that a large force of Xhosa was approaching the town, and he immediately went to investigate while the second in command, Captain Trappes, turned out the troops for action. There were not very many of them; half a Company of the 38th Foot (45 men), one Company of the Royal African Corps (135 strong), one Company of the Cape Corps (121 men) and thirty-two armed men unattached, plus artillery.[115]

The Xhosa appeared on a hill to the east of the town, which is still known as Makana's Kop – the whole district has been renamed 'Makana' today - sometime in the morning of 22nd April, 1819, but it took a considerable amount of time to get the warriors into a position to attack. This was probably due to caution and indecision on the part of the Xhosa leadership who had

---

[115] Theal, *History of South Africa* Vol.I, p.337.

never fought this kind of battle before. They were probably unsure as to the effects of massed musketry supported by artillery on a determined charge and unsure about how to attack a building as solid as the soldier's barracks. It is also possible that they were consulting a deserter from the Royal African Corps who may have been advising them on tactics.[116] The plan, once agreed upon, was to detach a force of 1000 warriors to act as a reserve and to intercept the missing Company of the 38th if it chose to reappear; two large divisions totalling 5000 warriors were to attack the main body of Colonial troops, while Nxele-Makana would take the remaining 4000 against the barracks. It was around noon before the Xhosa began to deploy into their positions.

Willshire was confident of his ability to defeat this attack, even though he was outnumbered so heavily, and drew up his main force on a slope that led down to a stream below Makana's Kop and which allowed him to site his artillery above and behind his firing line. Sixty men of the Royal African Corps under Lieutenant Cartwright were stationed in the barracks above the stream, where most of the civilians had taken shelter. Willshire was keen to act aggressively early on and, possibly fearing that the Xhosa delay in deploying was due to their awaiting further reinforcement, like Henry V at Agincourt, he *advanced* his line across the stream towards Makana's Kop in the hope of using his musketry to provoke the Xhosa to attack. The fact that he advanced a maximum number of 260 men against 10,000 warriors is indicative of the confidence that he held in his weapons and men. As an experienced soldier he would have been able to make the calculations necessary to appreciate his chances of success.

An analysis of the mechanics of this battle are instructive. It seems safe to say that there was no one great, heroic charge by the Xhosa which was narrowly repulsed by a thin red line. If the Xhosa took five minutes to charge down the Kop and across the stream, a distance of some two hundred metres, then Willshire would have time to fire off no more than 15 volleys at a standard rate of fire of three shots per minute. Multiplied by the 270 muskets that he had to direct (which excludes those in the barracks), this would mean that 4050 shots would be fired. If every single one hit their mark then there would still be 950 (out of 5000) warriors alive at the end of the charge and thus his men would still face odds of 2:1. Of course, even taking into account that these troops were experienced and may well have been better shots than average, a 100% hit rate is ludicrously high. Brown Bess muskets could not really be expected to be accurate beyond 100 metres or so and 60 metres would be a more realistic proposition. It is more likely, therefore, that there would be no more than three full volleys giving 810 shots discharged with a hit rate of 30% maximum overall. In short, the British volleys – even taking into account the effects of the artillery - were not enough to stop the Xhosa charge if it had been pressed home. It should have been a walk over for the Xhosa but instead it was a rout; accounts vary, but the battle seems to have lasted until 5pm and the Xhosa casualties estimated at between 500 and 1300 men, while the British had three dead and five wounded. The only way that this can be accounted for is that the Xhosa warriors would not fight.

---

[116] Mostert, *Frontiers*, pp. 475.

This needs to be explained if only to balance up the gleeful way in which British defeats are dissected by South African Historians (and we'll see plenty of this as we go on). Victories over large numbers of Africans by very small numbers of Colonial troops are usually brushed away as being the result of the Maxim gun being deployed against spears, or professionals against brave amateurs but in this case, these explanations just won't do. A thrown spear, especially if you have five or six of them, is a rough match for a Brown Bess. Furthermore, the Xhosa were experienced in warfare and had fought against the British, Boers and other Xhosa on numerous occasions and so probably had a fair idea of the strengths and limitations of both artillery and the Brown Bess.   Also, it isn't necessary to exaggerate Ndlambe's talents as a general – you get the impression from some quarters that he would put Wellington, Rommel and Stormin' Norman to rout – to say that he was an experienced commander who had seen plenty of service and must have been aware that a numerical superiority of around 25:1 launched against infantry in the open should have been more than enough to ensure victory (3:1 is reckoned a safe bet).

In the event, what seems likely is that one or two charges were made by certain sections of the Xhosa but never at any time were they massed or co-ordinated. We might conclude from this that the volley firing, backed up by shrapnel rounds from the artillery, had effect enough to deter any Xhosa advance after the first or second experience, especially as the most eager warriors would probably have borne the brunt of the casualties and that after that there would be a great deal of posturing and display but not much else. Ndlambe failed to motivate his troops and his leadership thus stands condemned but it still does not explain why the Xhosa would not respond to his urging and exhortation. Perhaps this was a symptom of the weak bonds that joined the Xhosa to their leaders; perhaps, assessing the possibility of loot as being not worth the risk of a bullet the average warrior decided to hang back (see the French knights at Agincourt; it was dishonourable to be killed by a knavish archer rather than a noble knight).

The one new thing in all this is the presence of Nxele-Makana, the chancer, prophet and seer, who promised whatever came into his head at the time to whoever was willing to listen. The assurances of *sangomas*, witchdoctors and holy men as to the ineffectiveness of a bullet are a feature of African warfare right up until the present and Nxele-Makana appears to have made several promises about the effectiveness of the magical protection that he could afford; apparently, British artillery would spray water rather than shrapnel.[117] My own view is that the majority of the Xhosa were not stupid and knew just exactly what that protection was worth, while their more hopeful compatriots were disabused of their belief in magic in the way that only a bullet can achieve. After those initial charges, that was that. The Xhosa retired out of musket range, Willshire was left in possession and when Boesak's 130 elephant hunters turned up and picked off three of Ndlambe's sons, the rest of the Xhosa took to their heels. It was an ignominious defeat. Within a few months, Nxele-Makana was aboard a ship bound for Robben Island, Ndlambe on the run, Hintsa warned in no uncertain terms that any

---

[117] Stockenstrom Vol 1 p.117

support he gave to further war would be met with retribution and Ngqika, almost permanently drunk these days, recognised as chief of the frontier Xhosa once more.

So why was this one of the *Seven Battles That Shaped South Africa*? There would be more battles with the Xhosa to come but this was a moment of decision because it halted the Xhosa colonists from moving any further westwards and so brought to an end the great Nguni-Bantu migration. At the end of 1819, when the area between the Fish River and the Keiskamma River was cleared of Xhosa colonists to provide a buffer zone between them and the British colony, that migration was effectively backed up and the Xhosa were contained. There was another reason that the Battle of Grahamstown was important for it was then that the decision was taken to ensure a separation between the unruly Trekboers and the equally unruly Xhosa by interposing a new body of settlers to keep them apart. These were the 1820 settlers and they represented the first deliberate attempt by the British to systematically colonise South Africa with British people.

It was a failure, just like every other attempt to settle that frontier. Between 1820-21, around 5000 settlers were shipped out to Algoa Bay at government expense and if the monument to them outside Grahamstown is to be believed, they looked like they had fallen off a Quality Street tin or popped out of the pages of a Regency bodice-ripper. It was intended that they should be primarily arable farmers, settled in a thick belt across the Zuurveldt rather than cattle ranchers like the Boers but this proved to be impractical largely because the settlers didn't have the necessary skills; they were townies; one of them was a poet. Within a year or two, most had given up and drifted into Grahamstown and Port Elizabeth ignoring an attempt to make them subject to the Pass Laws; wheat would not grow there and being forbidden to hold slaves, they were short of the necessary labour; some did succeed, given time but the scheme was not a success and nothing like it was tried again.

*

The March of Folly.

> A phenomenon noticeable throughout History regardless of place or period is the pursuit by governments of policies contrary to their own interests…. Self-interest is whatever conduces to the welfare or advantage of the body being governed; folly is a policy that in these terms is counter-productive. To qualify as folly…the policy adopted must meet three criteria: it must have been perceived as counter-productive in its own time, not merely by hindsight…. Secondly a feasible course of action must have been available…a third criterion must be that the policy in question should be that of a group, not an individual ruler, and should persist beyond any one political lifetime.
>
> Barbara Tuchman. *The March of Folly from Troy to Vietnam.*[118]

When the British expelled the Xhosa from the Zuurveldt in 1812 after the Fourth Frontier War, the Xhosa might have been forgiven for thinking that they still had a chance of

---

[118] Barbara W. Tuchman, *The March of Folly from Troy to Vietnam*, pp. 2-4.

overcoming British control of the area. Their defeat at the Battle of Grahamstown in 1819 removed any such illusion and the settlement held out to them by the British authorities offered them the chance of peace, trade and sovereignty, for which they had only to recognise the Fish River border and to desist from stealing cattle from the colonial side of it. If they agreed to the British terms they would be left to their own devices; if they continued to steal cattle, then there would be renewed war, defeat and further dispossession. Already patience was wearing thin; Cradock described the Xhosa as 'deaf to every reasonable proposal (however beneficial to themselves) and who seem only to exist for the annoyance of their neighbours'.[119] It was a simple decision and a real choice but the Xhosa refused to stop stealing cattle and in doing so embarked on the long march of folly that would lead them to destruction.

Was there a feasible course of alternative action? The Xhosa were rich in cattle, to the point that their demand for land was often the result of having too many cattle for the available pasturage. The surplus would have been gladly accepted in trade by the British to supply the demand for meat for passing ships and in this lay the basis for a potential partnership in trade which would enrich both parties. Opportunities for service as labourers in the colony – which many individual Xhosa had already availed themselves of[120] - would present further opportunities for the accumulation of capital while the wilder spirits might well have found employment in the Cape Corps or, conceivably, the navy. Within a generation or two, the Xhosa might well have emerged as a strong, independent polity armed with wealth and weapons enough to robustly defend their independence and to construct a relationship with the British similar to that enjoyed by the Indian Native States. Instead they chose theft, which within a generation, brought them ruin.

This policy of theft, or the refusal to restrain it, went across generations and across the different branches of the Xhosa polity and all attempts to change it fell by the wayside; many chiefs complained that they should not be held responsible for the actions of their people (a remarkable notion – *N.B. it's what government is for*); and when the British did visit fire and sword upon them in a series of attempts to get them to change their ways, the Xhosa embarked on the final folly of placing their trust, once again, in prophets who advised them to resist by destroying the basis of their wealth and culture in the great cattle killings. As a sovereign entity, the Xhosa collapsed out of sheer folly. It's hard to believe and even harder to accept but they really have no-one to blame but themselves.

Trouble began within 18 months of Ngqika agreeing terms after the defeat at Grahamstown when his sons, Maqoma and Tyali, re-crossed the Keiskamma and lifted 300 cattle from the new mission station on the Kat River. Ngqika proved defiant and when an attempt was made to seize him, he fled discredited and distrusted by both sides, and Maqoma asserted his leadership of the Rarabe, despite having no legitimate claim to it. A series of similar incidents followed to which the response was the construction of Fort Beaufort and Henry Somerset, the Governor's son, was put in charge of the military defence of the frontier. On

---

[119] Stockenstrom Vol 1 p.96
[120] S. Newton-King, "The Labour market of the Cape Colony, 1807 – 28" in S. Marks and A. Atmore (eds), *Economy and Society in Pre-industrial South Africa*, (London, 1980), p. 175.

5th December 1823, Maqoma's kraal was raided and 7000 cattle taken in reprisal. The aged and infirm, almost blind Ndlambe and the other frontier clans rejected Ngqika's overlordship too, which in effect meant that there was no single Xhosa authority on the frontier and given the traditional weakness of the Xhosa chiefs' authority, no effective way to restrain individual Xhosa from engaging in stock theft.

When in 1828 both Ngqika and Ndlambe died, the nominal leadership passed to Maqoma, a man of undoubted skill, bravery and intelligence but he was not able to prevent the continual theft of stock either; there is some doubt as to whether he thought it was even his duty to attempt it; like his father, he was already drinking heavily. Henry Somerset rather liked him and acquiesced in his re-occupation of land between the Keiskamma and Fish Rivers in what was now called the Ceded Territory. Andries Stockenstrom, Commissioner-General for the eastern frontier, distrusted him completely and was convinced that the cycle of theft and Commando would not be broken by such weak leadership.

We should pause here again, this time to consider the character of Andries Stockenstrom because he was accepted as the expert on all things frontier related for the best part of thirty years. He's also interesting because he doesn't really fit into any kind of stereotype. It used to be quite hard to get hold of his memoirs so you had to see him through the prism of other Historians and this was a bit of a problem because by the time I started researching South Africa that prism was firmly in the grasp of the Left. His entry in the Dictionary of National Biography was written by Stanley Trapido, a chap who was described in his *Independent* obituary as 'politically engaged'.[121] This means he was a white South African working at Oxford University doing his best to bring down Apartheid, for which he gets a Gold Star (he was pals with Bram Fischer, Nelson Mandela's lawyer). Unfortunately, he also got mixed up in the race/class nonsense which in turn meant that he was open to the charge of being biased against anyone who was white even if that person did not fit the mould of a racist oppressor, despite the fact that old Stan didn't fit the mould either (NB. You need to be able to perform some seriously complicated mental gymnastics to be a Marxist academic). Fortunately, the glories of the internet mean that you can download a copy of Stockenstrom Junior's scribbling and read it for yourself these days and make your own mind up. You don't even have to take *my* word for it either. One other thing; if old Stan thought the best fish and chips in the world were to be found at Kalk Bay, he was wrong. The fish is too bony. And don't even think of eating butterfish from the one in Hout Bay unless you are fond of food poisoning and the Great White Telephone. You need to go to Aldeburgh on the Suffolk coast of England for proper fish and chips.

Born in 1792 and educated in Cape Town – or 'tossed about from Arsaai to Kok,'[122] as he put it (they were tutors) – Andries was the son of the Llandrost of Graaff-Reinet. A chance meeting with Colonel Collins resulted in him accompanying him on his tour in 1809, and after service in the Cape Corps and with Burgher forces, he rose quickly to become the Llandrost of Graaff-Reinet and thereafter Commissioner for the Eastern frontier. Tough,

---

[121] http://www.independent.co.uk/news/obituaries/stanley-trapido-politically-engaged-historian-788505.html
[122] Stockenstrom Vol 1, p.52.

patient and wise for such a young man, he was a good hater of people who disagreed with him, had a chip on his shoulder the size of a Cape oak about his humble background, was eager for a quarrel and merciless in pursuing the very many that he had, an admirer of British law and constitutional practice but not the aristocracy or its system of patronage when it worked against him or his family. He was sympathetic to the Boers, sympathetic to the Xhosa, but regarded them as 'cruel barbarians,'[123] and sympathetic to the Khoisan. He was utterly opposed to Somerset's Spoor Law, utterly opposed to the lawlessness of Boer and Baastard frontiersmen, completely loyal to British rule and always willing to fight for it but thoroughly opposed to the expansion of the empire. As far as business or making money was concerned, he was a complete Bolshevik. He was of a profoundly liberal disposition too, was opposed to slavery while owning slaves, infuriated by injustices visited on the Xhosa and Khoisan (he particularly opposed the Pass laws) and scathing of those who justified such injustices on the grounds of advancing the bible and civilisation. This was all complicated by his conviction that the opinions of people who hadn't acquired a long knowledge of life on the frontier were worthless. Sometimes it feels as if his anger is going to leap off the page and throttle you. I dare say an acquaintance with him in the flesh was never dull. This is him on the Governor's son, Henry Somerset, who he hated from the beginning.

> From my profound respect for, and attachment to, his father, there are few sacrifices that I would not have made to serve the son and gain his good-will; but with an infatuated parent who could not believe it possible for his son to be in the wrong, who possessed despotic sway in the Colony, and all powerful influence at head-quarters, civil and military, it was but natural that the young aspirant Captain should become the focus of a set of hangers-on and flatterers, who, like himself, having made South Africa the *Champ de Mars* of their future glory, would not like to see a mere unpatronised Africaner jump over the heads of gentlemen of influence and blood so well adapted to give brilliancy to the crack corps. For me to speak kindly of Captain Somerset would be disgusting affectation.[124]

Much of this hatred began when the Cape Corps was reformed and in the general scrabble for places, Henry Somerset and his smart set displaced the previous officers now placed on half-pay. Stockenstrom was hoping for a Captaincy but instead was 'shoved into the Corsican Rangers'[125] a complaint that shows his talent for bile; the Corsican Rangers was a unit made up of French emigres long since disbanded. The regiment he was gazetted to was actually the 60th Royal American Regiment, who had a uniform similar to the Corsican Rangers. Never one to forgive a slight, he was still raging about it on his death bed.

This is him responding to accusations made by Dr John Philip of the London Missionary Society that he wanted to see the Khoikhoin enslaved.

> You were perfectly justified in telling Doctor Philip, or the Commissioners, or the Governor, that I had tried to find out which Hottentots, or any others, were living

---

[123] Stockenstrom Vol 1 p. 143.
[124] Stockenstrom Vol 1 p. 129.
[125] Stockenstrom Vol 1 p. 138.

> upon their industry or property, and which upon plunder and robbery, and you might safely have added that I am as hostile to the emancipation of the Hottentots and all other classes from *all legal and moral restraints,* as I am anxious for their emancipation from *bondage and oppression,* and that I cannot be a greater advocate for Christian conversion, or bear greater respect for the truly religious missionary, than I despise the fanatic or the hypocrite, who, abandoning the glory of his Maker, makes religion answer his own purposes.[126]

Ouch!

Here he is giving another of his very, very many opponents, a good trolling.

> I left the scurvy curs to scratch and growl, except on a late occasion when I thought the puppy's station rendered it necessary to check his insolence.... There are many whose approbation it has been the study of my life to obtain, but there are also some whose cordial hatred I have considered barely less desirable.... For the temporary torments which I once suffered from an infamous cabal, I was amply compensated by the heart-burning with which the disappointed tools vented their fury in impotent blustering and foaming rage, in full consciousness of my own and every honest man's contempt.[127]

What is interesting about him is that he never let theory or prejudice get in the way of a practical solution to a problem. He dealt with what was in front of him and spoke his mind – which is never a good policy. Here he is laying out his analysis of the situation the colony found itself in in 1826.

> My system is to do my best to get the white man hanged who murders a black; but I also do my best to root out any gang of robbers and murderers among the blacks.... our ancestors, and the Government have forced us into... [this] scrape we must either run away, sit still and have our throats cut, or defend what we have. Neither of the two former alternatives will benefit the blacks—either must ultimately ruin both them and ourselves; whereas, the third persisted in with firmness, strict justice and moderation, may in a country like this enable both parties to live in peace and plenty.[128]

Bad things had been done on both sides in the past, ran the argument, but it was not practical to erase the past. Nor was it practical to hold the present colonists responsible for those past deeds, so some sort of equitable solution had to be sought in the here and now.

> I am no out and out advocate of the native tribes. I never allow them to plunder and murder with impunity. They know it. They are neither angels nor devils. When I have to choose between destroying them, or being destroyed by them, I am never long in deciding, but I insist upon it, and repeat that a powerful government like that of England, by equitable treaties honestly and wisely drawn up, and faithfully kept in a

---
[126] Stockenstrom Vol 1 p. 233.
[127] Stockenstrom Vol 2. p. 2.
[128] Stockenstrom Vol 1 pp. 243-5.

spirit of candour and liberality, will soon have the chiefs so completely under its influence that its word will be law without appearing or pretending to be so.[129]

As to missionaries, his views again reveal a man who dealt in common sense drawn from experience rather than hope, zeal or faith in a cause.

> I consider them men like other classes, neither better nor worse. I know some of them to be very foolish and ignorant, apt to deceive you and the public by exaggerated reports of their efforts and their success, as well as of the virtues and long suffering of the blacks, and the vices and cruelty of the whites; but I have found some most excellent men among them, for whom I entertain the most sincere respect. In fact, I feel that every attempt to civilise the barbarians and savages without the help of prudent, wise, Christian missionaries, will certainly fail; but they, on the other hand, will not succeed without the cordial co-operation of and with the Government; and these two forces, combined, however powerful, will not civilise unless they make the native chiefs the principal levers in the operations on their people. If we gain the confidence of the chiefs, they, with the power of the Government, and the efforts of the missionaries, will influence the masses, and improve the state of society; but if you undermine the power of the chiefs you may scheme and plan systems, but the end must be the extermination and bondage of the natives. You will possess the land, and the present proprietors will be your drawers of water and hewers of wood; but the Christianisation and civilisation of the aborigines will be nothing more nor less than a tremendous sham for secret, ambitious, hypocritical, or rapacious purposes.[130]

Here then is Andries Stockenstrom in 1828. Appointed as Civil Commissioner for the Eastern Frontier he was at daggers drawn with the military commander, Henry Somerset, for whom the loathing was mutual. Ostensibly the dispute was professional; Stockenstrom thought the 'Spoor Law' system of 'patrol and reprisal' which was being used to police stock theft on the frontier ruinous, counter-productive and iniquitous; he was also opposed to the presence of Maqoma, the leading Xhosa chief, in the Ceded Territory on the Kat River. A bureaucratic turf war made things even worse; Somerset was in charge of the military but Stockenstrom was in charge of the Commandos so when Stockenstrom vetoed a Commando, Somerset would go behind his back to the Governor. Stockenstrom was convinced that the Xhosa were no real threat because the chiefs knew they would lose in any war; Somerset wasn't convinced. At bottom though, they just hated each other's guts and would cross the road to take up a quarrel.

In 1828, Maqoma attacked a Tembu clan in a dispute over grazing rights and so set off a series of alarms and disorders along the border. Stockenstrom was furious. The whole point of the Ceded Territory was to interpose a buffer zone between the Xhosa and the colonists; Maqoma should never have been allowed to settle there at all; and now the blasted rogue had used his base inside colonial territory to attack Tembu clans (then known as the 'Tambookies') outside it. Stockenstrom's solution was to reverse Somerset's original

---
[129] Stockenstrom Vol 1 p 247-8.
[130] Stockenstrom Vol 1 p. 246

mistake and boot Maqoma out of the Ceded Territories. Permission was gained, Maqoma displaced – those other clans who had quietly sneaked across the river and which had had the good sense to keep quiet and live peaceably were left alone - and the cattle he had stolen from the Tembu were restored. And then, in one of those remarkable shifts that Stockenstrom was capable of, he made the decision to settle the territory with new colonists on the 1820 model, only this time the colonists would not be English, but Khoikhoin.

The 400 square miles of the Kat River Settlement, as it became known, was divided up into villages of 4-6000 acres with each settler being allocated 4-6 acres of land. The model was an English village with plots, common land, education, irrigation, religion - and a ban on the sale of the liquor that had such terrible effects on those without the genetic resistance to it. James Read, one of the Bethelsdorp missionaries, moved in with his mixed-race family and the settlement rapidly became a thriving and prosperous community. It was Stockenstrom's way of making up a little for what the Khoikhoin had lost and he did it against the wishes of the white settlers who hoped to assuage a little of their own land hunger by swallowing up Maqoma's abandoned kraals.

The expulsion of Maqoma did not stop the theft of cattle and for the next two years Stockenstrom and Somerset wrangled over the best way to deal with it. Somerset wanted strict and rigorous application of the Spoor Law believing the Xhosa to be inveterate thieves and in need of regular demonstrations as to the consequences of their behavior. Stockenstrom believed that the Spoor Law just made things worse and that the only way to limit stock theft was for the Boers to take more care of their property and for the authority of the Xhosa chiefs over their own people to be recognized and supported. Somerset thought that Maqoma ought to be allowed back but Stockenstrom vetoed it. Somerset banged up two chiefs in Fort Willshire while two others were shot and Stockenstrom fumed that this would only serve to inflame tensions more. When the drought began to bite, Maqoma asked once more to be allowed back into the Ceded territory and Somerset allowed it on the QT. Stockenstrom decided that the only way to get some sort of order into the management of frontier affairs was to go to England himself and in 1833 taking six months leave, he took ship for the Colonial Office. While he was away, Maqoma was evicted once more but then, when Somerset came back from leave, allowed to return once more. Whereupon Duncan Campbell, Civil Commissioner for Albany, who had taken on many of Stockenstrom's functions while he was away, promptly ordered Maqoma out. Huts were razed, crops were burned, cattle theft continued, commandos took revenge and the whole cycle continued until the Xhosa exploded. In London, Stockenstrom tried to get the ear of the Colonial Office but to no avail. Under the reorganization of the government of the Cape, his post was abolished and he got the bum's rush. By the end of the year the colony was once more at war (the Sixth Frontier War 1834-5) with the Xhosa as 12000 warriors rushed down on the settlements of Albany and Grahamstown.

And, as the Duke of Wellington said of the French army, they came on in the same old way and they were driven off in the same old way. Within six months of December 1834, the Xhosa were defeated, pushed back off the Keiskamma River to the Kei, another 100 miles eastwards, and their paramount chief Hintsa, shot dead. His son Kreli was recognized as the new paramount. What was different, however, was an entirely new level of confusion in British policy. The new commander on the frontier, Sir Harry Smith, set up his HQ in Kingwilliamstown and prepared to clear the Xhosa clans out of the area only to be met with a reversal of policy from Governor D'Urban at the Cape. Now the Xhosa clans were to be allowed back and as many of them did not want to recognize Kreli, they could become British subjects in what was now to be called Queen Adelaide Province. Er...no, said the government in London, reversing the policy again; there would be no Queen Adelaide province and the whole kit and caboodle was handed back to the Xhosa and Stockenstrom was returned to the frontier.

'Vacillation is the History of this country' said one Edward Fairfield of the Colonial Office, fifty years later. He wasn't wrong. The people who *are* wrong are those Historians who imagine the History of the British Empire is one long tale of smash and grab as this episode so plainly shows. A short summary would read:

1. British colonists robbed of cattle by Xhosa colonists.

2. British colonists take cattle back.

3. British colonists attacked by Xhosa colonists.

4. British colonists defeat Xhosa colonists.

5. British colonists take land in compensation.

6. British government takes land from British colonists and hands it back to Xhosa colonists.

Why did the British government do this? Well, remember what I said at the beginning about the real importance of South Africa being a place to protect the trade routes to India? That's it. The view that Britain is interested in is not the pretty one looking out from the Fish River across to the misty Amatola Mountains but the one that goes out from the top of Table Mountain to the straight horizon and freezing waters of the Southern Ocean. Anything that isn't a port on the route to India is of little or no interest at all to the British government. That's what Galbraith's *Reluctant Empire* was all about.

And the lifting of cattle began again.

\*

1837

Now, things are going to get a bit complicated here because over the next fifteen years a lot happens in a lot of different places and a lot of what happens overlaps and so it's a bit of a tangled skein. In order to help see the different strands in that skein therefore, I'm going to put up a table of dates for ease of reckoning.

| | | |
|---|---|---|
| 1834 | 6th Frontier War starts between the Colony and the Xhosa. | |
| 1835 | Xhosa defeated. Queen Adelaide province annexed. | Voortrekkers start leaving the colony. |
| 1836 | Queen Adelaide province handed back to the Xhosa | Voortrekkers defeat Mzilikazi at Vegkop. |
| 1837 | | Piet Retief leaves colony. |
| 1838 | | Boers defeat Zulus at Blood River. |
| 1840-43 | | Republic of Natalia. Ended by British occupation. |
| 1845 | | Brits defeat Boers at Battle of Swartkoppies. |
| 1846-47 | 7th Frontier war between colonists and the Xhosa. Queen Adelaide province annexed as British Kaffraria | |
| 1848 | Orange River Sovereignty annexed to Colony | Brits defeat Boers at Battle of Boomplats. |
| 1850 | 8th Frontier War. Xhosa lose again. | |

One of the impressions created by a long study of South African History is that pretty much all the colonists were absolute bastards before the missionaries arrived and showed them the light. To be fair, I think that this is a function of the records again, because the London Missionary Society and others were good enough to keep lots and lots of reports, accounts, correspondence and the like which were often incorporated into the parliamentary Blue Books and so provide the hurried historian with an essay deadline to meet with a wealth of easily accessible sources. Also, they are in English and printed and so easy to read; the earlier ones are in Dutch, often illegible and produced by people for whom literacy did not come easily. However, I'm going to stick with Stockenstrom on this because, being such a bad tempered old bugger who was unwilling to temper his opinion or tack with the prevailing wind (and also being so hard not to like as a result), his words carry the weight of authenticity. He certainly seemed to retain the confidence of all sorts of people in the colony and he was tolerated by his superiors way beyond what might be expected, probably because of the forthrightness of his opinions as much as for his experience. You always know where you are with Stockenstrom; he wouldn't last five minutes today, of course, but I would love to see him in action at an Islington dinner party for Guardianistas; I can close my eyes and hear the sneers of condescension and howls of fake outrage from here (and I'm writing this at the top of the Montagu Pass).

The two issues driving the missionaries were first, evangelism and the desire to bring Christianity to the heathen and so gain converts and secondly, the campaign against slavery. With the first aim, few people had any qualms; religion was seen as a universal good and Christianity was seen as something necessary for the liberation of mankind from ignorance, base passions and bad habits and the promotion of virtuous behaviour, community and useful knowledge. It was the marked failure of the early missionaries such as Van der Kemp and Read at Bethelsdorp that raised the voice of the colonists against them rather than the actual idea of evangelism.

Something similar went for the issue of slavery and at this point we should just issue a trigger warning for those people too delicate to cope with the harsh reality of History. At the time that Van Riebeeck landed at the Cape, slavery was accepted as a fact of life. No-one wanted to *be* a slave, but the institution existed in pretty much every society in some form or other; some conditions of slavery were mild by comparison, others unspeakably bad. To illustrate this, all you need to do is read *Robinson Crusoe*; setting out in 1651, his first voyage ends in shipwreck, his second in him being enslaved by the Moors in North Africa; he then escapes with a fellow slave and then sells that slave to the captain of the ship that rescues him in return for a plantation in Brazil; he is finally and famously shipwrecked while on a journey to buy more slaves. Move forward a hundred years to the height of the Atlantic slave trade and although its scale has grown massively because the African rulers were more than happy to satisfy the demand and because supply creates its own demand (*Says Law*: Google it), the trade is still seen as pretty normal and the debate about it is was often couched in plain economic terms rather than humanitarian ones; is slave labour more efficient than paid labour? (Answer: paid labour is more efficient because the worker has an incentive to work).

Slaves began to be imported into the Cape from the East Indies, Mozambique and Angola from 1717 and contrary to the impression given by Alex Hailey's controversial 'History' *Roots*, slaves were not stolen by white people but purchased legally from black people. The book was controversial because he was awarded a Pulitzer Prize, when he had plagiarized an earlier work and, frankly, made up large parts of his supposed family History.[131] At the Cape, by and large, slaves were treated well mainly because there was no grinding plantation labour to be done, they were expensive and poor treatment encouraged them to run for the borders and also because most of the slave owners were reasonably normal people. Certainly, there was a Slave Code which sanctioned horrendous punishments but the arrival of the British put an end to that and in 1807, the Abolition of the Trade in slaves, but not of slavery itself, put the writing on the wall. Slaves were also given legal protection against ill-treatment and there were several cases where the law intervened on their behalf. Stockenstrom was of the view that the institution was likely to die out within a few years – a

---

[131] https://www.theguardian.com/books/booksblog/2017/feb/09/alex-haley-roots-reputation-authenticity

view shared by the public meeting of the Boers at Graaff-Reinet in 1826 - and the question was how to allow for it. Stockenstrom advocated that all children of slaves should be born free - an idea that was common in the early colony and often enacted if the children were baptised. Many of the colonists (and the London Missionary Society) wondered whether the abolition of slavery would end up adding to the vagrancy problem and if the provisions of the Hottentot Ordinance would be applied to the freed slaves. There was also the question of property, because slaves were 'property' in law and as property rights are fundamental to all freedom, prosperity and good government some form of payment upon emancipation would have to be made. The government could not simply emancipate the slaves without compensating the slave owners – or as some modern-day activists demand, making the owners pay compensation to the slaves (an absurdity; the *original owners* in West Africa would have to be hunted down and billed) – because this would violate the principle of property rights; if the government could take your slaves away without paying, then they could do it for your house, horse and farm and this would be throwing the baby out with the bathwater.

It was at this point that the missionaries arrived, full of holy wrath, righteous indignation, complete incompetence, ignorance of local circumstances and a firm belief that 'the conversations, generalisations, the plans of superior men are unintelligible to little minds'.[132] Step forward Dr. John Philip of the London Missionary Society who, armed with a salary that was not subject to the vagaries of drought, flood, locusts or the market (he was utterly ignorant of the realities of doing business) allowed him the feedom to pontificate about the iniquities of the profit motive and generally look down on the farmers who were. In this, Philip resembled many of the corporate barons of the African Aid industry who hold the same views about profit today; they are, of course, not averse to trousering those profits when they transmute into donations though (and as I write in February 2018, they are being exposed for the same reasons as Read was exposed; sexual misconduct; *plus ça change....*). From the outset he got the backs of the colonists up by misrepresenting them on a heroic scale and insulted all officialdom by claiming from the standpoint of his obviously superior knowledge, that they were all, pretty much from the Governor downwards, corrupt or stupid.

His *Researches in South Africa* published in 1828 was a Swiss cheese of a book and it wasn't necessary to read past the preface to realise that his 'superior' knowledge wasn't very superior at all; he claimed that slaves could be bought for a 'trifling sum'[133] when in reality, they were expensive articles, and that Missionaries were welcomed by Africans everywhere they went, which they clearly weren't. As far as Van Riebeeck's time was concerned, he declared that:

> All the records of the colony, during the first fifty years of the Dutch occupation, that I have seen…relate…that during the whole of that period, the natives had never in one instance had been detected in committing an act of theft upon the property of the colonist.[134]

---

[132] Dr John Philip, *Researches in South Africa* (London, 1828) Vol. 1 p.140
[133] Dr John Philip, *Researches in South Africa* Vol 1. p. xvii.
[134] Dr John Philip, *Researches in South Africa* Vol 1. p.4.

Inserting *that I have seen* in the passage, was an attempt at a get-out clause in case he was challenged on this. In fact, this was a straightforward lie because a couple of pages later on, he admitted reading Van Riebeeck's Journal, using it to claim that it was the Dutch who did the thieving.[135] Given this start, it is probably needless to say that his account of the Commando warfare in the later 18th Century was one-sided, to say the least, while the then present condition of the Khoisan – which he described as being one of indolence, gluttony, drunkenness and declining physique – he ascribed entirely to their treatment at the hands of the farmers.[136] He even trotted out that old chestnut 'No Entry to Hottentots or dogs'. Van der Kemp was given a coat of whitewash and, for good measure in the pots and kettles category, those who had criticised him were branded as liars.[137] Actually, it's quite a fun book to read because you can't help but snigger at his complete zealotry, paranoia, wide-eyed fanaticism, self-congratulation (complete with testimonials), huge over-statements, predilection for conspiracies and banalities: 'one set of laws for the rich and another for the poor'[138] and the 'system of oppression under which the Hottentot groans'[139] are just two examples. Much of his evidence is anecdotal on the lines of 'a bloke I once knew told me' and though doubtless some of the tales of ill-treatment are true, there are no counterbalancing anecdotes to add veracity – not *every* farmer and colonist was as complete a bastard as Philip would have us believe surely? And though the age was certainly more tolerant of casual violence than the present, it remains the case that happy workers are more productive than those kept under the lash and in a situation where labour was in high demand, application of the sjambok would tend to make a farmer's labour situation rather worse than better. Added to this are the frequent contradictions; one moment he is praising his flock as fine examples of the Noble Savage, the next excoriating them for being idle, feckless, filthy, licentious and depraved. He even claimed that there hadn't been a drunk or a brawl at Bethelsdorp in the six years that he had been overseeing it and that despite being horrendously oppressed by the colonial system, the inhabitants now lived in better houses, had better clothes and more comforts than either the Boers or the colonial Brits.[140] These were claims that could only be swallowed with a shovel full of salt, especially as he was also claiming that the Khoikhoin there couldn't afford to pay their taxes. Similarly, he excoriated the colonial government for making it practically impossible for the Khoikhoin to own land while then going into great detail (with documents) showing how that same colonial government had prevented a corrupt member of the LMS from ripping off land in their possession near Swellendam; the complexities of the case seem to hinge on Philip's own incompetence in neglecting to assert the LMS title to land while at the same time asserting that his demand for the removal of the corrupt missionary carried the weight of law. Indeed, for someone so incensed at the law, he seems to have been remarkably ignorant of it. All in all, it's hard not to discern from the construction and tone of the work that it contained that feature so often observed among the self-appointed, self-righteous defenders of the poor and oppressed - a very heavy hint that, considering his huge talents and pure genius, a large pay rise would not be out of place.

---

[135] Dr John Philip, *Researches in South Africa* Vol 1. p.17
[136] Dr John Philip, *Researches in South Africa* Vol 1. p.57.
[137] Dr John Philip, *Researches in South Africa* Vol 1. p.95
[138] Dr John Philip, *Researches in South Africa* Vol 1. p. 156
[139] Dr John Philip, *Researches in South Africa* Vol 1. p.159.
[140] Dr John Philip, *Researches in South Africa* Vol 1. p. 223.

Arriving in 1819, Philip was welcomed as a vast improvement on what had gone before and his early reports on Bethelsdorp bore out all the criticisms that the colonists and other missionaries had already made about that place (an inconvenience that he glossed over in *Researches*). There was also a certain wariness towards him because the LMS had friends in high places, good connections in parliament and the press and were connected to the great Tory anti-slavery champions, Wilberforce and Fowell Buxton. In particular, the idea of proselytizing among the indigenous people was not universally accepted. In India the saying was 'don't monkey with the local Gods' and the East India Company went out of its way to support both the Hindu and Muslim religions. As well as this, many people preferred their religion to be a quiet affair of hymns on Sunday, weddings, funerals and christenings rather than blood and thunder Methodism and fervent Evangelism and there were several missionaries who had already taken the decision to sever their connections with the LMS in favour of becoming country parsons. What was more, many of the colonists spoke Dutch and were quite happy with the religion they had.

The ground upon which useful work might be done seemed to Philip to lie beyond the colonial boundary on the Orange River and it was this that brought him into conflict with the authorities because what the British government in Cape Town did not want was people wandering off beyond the borders where they became a law unto themselves. For a start, it wasn't safe; Philip was a pretty tough character but it would be reasonable to assume that a couple of handy Oorlams would make short work of him and if they did, there would be all sorts of irritation in London.

Philip was a good hater too and being strong-minded and willful would not take 'no' for an answer. His response to the refusal of his request to go up to the Orange River was to take up the cause of the Hottentot Ordinance and the Khoikhoin. In 1821, getting Read to draw up another dossier of the sort of vague accusations that had been presented to the Black Circuit, he approached the Governor with what looks like a *quid pro quo*; let me go beyond the border or I'll cause you more trouble than you want. The Governor responded by ordering an inquiry into the dossier and the inquiry threw out the allegations. Irritated at Read's incompetence, Philip went to Bethelsdorp and miraculously stumbled upon all the evidence he needed to prove Read's allegations because the chief target of those allegations, Major Cuyler, had – again miraculously! - written down all the evidence to prove his guilt, in his own handwriting, and conveniently left it in a corner of Read's office. This was the same Major Cuyler, who had insisted as a matter of honour that a trained and qualified lawyer be assigned to the Khoikhoin who Read had jacked up to testify against him last time. In short, the evidence was nonsense; nothing more than a series of petty administrative disputes over the requisition of labourers for various public works, a type of *corveé* which at that time was perfectly legal, and the conscription of men for the Cape Corps, again perfectly legal. Philip, a man in search of a cause, had just found it and he wasn't too scrupulous about the methods that he was prepared to use to further it. The problem was that it wasn't much of a cause at all.

Philip began to send a stream of reports back to London critical of the treatment of the Khoikhoin and when the parliamentary commissioners engaged on enquiring into the state of the colony arrived at the Cape in 1823, he sent in a stream of information to them. Unfortunately for Philip, the parliamentary commissioners did not immediately roll over and do what he loudly and stridently demanded of them and nor were they convinced by his constant accusations that the Dutch colonists were horribly prejudiced and the British colonists well down on the same road. Neither did Lord Charles Somerset or the Governor, Lord Bathurst, give much backing to his charges, in part, no doubt because Philip was not above dishonest exaggerations - when one of his flock was drafted into the Cape Regiment at Grahamstown in 1822, Philip claimed that he had been 'violently seized' which is not the same thing at all.[141] Philip also made a series of wild accusations against Stockenstrom, including the charge that he deliberately shot down Bushmen to get at their children.[142] The commissioners brought several of these accusations up with Stockenstrom; they went away with the customary flea in their ear. Stockenstrom pointed out that he had scrupulously upheld the 1809 Hottentot Ordinance and refused to allow any child to be apprenticed unless they had no other means of support. Were the colonists entirely innocent of the charges? Of course, not.

> They have often been attacked with savage ferocity, it is true, but they have not always been without shame.[143]

However, that said, he denied 'that there was a general feeling against the freedom of the Hottentots'. He also stated firmly that he had been supported at all times by the Heemraaden (his local council) in the proper upholding of the law, and that the vast majority of the people of his district were convinced of the unjust aspects of the laws long before Philip had put a foot in Africa.[144]

Getting nowhere in the Cape, Philip went off to see if he could get his voice heard in London but arriving there in 1826, it seemed that the LMS had not been convinced by his reports either. Desperate to find someone who would believe him, he then turned to Fowell Buxton of the Anti-Slavery Society and pressed on him the idea that the Hottentot Ordinance was no different in reality to the condition of slavery. This was nonsense; slaves don't get contracts; slavery is not driven by notions of paternalism; a slave does not own his own body. With the outrageous overstatement of the spittle-flecked zealot, Philip had just tarred every single person in the colony who employed Khoikhoin as a slave master. No wonder he was reviled and his *Researches in South Africa* met with disgust.

It was met with disgust because in July 1828, while Philip was hyperventilating in London, Stockenstrom got the famous 50th Ordinance enacted at the Cape without reference to him. At a stroke, the Cape Colony, at that time undergoing a thorough legal reform, adopted the basic principle of English Law that all men possess equal rights. The Hottentot Ordinance

---

[141] Dr John Philip, *Researches in South Africa* Vol 1. p. 310.
[142] Stockenstrom Vol.2 p.26.
[143] Stockenstrom Vol 2. p.7
[144] Stockenstrom Vol. 2 p.9.

was swept away, freedom of movement guaranteed, the right to own and purchase property enshrined and though slavery was still legal, it was recognized that this was something that would be tidied out of the way in the near future. Stockenstrom was a great believer in the English Common Law; it was colour blind; it was capable of moving to reflect the customs, changing circumstances and beliefs of the day; it did not need to be deceived into doing the right thing by noisy and unscrupulous agitators. And neither did the colonists feel the need to be lectured about their manners by noisy, ignorant prelates who felt entitled to stride into their house and complain about the hospitality. And when his accusations were put to the test of legal proof, it was Philip who lost the libel case brought against him. Stockenstrom was, as usual, quite right in his beliefs.

*

The legal reforms enacted at the Cape during the 1820s were just one aspect of a process that began to look like Anglicisation. In 1828, the old Roman-Dutch criminal law was replaced by English law although the civil law remained unchanged. The local government system of Llandrost and elected Heemraaden was abolished and replaced with that of the Civil Commissioners who administered without recourse to elected help, and Resident Magistrates to administer justice. Central government was also reformed with the abolition of the elected *Raad* in Cape Town and its replacement by a Legislative Council made up of non-elected officials and non-elected appointees (of which Stockenstrom was one). Land reform followed too and the practice of handing out Loan Farms was ended and replaced with the sale of Crown Lands by public auction. On top of this, a flood of teachers arrived in the colony raising the prospect that Dutch speakers faced marginalisation or Anglicisation through the spread of English medium education and, quite bizarrely, according to Stockenstrom, a rumour that everyone was to be forcibly converted to Roman Catholicism. For the British, of course, Anglicisation was no fixed policy but rather a series of pragmatic reforms intended for the better administration of the colony but for the Dutch it looked as though their heritage and identity was under assault, an impression that was given further depth by the insults rained down on them by Dr. Philip and his missionary friends.

With the passing of Ordinance 50, the question of slavery came up once again. Just about everyone knew that abolition was coming and it was the mechanics rather than the rightness of abolition that caused misgivings. When the word came that as of 1$^{st}$ December 1834, slavery would be abolished, the freed slaves to be apprenticed to their former masters for four years and compensation would be paid, there was a general acceptance. It would allow the farmers to adjust, prevent the slaves being turned away and driven to vagrancy and not least, give the slaves themselves time to prepare for an independent life. Again, this would not be acceptable today but by the standards of the time, this was a remarkable piece of legislation, and probably unprecedented in the History of the world. The question of slaves being 'property' was answered by the government making a compulsory purchase of that property and then, being free to do as it pleased with its own property, set it free. It was a brilliant solution; the consequences of the alternative, of emancipation without compensation, was seen thirty years later on the battlefields and burned out cities of the United States of America.

I remember making this point during my studies in Multicultural Education; Britain certainly played a large and ignominious role in the slave trade but surely, we deserve some credit for being the first country in the world to abolish it and then commit the resources of the Royal Navy to its suppression for the best part of a century at quite staggering cost and no practical or personal gain? This was met by the full Islington sneer, which if you haven't come across it (an unlikely prospect) entails the drawing in of the stomach, a narrowing of the eyes, the elevation of the nose to an angle that would not disgrace a Roman Emperor looking down on the mob, followed by a dismissive toss of the hair which says *Do I really have to dignify such a statement with an answer?* and then an expressive, wearied sigh. 'Black people liberated themselves,' intoned the tutor.

'No, they did not,' I replied. 'Slavery was ended by the Union Army in the American Civil War and the Royal Navy.'

I wonder to this day how I managed to avoid being booted off that course. I'm trying to be humorous here but it's a deadly serious point that I'm making. The pushing of the idea that the British Empire was irredeemably bad by people who believe that no culture is more valid than another – the essence of multiculturalism – is antinomian. And it is also in essence a lie; if all cultures are equal, then that includes Britain and its imperial past. In practice, multiculturalism does not see all cultures as equal; it sees British/European culture as decidedly inferior, guilty of the original sins of imperialism and the slave trade, and in need of serious correctional services by the elevation in status of any and all other cultures. *Antinomian*; that's a big and possibly unfamiliar word but it means that people who consider themselves on the side of virtue are exempt from the normal rules of a good and bad behavior and it is this belief that allows them to peddle any bullshit they please on the grounds that when pursuing what they see as a virtuous goal, the end justifies the means. It's the way of the purge, the re-education camp and the Gulag – and they know it and they're willing to see you in it and sooner rather than later, excuse the firing squad that purifies the world of your unclean existence.

On with the show. The principle of abolition was accepted by all but the most hard line Boers but when the mechanics went awry, anger was widespread and justified. Firstly, when the compensation payments were announced, they were set at a level way below the monetary value of the slave (property rights!) and secondly, the payments were to be made in London. Anyone who wanted to make that journey would bear their own costs which meant that a man who owned one or two slaves would probably be a long way out of pocket if he went to the time and expense of trekking all the way to the Cape, making the dangerous voyage to Mud Island and back (Stockenstrom had been quarantined after a smallpox outbreak on the ship he was travelling in) and then trekking all the way back up through the Karoo to Graaff-Reinet. The only alternative was to sell the entitlement to compensation to an agent at yet another discount. Most reasonable people reckoned they had been bilked and those people were correct.

The other group of people who found it difficult to accept the Abolition of Slavery were the Xhosa who had enslaved the mFengu people when they had fled Natal to get away from war and famine. In one of his most brilliant displays of semantic acrobatics, Noel Mostert attempted to play down the enslavement of the mFengu by the Xhosa by describing it as 'a bond mutually agreed and accepted according to established tradition'.[145] Paramount Chief Hintsa was more honest; he called the mFengu 'his dogs'.[146] The mFengu were even more honest; when Harry Smith invaded Hintsa's territory, they deserted the Xhosa on mass and from then on would serve as regular allies to the British Army. On 9th May 1835, a column one and a half miles wide and eight miles long made up of 17000 mFengu men women and children along with 22000 cattle were given permission to come across the River Kei to settle in the Cape Colony in freedom. Those who preferred the 'bond mutually agreed and accepted according to established tradition' were killed by Hintsa's warriors. It's a good job I didn't know this when I was doing the course in Multicultural Education; that full Islington sneer would no doubt have been supplemented by the full *Guardianista* witch-hunt (or should that be 'traditional healer and purveyor of decolonized knowledge no platforming'?).

The 1835 Frontier War did nothing to allay the mounting frustration that many of the Boers were beginning to feel at the actions of the British government. The back and forth way of dealing with Maqoma, the establishment of Queen Adelaide Province and then its abandonment, gradually built up a conviction that the government in Cape Town or London or both had no idea as to the circumstances that those on the frontier faced on a daily basis – cattle theft, invasion, drought. Were they heartless? Uncaring? Distracted? Incompetent? No-one knew and as the Heemraaden had been abolished there was no way in which their concerns could be transmitted to the government in such a way as to expect some action or redress. Stockenstrom, as usual, had his finger on the pulse.

> The destruction of the link which had so long existed between the Government and the governed, became to me very glaring. The most thinking and sensible of the old inhabitants, in their accustomed familiar intercourse with me, lamented despondingly the loss of those "Voorstanders van't Volk" (leaders and defenders of the people) who always knew at least something of the views of the Rulers, and to whom the most ignorant of the people could apply for information or advice as to a Father, Brother, Uncle, or other friend—at least as to an equal. "Now," said some of the old leaders, "We have a Civil Commissioner to receive our money for Government and for Land Surveyors, a Magistrate to punish us, a Clerk of the Peace to prosecute us, and get us into the Tronk, but no Heemraad to tell us whether things are right or wrong, when we can make neither head nor tail of them, for our oldest and wisest men know as little of the Government as we do. The fact is that many of us begin to think that the old Dutch Boer is no longer fit for this country. The Englishman is very learned, and we are very stupid. They and the Hottentots will squeeze us all out by degrees.[147]

\*

---

[145] Mostert, *Frontiers* p. 698.
[146] Mostert, *Frontiers* p. 698.
[147] Stockenstrom Vol. 1. p.391.

Graaff-Reinet is a really pretty town, nestled in a bend of the Sundays River under the Snowberg and the massive shoulders of Spandau Kop. It's full of Cape Dutch gables, agreeable guesthouses with yellow wood floors, riotous bougainvillea in orange, pink and yellow; red flame trees and purple jacarandas shade the wide, white streets and slap bang in the middle of it a very large church that is said to have been modelled on Salisbury cathedral. This is a fiction that can only be sustained if you've never seen Salisbury cathedral but it's still a nice church and you can look at it while you have breakfast in the *Spur* just by the Drostdy. Looking around you can see that like very many other small towns in South Africa, it gets a little shabbier every time you visit and the need for a lick of paint on a wall and a barrow load of tarmac in a pothole becomes more and more apparent and though there is a fierce optimism among the 25,000 inhabitants, it seems to me that the spirit is of the Dunkirk variety, rather than of Overlord. The town is gradually retreating rather than bravely advancing.

I'm told that the impact of Apartheid here was negligible and that the school was segregated more in theory than in practice. Long term residents told me that the ANC was so unsuccessful here that supporters had to be bussed in whenever there was a demonstration. This I suspect is only the half of it; during the 19th Century the town had provided a refuge for a body of slaves liberated on the high seas by the Royal Navy but Apartheid had ensured that the black people were relocated from the centre of the town to a 'Location' just to the north of it. In 2016, the ANC took 55% of the vote in the Municipal elections with the opposition Democratic Alliance on 42%. Still, it is a quiet town and though the traders of the 'informal' market at the eastern end of town seem to be unable to carry out the business of flogging fruit and veg without the accompaniment of awful music played at industrial volumes, it has avoided the terrible fate of becoming 'vibrant'. I've wandered home mildly plastered several times after beer and bobotie at the *Pioneers* Restaurant, happily weaving past Somerset, Bourke, Cradock, Caledon and Stockenstrom Streets without feeling anything more than the mild anxiety that goes with walking anywhere after dark in South Africa. Joburg it ain't.

One of the things that keeps me coming back to it is the road up to Colesberg that goes from here. It is 200km of spectacular desert scenery, of flat plains, rocky outcrops and sparse blonde grass, two passes, the Naudeberg and the Lootsberg one higher than the next, both of which come with snow warnings in winter and which, when you pull over, look back over a landscape like a turbulent sea. These roads aren't busy so there is always time to stop and stare and it's always worth doing just that, but they are steep and the 1.1*l* engine that the hire company is all too keen to foist on you means that you're often in third – second sometimes – and willing the blasted car up the hill with your stomach muscles. During the 1830s, the whole area was awash with game; Stockenstrom claimed to have seen a Springbok migration through the Karoo that numbered more than a million animals and this is no exaggeration. Every year, vast herds would sweep down across the whole of the Karoo and across to the Atlantic coast, nibbling away every last bit of grazing and raising dust storms as dense as sandstorms. The place was also infested with lions.

Middelburg is a dump which seems to consist mainly of an unfinished bypass, an endless diversion and a prison but I never stay long enough to find out whether I'm being unjust or not because after Middelburg comes the Carlton heights and that too is an amazing, long, steep right-handed climb with views that go all the way to the purple horizon where ridges run like steam trains in the distance. A little further on is Colesberg, dominated by its own miniature version of Table Mountain, where the N1 Cape Town to Bloem road joins the road up from Graaff-Reinet and you're back in the 21st Century cursing the truckers and dodging the boy racers. It's taken you two hours or perhaps a little more and you have come up from a height of 741m/2431ft above sea level at Graaff-Reinet to a height of 1357m/4452ft and most of that gain in height has been done in those three lifts at Naudeberg, Lootsberg and Carlton. In between the land is pretty flat so it's comparable to climbing stairs. It isn't a long journey and when I do it the other way, I stay in the Horse and Mill pub, get up early and drive it before stopping for breakfast at the aforementioned Spur for breakfast. To me, it is one of the finest and most spectacular roads in the world.

'OK', I hear you say. 'It's pretty but it's hardly the Alps or the Himalayas or anything, is it?' This is correct but the thing is that I drove up in a crappy hire car and it was bad enough; the Trekboers who came up it in the 1830s came up it in an ox wagon and that is a very different thing indeed. Basically, speaking this, the preferred mode of transport of the Trekboer, was made up of a span of eighteen oxen covering no more than roughly 20km per day as an absolute maximum. Going slower than walking speed because the animals required plenty of time to graze, it would often take two or even three span of oxen to get up a steep slope and though oxen can go for two or three days without water, water they must have. There aren't any major rivers until the Orange after Colesberg and precious few *spruits* or streams so the Trekboers had to rely on finding *vleis*, small marshy areas where the water would stand after the rains or springs, *fonteins,* which often were the difference between life and death. Look at any map of South Africa and you'll see those words everywhere where water is scarce; *Bloemfontein, Bronkhurstspruit* are written into the History of the country but I suspect that *Fonteinjie*, the 'little spring' atop the Carlton Heights and a little further on *Rietfontein,* another *Fonteinjie,* and *Hartebeesfontein* were more famous long before the other two earned their names.

Going on beyond Colesberg towards Bloemfontein, the scrub of the desert begins to give way a little and there is more grass, more grazing, to be seen but the water is still the thing; *Springfontein, Jagersfontein, Gomvlei, Fouriespruit, Waterkloof.* After that, going eastwards to the great sea of grass that stretches out from Bethlehem all along the edge of the Drakensberg to the heights of Natal, the names thin out; there is still *Tweespruit* and *Vekeerdevlei* but it isn't until you come to *Sterkfontein* at the top of Van Reenan's Pass and look down at the mint, myrtle and emerald of the lands below does the presence of abundant water diminish the need for the names. Keep going north from Bloemfontein and you can hardly pin a donkey's tail on the map without pricking a *spruit,* a *vlei* or another *fontein.* And this is important because these names mark the routes of the Trekboers – or *Voortrekkers* as we must now call them.

\*

The Great Trek is the great founding myth of Afrikaaner Nationalism and the story runs roughly like this. In 1837, Piet Retief disgusted by British rule led the Boers out of Cape Colony to seek new lands beyond the Orange River. To their surprise and delight, up there on the Highveldt beyond the Karoo and far from the reach of the British was a land of milk and honey, empty of people, free for the taking and take it they did. Descending into Natal, they then came upon the Zulus who treacherously murdered Piet Retief and then attacked the Boers with the intention of exterminating them. At the Battle of the Blood River, 16th December 1838, facing annihilation at the spears of the heathen, the Boers prayed for deliverance and God heard them and presented them with a victory as overwhelming as it was unexpected. Thus, was the Afrikaaner claim to the land of South Africa established by Divine Will and Right of Conquest.

Now, this is a myth as everyone recognizes. The truth was far more provisional and complicated but like all myths, there is a grain of truth at the bottom of it, and that grain of truth is that when the Boers trekked up onto the Highveldt, they did indeed find a land empty for the taking and this allowed them to claim that their ownership of the land pre-dated the claims of black South Africans to ownership. This became an axiom of Afrikaaner Nationalist belief and one that was held onto with great tenacity and therefore many South African Historians decided that this version of History needed to be looked at very closely indeed.

The first question that they asked was why the lands were empty and this prompted two very different responses which, when the necessary research and honest study was completed, turned out to be two sides of the same coin. The first answer put forward the idea that there had been some terrible drought or other environmental disaster that had driven the indigenous people off the land and, given that there *was* a terrible drought around 1830, this was an idea that had some legs to it. The second idea was put forward by Professor J.D. Omer-Cooper during the late 1960s and he argued that this disaster, which went by the name of *Mfecane*, the 'time of the crushing' was the result of the rise of the Zulu empire and the military revolution that went with it. When Shaka Zulu began his career of conquest, he argued, a chain reaction of migration, flight, crop failure, stock theft and starvation resulted in the depopulation of the Highveldt at exactly the moment when the Voortrekkers were leaving the British colony. Both of these ideas were complimentary and worked well together. They seemed uncontroversial; but buried deep in Omer-Cooper's work was a worm that if left alone would eat through the whole apple of Afrikaaner Nationalist History because his aim was to give an *Afrocentric* view of South African History which said that *internal* African dynamics – the rise of the Zulu empire - had more important consequences than whatever the Europeans were up to and that Africans were not simply passive objects impacted upon by British and Boer interlopers. *Black Africans*, by implication, were *South Africans* too and as entitled to a say in what happened in their own country as were white people.

So far so good. Have a Gold Star Professor Omer-Cooper because *real* historical study and research is essential to understanding the past and how we arrived in the present. And then, in 1988, Julian Cobbing stepped forward with the idea that Omer-Cooper was really just an apologist for Apartheid because he blamed the *mfecane* on black people; the Zulus could not be responsible for bad things because they were black and oppressed; ditto the 40,000 warriors of the Mantatisi Horde (aka the baToklwa) that swept across the continent and devastated it. The real reason for the *mfecane*, he claimed, was a load of Portuguese slave traders working out of Lourenco Marques (modern day Maputo in Mozambique) and Griqua slavers operating at the behest of the Cape Colony authorities. It was *white* people who started off the *mfecane*. It was *white* people who were responsible for all the trouble in South Africa.

Now, I read Cobbing's original article before I had travelled much in South Africa and I thought it was very possibly an attempt to make sure of Dr Cobbings' continued university employment when the ANC took over. Since that time, I've been in Mozambique and I would say that any slave traders attempting to make the journey down and back through those malarial forests, awash with tsetse fly and devoid of roads, would be bankrupt in no time. The Arab slave trading networks centred on Zanzibar had taken centuries to build up; new entrants to the business would have to get past the armed and dangerous Swazis too. Similarly, the idea that the Cape authorities could exercise any sort of control over the Griquas struck me as fanciful too.

I wasn't alone in my scepticism either because in 1991 the whole of the historical establishment descended on the University of Witwatersrand for a conference aiming to examine what had become known as the 'Cobbing Hypothesis'. This, it seems, brought Cobbing out in hives and he demanded that he be granted editorial control over the final conference report and when this was refused, declined to take part. Not surprising, really. The report, when published as *The Mfecane Aftermath*,[148] junked the whole hypothesis and only just stopped short of accusing him of writing fiction. And this was a thorough job too; one of the contributors went all the way through his footnotes which, after being the proof reader for the latest collection of Marxist thought (or what passes for it), is possibly the most tedious job known to man. 'History is political' argued Elizabeth Eldridge, one of Cobbing's most vocal defenders, and it had been 'systematically distorted' to suit the justification of Apartheid. That the History had been distorted to justify Apartheid was true; what was not acceptable was the 'systematic distortion' of History to support the destruction of Apartheid or any other favoured cause. The end does not justify the means. 'That road,' said J.D. Omer-Cooper, hitting the nail squarely on the head. 'Must soon leave all honest scholarship behind.' Unfortunately, honest scholarship has never been the first concern of the Left; History must serve the Cause; the end *does* justify the means and this has been the case since Marat declared that the guillotining of 250,000 aristocrats would complete the French Revolution and usher in Utopia.

So, what did happen up on the Highveldt in 1837? Fortunately, we have a guide in Professor John Laband who during the 1980s and 1990s quietly and steadily built himself into the best historian the Zulu people have ever had. Tall, austere, he had done his National Service as an

---

[148] C. Hamilton (Ed), *The Mfecane Aftermath*, (Witwatersrand University Press 1995).

infantryman and hated it because he did not have the co-ordination to jump out of a moving truck while holding the baseplate of a mortar. I heard him speak several times, spoke alongside him in a couple of conferences and each time I learned something more. In the end, we disagreed, but I never, ever found cause to doubt his integrity. His best work *Rope of Sand* (my copy is signed and it is precious) came out in 1995 and stood out because it was firmly in the Africanist tradition of Omer-Cooper. Laband wanted to explain the world from the Zulu point of view and his books are outstanding because they read like real History books. They treat the Zulu people as people like any other; not *black*, not *oppressed*, not *victims*, not *helpless*. The Zulus were politicians, had policies, interests and acted rationally; I found myself reading those books just as I would read a History of France or Germany. He treated the Zulu kings with the same seriousness as the Russian Tsars, pointed out their characteristics and their failings and applied to them the same rigorous academic standards that a decent History requires.

*

The Zulus rose to prominence among the tribes that inhabited the lands that lay at the bottom of the escarpment between modern day St. Lucia and the area just south of Durban. Like the Xhosa they were essentially pastoral but occupying more fertile and well-watered lands they were more numerous, more prosperous and ultimately more warlike. Pressure on land meant that the age-regiment system became more formed, stricter, more regulated under stronger authority and much more effective as a military force.

This was perhaps the main achievement of Shaka who led what was an insignificant clan to pre-eminence in the first two decades of the 19th Century. Cruel, capricious and tyrannical he was, but also intelligent, shrewd, a brave warrior and skillful diplomat. By 1824, his wars and cattle raids were already forcing other clans to take the long road up the Drakensberg in the hope of escaping the wrath of the Zulu and there they came into contact with the Griqua, who with their horses and guns, were already making their presence felt. In that same year, Henry Francis Fynn and Francis Farewell arrived at the bay now known as Durban, named it Port Natal and set up a trading post. This was done with the knowledge of the Cape authorities but strictly on the understanding that there would be no protection offered and no annexation considered. The traders therefore opened up negotiations for occupation of the land with Shaka himself, which was granted, and they promptly settled down, married into the local community and by 1835, were almost indistinguishable from any other Zulu chiefs. Indeed, they accepted Shaka's overlordship and in 1826, Farwell took the men under his command and accompanied Shaka's *impi* to the battle which routed his main rivals, the Ndwandwe. In 1827, James King, another trader, and his muskets were called upon from Port Natal to help Shaka destroy the last of his external rivals. Alas, the victory was not enough to secure him from his internal enemies; Shaka seems to have been mentally unbalanced by the death of his mother – some said he murdered her in a very gross way– and he made enemies with an abandon that would have amazed even Stockenstrom. In 1828, he was assassinated by his half-brothers, Dingane and Mhlangana.

What followed was a bloodletting on a scale that was unimaginable to the Xhosa. Dingane first outmanoeuvred his fellow conspirators and had them killed and then, having invited his royal half-brothers into his *isigodlo* (a sort of harem), had them and the women involved killed too. This was sensible in stark terms; by killing off potential heirs he killed off potential rivals. It is a tactic as old as time; I remember going into a classroom in Abu Dhabi in 1995 to find a number of Qatari children in a terrified state; having just heard the news that there had been an intra-family coup in Qatar, they really were in fear for their lives. At the time, I thought it an over-reaction but then, later in the day when I saw the Intercontinental Hotel cordoned off by the French Foreign Legion because old man Al-Thani had fled there, I had to admit they might have had a point.

Dingane was not afraid of using such indiscriminate murder to further his position. Other killings aimed at consolidating his power followed; they never ended. Dingane was a firm believer in using random killings to maintain a pervading sense of fear; 'The killing of people is a proper practice,' maintained his adviser Nzobo. 'For if no killing is done there will be no fear.'[149] If this was Machiavellian (or perhaps, *Mugabian*) in essence, the scale of it was something unusual in African societies. Indeed, there is something harder, more ruthless, more extreme, more of the *Might is Right* in the Zulu state than is to be found in other South African tribes and although attempts have been made to discredit the principle witnesses of Dingane's atrocities – the memoirs of the Port Natal settlers – the Zulus themselves record through their praise songs a picture of 'shrewdness, cruelty, resilience, implacability and fathomlessness'.[150] It is tempting to regard him in the same light as that litany of African rulers who have so disgraced the continent since the end of colonial rule and come to regard him as just typical of African leadership in general. This I think is a mistake; thugs like Idi Amin and Foday Sankoh are not the same as the kleptocrats Mobuto and Dos Santos and we cannot put Dingane in the same box as Zuma. I think, however, that we may put him into the same category as Robert Mugabe; there was a cynical and perhaps sociopathic use of violence as a means to an end; rewards to the military and the leading men of the kingdom were generous; the judicial process was subverted to his own ends and execution public and horrendous – impalement, slow strangulation for women (and by slow, I mean slow enough to make her eyes come out of her head), bludgeoning. Mass, targeted violence was employed to 'send a message'; on one occasion, sixty young women were taken from the homestead of an offending chief and slaughtered. In war, too, there was a violation of the (almost, almost) worldwide taboo that women and children should be spared; Dingane's *impis* slaughtered everyone. It is probably fair to say that Dingane ruled by fear rather than eliciting the love of his people; there was a steady stream of refugees from his rule into Port Natal.

He was also a damned uncomfortable neighbour to have. Right from the beginning he sent his *impis* up into southern Mozambique and down beyond Port Natal. In 1831, he sent them into Port Natal itself, scattering the traders before realizing that without them, the guns he so desired would be unobtainable. He patched up a deal and then, like Shaka before him, called on Port Natal to supply him with commando contingents; in 1837, with their help he took

---

[149] J.Laband, *Rope of Sand* (Jeppestown, 1995) p. 55.
[150] Laband, *Rope of Sand* p. 58.

15000 head of cattle off the Swazis in the Lubombo mountains to the north. The most significant of his attacks, however, was against Mzilikazi in 1830.

Mzilikazi was a Zulu chief who had owed allegiance to Shaka but who had fled up onto the Highveldt in 1822 after a dispute over captured cattle. In 1825, he moved onto the Magaliesberg – near the modern-day Sun City – to put more distance between himself and Shaka and began to build up an independent kingdom of the *Ndebele* or *Matabele* by raiding everyone within reach in all directions. This was the beginning of the *mfecane*; the presence of Zulu raiders was remarked upon by Stockenstrom in the 1820s. Bertram Mitford, a journalist working in Zululand in the late 19th century, wrote a whole novel *The King's Assegai* (1894) about Mzilikazi's campaign of flight and conquest which, though fanciful, he seems to have got the bones of from his conversations with Zulus. In 1830, Dingane hit him hard and hard again in 1832 which, combined with the increasing resistance he was experiencing from the Griqua, persuaded Mzilikazi in 1833 to shift his people a hundred or so miles westward to new lands on the Marico and throw the resident Tswana off it. Once established in his new colony, he began raiding once again.

For a while, anyway. In 1836, noting the increasing number of Voortrekker groups moving north of the Vaal, he sent 6000 men against Andries Potgeiter's laager at Vegkop in October 1836. Advancing in the famous 'Horns of the Buffalo' formation, his warriors broke in the face of a mere forty Boer muskets; they lost five hundred men to Potgeiter's two. This was an ignominious defeat and was promptly followed up in January 1837 by a Commando of 107 Boers and 40 Griqua and Tswana directed at Mzilikazi's 'capital' at Mosega. The Ndebele were outclassed and outgunned and, when attacked once more by Dingane in June 1837, fled northwards across the Limpopo into modern day Zimbabwe – which they promptly colonized at the expense of the Shona people and began a fifty-year reign of terror there.

Here then is the real fact of the 'empty lands' across the Orange River that form such a major part of the Afrikaaner Nationalist myth; devastated by the *mfecane* they were; but empty? They were not – everywhere were wandering bands of displaced people, some heading for the mountains, some starving, some resorting to cannibalism, some being preyed upon and preying upon others in their turn and all in the process of being *conquered and colonised* by Mzilikazi. The real disaster of the mid-1830s - and this was the greatest disaster to hit South Africa in all its recorded History - was not occasioned by the Boers but by the Zulus.

*

Enter the Voortrekkers. When Piet Retief, a man whose portrait bears more than a passing resemblance to Ian McShane in *Deadwood*, published his manifesto in the Grahamstown Journal in April 1837, it was less the act of a man making a declaration of independence (though that is what it was) than a respected Commandant imitating the actions of Martin Luther nailing his *Ninety-Five Theses* to the door of All Saints Church in Wittemburg three hundred and twenty years before. 'We despair of saving the colony,' he raged. 'We complain of severe losses [due to Abolition] …. of the continual plunder which we have ever endured from the Kaffirs…. of the unjustifiable odium which has been cast on us [by the missionaries] …. We quit this colony under the full assurance that the English government has no more to require of us…'

Estimates as to how many Afrikaaners left on what became known as the Great Trek vary mainly because there was no single Great Trek. Instead, various groups of trekkers set off through the Karoo generally converging on Colesberg crossing over the Orange River before following a route eastward along the Drakensberg. Probably, there were no more than 6000 to begin with, although probably the same number followed in later years once they had been seen to be successful. Many of their black and Khoisan servants went with them, some because they were old retainers, others because they had no other means of support and still others, we must presume, because they felt themselves to be members of a clan which, though different from ones they had been in before, were still recognizable as clans in the African tradition. As to routes, the Voortrekkers followed their noses and the grazing as much as anything else. Traders, hunters and earlier treks had indicated that the land eastwards was better, perhaps emptier this way; the west had already been colonized by the Oorlams, the Griqua and the Tswana; going north meant uncertainties with water and Mzilikazi. And it was a beautiful land. Take the R26 from Aliwal North and you run through a gentle, gentle landscape, well-watered, with the mountains rising up on your right until you come to the magnificent sandstone sentinels and rich green valleys of the Golden Gate. There are wild horses there today but in the 1830s these valleys were thick with an endless supply of game.

For the Voortrekkers, it seemed to be a blessing of Biblical proportions. The Afrikaaners were a deeply religious people; many still are – my old Pal, Thielman, carries verses from the Bible in his pocket when he goes about his daily business and never passes up an opportunity to attempt my conversion, once he's had a beer or two. Their religion was still based on Calvin and the liberalism of the Enlightenment had passed them by. Today, we would call them Fundamentalists, in that they took the Bible quite literally and if this meant some confusion (as indeed it must, the text being so contradictory) well, this was all part of God's mystery and something to argue about around the camp fire. Not that most Boers were concerned with doctrinal disputes; like most people, Sundays, weddings, funerals and Christenings were just part of the round. The problem was that a dominant minority of this minority of Afrikaaners – and the Voortrekkers *were* a minority, perhaps 10% of the Cape Dutch – held very firmly to that part of the Bible that declared black people to be the Children of Ham, condemned to be the hewers of wood and the drawers of water for the Afrikaaner Elect. That the English law should hold all men equal rankled at a visceral as well as religious level; so much so that many left good property and substantial land holdings behind them. It is here, not in the Cape colony, that the beginnings of Apartheid are to be looked for.

The Treks were led by men chosen for their experience and ability but leading the individualistic Boers was like herding cats. Men used to making their own decisions, men who had left everything behind to get away from the very notion of government, were unlikely to make model citizens respectful of the collective will and they argued over who would be Veldkornet, who would be Heemraaden, who would be the Minister – especially over who would be the Minister – and in which direction they should go. Andries Potgeiter, a famous Commando leader, convinced now that Mzilikazi was a paper tiger, favoured Delagoa Bay, for it was there that the outlet to the sea lay and without that outlet they would want for coffee, sugar, tea and most importantly, guns and ammunition. Piet Retief agreed on the necessity for a port but favoured Natal and in this he was supported by Gert Maritz, a wagon-maker and solid administrator from Graaff-Reinet, and Piet Uys, a farmer from Uitenhage who had trekked through the Eastern Cape in 1834 as far as Port Natal. Towards the end of 1837, the Port Natal option was generally accepted and the Boers began to meander in that direction but Potgeiter went his own way, hammering Mzilikazi at the very moment when Piet Retief had reached the Olivershoek Pass at the top of the Drakensberg that led down to Zululand.

Down at the bottom of the pass, Dingane watched and wondered how he was to deal with the warriors that had so easily defeated Mzilikazi. When Piet Retief arrived at his Great Place uMgungundlovu in November 1837, his first instinct was to impress upon the Boers the extent of his power and his wealth through displays of his warriors and his cattle and then to tempt the Boers with vague promises of land in the area south of Port Natal. Next, he offered a deal; Sekonyela, chief of a Tlokwa clan in the Caledon valley area, a man who had quickly adopted the horse and gun tactics of the Griqua and the Boers, was alleged to have stolen some of Dingane's cattle; if Retief got them back then some land would be given up in return. Retief accepted the deal, brought his people down the passes into laager and then took a commando back up the Drakensberg to recover the cattle. By January 1838, he was back with the booty and in February 1838, at the head of a hundred-strong commando (a third were non-white) presented himself at uMgungundlovu. Dingane duly obliged and put his mark to a paper that ceded Port Natal and the areas south and west of the River Tugela to the Boers (today, roughly KwaDukuza to Ladysmith) but the reality was that Dingane intended to fall back on his standard method of dealing with potential rivals. Just as he had killed his half-brothers, so he invited the Boers to a party (no girls this time, just beer, leave your weapons outside) and on 6th February 1838 killed them all. Later that day, he dispatched his warriors to kill the rest of the Voortrekkers, along with their families.

You can drive the routes that the Voortrekkers and their families took down the pass. Olivershoek is on the R74, and it is a spectacular run past the inland sea formed by the Sterkfontein dam (there's always a chap there selling really smart little clay models), through little Switzerland to Bergville; I did it once when the road was closed for repairs and grounded on the gravel several times. My bad – it was a hire car. Either that or you can take Van Reenen's pass which is the route that the N3 takes and is equally spectacular; the grass is so bright, so green that it almost blinds you, especially if you have come up from the scrubby areas around Spion Kop or you've got used to the red and ochre tints of the Zululand earth. And then, when you study the map, you start to see the scars; History really is written in the landscape for here is *Weenen* – Weeping County – and just by it, the *Moord*, the Murder River, *Veglaer*, the Lower Battle, *Bloukrans* and *Van Rensburg Koppie* are not so obvious but the biggest one of all is unmistakeable; *Blood River*.

During the night of 16th February 1838, the Zulus swept through the scattered laagers and outspans of the Voortrekkers in a merciless rampage of blood, theft and fire. Those wiser and more cautious Boers who had established proper laagers fared relatively well for the brave Zulu warriors preferred easier targets than armed men, grim, determined and confident in their weapons. In what was to become the Weenen district, the wagons were scattered; 40 men, 56 women, 185 *children* as well as 250 mixed race and black servants were killed and many more were wounded that night. 'Wagons were literally awash with blood, the grass matted with gore, household possessions scattered in all directions, and vultures and crows were gathering, greedy for the feast.'[151] At Bloukrans, Mevrou Steenkamp saw 'on all sides…tears flowing and heard people weeping by plundered wagons painted with blood, tents and beds were ripped to shreds; pregnant women and little children had to walk for hours together bearing the signs of their hasty flight.'[152] There is sometimes a sort of adulation for the Zulu warrior in South African History and there is no doubting that he could at times show great bravery; but not on this night. And what he got meted out in revenge a few months later, he had coming.

As soon as it was light, the Voortrekkers formed up in their improvised commandos, went out to fight the Zulus now retreating towards the Tugela and though they inflicted perhaps 500 casualties on them, they could not defeat such numbers with what they presently possessed. All that could be done was to gather up the survivors, go into laager and hope for help. It was the rainy season and nothing much could be done until it was over; 640 men, 3200 women and children and 1260 black and mixed-race servants put up the canvas and prepared to see what God held out for them.

Something that has always struck me about the Europeans and their black and mixed-race allies who went out to fight the Zulus in these years is their sheer disregard for the odds stacked against them. Dingane could field probably 20,000 warriors; when John Cane, a settler at Port Natal, decided to launch an attack in March to take some pressure off the Boers, he went out with 2100 men – and came back with 6000 cattle. In April, Piet Uys and Andries Potgeiter with 347 men went up against several thousand Zulus, were bested and forced to retreat leaving Piet and his fourteen-year-old son, Dirk, to be killed, but no-one seemed to question the wisdom of sending so few out against so many; that expedition became known derisively as the *Vlugkommando* or 'the Commando that ran away'. Military theory holds that the basic ratio needed for an attack to be successful against a comparable defender is 3:1. Certainly the greater mobility that the Boers possessed gave them an advantage in open country, for they could quickly ride into range, form a firing line, start shooting and then retire just as quickly when threatened. It sounds simple enough, but the discipline needed for this is remarkable as is the horsemanship required to prevent the mounts becoming blown. This isn't the whole story either though; even when the Boers were attacked in broken country, they almost always managed to fight their way out. Nor would the Zulus attack anyone standing behind a barricade; at Veglaer in August, 10,000 experienced warriors spent three days trying to overrun the inhabitants of a laager that they

---

[151] Laband, *Rope of Sand* p.91.
[152] Quoted in G. Mills and D. Williams, *Seven Battles that shaped South Africa*, (Cape Town, 2006) p. 25.

outnumbered by more than 20:1. Accepting that the Boers were not supermen, you can't help wondering if there was more than a little reluctance among the Zulu warriors to face actual fighting men; in April they had beaten and killed John Cane's 446 men, but only after 400 badly trained black levies had broken and run, and had then shown their metal by sacking Port Natal for nine long and very thorough days.

In November 1838, Andries Pretorius arrived with reinforcements; a whole sixty men. Yet the Voortrekkers considered this plenty and in December decided it was time to advance. Just short of 500 men, including 120 black men from Port Natal, intending to take on 16000 Zulus advanced through present day Winterton, Ladysmith and Dundee and then laagered up on a stretch of veldt against a puddle of a river about 35km eastwards. You can go there today. It's a drive down a dirt track so you have to check with the Hotel to see if it's OK for a saloon car because when the rains come down, the dirt roads in this part of the world turn to porridge a foot deep and then it's second gear, slide, hope and pray but the trip is worth it in any weather for the monument to the Battle of Blood River is awesome.

And I mean *awesome*. There is a laager of bronze wagons, faithfully reproduced and laid out in a rough circle on the site of the actual laager. They look out across a perfectly level plain of dun grass eastwards towards a line of hills across the river and northwest towards a conical hill but the main feature is the donga that encloses the laager in its arms from east through the south and round to the west. When the river is full, the northern approaches to the laager are the most vulnerable but the truth is that it's a lonely spot, the ground ideal for moving large masses of infantry beyond effective musket shot and a betting man would say that the odds were heavily stacked in favour of the Zulus. This was absolutely backs-to-the-wall stuff; the Voortrekkers knew there would be no mercy shown if the Zulus got inside that laager, but their motivation was strong. They wanted revenge for all those dead children, for the betrayal of Piet Retief and his hundred men and they had reached down into their deep religious feeling to ask for Divine help. Pretorius and Sarel Cilliers came up with the idea of The Vow, a Biblical Covenant with God, which tapped into their Calvinistic beliefs that they were special, God's Chosen, the Elect. It was a powerful prayer that was repeated at services morning and evening.

> Here we stand
>
> Before the Holy God of heaven and earth
>
> To make him a vow that
>
> If he will protect us
>
> And deliver our enemies into our hands,
>
> We will observe the day and date each year,
>
> As a day of thanks, like a Sabbath.
>
> And that we will erect a church in his honour

> Wherever he may choose
>
> And that we will also tell our children
>
> To join with us in commemorating this day,
>
> Also for coming generations,
>
> For His name will be glorified
>
> By giving Him
>
> All the honour and glory of victory.

Just outside the Visitor's Centre there is a granite monument erected in 1947 – the bronze wagons were completed in 1974 – on which are a couple of friezes depicting the Voortrekkers before and during the battle. The Boers at prayer are not ramped up wild-eyed fanatics but quiet men, serious, devout in that 'religion should be kept for Sundays' way. The Boers during the battle are serious in a different way. What is most striking is their faces; there is no wild joy of battle or the triumph of victory, just a terrible, merciless implacability; only the horses look afraid; the faces of the Zulus trampled down beneath their hooves, I could not read.

The Zulus approached the laager during the evening of 15th December but declined to attack as there was a thick fog coming up from the river which they hoped would dampen the Boer powder. Pretorius lit fires to keep the fog off and held a prayer meeting; the hymns were met with the martial chants of the Zulus, which I can vouch for as being pretty impressive; the Zulus described the Boer hymns as the sound of weeping. In the morning, one of those fine, bright, clear Natal mornings where the sky is azure blue, high, wide and brushed with cloud into eyelashes, the fog lifted to reveal several Zulu regiments squatting within forty yards of the north and west faces of the laager. The *iciLongo* – think vuvuzela – was blown and the regiments banged their spears on their shields, shouted their war cries and charged.

It was to no avail. The most important thing a commander can do in a battle is to control the fire of his troops and Pretorius was brilliant that day. A black powder musket discharges a cloud of thick, dense, yellow-white smoke about the size of a beach ball which quickly builds up into – literally – the fog of war. The rate of fire of a musket is only two shots per minute and its effective range fifty yards; just enough to hit a barn door. This means that fire must be concentrated to produce a short and devastating blast which will topple a charge over on itself, discourage those behind from following and, crucially, give those at the rear and sides an excuse to retreat; studies from the Napoleonic wars show that it was only necessary for the British line to shoot away the head of the French column to send it back, largely because those packed in the middle started a panic which spread to those at the sides and rear who actually had some chance of escape. We might imagine that this was the case with the Zulu charges, human nature being common to all. To achieve this panic, Pretorius had his men load more than one musket and then issued them with *loopers*, a sort of buck shot which burst at forty yards which impacted with terrible effect on a target as dense packed as the Zulus. And they were densely packed because restricted to an area away from the donga and the river, their charges were forced into an ever-narrower area. In short, Pretorius had engineered a situation which would make that barn door impossible to miss even for a blind man.

The Zulus tried to attack across the dry donga; Sarel Cilliers led some men down and killed *all* of them. Flip Coetzer, a fluent Zulu speaker, stood on a wagon and tried to taunt them into attacking again: 'This is no more a case of Bloukrans. Are you afraid to start the attack?' For an increasing number, but by no means all at this stage, the answer was *yes*. A number of further charges were attempted but the moral balance had shifted; Pretorius sensed this and sent out a mounted commando of 100 men. The Zulus began to waver and when those Commandos got in behind them and began to hunt up and down the river, it was all over. The Zulus broke and fled in all directions. By the end of the day, 3000 Zulus lay dead; three Voortrekkers had suffered minor wounds. It looked like God had taken the deal.

Blood River was recognized as a turning point long before the Afrikaaner Nationalists began to turn it into a central plank of their justification of Apartheid. Remarkably, in 1866 a meeting was held between Afrikaaner veterans and Zulu veterans whom were led by none other than King Cetshwayo himself and it was then that the original memorial was built, a simple cairn of stones. After Apartheid was swept away, the 16th December ceased to be the Day of the Vow, or more popularly 'Dingane's Day', and became the Day of Reconciliation in the hope that reconciliation would indeed follow. During the 1990s, another memorial was built in a dedicated visitors' centre and you can go and visit the fine mural painted there; but the centre is tired already and the road was shocking when I went there in 2013. Perhaps the most interesting thing about the painting is the party of modern day people superimposed on the battle scene; they are heading towards a bridge that connects the Boer memorial to the Zulu centre. The gate on that bridge has been locked since 1995 and when I tried to find someone with a key, I could get no answer.

*

A few days later, the victorious commando descended on Dingane's abandoned Great place at uMgungundlovu and there they found among the bones of their slaughtered compatriots, Piet Retief's hunting bag. Opening it up, they found the piece of paper that Dingane had put his mark to ceding the lands of Natal over to them. Now to say that this fortunate find has opened up some controversy over the years would be to understate things a little. The paper on which Retief's treaty was written was in a remarkable state of preservation considering it had been left outside for eight months but Andries Pretorius and four others swore under oath that what they found was authentic and it is fair to say that these were men who took oaths seriously. The original was lost during the Anglo-Boer War 1899-1902, but three tracings were made of it in 1891 and lithographed and these confirmed the outlines of the agreement. What made the paper problematical was that although Dingane had indeed made his mark, the other 'signatories' were only attendants and not the great councilors of the realm who might expect to be consulted. My own instinct, and it is only that, is that Dingane knew what he was doing when he signed off on the deal but had no intention of keeping to it because once Piet Retief came back with his missing cattle, he intended to kill him. It is another thing that we can't really know. Anyway, it is academic because the Voortrekkers never got their land.

For the Boers, this piece of paper was not just proof that the land belonged legally to them but just as powerfully pointed out that the land did not belong to the *English*. This is important because an important dynamic in South African History is the rivalry between Briton and Boer, a dynamic that even during the Apartheid years was arguably as important as the rivalry between black and white people. Examples of this abound and it doesn't take long to wind an Afrikaaner up into paroxysms of rage about the *bladdy Rooineks*. 'Why did the sun never set on the British Empire?' asked one fearsome group of traditionally-whiskered and suspicious academics from the University of Pretoria Theology Department. I stifled a yawn: I hadn't heard the joke for at least, oh, two days. 'Because God would never trust you *Bladdy Engelse* in the dark!' Chortle, chortle and pass the Smirnoff Ice (yes, really; that's what they were drinking). The artist, Jason Askew, who grew up in South Africa tells this story about going to visit Rorke's Drift as a boy:

> My father asked directions at a petrol station in a local one-horse *dorp* (being an Anglo-Zulu battlefield, Rorke's drift was barely even on the map back then and Isandhlwana may as well have been on the moon). The obese *verkramte tannie* (old lady) there replied with that singular Afrikaaner contempt, disdain and hostility towards anything remotely English: 'Ag! I don't know hey – but there is a very good road to Blood River.' My father answered with measured gravity and politeness: 'Thank you, that's good to know – but we want to visit the important places first…'[153]

A peace with Dingane was brokered by the British in March 1839 where a detachment of troops had arrived to secure Port Natal. The Boers got their land south of the Tugela and the return of some of the horses and cattle that they had lost and immediately began to lay out farms of a size they considered decent. Pietermaritzburg, named for Piet Retief and Gerrit Maritz, was laid out and the Church of the Vow was begun. Dingane turned northwards to attack the Swazi in the hope of compensating for his losses in the south. It seemed to the Boers that they had indeed fled Egypt, crossed the desert, defeated the Canaanites and come down into the Promised Land.

They probably did not realise it, but the Boers had now entered into the calculations of the Zulu people in an unexpected way. There were several factions who opposed Dingane, not just for his failures against the Boers and for his murderous proclivities but also for his decision to turn north against the Swazis. Those in the south of the kingdom saw no reason to want to move to the malarial areas north of the Pongola River, especially when there was the prospect of trade through Port Natal and peace with the Boers. In particular, Mpande, Dingane's only surviving half-brother who, like Queen Elizabeth I, had spent all his life

[153] Posted on Facebook.

trying not to be put to death for who he was and what he represented, saw his chance. When Dingane was defeated by the Swazi in June-July 1839, and demanded reinforcements, Mpande led his people south over the Tugela in the hope of allying with the Boers to overthrow the king. In October, the deal was done; in return the Boers would get their outlet to the sea in the bay of St. Lucia.

The British withdrawal from Port Natal at Christmas 1839 and the running up the flagpole of the colours of the Republic of Natal removed the last obstacle to the overthrow of the hated Dingane and in the New Year, the war began. Mpande defeated Dingane on 27th January at the Battle of the Maqongo hills (without Boer help) and the old king fled towards Swaziland where he was killed by them. In February 1840, Pretorius declared, *by the power of the Volksraad*, Mpande to be the King of the Zulus and that all land south of the Black Mfolozi River was now to be incorporated into the Republic of Natalia. Mpande might have won his crown without Boer help but if he wanted to keep it on his head, he could do nothing but kowtow to them. Fortunately, for him, this was not something he had to do for long because within three years the Republic of Natalia had been extinguished and the colony annexed to the British Empire.

That there was a contradiction here huge enough to cause the head of even the mildest mannered Boer to explode was obvious: Queen Adelaide province had been given up and yet Natal was to be annexed? *Why? And by what right?* As far as the Voortrekkers were concerned, Natal had been ceded legally (and however suspect the paper found in Retief's bag might be, there was no doubt that some sort of deal had been done with Dingane) and that concession had been asserted by right of conquest and then endorsed by Mpande. If the British wanted more land, why did they not just keep Queen Adelaide, which they too had earned by right of conquest? When the Republic of Natal had been proclaimed, the British had removed their troops and now they were back. *Why?*

These were fair questions and the answer lay in the fact that however bad the sand bar at Port Natal (now renamed Durban) was, it remained a port and when ships called there, the possibility arose that they might sell arms and ammunition to the nascent Republic. This could not be allowed because this was the one firm grip that the British had on the Boer collar. On the friezes of the Voortrekker Monument in Pretoria, Louis Trichardt is shown reaching Lourenco Marques after an epic trek and the things he is buying from the Portuguese are the muskets and powder that guarantee independence; Louis Trichardt had actually been a gun-runner supplying the Xhosa before the 1834-5 war and did a sideline in stirring them up to attack the British.

The second reason was that in March 1842 a Dutch trader from the Netherlands turned up in Pietermaritzburg talking about a treaty between the two countries – something that he did not have the authority to do – and was welcomed with open arms. This was simply unacceptable; the Cape was on the route to India and that is what the occupation was about. No power, European or American would be allowed any influence whatsoever. Two years earlier, Lord John Russell had been approached by the French as to how much of Australia Britain actually laid claim to and had responded, off the top of his head, with: 'All of it.' That went for the coastlines and ports of southern Africa too and no lawyers' quibbles, appeals to justice, sentiment or whatever would change that.

These were not answers that the Voortrekkers cared for however. Some of the cooler heads realized that their *Volksraad* was so chaotic that the colony could never survive and welcomed the arrival of the British. Most thought they had been robbed. Where before they had been simply bitter at the British, now they were incensed.

*

There is something else that strikes me about the tale of the Great Trek, the murder of Piet Retief, the Bloukrans Massacre and the Battle of the Blood River. Before the Trek, it is possible to see the Trekboers as defensive creatures, fighting for survival on frontiers that demanded toughness; parochial, pragmatic certainly but also mindful of authority, respectful of the law and decent citizens not a great deal different from citizens anywhere else in the world at that time. After the trek and the failure of the Republic of Natal, something seems to have changed. There is a new, much harsher quality prevalent; a stripping away of empathy and compassion and its replacement by a Darwinian ethos. The Afrikaaners that head back up onto the Highveldt become a nation on permanent campaign, their white covered wagons like battleships on the sea of grass. Their hands are always on their guns, quick on the draw and ready to pre-empt trouble in the simplest way: *do unto them before they do unto you; get your revenge in first; it might be a sledgehammer but it's guaranteed to crack the nut; nip trouble in the bud.* And I wonder if the people who saw the wagons full of blood in Weenen and then the Union Jack flying at Port Natal decided that if all their sorrows, labours and struggles were not to be in vain, then they would have to become as cruel as Dingane and as relentless in the pursuit of their self-interest as the British. I think we can point to one of them that did, for fourteen-year-old Paul Kruger was in the laager at Blood River on 16th December 1838.

*

### The March of Folly. Part II

North of the Orange River, the world had been in a state of chaos since the 1830s. The Highveldt, marked by the line of the Drakensberg to the south, the line of the escarpment on the east to the Limpopo and the Kalahari Desert on the west was now a wasteland of burnt crops, ruined villages, wandering bandits and bewildered refugees. In an area roughly 750 miles long and 400 miles broad, there was no law and no security beyond the reach of an assegai or the range of a gun. Today those journeys would take the best part of 13 hours and 7 hours by car respectively, on black top, no stopping; that's Land's End to John O'Groats and London to Leeds and back. Dominating the western part (roughly where modern day Kimberley lies) were the Griquas, their horses and guns enabling them to protect their flocks and enslave their enemies; north of them were the Tswana, holding their own and watching warily. In the south the Basuto were gathering up the lost, the bewildered, the defeated and the desperate and forming up in the high valleys and moorlands of modern day Lesotho. Close by were Sekonyela's Tlokwa. Mzilikazi was fleeing northwards, the Zulu were defeated and the Swazi, and north of them, the Pedi, were holed up in their mountain retreats. Into this came the Voortrekkers to give an extra stir to the devil's brew in this terrible melting pot.

What were the British to do? The thing they most desired was a frontier that was fixed, settled and peaceful so that they could get on with the real business of victualling ships at the Cape. They had attempted to fix the eastern border on the Fish River but the endless stock theft had driven them forward onto the Keiskamma in the hope that this would be a buffer zone. When this had not worked and war had once more broken out, Governor D'Urban had tried it again, this time by driving the Xhosa back to the Kei and annexing the buffer zone as Queen Adelaide province, only to have the annexation overturned in London. What next?

Up on the northern frontier, the stabilization of the frontier had been achieved (sort of) by recognizing Andries Waterboer as an independent Griqua chief and sending up a missionary to act as the government's agent there. The deal was that as long as the Griquas kept the peace, returned British subjects to the colony and co-operated in the suppression of stock theft, they could expect to be left alone. D'Urban had hoped to extend this situation to the eastern frontier, but the Xhosa invaded before he could get up to the frontier and negotiate with Maqoma and Hintsa. In 1835, the Cape Punishment Act was also passed in an attempt to stop treks leaving the colony; wherever you went, and whatever you did, whether under the jurisdiction of an African chief or not, if you were a British subject south of Latitude 25S (roughly from Lourenco Marques, through modern day Johannesburg to the Atlantic), the law applied to you. The last thing the British wanted was their subjects disappearing off into the lawless interior where they might come to harm and need rescuing, or stir up trouble over stock theft and precipitate more war; in 1830, Stockenstrom had been sent up to the Orange River to bring back a party of Trekboers with their eyes set on the wide blue yonder but his success was exceptional. There was simply no way of preventing people heading over the border northwards in normal times; when Queen Adelaide province was retroceded, the disgust with the government was so great that it could not have stopped the Great Trek if it had wanted to.

The decision to abandon Queen Adelaide province was met with such outrage in the colony because Lord Glenelg, the Colonial Secretary (1835-39) was thought to have been unduly under the influence of the London Missionary Society in the form of the irritating Dr John Philip. It was him that they blamed for the document, which a later commentator described as 'inspired in every line by crass ignorance, pharisaical self-righteousness and bitter prejudice'[154] that pulled the rug from under the feet of D'Urban and added insult to injury by blaming the colonists for the outbreak of the war in the first place. Certainly, Glenelg was attracted to humanitarian causes, was a friend of Fowell Buxton and he had sat on the 1835 Aborigines committee to which Philip had provided such alarming testimony, but this was not the whole story. Just as the colonists despised Philip, there was much repugnance in Britain towards the missionaries. Their 'arrogant self-righteousness' and claim to a 'monopoly of religious zeal'[155] were as deeply offensive to ordinary churchgoers in England

---

[154] Leo Amery, *The Times History of the War in South Africa 1899-1900* (London 1900) p.32.

as they were in the Cape; it was often remarked upon that they were willing to walk past the London poor that they came across daily, but their numbers and organisation allowed them an influence that made governments and governors take notice of them (in the same way that modern day Aid workers prefer the glamour of 4x4s and 5 Star Hotels in Africa to a slum in Wigan). The May meetings at Exeter Hall on the Strand were always full (capacity 5,000) and the campaign against slavery provided a unifying, crusading force to their activities.

But it was only an influence; Britain was a parliamentary democracy but that did not mean that Britain was ruled by anything as nebulous as 'the people'. The brains at the Colonial Office in these years belonged to Sir James Stephens, a capable workaholic control freak whose accomplishments included drafting the 1833 Abolition of Slavery over a weekend when his boss, Lord Stanley, had thrown the towel in, it being too difficult for the poor chap. Stephens was no policy maker, but his influence was as great as anything the Exeter Hall crowd could exert, firstly, because he did the paperwork and administration is always nine tenths of the policy and, secondly, because the advice he gave to ministers was informed by great knowledge; he read *all* the dispatches that arrived in the office personally. Like many others, he was a devout evangelical but this never overrode his analysis of a particular situation; though he opposed the expansion of empire in South Africa, he was quite willing to see it happen in Australia.[156] Within the Colonial Office, therefore, the view was that Queen Adelaide province served no purpose; it would be expensive to administer, the Xhosa were impossible to convert and it would probably result in more wars that would do nothing to improve the essential security of the Cape.

So, what to do with these turbulent borders? It was Stockenstrom who provided the answer. The chiefs' power and influence would be strengthened; they would be treated as sovereign powers; they would be provided with government agents to act as ambassadors; the Spoor Law and Commandos would be abandoned but all reasonable force, including lethal force, would be allowed in the defence of property, flocks and herds from theft; from now on all claims of theft had to made on oath before a local official and any expeditions would be carried out by troops assisted by and with the full agreement of the Xhosa chiefs, but any group of armed Xhosa entering the Colony without permission would be fair game. It was a good, reasonable, practical and pragmatic solution that might have worked before the Xhosa invasion of 1834-5, but was doomed to fail on three counts.

Firstly, Glenelg's Queen Adelaide dispatch had destroyed the faith of both Boer and British colonists on the frontier that they might get a fair hearing for their grievances because they firmly believed that the government was in the pocket of a corrupt bunch of babbling, dishonest religious maniacs who thought that it was as simple a matter to apprehend a cattle thief on the Fish River as it was to nab a Lincolnshire poacher; this was Philip's real achievement. Secondly, the corollary of this was that because Stockenstrom had given evidence before the 1835 Aborigines Committee, he was tarred with the same brush; the Boers would no longer listen to him and his influence with them was gone. Neither would

---

[155] Galbraith, *Reluctant Empire* p.72.
[156] Dictionary of National Biography

the British settlers countenance him; an attempt was made to bring him down with a trumped-up murder charge going back twenty years to when he was on Commando and though he survived this, he foolishly attempted to kill off the rumours with a suit for libel before the enquiry, which he lost. As he complained;

> The triumph of the conspirators and of Stockenstrom's enemies now knew no bounds; the *Graham's Town Journal* especially was virulent….it denounced him as a murderer, a liar, a traducer, a slanderer, a mock philanthropist, until the English language was pretty well exhausted of bitter and opprobrious terms with which to vilify him, and they would have danced with fiendish joy round the gallows if they could at once have hung him for murder.[157]

One of the unforeseen results of this unholy row was that our old friend Donald Moodie[158] was employed to produce *The Record*, he being generally accepted as honest, impartial and most importantly, not in the hands of Exeter Hall after winning his case against Philip's man, Fairbairn, in another libel trial in 1837. Such was the state of opinion in the Colony, however, that Stockenstrom could not be kept in a position where neither his officials nor the population at large believed him to be impartial. In 1839, the incoming ministry in London decided that he must be relieved and handed him a Baronetcy wrapped up in the sack. Stockenstrom was, as ever, outraged even though he had already tendered his resignation, and claimed he had been the victim of '*dismissal for unpopularity*';[159] which of course, was true.

Thirdly, and most importantly, Stockenstrom was gambling on the ability of the Xhosa chiefs to prevent their people from lifting cattle and he had more chance of being struck by lightning in a condom factory than he had of achieving this.

\*

The peace that followed the Queen Adelaide war was an uneasy one. The British settlers and that majority of the Dutch who remained in the colony were still faced with armed bands of Xhosa acting in defiance of their own chiefs to lift cattle and were smarting from what they regarded as a humiliating peace imposed on them by a distant government that had snatched defeat from the jaws of victory. Many of them had outstanding claims against the government for cattle, horses and oxen that had been impressed by the military for the war. Many more of them faced the prospect of rebuilding razed homes and destroyed property and the simmering hatred and resentment that resulted should not be underestimated. I caught a glimpse of this among the British ex-pats who had lost everything during the Iraqi invasion of Kuwait in 1990; some could not go back; some that did reported that their homes had been sacked and abused in the most wanton of ways; wedding photos ripped up (why?), turds dumped in the middle of the living room carpet (why?); one person bought an expensive

---

[157] Stockenstrom Vol II p. 147.

[158] Donald Moodie: South Africa's Pioneer Oral Historian. V. C. Malherbe *History in Africa* Vol. 25 (1998), pp. 171-197.

[159] Stockenstrom Vol II, p. 207.

bottle and laid it down for when Saddam Hussein died; she waited a long time, but did eventually have the satisfaction of drinking it. They also reacted with disgust when the Embassy officials and Foreign Office wonks handed each other medals and awards for their sterling service. For those who survived the 1834-5 Xhosa war, there were no reparations either.

There was something else too. It is often said that travel broadens the mind but it is also true that living alongside another culture can also narrow it. People who visit another culture on their holidays will delight in the different foods, dress and customs of the host country and will come away with beaming tales of how wonderful those nice people are and how rubbish their own culture is by comparison. The reality can often be very different; generally speaking there are good, bad and indifferent people in every culture and the occasional tourist is unlikely to come across anyone more irritating than a rip-off merchant with an irritating sales pitch. If you actually live in that culture for any length of time then the downsides can come crowding in at a level of culture shock that can lead to revulsion. What seems normal and reasonable in one culture is often anathema to another and the reaction is to retreat from contact, very often, and to enter into what is often known as the 'Expat bubble' where it is possible to live a life with only minimal contact with the host culture. You can see this with the Westerners in Dubai and the Pakistani-British in the towns of northern England. In historical terms, the cantonments of the British in India are a good example and in South Africa, we would definitely be looking at Grahamstown and the District of Albany.

Philip, Read and the other missionaries had fed the Grahamstown settlers' growing alienation by their lurid and one-sided accounts of mistreatment of Africans until the missionaries were regarded as purveyors of 'that spurious philanthropy which, like the canker worm, has eaten to the very core of this settlement'.[160] The resentment they caused fed a sense that in their dealings with Africans the settlers might as well be hung for a sheep as for a lamb, so little chance would they get at a fair hearing or any sort of justice. Many of them threw up their farms and headed back towards the security of the Western Cape – a trek that went largely unnoticed. Those who remained had been so beaten with the stick of moral righteousness that they retreated into a sort of mental laager from out of which the *Grahamstown Journal* fired off volleys in their defence.

> We had the melancholy task of witnessing a few days ago a party of British settlers of 1820, with their wives and little ones, on their journey from their late flourishing settlement in search of a more peaceful and secure abode. We understand that it is not their intention to quit the colony, but to remove into the western province, and we doubt not, wherever they go, but that neighbourhood will be benefited by the same active industry which has always been displayed by them since their first arrival in the colony 17 years ago. We are informed that many others are preparing to follow them, so sensible are they of the jeopardy in which they are placed by the absurd measures which have been lately adopted towards the Kafir tribes. It may be very well for people at a distance to speculate on this subject, but to men who find the same Kafirs

---

[160] *Grahamstown Journal* 27th April, 1837.

who have recently spread death and ruin through the land, brought to their very doors, who see bands of these barbarians wandering armed through the country and hovering about their dwellings, and whose families are obliged, when they make the demand, to supply them with food and submit to their menaces, - it is the height of folly to talk of security, and to require them to wait patiently the result of the experiment. No man in his senses will live in such a state of anxiety; and hence it is certain that this part of the frontier will again shortly be abandoned.[161]

The fact that new missionaries, less partisan and more realistic than Philip and Read, and certainly more sympathetic to the colonists began to appear in South Africa also contributed to a hardening up of settler attitudes. Within the London Missionary Society, there had always been a great deal of scepticism regarding Philip and Read and with the arrival of Henry Calderwood at Cape Town in 1838 that change in attitude became firmer. For a start, he was not prepared to turn a blind eye to those Xhosa practices that he found abhorrent and within a very short time of establishing his mission at Chief Maqoma's village at the foot of the Amatola Mountains, he was at loggerheads with him. One of Maqoma's wives had involved herself in an adulterous relationship and given birth to a child. Maqoma ordered her to *bury the child alive* and sent an armed guard to ensure she did it. Calderwood objected but Maqoma insisted and infanticide was committed – not for the last time, either; a few years later, he killed another child in a drunken rage.[162] Calderwood also gave sanctuary to one of Maqoma's sisters and one of his concubines, taking them away to Cape Town. Maqoma, now deposed as regent by his nephew Sandile, was drinking heavily too. Within a very short time, Calderwood began to realise that beyond a few waifs and strays the Xhosa were highly unlikely to be converted; he also realized that Philip and Read had been less than candid about the extent to which they had turned a blind eye to these practices: *infanticide*! They also saw the reality of Glenelg's system for dealing with cattle theft at first hand:

> The chief may pretend to punish theft when compelled to do so by British power and, in some solitary cases he may even be sincere; but they who know the real state of things know this, that the great guilt of stealing among the Caffres generally is simply that of being found out.[163]

The fact was that those missionaries who were active in Xhosa territory saw at first hand the smellings-out, the terrible tortures that followed, the destitution of the families of the accused[164] and the arbitrary power over life and death that the chiefs so abused. Not just the missionaries either; in September 1844, one lucky soldier was invited into the bush by a Xhosa girl for a pleasant afternoon's entertainment only to be threatened with murder by 500 of her countrymen after some weaselly little Peeping Tom reported her. Later that night, the girl was slowly burned to death in a bonfire constructed for the purpose while several

---

[161] *Grahamstown Journal* 2 March, 1837
[162] Ward p. 149.
[163] Calderwood, Henry. *Caffres and Caffre Mission: with preliminary chapters on the Cape Colony as a field for emigration, and basis of missionary operation.* London : J. Nisbet, 1858 p.61

[164] Calderwood, Henry. *Caffres and Caffre Missions :with preliminary chapters on the Cape Colony as a field for emigration, and basis of missionary operation.* London : J. Nisbet, 1858 p.43

thousand more of her countrymen cheered the proceedings on. Such things led an increasing number of reasonably minded missionaries to the conclusion in good faith and in their duty to humanity that the ordinary Xhosa people would be far better off under British rule than under that of the chiefs.

In short, the missionaries had their idealism mugged by reality.

This was a huge leap. Stockenstrom never believed that the Xhosa could be ruled according to the principles of English Law and had always argued that it was the *weakness* of the chiefs that was the cause of most troubles. There was no point in trying to rule the Xhosa *in toto* because their way of life was so different that they could never be assimilated. His was the 'long run' argument; that if the chiefs' authority could be sustained and upheld, even at the cost of all sorts of unpleasant practices, then the Xhosa would gradually be brought to improve their government, law and general circumstances through a process of osmosis. The newer missionaries' argument was that people were being killed *now* and that waiting for a gradual improvement meant more deaths of real, live *individuals*. And these arguments were irreconcilable and remain so to this day.

The Victorians were nothing if they were not confident; they were not afraid of making a decision; most were convinced that Magna Carta, parliamentary democracy, individual liberty and the rule of law, Christianity and capitalism constituted a set of values that were universal in application and many (but not all by a long chalk) believed that they were fully justified in sweeping out of the way obscurantist despots so that the ordinary people of the world might enjoy the benefits of self-help, improvement by individual effort, a religion of hope and redemption, free trade and just law. What this meant on the frontier was a narrowing of the gap between the settlers and the missionaries and the growing belief that the chiefs in particular and the Xhosa in general were due to have their hash settled once and for all.

Calderwood and the other missionaries have come in for a massive battering from the Left for taking a different view to that of Philip and Read, despite the fact that the latter were widely distrusted and reviled by their contemporaries. The problem for the Left is that the missionaries provide first hand evidence gathered by men of education, experience and intelligence for a less than flattering view of the Xhosa. If Calderwood had spent three decades and more on the frontier praising the Xhosa then his views would have been treated as Gospel, if you'll excuse the expression, but he did not and so to fit the narrative of black=good and white=bad it was necessary to discredit him. In the absence of much actual evidence to achieve such a thing, this was done by means of 'reading against the grain' primarily; the trick to this is to use the same information used by the writer but draw opposite conclusions from it and it's a perfectly legitimate intellectual technique. As it's the only way I can find real value from reading him, I use it all the time with Mostert, who glides over Maqoma's infanticide without comment and then expends thousands of words on how brilliant a debater he was. The other way is the resort to the old mental acrobatics which is what one dude from the University of Maryland, which I can't quote or cite without permission so I won't, resorted to in arguing that the missionaries actually learned to be ignorant about the Xhosa. *Learned to be ignorant*? That is a very good trick: imagine it; 'right Reverend Fathers, today we're going to be forgetting everything we have ever learned and discounting the evidence of our own eyes, long study, wide experience and deep meditation about the Xhosa in our search for a profound lack of information, understanding or knowledge. Pay attention at the back!'

*Learned to be ignorant.* No doubt this piece of specious drivel was delivered to the thronging horde with the same earnest menace as Orwell had the Ministry of Truth declare that *Oceania is at war with Eurasia; Oceania has ALWAYS been at war with Eurasia.* Inventing new, and usually empty terms, is a favourite trick with the politically correct. I once knew a female teacher in the small town of Al Ain in the UAE whose unpromising Arab male students' work not only suddenly leaped in a positive direction but also, most serendipitously, their exam essays appeared to have been written down in an almost identical outburst of sheer genius. It was down to, she declared, her gimlet eyes daring the room to disagree as she reached for the Racist gun, 'a cultural sharing of knowledge'. The rest of the staff called this 'cultural sharing of knowledge' by its correct term; 'cheating'. A few months later the same female teacher was dismissed and deported after another incident of 'sharing of knowledge' with her young male students, only this time that knowledge was of the carnal variety rather than the cultural. Ho hum.

The way in which this sort of nonsense is mainlined into the academic body politic was explained to me many years ago by a South African historian of great standing but whose blushes I will spare. Basically, Professor Trot writes up some old pony which is then quoted in an article written by Dr. Orc and published in a Journal edited by Professor Swivel-Eyed Fanatic. Then Professor Trot then writes another load of old pony which quotes Dr. Orc's *seminal* and *ground-breaking work* which is then published in a Journal edited by Dr. Marxenengels. This article is then quoted by Professor Swivel-Eyed Fanatic in another article, which also references Professor Trot and Dr. Marxenengels, and then quoted by the *emerging authority on the subject* Dr. Orc and before you know it there is *an exciting new School of Thought* (or what passes for it). Marvellous! Academic Tenures all round! And poor old Jimmy Nosegrinder, who knows it's all a load of pony and can prove it, having been burning the midnight oil in the search for truth, justice and academic beauty for years doesn't get a look in because neither Trot, Orc, Swivel-Eyed Fanatic or Marxenengels will quote him or publish his work. All names have been changed to protect me from a libel suit from the guilty, but that's the way it works. The net result is that Calderwood and the other missionaries have been branded as racists and by extension therefore their testimony is about as valuable as Mark Furman's was in the O.J. Simpson trial. A neat trick – especially when you consider that racism hadn't been invented back in the 1840s (and we'll get to that too) – but that's how the Left do their stuff.

But the missionaries aren't racists; they are good, solid witnesses.

\*

Form Ranks and Quick March: farming was always a precarious business in the Eastern Cape. Long laid fruit orchards could be stripped bare by hailstorms that appeared from nowhere and took no more than minutes to destroy a crop and undo a years' hopes. They were worse than baboons. I owe my life to a last-minute decision to take the car rather than walk to that Piet Retief restaurant in November 2016; the hail came down the size of eggs, broke nine windows in the restaurant, dented the car bonnets, set off all the alarms and left a litter of Jacaranda leaves, twigs and branches all down the street to the church. Just one hit on the head would be enough to see you on your last walk to the final pavilion, I reckon. In the Eastern Transvaal, literally *hundreds* of transport oxen were killed during military operations in the late 19th Century due to hail and lightning. Here is Harriet Ward's description of the Eastern Cape weather; I've never come across a better one,

> Everything in Africa is in extremes. The air is at one moment perfectly calm, the next wild with terrific storms. The sky so sweetly serene at noon, before half an hour passes is often darkened by clouds which shroud the land as with a pall. For months, the long droughts parch the earth, the rivers may be forded on foot, the flocks and herds pant for refreshing waters and green herbage. Suddenly, "a cloud no bigger than a man's hand" appears on the horizon, and lo! the elements rage and swell, thunder booms upon the air, darkness covers the land, the arrows of the Almighty dart from the angry heavens, striking death and terror wheresoever they fall. From the far desert an overpowering torrent of sand comes sweeping on, obscuring the air, and making its way into your very house, in such profusion that you may trace characters in its dry-depths on the window-sill. The skies open, the floods descend, the rivers burst their bounds, trees are uprooted from the saturated earth, and through the roof of your dwelling the rain beats heavily, the walls crack, the plaster falls, the beams that support the thatch groan and creak with "melancholy moan," the voices of angry spirits seem to howl and shout around you, the poor birds on frightened wing wheel past your windows, the cattle disturb you with their lowing, the dogs howl, and the unearthly tones of the Kaffir or Fingo herdsman's song are no agreeable addition to the wild scene stirring before you, The tempest, however, subsides as suddenly as it arose, the voices of the storm-spirits die away in the distance over the mountain-tops, the dark pall of clouds is rent by a Mighty Hand, the swollen rivers rush on, bearing evidences of devastation, but subsiding at last into a more measured course ; the sun lights up the valleys and the hill sides, the air is clearer, the sky brighter than ever; and, but for the History of devastation and oftentimes of death, and the knowledge that for weeks the country will be subject to these violent convulsions of nature, the terrors of the tempest would soon be forgotten. Such is the climate of South Africa. Lovely indeed it is for part of the year; for the rest experience is necessary to teach you whether it be agreeable or not. At one time of the day, I have known the thermometer 120°; at sunset, it has been so cold that a fire has been necessary; nay, I have known it 92° in a room with the air kept out at noon, and at six I have wanted a shawl, or cloak, during my walk. In the morning, you are scorched and blistered by the hot wind, while the vegetation is withering under your feet, and at night you must wrap yourself well up, and put your feet in shoes impervious to the dew.[165]

Unexpected frosts and locusts that wiped out the wheat crop were to be contended with too but the farmers were nothing if not resilient and innovative. During the 1840s, sheep farming became popular as merino sheep were introduced to replace the local, fat-tailed variety (the tail was rendered down for a kind of butter). They were more profitable as they would bear both meat and wool and easier to keep than pigs, whose lack of sweat glands made them unsuitable for the heat. These were also the years of the 'hungry forties' in England and so a steady stream of emigrants made their way out to the Eastern Cape, though never in the sort of numbers that went across the Atlantic. The advertisement columns of the *Grahamstown Journal* gave an impression of hopes, small but realistic, among the business community with new hotels, new products, new people coming in to replace the frequently mourned deaths of the older 1820 settlers.

On the other side of the Fish River, these were also prosperous years as the Xhosa rebuilt their herds and re-occupied the lands that they had been granted by Lord Glenelg. In a way, they were too prosperous; the size of the herds increased steadily and so increased pressure on the available grazing and as the Xhosa raised cattle for reasons more related to culture and status than business there was no commercial slaughter or export to relieve that pressure. The population was also growing; many Xhosa were beginning to drift across the Fish River in search of work as their access to land and cattle was restricted. Others talked of emigrating across the Orange to join with the Tswana or with Chief Moshweshewe in Basutoland (Lesotho). There was also the issue of *lobola* whereby a man must pay a dowry of cattle to obtain a bride. This is a custom that is still common in modern South Africa; at New Year 2017, I stayed in a guest house in Rustenburg with a man who had been forced to pay way over the odds for his mPedi bride because her dad was prejudiced against Zulus (I should note that he was sensible enough to let *her* tell this story). *Lobola* was vital and because young men routinely let the little head do the thinking for the big head, another impetus was given to cattle theft.

And on both sides of the river, drought added an extra, desperate burden; there was never enough rain, and when it did come, it was too much, turning dry beds into raging spates; once, when Mary Moffat did the school run from Kuruman to Graaff-Reinet (a mere 450 miles) to pick up her daughter, she found the Orange River so full that she had to camp by it for a month before it was fordable. Harriet Ward had to wait two days at Trompeters Drift on her way to Fort Peddie to cross over the Fish River in 1843 due to an unexpected deluge; it wasn't unknown for both ferry and wagons to be wrecked even at established crossing places.[166]

*

The men in the Cape government who had to manage these problems were usually tough, independently minded soldiers who knew what war meant and were reluctant to engage in it when there was the possibility of another solution. It's one of the tropes employed by many South African Historians of both Left and Right to portray British administrators or soldiers as blithering idiots, bumbling about in a port-filled fog of upper class twittery yet this

---
[165] Harriet Ward *The Cape and the Kaffirs* p.93.
[166] Ward, p.65

ludicrous caricature is rarely born out when put to the test. The man who won the Xhosa war of 1834-5 was Sir Harry Smith, veteran of Badajoz and the Peninsular War, the man who had eaten the President of the USA's dinner while it was still warm after storming Washington in 1812 and who, aged 46, rode the 600 miles from Cape Town to Grahamstown in under a week to get to the scene of the action. The man who took over from D'Urban to manage Glenelg's system was Sir George Napier, who lost his arm storming yet another breach in Spain; no great loss, I suppose because it had already been broken in three places while he was fighting a battle a couple of days earlier. His Lieutenant-Governor on the frontier, Colonel John Hare, had served in Holland, Egypt, Naples and Spain before getting his Colonelcy at Waterloo. When Napier went, he was replaced by Peregrine Maitland, a name to set all the upper-class twit-baters spluttering with glee; except that he first saw action in 1794 and, *nineteen years* of war later, was the man who destroyed the French Imperial Guard at Waterloo ('Now Maitland. Now's your time.'). No matter which way you cut it, these were tough men of experience, qualification, distinction and decision and you would be hard put to find better.

So, when Colonel John Hare decided that the system he inherited from Stockenstrom wasn't working, it is probably fair to say that he had a point and his 1844 decision to re-occupy forts in the Ceded Territory to attempt to stop cattle lifting was done after long thought. That Maitland should go further and reinstate the Spoor Law was probably the result of exasperation at the inability or unwillingness of the chiefs to end cattle theft. That he did so unilaterally, may also be seen as a result of that same exasperation; if the chiefs could not control their people, what was the point of negotiating treaties with them? Again, what the British wanted was a peaceful frontier so they could concentrate on the Cape naval station but it was this that the incompetence of the Xhosa chiefs continually denied them.

That this hardening of policy against the Xhosa was *emphatically not* driven by race or a desire to grab more land may be seen in the fact that in 1845 Maitland went up beyond the Orange River to intervene in the hostilities then raging between the Boers and the Griqua. His aim was to enforce a couple of treaties that Napier had signed with the Griqua and the Basuto, both of which were firmly aimed at getting that settled frontier; when the Boers demurred, Maitland first sent the Griqua arms and then British regulars in support. The 1845 Battle of Swartkoppies (although 'skirmish' would be a better description) was 'one of the feeblest performances ever mounted by a Boer force against British troops' and 'a triumph of professional over amateurish soldiering' according to the South African Military History Society[167] but it was also a strong marker that British policy was about security, not the colour of a person's skin.

All that was required for peace on the eastern frontier was for the cattle lifting to end but the new Xhosa chief, Sandile, was incompetent; Theal said his only qualification to the title was birth – and then questioned his paternity;[168] even the most sympathetic observers could find little to say that was positive about him and one would need to deploy some pretty selective

---

[167] DY Saks, *Skirmish at Zwartkoppies*, SAMHS Military History Journal Vol. 10 No.1. June 1995
[168] Theal, *History of South Africa 1872-1884* p. 132.

quotation to hide the fact that he was not above a little petty thievery and begging with menaces.[169] He was weak, indecisive, often on the bottle and with a club foot did not look the part in Xhosa eyes. When the younger warriors formed a war party, he could not face them down even with the support of the older councillors. These men wanted to expand their own colonial project and needed the land over the Fish River for their own herds and as far as they were concerned, a runt like Sandile was not going to stop them. As cattle theft began to reach ever more ludicrous levels, the farmer John Mitford Bowker complained of the realities he faced.

> And this is frontier life. The anxieties – the watchings – searchings –listening – dogs barking etc. I cannot describe, neither can you wholly conceive. This is the life that destroyed the loyalty of the Boers, and is ruining as fine a country as any under the crown.'[170]

That the Xhosa's inability to stop stealing cattle had sent them fully kitted, wide eyes open and at the double on the March of Folly was evident to everyone. The missionaries and frontier colonists had long recognized it but their fears had been dismissed and discounted at the time and to this day they are reviled as mistaken and malevolent racists. Who are we to believe? Perhaps we should turn to the Reverend James Read, the original scourge of the colonists, for an opinion that even the aphasiacs of the Left might believe?

> The thefts increased greatly. Thieves became more and more daring, and the chiefs less active to prevent them, and at last almost determined not…to give compensation under treaty…The colonists were very dissatisfied…They conceived a war preferable to existing circumstances….[171]

Or perhaps we might alight on John Fairbairn, the philanthropist editor of the *South African Commercial Advertiser*, a friend to the Xhosa throughout his life and the son-in-law of John Philip? He declared that when war did break out, Maitland was going to the frontier 'not to exterminate savages, but to subdue anarchy and to establish the reign of justice'.[172] In the event Read, and his son Joseph, gave his full support to the war because his parishioners in the Kat River Settlement had been robbed blind like everyone else – another case of idealism being mugged by reality. Stockenstrom came out of retirement too and took up his position as a commando commandant. Even the arch-mouth himself, Dr. John Philip, could raise no voice in the defence of the Xhosa; after the 1834-5 war he found out that one of his few Christian converts, a man who he regarded as a model and who he had taken to England, had been involved in the rebellion and the murder of a number of mFengu women and children. He never campaigned again.[173]

\*

---

[169] Compare Ward p.69 with Mostert p.837 if you don't want to take my word for it.
[170] Quoted in Mostert, p.866.
[171] Quoted in Mostert, p.871.
[172] Quoted in Mostert, p.872.
[173] Theal, Vol III, p. 60.

The Seventh Xhosa War got its contemporary name the 'War of the Axe' after the attempted theft of the said item from a hardware store at Fort Beaufort near the Kat River Settlement in 1846. The thief was caught but then liberated by his pals before he could come to trial and disappeared into the Xhosa kraals. Colonel Hare demanded his return only to be rebuffed; it was the last straw and a vast column of wagons set off to make camp in the Amatolas with a view to forming a base from which to attack this Xhosa stronghold. Unfortunately, in a three-day running battle a large part of the convoy was destroyed by the Xhosa and though the troops came back with the ammunition supplies intact and two thousand head of cattle, the opportunity for the swift knock-out blow was gone. The Xhosa now armed with muskets and plentifully supplied with stolen horses invaded the colony and a long, pointless war of small skirmish, cattle raid, endless patrolling and slow grinding down of resistance began, all of which was exacerbated by a dismal drought. Whenever the Xhosa stood, they were defeated by the mixed forces of British regular infantry and dragoons, Burgher commandos called up from the Cape, the excellent Khoisan professionals of the Cape Mounted Rifles, Native Infantry raised from the liberated slaves, the *amabutho* of the mFengu and on occasion, the Bushmen themselves.[174] As the season for planting approached and the Xhosa were increasingly reliant on burning off the pasturage to prevent the British advance – a tactic that also denied their own cattle forage - many of the Xhosa chiefs, including Maqoma who was now almost permanently drunk, began to call for peace but realized only too late that the British relentlessness in war was now coming to the fore. No matter how badly the commissariat broke down, no matter how severe the drought, no matter how many farms and kraals were burned, no matter what the hardships to the troops or the civilians, the Xhosa would be defeated, their banditti rounded up and booted out of the colony and only when a peace that guaranteed the security of the colonial border was in the offing would any sort of let-up be countenanced. Harriet Ward touched the nerve in her description of a farmstead outside Grahamstown in 1846.

> The settlers, a man and his wife, perfectly English in appearance, but pale and harassed, stood surveying their miserable homestead. This, too, from its open position, had escaped the brand; but the windows were shattered, the door swung on imperfect hinges, the steps were broken and grass grew between them; the little garden laid waste; and, as if in mockery, a scarlet geranium streamed garishly over the crumbling embankment; rank weeds filled the place of other plants under the broken boughs of the apricot trees, and a few poor articles of furniture which had been borne away to Graham's Town, on the family flitting, stood in the open air, awaiting more strength than the exhausted mistress of the place could command. Her husband had been trying to bring a piece of ground into some sort of cultivation, but it was heavy work; the long droughts had parched the earth, and the mimosa fence was scattered over the face of the patch, which had once yielded vegetables.[175]

For the British war was not a pastime or a ritual or a rite of passage or something that could be switched on and off at will; it was something that had to be won if these scenes were not to

---

[174] Ward p.158
[175] Ward p. 169.

be endlessly repeated. By the end of 1846, it was clear that the 70-year-old Maitland could not be expected to continue in the field and Hare, too, had had his health broken (he died four days after leaving the Cape and was buried at sea) and the two were replaced by Sir Henry Pottinger and Lt-General Berkeley with orders to bring the war to an end at the earliest. With these men arrived a new hardness, a determination that made short work of any idea of laxity or compromise; cattle that encumbered the troops would be shot; anyone trading with the enemy in any way shape or form – but especially those running guns and ammunition – would be prosecuted for treason; Sandile was to be arrested. The mouth of the Buffalo River was occupied (now East London) and a chain of forts run up it; this would do away with many of the supply problems as well as bisect the Xhosa territories. By October, the patrolling had done its work and Sandile surrendered.

So ended an unnecessary war; the Xhosa lost again; the land was devastated again; and the Xhosa plan to conquer and colonise west of the Fish River resulted in the loss of even more pasturage; and Kingwilliamstown once more became the base for a garrison in the re-occupied Queen Adelaide province, now re-named British Kaffraria.

The appointment of Sir Harry Smith as Cape High Commissioner in December 1847 was hugely popular and not just because Pottinger was a dirty old man whose licentiousness had scandalised Cape Town society.[176] For a start, both Boer and British settlers were convinced Smith understood their problems and thoroughly agreed with his re-annexation of the Ceded Territory and even more enamoured of his decision to annex all the land as far as the Kei River. The Ceded Territory was re-named Victoria East with part of it granted to the mFengu and the rest auctioned off, while the land up to the Kei became British Kaffraria. There the Xhosa would reside under their own chiefs but the Paramount Chief would now be the British Governor; smelling-out was banned, which was a boon for everybody, but the banning of *lobola,* though motivated by a desire to stop young men thinking with the little head and stealing cattle from the colony, was an unnecessary imposition.

It is hard not to smile at Sir Harry Smith. His entry in the Dictionary of National Biography describes him thus:

> Smith was not devoid of the self-assertion characteristic of men who fight their own way in the world and owe their successes solely to their energy and ability; but he was popular with his colleagues and subordinates, who were fascinated by his daring energy, histrionics, and originality, and who admired his rough and ready wit.

His comments on the autobiography he had begun writing in India reveal much: 'I have never read a page of it since scrawling over it at a gallop'[177] which is probably a fine description of how he lived his life. Hyperactive ain't in it; he lived his life so fast that he couldn't remember the year he was born or how old he was. The book is a delight.

---

[176] Theal, *History of South Africa* Vol III, p. 52.
[177] The Autobiography of Lt.General Sir Harry Smith (London, 1901) Vol. I. p.v

> It was barely fourteen months since the Battle of Toulouse. I had crossed the Atlantic four times to and from America; fought a gallant action and captured the metropolis of that world; brought home dispatches and received £500; was in communication with ministers, and honoured of a long audience of His Royal Highness the Prince Regent; again went out; was under fire for three weeks, and in the sanguinary disaster at New Orleans; was in the Battle of Waterloo, and had been promoted from Captain to Lieut-Colonel and the Companion of the Bath; without a wound.[178]

Not bad for the son of a country surgeon. Here he is bidding farewell to his wife before going into battle during the Peninsular war:

> She looked very sad, and I said "Hallo, what's the matter?" "You or your horse will be killed tomorrow." I laughed and said, "Well, of two such chances, I hope it will be the horse."[179]

The horse was actually killed.

This is an extract from his account of his extraordinary 600-mile ride from the Cape to Grahamstown in 1835.

> My first horse from Swellendam had a 20-miles stage, but through having to go up the river to ford, this noble little four-year-old had 30 miles, which he did, crossing the river too, in two hours and twenty minutes, I was so pleased with him, I wrote to Rivers to buy him and bring him up with the Burghers. He bought him for £18 5s. I afterwards rode him very hard for two years, and sold him to Sir George Napier for £50.[180]

Here he is on diplomatic relations with Hintsa.

> After a day or two's shuffling, Hintza sent into camp his Prime Minister, Kuba, a sharp wolf-like looking fellow, with the cunning of Satan. I would back him eating beef-steaks against any devil.[181]

His way of dealing with the Xhosa chiefs was theatrical to say the least and the ceremonies he designed to impress on them his status as Lord and Master would raise more than an eyebrow today, but his view was that the Xhosa were capable of improvement if only they could be brought to accept the rule of law and abandon superstitious nonsense like rain-making and witchcraft. To him, the existence of a social compact was essential; in any successful society there was a hierarchy defined largely by education, but those at the top had a responsibility to those at the bottom and all were worthy of respect[182] and these were features that Xhosa society lacked. This extended to his view of empire:

---

[178] Smith, *Autobiography* Vol I, p. 294.
[179] Smith, *Autobiography* Vol I, p. 144.
[180] Smith, *Autobiography* Vol II, p. 13.
[181] Smith, *Autobiography* Vol II, p. 33.
[182] Smith, *Autobiography* Vol I, p. 331.

> Conquest must be achieved by force of arms, by the display of irresistible power; then held by moderation, by a progressive system of amelioration of the condition of the people, by consistency and uncompromising justice. In this way the great movers of mankind, Fear and Self-interest, perpetuate subjection.[183]

He seemed to like the Xhosa and they in turn found much to like in him; he might have been eccentric, over-bearing and loud but he was straight, honest, fair and consistent which was probably an improvement on what they had to put up with from Chiefs like Sandile and Maqoma. This is him administering justice in 1835 for a man severely burned after a smelling-out by Chief Umhala.

> "Umhala, did I not give the word—no more witchcraft?" He boldly answered, "You did." "Then how dare you, Umhala, one of my magistrates sworn to be obedient to my law, infringe the Word?" He stoutly denied it. I then brought in the poor afflicted sufferer, and roared out, "Umhala, devil, liar, villain, you dare to deceive me. Deny now what I accuse you of." He then confessed all, and began to palliate his conduct. To this I would not listen, but seized my wand [a large cane with a gold knob on it] to give the Word. "Hear you, Umhala! You have eaten a man up. Give back every head of his cattle, and ten head of your own for having eaten him up. And you forfeit ten head more to me, the Great Chief, for my government."[184]

Umhala demurred and was forced into submission by the dispatch of troops. When he came back in a more penitent mode, Smith forgave him with equally theatrical generosity. It's hard to escape the impression that he thought he was training puppies by means of a rolled-up newspaper and a doggie choc. That he was capable of over-doing this is true; one colonist said of him that 'It is true, when under excitement, he employed somewhat strong expletives, which, like sheet lightning, are terrifying yet harmless';[185] when he arrived at Port Elizabeth in December 1847, he found Maqoma, abandoned by nine of his ten wives, drunk and trussed up in an old dragoon uniform complete with brass helmet, and instantly threw him down. Putting his foot on his neck, he declared that 'I am come hither to teach Kafirland that I am chief and master here, and this is the way I shall treat the enemies of the Queen of England.'[186] Even the editor of his Autobiography thought he had gone overboard here as indeed he had.

The problem with Sir Harry's *Autobiography* is that the part written by him ends in 1846 and the chap who edited it was forced to pad out the rest of it with all sorts of odds and ends. In this respect he was fortunate to have to hand the great *History of South Africa Since 1795* written by our old pal George McCall Theal. Theal was a teacher at the Lovedale Seminary in the Eastern Cape where he taught missionaries of all denominations as well as Africans but his real passion was for History and when he was offered a job in the Cape Treasury in 1877, he leaped at it because he knew he could get at the records stored there. After that, there was no stopping him and he scribbled away with a passion. His volumes are detailed, balanced

---

[183] Smith, *Autobiography* Vol II, p. 121.
[184] Smith, *Autobiography* Vol II, p. 84.
[185] Smith, *Autobiography* Vol II, p. 293.
[186] Smith, *Autobiography* Vol II, p. 228.

and in some cases exhaustive and are therefore hated by the Left who dismiss this sort of real research as 'Settler History' but the fact is that he can't be ignored. He wrote both as a first-hand observer, as someone who interviewed many of the Xhosa chiefs personally and as someone who could read the official documents both past and present to clarify and expand his knowledge. He also had missionary sympathies and believed in the 'civilisation' of the black people of Africa (by which he meant, in the modern parlance, 'development') through education, work, religion and justice. To this end, he produced Xhosa language works, a local Xhosa-language newspaper from the printing press at Lovedale, and collected and published Xhosa stories; Christopher Saunders (a proper historian) says he was 'the only white South African historian for a century to have written with an African readership in mind'.[187] His was the first truly South African voice (even though he was born in Canada) because he wrote from the perspective of the colonial; an idea of how balanced he was can be gained by the assessment of *The Spectator* in 1889 that he was very much pro-Boer rather than pro-British,[188] while also being accused of being pro-African, anti-Dutch, pro-missionary (and anti-) and just about everything else in between. He was also honest enough to admit when he was wrong and when he changed his mind, which is a quality pretty rare among Historians, so with this fine man as a guide, we'll crack on.

With British Kaffraria annexed, the good Sir Harry turned his attentions to the chaotic situation on the Orange River. He had already declared all land south of the river to be British territory, an addition to Her Majesty's possessions at least a dozen times larger than British Kaffraria, and now headed up into the great emptiness beyond that river in the belief that he could persuade the Voortrekkers to come back into the colony. In this he was mistaken, as Theal made clear.

> Twelve years of wandering and suffering had produced such a change in these people that they could no longer be dealt with like the men he had formerly known and respected. Attributing their losses and hardships to the action of the imperial government and the London missionary society, their antipathy to English rule had become so deep that willingly but few of them could ever be brought to submit to it again.[189]

Their experience had taught them self-reliance, their children had grown up ignorant of any knowledge of Britain except the certainty that English law always favoured the black over the white and the power of the English government was always directed towards the oppression of the Boers. The only contact many of them had with the British was in the form of those criminals, renegades, deserters and adventurers who had quit the colony and girded up in the armour of desperation were willing to commit any act that might ensure survival; none of those fellows would welcome the return of British rule, if it meant the noose or the firing squad.

---

[187] Christopher Saunders, *George McCall Theal and Lovedale*, History in Africa Vol. 8 (1981), pp. 155-164.

[188] http://archive.spectator.co.uk/article/19th-october-1889/23/History-of-south-africa-1854---1872-by-george-mcca

[189] Theal Vol III, p. 260

None of this deterred Sir Harry though. In 1848, he first demanded that Adam Kok and his Griquas should give up their independence and become subsidiaries of the Crown, throwing a rope over a beam to clinch the argument. Moshweshewe (also known as Moshoeshoe and/or Moshesh), the powerful chief of the Basuto, was induced to accept British paramountcy for the advantages it would bring in controlling the Europeans who were endlessly encroaching on his lands. After that Sir Harry leaped upon his steed and flew across to Natal where Andries Pretorius was preparing to trek for the Transvaal and there hit the buffers. Both sides disputed what happened at the camp at the foot of the Drakensberg but the balance of the evidence pointed to Pretorius' version being closer to the truth than that of Harry the Hotspur. Smith claimed that Pretorius had agreed that all the land south of the Vaal River should be taken over by Britain and incorporated into a thing called the Orange River Sovereignty but the land north of it should remain open unless the majority of the Boers there wanted otherwise. Pretorius claimed that the land south of the Vaal should only be annexed *if* the majority of the Boers there wanted it but Smith went right ahead and issued the proclamation, confident that he had the support of those Boers he had already conferred with at Bloemfontein and Winburg. Another 60,000 square miles was thus added to the empire.

Who was right? Pretorius; roughly two-thirds of the Boers now in the Orange River Sovereignty preferred their independence to British rule and in July 1848, Pretorius gathered up a commando from across the Vaal and invaded. Major Warden, the British authority in Bloemfontein was then persuaded to take his force of 60 Cape Mounted Riflemen down to Colesberg and out of the new republic and once that happened, a collision was inevitable.

Smith came galloping up as expected and put his force of British Regulars, Griquas, Khoisan Cape Mounted Rifles and a substantial Boer contingent up against Pretorius' commando at a smudge on the map called Boomplats on the road to Bloemfontein. There was a skirmish. The British won. Those Voortrekkers who could not stomach British rule went north over the Vaal. They had left the Cape; they had fought for and then been ejected from Natal; now they had been pushed off the Orange; all their prejudices against the British had been confirmed once more; they were *furious*.

They weren't the only ones because in December 1850 the Xhosa rose in revolt again. Why? Theal thought that the main reason was the abolition of smelling-out and put forward the view that the practice was so deeply embedded in Xhosa culture that it was impossible to stop. The people believed that bad luck, illnesses and ailments were due to the presence of evil spirits and without the witchdoctors to smell them out those evils would mount up; it was better to have a few people grotesquely murdered than face this fate. It's possible that this belief was reinforced because yet another drought hit the area in 1850 and with it came a prophet called Mlanjeni. It was rumoured that Mlanjeni was Makana (of the defeat at Grahamstown in 1819 fame) returned and though this should have been enough to put the Xhosa completely off him, they took his assurances that chewing on a bit of *pelargonium* was a sure-fire way to prevent a bullet wound. Mlanjeni was supernatural, it was said, and the people began to flock to him.

One of the other causes that Theal pointed to was the loss of the chief's power and influence, especially when the ban on smelling-out meant that they couldn't augment their wealth by having a prosperous man duly done over to take possession of his cattle. Sandile saw the potential of this prophet and by October 1850 had him in his pocket. The frontier farmers heard the rumours and saw their Xhosa workers deserting their farms; loyal Xhosa clan chiefs passed on the warnings so that Sir Harry called a meeting of the chiefs at Kingwilliamstown at the end of October 1850 to try to nip this in the bud. Sandile, and Maqoma now back in Xhosa territory, refused to attend; this was an act of defiance equal to a declaration of war so Smith promptly deposed Sandile as chief. It made no difference whatsoever. At Christmas, the Xhosa rose, ambushed a few troops, massacred a few colonists, burnt a few farms and mission stations, besieged a few forts and then entered the colony in pursuit of cattle to steal.

It was all so depressingly familiar and all so depressingly stupid because they had no concept of just how vulnerable they were. During previous conflicts they had been able to rely on drought, the burning off of grazing and distance to slow down the British to a crawl and then head up into the almost impassable Amatola Mountains where they could hole up and hold out. With the opening of the port at East London, however, Kingwilliamstown at the foot of the Amatolas was only 35 miles away. Pato, chief of the Gqunukhwebe Xhosa, whose lands were right on that supply route understood this well enough and having fought long and hard against the British in the previous war, knew that if they couldn't be beaten last time, they certainly couldn't be beaten now; he joined up with Sir Harry in short order.

What was new and extremely disturbing was the rebellion of the Khoisan at the Kat River Settlement and the desertion of a substantial number of Cape Mounted Riflemen. Led by a man of some talent and an ambition to found his own independent nation, the Khoisan under Willem Uithaalder made up a formidable band of trained soldiers a thousand strong. In earlier times, he might have shot his way northwards and away over the Orange River like the Oorlams or the Griquas but again, times had changed. Why they revolted is disputed too; Theal, like many of his contemporaries, blamed it on the likes of James Read and other missionary agitators and resentment against the mFengu who had moved in nearby and were competing commercially with them. It may have been the result of a build-up of grievances stemming from the amount of time they had been kept under arms and the arduous service that they had seen. This seems to me to be plausible for the Khoisan in the western areas of the Cape not only stayed quiet but joined up in the British forces. That such a 'model' settlement should revolt was bewildering but by throwing in their lot with the Xhosa, they were signing their own death warrant. Perhaps it was just an outburst of desperate final rage after a century of decline; understandable but ultimately futile.

A year of skirmish, ambush, raid and counter-raid went by before the government in London lost its patience with the dashing Sir Harry. They had given him his head because he had been such a successful and daring soldier, an intelligent and just administrator and because he had the confidence of the colony but his widespread annexations, which probably amounted to an area greater than the size of the United Kingdom in total, had worried them. The revolt of the Boers and the Battle of Boomplats gave the lie to his idea that extending British rule would mean fewer disorders, especially when in 1851 war broke out with the Basuto. The failure to put down the Xhosa revolt quickly was the last straw and in January 1851, he was recalled and replaced with another soldier, Sir George Cathcart. Cathcart changed the tactics, put in some more troops and by October 1851 had defeated the Xhosa and taken the Amatolas away from them. The Kat River Settlement was handed over to European settlers. Another pointless and avoidable war came to an end formally in 1853, just five years after the last defeat; the Xhosa were not yet at the end of their March of Folly though. They had one more hideous stupidity hidden under their cloaks.

Poor old Sir Harry. At the end, he was just too old. Too many battles, too many slugging matches and the wear and tear of *anno domini* had blunted his ability to come up with a new answer to the old problem of the Amatola stronghold. Cathcart got it in one; small forts to occupy ground won which could not then be re-occupied acted to slowly strangle resistance. Sir Harry always wanted the pitched battle, the form of warfare in which he excelled - look up Aliwal or Ferozepore, where he was magnificent – but he never got it. He left his name behind at Harrismith at the top of Van Reenen's pass into Natal and at Ladysmith, at the bottom. There's also Smithfield and Aliwal North, a couple of hundred kilometres east of Colesberg, where you can sit on the veranda of the pub, eat *varkeribbetjies* and watch the very orange water of the Orange River go past. The greatest thing he left behind had nothing to do with war though; it was the constitution for the self-government of the Cape.

*

The British ruled the Cape by appointing a suitable Governor who would preside over a Legislative Council made up of appointed officials and 'non-official' members who were chosen from among the leading men of the colony. This was known as 'representative government' because the non-official members were supposed to represent the general opinion of the colony and it worked well where colonies were small, vulnerable and not really equipped to administer or govern themselves. The experience of the American War of Independence showed, however, that when colonies were big enough and strong enough then representative government fell well short of what British people expected. As it was widely thought that the colonies would go their own way rather sooner than later, it was also thought that it was probably best left to the colonists themselves to decide what form of government they desired rather than have an unpopular form imposed. In 1843, a rebellion among the French Canadians brought this truth sharply into focus and Lord Durham was dispatched to investigate, report and recommend. What he came up with was 'responsible' government. This meant that an elected parliament would replace the Legislative Council and a Prime Minister and Cabinet on the British model would run the administration. The Governor was reduced to a more formal role but would retain substantial powers as, effectively, the voice of the British government who, in the last analysis, would be supplying the troops and paying the bills. Australia, Canada, New Zealand and South Africa, variously known as the 'settlement colonies' all quickly took up responsible government. India didn't because it was not a colony of settlement and the East India Company government operated more according to established Indian modes of government; hence the name 'The Raj'. The rest of the empire was governed according to what was deemed to work best in a particular circumstance, largely because the Colonial Office permanent secretary thought it absurd to impose any one system on such a disparate collection of territories. The term 'Crown Colony' covered a multitude of sins ranging from a fairly autocratic rule by an appointed Governor to those which had elected assemblies or nominated councils. As it turned out, for the next twenty years, South Africa got a hybrid; an elected two chamber parliament but overseen by the Governor and the Legislative Council.

South Africa had never been short of people with an opinion on how the place should be governed and the shift from a 'Dutch' to a 'British' form of government had caused much resentment among the Trekboers. Out towards the Eastern frontier, there were growing calls during the 1840s for a separate administration mainly on the grounds that the government of the Cape was too remote and didn't understand or ignored the plight and problems of the colonists hard up against the Xhosa. There were also those who thought the capital of the colony should be moved to Grahamstown, now its second 'city'. This was all evidence that it was time to look at the way in which the people were represented.

The response from Sir Harry Smith and from London was entirely positive. Smith arranged for representatives to come forward to discuss the matter and the wrangling over the details began. The most important dispute was over who should actually get the vote with one party demanding that the franchise be limited to those who could prove their worth by the display of capital. This 'property qualification' would be seen as oppressive and absurd today but at the time it was thought quite sensible to limit the vote to those educated enough and independently wealthy enough to use it wisely. 'Democracy' was associated with French mobs and guillotines and without such a property qualification the natural result would be a mob of the great unwashed voting themselves a vast array of benefits to be paid for by their hard-working, honest and successful betters, which is a pretty accurate description of the manifestoes of modern European and British social democratic parties. The end result of this would be ruin because the successful, hard-working businessmen and farmers would either tire of being bilked to keep the idle in grog and move elsewhere or raise an army and rebel in defence of their own property, which is obvious but still something that has not yet dawned on those same European and British dimwitted social democrats. So the debate revolved around what level the property qualification was to be set at; Stockenstrom and Fairbairn wanted it to be set fairly low while the majority of the council wanted it set rather higher.

At the heart of the debate was whether the franchise would allow black people the opportunity to gain the vote and on this the government in London was absolutely firm.

> In conferring upon the colony the boon of a representative constitution it would be exceedingly unadvisable that the franchise should be so restricted as to leave those of the coloured classes who in point of intelligence were qualified for the exercise of political power practically unrepresented....It was the earnest desire of Her Majesty's government that all her subjects at the Cape, without distinction of class or colour, should be united by one bond of loyalty and a common interest...the exercise of

political rights enjoyed by all alike would prove one of the best methods of attaining this object.[190]

Those on the frontier were not so sure that it was a wise thing to hand out the vote to those black and Khoisan people currently in open revolt against it, which was a fair point, but their objections were overcome by a huge outburst of popular agitation among the British and Dutch people of the western Cape for the more liberal franchise. In 1853, they carried their point with 85% support, as Theal made clear.

> For the franchise no distinction was made between classes and creeds, between white men and blacks; the Hottentot, or freed slave, or prize negro, or Fingo clothed in nothing but a blanket, was to be as free to go to the poll as the astronomer - royal or the richest merchant in Capetown, provided he was a subject of her Majesty, twenty-one years of age, an occupant for a year of premises worth £25…or who had been for twelve months in receipt of a salary at the rate of £50 per annum or £25 per annum with board and lodging. No education was needed, for the voting could be entirely by word of mouth.[191]

This is astonishing to those who point sharp fingers at the British Empire as being (insert your favourite *–ism* or *–ist* here), mainly because it shoots down all their tired prejudices. Let me emphasise; within twenty years Britain had voluntarily abolished slavery and thereby gained the much unheralded distinction of being the first civilization in human History to do so, committed the most powerful warfighting machine on the planet, the Royal Navy, at its own expense to abolish the slave trade worldwide and had then granted a constitution to a colony extending the franchise to black people, most of whom had no idea or experience of anything approaching political representation, with the active and willing support of 85% of its white colonists at a time when those black people outnumbered the white people by 210,000 to 140,000 and way before comparable British people in the UK got the vote.

\*

The problem with South African History is that the further you get into it, the more spread out it gets. Each theme gets more and more separate from the next the further you get towards the frontier and some of them disappear into the blue because they head off beyond the reach of the records. This means that a strictly chronological approach is impossible because so much is going on at the same time and in several unfamiliar places and in several unfamiliar languages with names that keep changing – is that a *Frontier* war, a *Kaffir* war or a War of *Resistance*? - that the reader is easily bamboozled. I've hardly touched on Natal, for example, but we'll get there eventually, and only briefly on British imperial policy because I've tried to focus on what was most important at a particular time. That means the Bushmen, the Boers and then the Xhosa as the colony expanded but from around 1850 all sorts of things start happening at once. The person most neglected so far is Moshweshewe of

---
[190] Theal. Vol.III, p. 128.
[191] Theal. Vol.III, p. 132.

the Basuto and so, with due apologies to the wily old bugger, we'll now turn our attention thither.

Moshweshewe was one of the great survivors of the *mfecane*. His base was at Thaba Bosigo, near modern day Maseru in Lesotho, tucked away inside the Drakensberg mountains, difficult to get to and easy to defend and as the terrible disruptions and dislocations proceeded, he built up his clans from those refugees and displaced clans desperate to escape the disaster. In 1831, he managed to defeat Mzilikazi which cemented his control and then began to play off his rivals in order to further expand and consolidate. By the time the Orange River Sovereignty was established, his writ ran as far east as the Oliphantshoek Pass, westwards towards Smithfield and Aliwal North, northwards almost as far as Winberg and throughout the Drakensberg. It was good grassland, fine mountain uplands, well-watered and relatively safe. The supreme realist, Moshweshwe never overestimated his power over his own clan leaders, never allowed hubris to lead him into thinking he could match British power but did pay attention to the way in which the horse and gun had overtaken the shield and assegai; his warriors rode and carried guns as well as assegais and unlike most of the Xhosa and the Zulus, they actually learned how to shoot straight. When the missionaries (mainly French) turned up he accepted them as another new thing, watched them, allowed them to do the good things that they did, but he would not abandon his own beliefs in a spirit world; he actually saw no incompatibility between the two beliefs.

Like everyone else on the Highveldt, his biggest problem was dealing with the constant cattle raiding and intrusion of bands of wandering desperadoes. To his north east, in the area that we would now identify as the Golden Gate National Park, was Sekonyela of the Tlokwa and to the north-west was a second rival, Moroka and his Barolong, on the Platberg. Adam Kok's Griquas based at Philipolis stretched out between the Orange and Riet Rivers while on the south bank of the Vaal were the Korannas. All were fractious neighbours quick to steal and quick to arbitrate at gun point. Actual borders were fluid and disputed; at times Moshweshe struggled with the concept of what a 'border' constituted, while claims flew thick and fast for farms and grazing and locations. Everything in between was supposed to be open to settlement, but vast areas were either empty, devastated or plagued by Bushmen and bandits.

His other problem was Major Warden, the British officer who had been given the unenviable task of maintaining order over this monstrous chaos, and who was inclined to see Moshweshwe's Basuto as part of the problem rather than the solution. Dealing with Warden was difficult because quite a large number of Basutos thought they were more than a match for the small forces that he had at his command and were itching for a fight. It duly came over yet another cattle dispute which when rolled into the spillover from the fighting of the 8th Xhosa/Frontier war resulted in Warden, against all entreaty from Moshweshwe, sending armed force against him. The motley crew at his disposal were repulsed with some slaughter at Vierfort in June 1851 whereupon the Basuto followed up with raids that ranged from Harrismith to Winberg to Bloemfontein to Caledon. Moshweshwe probably didn't realise it, but he had struck a fatal blow to the Orange River Sovereignty because when news of the situation reached London, an exasperated government looked at a map and asked themselves the question: *why the hell do we need to be fighting Basutos in Bloemfontein if all we want is the port at Cape Town?* The answer was, of course, *we don't.* In January 1852, Commissioners were sent out from London, met with Andries Pretorius and agreed the Sand River Convention which basically revoked all pretence at British control of the area north of the Vaal River. Immediately, those Boers in the Orange River Sovereignty who resented being under British rule packed their traps and headed straight over the Vaal.

The apparent disintegration of British rule on the Highveldt provided Moshweshwe with both threats and opportunities. It was clear when negotiations were opened up that the British were keen to do a deal because the Commissioners told him they were going to sack Warden for starting a war in the first place. He then made contact with Pretorius offering a general alliance, an offer that was eagerly accepted. This provided him with opportunity to settle Sekonyela's hash, which he did in May 1852 and followed this up in July with the crushing of the Barolongs. Warden, who had been implicated in supplying ammunition to Moshweshwe's enemies, was duly sacked.

The threat came from the fact that the British had been beaten and, on all past experience, as well as the present spectacle of Cathcart's defeat of the Xhosa, they would not stay beaten and when fresh British troops appeared on the Caledon River in November 1852, Moshweshewe turned his attention to this threat. The last thing he wanted was war, he insisted at a series of meetings with Cathcart in December 1852, but he doubted whether he could accept terms that his own clan leaders would refuse and which his pumped up young warriors would hardly accept. Cathcart would not back down and ordered the troops forward.

On 20th December the two sides met at Berea Mountain and in a series of skirmishes took each other's measure. The British were surprised at the skill in which the Basutos moved quickly and used their local knowledge to mount effective ambushes. The Basutos were utterly unused to and (very wisely) unwilling to fling themselves at a line of disciplined redcoats backed up by Lancers. Casualties amounted to around fifty killed and wounded on either side; both sides considered whether another engagement was worth it; the Basutos were talking about retreating higher up into the Drakensberg but the British troops were talking about getting a really decisive victory.

And at this point, Moshweshwe came up with an idea that was as brilliant as anything Talleyrand or Palmerston ever came up with. At midnight he sent a messenger to Cathcart with the following note.

> This day you have fought against my people, and taken much cattle. As the object for which you have come is to have a compensation ... I beg you will be satisfied with what you have taken. I entreat peace from you,—you have shown your power, you have chastised,—let it be enough, I pray you; and let me be no longer considered an enemy to the queen. I will try all I can to keep my people in order in the future.[192]

---

[192] Theal, Vol III, p.332

He had built a golden bridge for Cathcart to retreat over and Cathcart, who had no interest in expending further blood and treasure in a very difficult undertaking to conquer a territory that would be given back by London even if the attempt was successful, took it. At the same time, Moshweshwe sent out messengers to all his clan leaders telling them that his men had won a great victory and offered up as proof the withdrawal of the British. And just to underline this, he sent another expedition against Sekonyela which finally broke him. He had established his reputation, protected his land and people and successfully navigated a diplomatic minefield with the most powerful government on the continent. You have to salute Moshweshwe.

The Orange River Sovereignty was finally given up in 1854 by the Bloemfontein Convention. That it took more than a year to get the papers drawn up and settled was due to another unwelcome intervention by irritating missionaries. This time they objected to the British *giving up African territory* on the grounds that Africans were better protected under British rule than they were under that of the Boers. They had a point, of course, but their old tactics of vilifying a whole people for the misdemeanors of a few based on evidence that was questionable at best and made up at worst meant that they persuaded no-one, caused the usual resentment and destroyed much of their own credibility.

*

## The March of Folly III

Vodka poured over cracked ice and then topped up with coffee liqueur; a Black Russian. I can't think of this cocktail without immediately associating it in my mind with the incredible, appalling, tragic, stupid and utterly, utterly foolish events that I'm now going to describe. It is the last leg of the March of Folly that the Xhosa nation had been engaged in for fifty years. They had stolen and stolen beyond all reason. They had fought endless wars against the British and lost. They had followed prophets who had been shown time and time again to be charlatans. They had adhered to chiefs who were, as leaders, almost entirely devoid of the qualities required for leadership. They had allowed themselves to be manipulated, robbed and murdered in the fearful circumstances of the smelling-out ceremonies. And all the time, they had before them in the shape of the Cape colony an alternative way of life, a way of life that was thriving and growing daily in strength and vitality, a way of life brimming with opportunity and only too ready to trade with them, employ them and, in time, even give them the vote. Peace, security and prosperity was within their reach if only they would give up their colonial ambitions and stay east of the boundary. Instead, they chose suicide. You might think the connection with a cocktail is flippant and it is, but if you don't need a bucket of triple strength Black Russian at the end of this section then you have a harder heart than mine.

In May 1856, two young girls by the name of Nongqawuse and Nombanda came back from a pool at the mouth of the river saying that they had been approached by two strange young men with a message. A great day of resurrection was about to occur, they were told, but to ensure that it came about all living cattle were to be killed and all the grain pits emptied and scattered to the winds. Once this was done, the 'new people' would arise out of the water, bring with them new cattle from an underground cave, and then sweep the whites and their mFengu allies into the sea. Now most sensible Xhosa, and there were a lot of them, would have seen this for what is was; too much *dagga* or a sly story to excuse an illicit tryst. Their uncle Mhalakazi, however, made his living as a prophet and seeing an opportunity to reap some fame and fortune from this nonsense – and similar nonsense had already been rejected from a slew of similar conmen – started to spread the word. The word caught fire, mainly because there was an outbreak of lung sickness that was devastating the herds of both the colonists and the Xhosa and the people were desperate for hope.

Still, a bit of leadership from the chiefs would have put an end to this garbage in no time but, as we have so far seen, leadership had long been at a premium among the Xhosa chiefs and in, Sarili, the heir to Hintsa it was a quality that was entirely lacking. A sickly boy, he had never been regarded as particularly bright, though Theal later interviewed him and found him to be a mine of folklore. Mostert, though laying on the glaze with a trowel, admitted that he was 'deeply impressionable'[193] as well as hating white people to the point of what we would call today outright racism. What he had picked up, however, was that the ever-victorious British had got a pasting off Moshweshwe and, wonder of wonder, such a beating from the Russians in the Crimea that even Cathcart had been killed. When he heard the good news about the 'new people', his prejudice against white people naturally led him to put two and two together and get three; the Russians must therefore be the 'new people'; Black Russians. He ordered his people to begin killing the cattle and began what Mostert called 'the greatest self-inflicted immolation of a people in all History, the saddest and most overwhelming of all South Africa's many human tragedies'.[194] And for once, Mostert is undeniably right.

Charles Brownlee, son of a missionary who had grown up among the Xhosa and spoke the language at mother tongue level was one of the colonial agents attached to Sandile of the Rarabe-Xhosa. Picking up the rumours of this remarkable prophesy and the wanton slaughter of cattle, he quickly got among the Xhosa and over the following period made strenuous efforts to dissuade them from this madness. He answered 'never' so often to the question of when all these wonders would arrive that he earned himself the nickname 'napakade'. When he first reported the rumour to his superiors, his wife thought he had gone mad and tried to dissuade him from sending the message.[195] When his reports arrived on Lt-Governor Maclean's desk, he too was incredulous; was this some sort of plot to foment war? He didn't know, but he sent a message to Sarili ordering him to desist on the instant or he would come with troops, but Governor Sir George Grey at the Cape rescinded the order for fear that such an action would indeed provoke a war. Surely the Xhosa would come to their senses?

The prophet Mhalakazi was now caught up in the success of his own lie and as the killing continued, he was repeatedly asked to name the day on which this army of black Russians was to arrive and as each date he named came and went, the lie got bigger. Unless *all* the cattle were killed – no exceptions – the new people would not come; and anyone who didn't

---

[193] Mostert, *Frontiers* p.1184
[194] Mostert, *Frontiers*, p. 1187
[195] C. Brownlee, *Reminiscences of Kaffir Life and History*, (Lovedale, South Africa) 1896 p. 137

believe this needed to be brought into line quick if the new people were not to go back to where they came from; but if all the cattle *were* killed then to the grand alliance of 'new people' and the black Russians would be added all the ancestors; and everyone who was sick or blind or lame would be healed and the old people would be rejuvenated; and everyone would get new cooking pots and no-one would have to go to work; and a hurricane would sweep the English away or possibly the sky would fall in on them.

Some of the clans had now slaughtered all their herds, emptied all their grain pits and were turning on those of their more sensible neighbours who had so far dismissed the hysteria. Brownlee was determined that the madness should not infect British Kaffraria and turned to Sandile in an attempt to get him to persuade Sarili to stop. Instead, Sandile joined in, as did the drunk Maqoma. By December 1856, the fate of the Xhosa was settled; they had killed the cattle, emptied the grain pits and had missed the rains that would allow them to sow for the next year's harvest; and still the miracles had not happened. Mhalakazi kept hope alive and death certain; the date for miracles would be January, or possibly February at the latest. Brownlee and the colonists began to stockpile food against the inevitable as a steady stream of clear-sighted Xhosa began to seek work and refuge among the farms of the Cape.

The date was set for 17th February 1857 and the Xhosa people duly gathered. On that day, a blood-red sun (or possibly two of them) would rise and immediately set (or wander about the sky for a bit possibly) in the east. Neither of them did. The same old sun came up, went across the sky and set in the west as, in their heart of hearts, everyone knew it would. And the Xhosa nation died.

You've seen the pictures of what a famine looks like on TV. This one was just the same but without the aid convoys or helicopters or C-130s dropping pallets full of food and medicine. There were no blue tents or field hospitals or refugee camps. Just a few missionaries doing what they could, frantically boiling up maize and sago to put a spoonful of mealipap into a dying child's mouth. Just a few British soldiers cursing the stupidity as they shared out their rations to the walking skeletons that collapsed around their posts. The colonists did what they could to accommodate the refugees, finding them employment on farms and road gangs; the population of British Kaffraria dropped from 105,000 to 37,500 in that terrible year of 1857; 25,000 went to the colony and probably 15,000 died. In the Transkei, there were probably 40,000 deaths. Another year would see a total of 150,000 Xhosa dispersed. Maqoma gave himself up to the colony and was sent to Robben Island. Sarili was booted off his land as punishment for his part in the massacre and Sandile lost so much of his clan that his status as a chief was virtually finished; most of the other chiefs accepted pensions from the British in return for shutting up; there was also the final extinction of those Bushmen who still eked out a living up in the mountains. Perhaps the only consolation was that Mhalakazi starved to death too. Nongqawuse survived and was taken to the colony where, beyond making a brief statement, she never said a word about the famine ever again.

Now pour the bloody vodka.

*

## The Transformation of South Africa

Up until the end of the 1850s, roughly speaking, South Africa would be just recognisable to someone who came out with Van Riebeeck and stayed around to see the 19th Century in. Of course, there would be differences, the most obvious being the disappearance of the Khoisan and the extension of the colony but you could probably drop down Old Jan in a Voortrekker wagon and he would probably recognise the place. You could give him a job on a farm and he'd know how to work the tools, how to keep the cattle, when to plant and when to harvest. You could take him to the harbour and he would be able to manage the surfboats bringing the cargo ashore and although he might gasp in wonder and amazement at the new-fangled steam ships, he would still be comforted by the fact that the vast majority of vessels were still powered by wind and steered by sextant and stars. He would understand the politics too; that the British were in charge now would make little difference to him because he would soon hear about how reluctant the government back home was to spend money on the defence or development of the colony in the same way that the VOC had been. He would be conversant with the topics that galvanized everyone; land, how to get it, how to hold onto it, and how to stop his kit, cattle and caboodle being lifted by the locals. After 1850, however, things would become less and less familiar and you would find him retiring to his *stoep* with his *mampoer* and tobacco and wondering where the years had gone and boring everybody rigid with his stories of what Cape Town was like before it ever became Cape Town (I know; I do this. So do you, probably. I went to Aiyu Napa when it was still Nipple Beach: I met my first South African there).

For a Xhosa, the change was more abrupt. Before 1850, his life was radically different than the one that he embarked upon after the killing of the cattle and although aspects of that life lived on for a little while in parts of the Transkei, in Basutoland, Natal, it was only over the Tugela in Zululand that it remained unchanged in everything but the minor things. From now on, for the average Xhosa, Andile and Akhona, life would be barely recognisable. For a start, they would probably not be under the authority of their chiefs for anything beyond minor matters because their new chief would be a 'resident' or 'magistrate' appointed by the British government. They might work for longer or shorter periods on European owned farms and these jobs would not be defined by gender; men would plough and hoe now as well as keep the cattle while women might enter service or work in any of the growing number of new occupations opening up. They would have a European master to direct their work and for at least part of the year, work they must for there would be a Hut tax to pay. A lot of things would be better; there would be relative peace, no more smellings-out, no more arbitrary rule by a chief who thought the law was his will and his will the law; there would be mission hospitals and schools; a wider and more varied diet – it seems incredible that most Africans would eat neither fish nor fowl back then - the chance to be his own boss. Some things would present a less attractive appearance; being your own boss meant accumulating capital and this could only be done by hard labour and thrift and as the accumulation of capital is the hardest thing in the world to achieve for a young person who doesn't have a large inheritance and a trust fund, the years ahead would mean grind. Andile would have to put away that old life of sitting in the sun drinking beer and watching the cattle while his wives cooked, cleaned and grew his crops; he might actually just have to content himself with just the one wife. He would also have to learn the ways of the Europeans of which he knew very little and, having little or no education, was ill-equipped to master; he could not start his life as a clerk in a warehouse as he was largely illiterate so the opportunities open to him were rarely greater than that of the common labourer; he would have to learn the uses of money rather than barter (it took the khoikhoin at the Cape twenty years to do this) and this under conditions of being poorly paid; and in front of him were the dangers of alcoholism presented by brandy and beer that was stronger than anything he was used to; it's still a curse today and Saturday night in a Karoo shebeen is as unattractive as anything you'll find on a pub crawl in Benidorm. He would also have to get used to new laws, laws which held him individually responsible for his actions rather than collectively - collective responsibility was an aspect of *uBuntu* which had both pros and cons to it - and he would have to get used to the ignorance of Europeans of his customs and traditions. Theal gives the example of a European stopped from shooting a *boomslanger*, a tree snake, at the last moment; for the European an obvious precaution, for the African, it was an attack on an ancestral spirit.[196] Increasingly, he would also have to stay put in the location assigned to him by the magistrate for the days of wandering off over the nearest border were coming to an end. For men of substance and intelligence and previous independence, this was surely a galling experience.

The population of the Cape now stood at roughly 350,000 people of whom about a third were European. Its principal exports of wool, hides, wine and food were worth £750,000 approximately but came nowhere close to meeting the cost of its imports which stood at about £1,400,000 carried in the 900 ships that called in at the Cape every year. Still, the situation was improving and by 1860, exports had doubled in value. Road Boards were established to replace the rough cart tracks with decent roads opening up the Karoo to commercial agriculture and newer, more accurate maps were being printed to aid the traveller, soldier and missionary; the biggest single item of expenditure in the Colony's accounts was on roads and bridges.[197] John Montagu, Charles Michell and Andrew Geddes Bain and his son Thomas Bain were the driving forces here;[198] Michell built Sir Lowry Coles pass in 1830 and so removed the century old necessity to either ruin your oxen by going straight up the mountains or head eastwards by first going north to Tulbagh; today you can stand at the top and watch the hang gliders – from above. Bains put in the Bainskloof Pass (gulp: 1800 feet of switchbacks and hairpins up a mountain that had been thought unpassable for two centuries) into Tulbagh and then Michells's pass from Tulbagh to Ceres and the amazing Piekeniers Pass from Picketberg to Citrusdal before handing over to his son, Thomas who subsequently built twenty-three major passes, including the Prince Alfred (hair-raising), the Tradouw (wild), the Pakhuis (staggeringly beautiful), and the Seven Passes road from Knysna (which town he laid out) to Plettenberg Bay. The Montagu pass was built with convict labour and opened in 1847 and since the 1980s has been beloved of lunatic mountain bike enthusiasts – and with Herold, there's a great wine farm at the top; Montagu was the administrator who got the Central Roads Bureau working to enable these fantastic

---

[196] Theal Vol IV, p.29
[197] Theal Vol. III, p. 137. All the statistics in this section can be easily accessed in Theal.
[198] David Fleminger, *Backroads of the Cape* (Joburg, 2005) p.100

developments. Some of this work was spectacular and anyone who hasn't got a drive through Meiringspoort, the great slashed passage through the Swartberg, on their bucket list will be much the poorer for it. The massive rocks were cracked out of the way by first clearing the vegetation, piling it on the rocks and burning it and then splitting them by rapid cooling by water. The ridge line looks like a great, crispy *mille feuille* that has been picked up and cracked by hand to expose the million different layers of crumbling rock. The railways were begun too in 1859 to provide a rapid and cheap form of bulk transport that the absence of any navigable river and the impossibility of building canals had previously forbidden. For the first time, goods might travel at a speed faster than 2mph.

More importantly, the nascent economy was approaching a point at which it might move beyond subsistence. South Africa was never a wealthy colony but in the things that mattered – plentiful food, enough work, financial stability – it was progressing to the point where it was possible for emigrants to arrive and not fear destitution. Perhaps most importantly of all, a local banking system had bedded in and had connected itself into the wider financial system based in London that was busy enabling the commerce of the world to grow like Topsy. This aspect of History is often neglected by Historians and especially economic Historians whom I shall now tarnish by pointing out that although they show admirable ability in being able to prove all sorts of things through the deft collection, collation, manipulation and presentation of any number of statistics, none of them seem to have ever understood the difference between economics and business. Indeed most of them appear to suffer from what the English philosopher Roger Scruton called 'the professor's constitutional disdain for the empty life of the executive'.[199] Business History as a discipline was virtually unknown until the 1980s and as a knowledge of finance was regarded among Left wing Historians in the same way as a dose of clap in a monastery, it was left to a Naval Historian called Nicholas Lambert, a man small in stature but tall in merit, to explain just how vital the financial system was to international trade.[200] (I met him when I gave a paper at the US Naval Academy in Annapolis: he asked an audience of the world's leading naval Historians if anyone knew who Robert Giffen was. I knew the answer but I was too shy to speak out in case I got it wrong in such august company. Answer: 19th Century Treasury statistician. I missed out on a Gold Star there).

This is how it worked. Let's say that the Clogs Mill Company in Yorkshire, England wants to buy a cargo of wool from the Grahamstown Wool Company. The first problem is that the chaps in Grahamstown want to be paid immediately but Clogs Mill needs to get the consignment shipped, spun, made into Norfolk Jackets, frock coats and knickerbockers and sold before they can pay. This is what is known as a Cash Flow problem and until it is resolved there can be no trade. Step forward those ever-helpful bankers to grease the wheels of industry and ease the flow of trade. Clogs goes along to a Merchant Bank and opens up a Line of Credit which allows the Merchant Bank to issue a time-dated Bill of Exchange (for a consideration of course). The Bill of Exchange is then sent by fast mail steamer to the Grahamstown Wool Company which, upon receipt of it, then puts the wool aboard a ship and

---

[199] R. Scruton, *Fools, Frauds and Firebrands: Thinkers of the New Left* (London 2015) Ch.3.
[200] N. Lambert, *Planning Armageddon*, (Harvard University Press), 2012.

obtains a Bill of Lading as proof the goods have been dispatched. Taking the two Bills in his hot little hands, the wool merchant then goes to his local Grahamstown bank and gets paid (minus a consideration). The banker then sends the Bill of Exchange and the Bill of Lading back by the fast steamer to the London Merchant Bank who cashes the Bill of Exchange up and forwards the Bill of Lading to Clogs Mill (for a consideration), who promptly nips down to Liverpool docks and picks his load up. Clogs Mill gets the wool, spins it up into the desired collection of Norfolk Jackets, frock coats and knickerbockers and flogs it for a tidy profit, Grahamstown gets his cash and the banks take a slice off both sides for providing the service, which then allows them to lend out capital to those who don't have it, but do have the ideas and skills to create a business, introduce new or improved products, provide employment and pay taxes. Problem solved and everyone's a winner, except the sour-faced old Marxists who hate to see anyone making a few bob but aren't averse to trousering the sweat of other peoples' brows in the form of the taxes that honest capitalists pay to keep those idle, dishonest and snobbish bookworms in clover.

Now this simple, secure and reliable system meant that trade could take place over vast distances without either the vendor or the purchaser ever fearing that he would never be paid or never get his goods, for that Bill of Exchange was as good as cash and that Bill of Lading was as good as a maiden's promise. So, it was for this reason that the Cape government wanted to build a breakwater and improve the dock facilities at Cape Town and was willing to pay a subsidy of £33,000pa to Donald Currie's Union Castle shipping line to carry the mails to and from Britain; the mails might have contained pink, scented wishes, birthday greetings and reams of advice from well-meaning aunties but the important part were those Bills of Lading and Exchange; the cost of a lighthouse or two was also thought worth the expense. The Cape government eagerly backed railway development for the same reason; the faster mails and goods went between the coast and the interior, the more business could be done, the more people employed, and the more profits made meant the more taxes were paid. That's how the capitalist system worked and as a method for enriching the world, it has never been bettered.

Getting people was always a problem for the colony. Despite the fact that there were abundant supplies of Xhosa labour available on the doorstep of the colony, they could not be induced to give up their less productive but more amenable lives around the cattle kraal in sufficient numbers. When they did apply for jobs, they tended to work for only as long as they needed to obtain the money to satisfy their immediate wants and then when that was done, they went back to the kraal. There were also issues of pay day; Europeans tended to work by Calendar month but Africans demanded payment by Lunar Month which added roughly 8% to the cost of labour (there are twelve Calendar months in a year as opposed to thirteen Lunar: if possible, young man, always insist on being paid weekly rather than monthly). Several farming schemes failed because of this; neither the cotton, tobacco or cane farmers could succeed because they needed a mass of labour for a short time only but at a specific time. Cane needs to be harvested *now now* not *just now*; leave it in the fields and the sugar content evaporates; drive down the N2 from Mtubatuba towards Durban today and you'll see dedicated lodges for the gangs of sugar cane harvesters who move up and down the coast as needed. Shortage of labour was less of a problem after the Xhosa cattle killing for obvious reasons and many refugees were employed on public works such as the building of roads, courthouses, prisons, schools, hospitals etc.

During the mid-1850s, however, the answer seemed to lie in promoting emigration from Europe and in 1855 an Act in the Cape Parliament was passed to do just this. It was hoped thereby to bring in skills, labour and add to the available manpower for the defence of the colony and although there was an element of 'race' involved here, too much should not be read into it as evidence of the roots of Apartheid; nothing of the kind was envisaged. Several hundred Dutch orphans were shipped in and apprenticed out to the farmers, free passage was offered to British settlers, Emigration Agents were employed and Immigration Boards set up to receive new arrivals. After the Crimean War, members of the German Legion who had been recruited to fight for Britain were offered plots of land and left their mark on the landscape in places like Stutterheim in the Eastern Cape and New Germany in KwaZulu-Natal. In 1858-59, 6343 British settlers took up the offer and quickly applied for their families to follow. This was a remarkable influx. When it was combined with the spread of government (still ridiculously light-touch when compared with 21st century Britain) in the form of magistrates, district councillors, the surveying of land and the fixing of weights and measures, it all added to the feeling that the colony was now 'settled' and 'advancing in civilisation'. By now, it was also raising its own regular defence force, the Frontier Armed and Mounted Police based at Grahamstown and manned largely by English settlers, which followed the Commando model but was wholly paid for by the Colony rather than the imperial government. By and large, the Cape was beginning to look European, rather than African, an impression that is maintained today both in demographics and architecture; Karoo towns like Montagu bear resemblance to Andalucia, Cape Dutch architecture is distinct but Germanic, and the white-washed, thatched cottages found all the way from the Cape to Grahamstown remind you of Cornwall.

Natal was rather different as it contained a much larger proportion of Africans to Europeans but those Africans tended to belong to clans that had been shattered by the *mfecane* and so were much more willing to accept being allocated 'reservations' or 'locations'. Again, these words have acquired negative connotations and have come to be associated with Apartheid over time but they should not be taken as evidence of some deep colonial plot. Rather the aim was to settle the people and let them get on with their lives in whichever way suited them best – minus smellings-out and the rest of it – overseen by a European magistrate. Interactions between Europeans and Africans were necessarily more frequent and it is one of those interesting facts that even those Europeans who grew up under Apartheid prided themselves on being 'Natal boys' who could speak isiZulu.

*

Outside British territory, not much did change during the 1850s. The creation of the Orange Free State in 1852 relieved the Cape of the immediate responsibility for all the problems of lawlessness, cattle theft and commando but it did not solve them. However much the inhabitants of the Free State wished to conciliate their much more powerful neighbour,

Moshweshe, his ability to restrain theft from his side of the frontier remained strictly limited. Nor were the Oorlam, Koranna, Bushmen or the Griqua leaders much interested in maintaining order when they had previously made quite a good living out of disorder. It was for this reason that the leaders of the Orange Free State began to make overtures to be readmitted to the Colony; fifteen thousand Europeans were just not enough to form a functioning state. The suggestion, however, was simply not countenanced in London where the view remained that the only thing of value was the Cape naval facilities. The emigrant farmers were welcome to move back to the colony and take up employment any time they chose to but there could be no advantage whatsoever to either Britain or the colony in further expansion into a troubled and unpromising interior. They then turned to the Transvaal for help and proposed unification with them but this too came to nothing when it was realized that such a move would bring an end to the Sand River Convention.

The precariousness of the position of the Free Staters was clear and then made doubly so when war broke out with the Basuto in 1858 over the usual issues – land and cattle theft – and Moshweshwe roundly thrashed them. The fact that he chose not to wipe the whole country off the map was because he was shrewd enough not to bite off more than he could chew; further intervention would bring in the Boers from the Transvaal and quite possibly the British too and though he now knew how to make his own gunpowder and had started to acquire artillery, he was very aware that he would have a thin time of it if both the Transvaal and the British came against him.

From then on, the Free Staters were embattled. The Basuto held the whip hand and did as they pleased while Moshweshewe restrained his wilder clan leaders only so far as to maintain his authority and avoid provoking the British. Frontier farms were robbed and wrecked. Basuto colonists moved into wide areas around Harrismith and Winberg. Appeals for the British to intervene, adjudicate, mediate were all rejected. When the British were finally persuaded to get involved in demarcating the border, Moshweshewe paid lip service to Governor Wodehouse' award and then ignored it. Robbery, cattle-lifting and squatting became general. Inevitably, the Free Staters began to go into mental laager; in 1864 a new constitution was promulgated in which the franchise was restricted to whites only. A year later, with nothing left to lose, they declared war on the Basuto.

*

Things were not much better in the Transvaal where, among the fractious and independent inhabitants a rough divide had opened up between the followers of Andries Pretorius and those of Hendrik Potgeiter. Actual formal government was almost non-existent; there was little revenue, taxes were optional, barely a currency and when Potgeiter died in 1852 followed by Pretorius in 1853, no real leadership; Theal reckoned that few people outside of southern Africa were aware of its existence;[201] there wasn't a constitution until 1856 and though it had a capital at Potchefstroom, it hadn't drawn up any boundaries. And no sooner had it elected its first president, Marthinus Pretorius, son of the late Andries, than there was a

---

[201] Theal, Vol IV, p.27

rebellion against it by the Boers up in the Zoutspanberg and the Republic of Lydenberg became the instant rival to the South African Republic (ZAR) and was followed by the district of Utrecht, which also claimed to be independent. None of these Republics were worth a tinker's cuss and when Pretorius invaded the Orange Free State to try to dragoon it into union, the Free Staters resisted with the aid of a Commando from Lydenburg. It didn't come to blows in the end as Paul Kruger brokered a peace deal which left the Free State, er, free, and an attempt at kiss-and-make-up with the Lydenburgers resulted in re-unification in 1858. Within a couple of years, however, the ZAR had broken up in civil war – well, 'civil skirmish' anyway; no more than a handful were killed during the three years of strife (1861-4). What this meant was that the Free State became ever more determined to stay out of any union with the Transvaal.

What united the Boers though was their sense of isolation amid terrible danger and their increasing willingness to use extreme violence in defence of themselves, a facet illustrated by the events that took place at Makapan's Poort in 1854 when Hermanus Potgeiter, brother of the late Hendrick Potgeiter, went on a winter hunting trip. The details of what happened are necessarily obscure; Hermanus was said to be a man of 'violent temper and rough demeanour'[202] while Makapan (or *Mokopane*, more properly) was of 'ferocious disposition' and so the possibility of trouble was high up on the cards. When Hermanus gave some offence, Makapan responded by massacring and mutilating his whole party of twenty-three men, women and children and, so it was said, flaying Hermanus alive and using his skin as a kaross. A Commando was called out and Makapan fled into the caves that now bear his name at the Makapangat World Heritage Archeological Site, about an hour's drive north of modern day Pretoria. The caves are large and tortuous perhaps 600 metres deep and 120 metres wide in places and into them disappeared Makapan and 3000 of his people. An attempt was made to get into the entrance of the cave but when this proved impossible, Field Cornet Paul Kruger was among those who decided to block up the mouth of the cave and lay siege to it and for twenty-five days anyone who came out in search of water was shot down. By the time, Kruger went back in 1800 people were dead of dehydration, starvation and gunshot. Legend has it that Makapan got away by strapping himself under a cow but the real significance of this terrible encounter is that the level of violence on both sides had reached appalling proportions.

Nor was this an isolated incident. Referring to the revolt of the Bamapela clan in 1858, Theal's language betrays a real weariness at the endless cycle of ever escalating violence: 'The outbreak began in the *usual* manner, by the murder of a party of Europeans and the seizure of their property. But it was speedily suppressed.' [203] *Speedily suppressed*: Kruger, now promoted from Field Cornet to Commandant led a Commando that killed 800 men for the loss of only one of his, which suggests a sustained, brutal and merciless assault. Cruelty, it seems, was *normal*. What is perhaps just as concerning is that in after years that cruelty was celebrated; the town of Potgeitersrus was later named after Hermanus' son who was killed

---

[202] Theal, Vol IV, p.28.
[203] Theal Vol. IV p. 126. My italics.

during the siege of the caves only to have its name changed years later, when the ANC took over, to Mokopane.

Added to this was the ongoing problem of trying to get the country settled and by that I mean 'trying to end the disruption of the *mfecane* and giving everyone a place to live'. In both the Boer Republics, there were still substantial groups of individuals and clans who struggled with the concept of land ownership and who were willing to sell up the lands allocated to them for greater or lesser sums. Many clans held the view that migrating from one place to another might provide better prospects than farming the land they actually occupied and as a result the countryside was riven with theft, vagabondage and murder and the only law in day-to-day usage was the appeal to superior force. The Zoutspanberg was so troubled by disease, tsetse fly, European renegades and quarrelling clans (who might be variously described as Venda or Shangaan but were, like Moshweshwe's people, a complete mix), that it was almost abandoned during the later 1860s and those Boers who remained were paying tribute to the local clans to avoid being burned out. The Swazis added to the problem by being utterly ruthless in the defence of their territory and willing to commit huge atrocities to achieve this; during one incident alone in June 1864, a Swazi *impi* fell upon the clan of Malewu and killed 854 men plus 2840 women and children and turned those who survived into yet more refugees.[204] The ZAR sought to bring an end to this chaos by assigning locations to the various African clans on the understanding that good, quiet behaviour would guarantee occupation. Actual ownership was denied to prevent sale to the more rapacious European adventurers and carpet-baggers who were an added plague in both Boer republics; from then on, a contract between a European and an African was only valid if given the nod by the Field Cornet. Individuals were also required to settle and if they had no clan they were assigned to a particular Boer. The sale of guns and ammunition to Africans was prohibited (again) as was booze and slavery.

This last law was controversial because although the British had insisted on it as part of their allowing the Boers to go their own way at the Sand River Convention, many Boers were not opposed to the practice on religious or economic grounds. In practical terms too, the emancipation of the slaves had merely resulted in people with no sellable skills facing the prospect of being turned out of their positions and set upon the highway and so new forms of dependency and subordination had emerged to fill the gap. The most common of these was the 'apprenticeship' system already discussed and although the trade in apprentices was theoretically forbidden, this was a law easily evaded. 'Slim' Piet Joubert, one of the most prominent of the Boer leaders bought and sold apprentices in complete defiance of the law and with pretty much complete impunity. Having said that, Theal quite rightly points out that when the ZAR was annexed by Britain in 1877, no slaves were emancipated because none could be found. He also said, and he never said a truer word, that the answer to the question of whether African children were better off apprenticed to the Boer or brought up as slaves of the conquering African tribe was 'answered in 1864, and will be answered to-day, according to the bias of the individual.'[205] It's a rare thing to see someone change their mind.

---

[204] Theal. Vol IV, p.148
[205] Theal, Vol. IV p.158.

## Sea Change

One of the problems with writing History lies in the matter of boundaries. The fact is that you can't cover everything and everything is, to a greater or lesser extent, connected. The problem is usually resolved by writing books with titles like *A History of England* or *Germany 1870-1945* which give you a strong indication that the writers have decided to plump for a boundary line equivalent to a national border. Other writers set their boundaries with titles like *Europe 1789-1914* or *The Pacific War 1941-45* which imply that the subject matter is not going to be restricted to a discussion of any single country. When it comes to writing about the British Empire, well, wider still and wider shall those bounds be set and so Historians specialise in all sorts of ways to try and make sense of either a bit of the Empire or to see it in its totality.

Writing about South African History poses the same problems but because Apartheid South Africa was cut off from much of academia those problems are a little deeper. As we have seen, most South African Historians working during the Apartheid era were doing their best to understand how they found themselves in their present predicament, while back in Blighty the emphasis among serious Historians was on how Britain acquired its empire, how it worked and why it disappeared, while the non-serious Historians (the Marxists) were mainly engaged in shouting slogans about racism, oppression, the inevitable triumph of the workers and ignoring any evidence that contradicted their conspiracy theories. No-one seemed to give much more than a passing nod to the wider international situation of the 19th Century and whether events in the rest of the world affected what happened in South Africa. Somewhere, it seemed to me, the essential fact of the Cape's value being primarily as a naval station had got lost and so I decided to see if there was a stronger connection between the significance of that fact, what was going on in the wider world and what was going on in South Africa itself.

I started off investigating the Anglo-Zulu War of 1879 and immediately stumbled on some pieces of information that sparked my curiosity. The first was that the chap who started the war, Sir Bartle Frere, had spent most of his life as an administrator in the Indian Empire, was a defence expert and had been sent out to the Cape just as a global war was brewing over a crisis in the Balkans. Surely these things were connected? To my mind they were. The second piece of information that came to hand was the fact that before 1870-ish, the common view of the Empire in Britain was that it was a bit of a hangover and was probably likely to shake itself loose and disappear over the horizon in the not too distant future. This was clearly not the view of the later Victorians, so what and how did that all change and what effect would that have on South Africa? My conclusions were presented in *The Zulu and the Raj: The Life of Sir Bartle Frere* and *Imperial Defence and the Commitment to Empire*, two tomes of such staggering brilliance – 'a brilliant exposition' is what the brilliant historian Stephen Badsey said of my brilliant conclusions as we bounced down the track to Rorke's Drift in 2009 under the brilliant sunshine - that you will be unable to resist acquiring copies; (they are available on Amazon for a song). To save your pocket, however, what follows is a condensed version of some of the arguments made in those books.

\*

Basically speaking, from 1815 up to around 1860, the strange conglomeration of territories, colonies and protectorates that was the British Empire was strategically secure from any real threat. Certainly, it had to be defended by the expenditure of blood and treasure on a regular basis, but the fact that British troops and sailors had, at various times in the living memory of those around in 1860, occupied Paris, burned Washington, Delhi, Peking, Sebastopol and, almost, St. Petersburg (the Russians surrendered just in time), in pursuit of a measure of security indicated Britain's ability to hold her own in a dangerous world. As a result, before the 1870s, there was little interest in the empire beyond its capacity for adventurous entertainment, and the overwhelming assumption held by the political classes was that it would disintegrate as the settlement colonies gained ever greater self-government[206] and India, later rather than sooner perhaps, regained the sovereignty that the Moghuls had squandered. Perhaps a warning note should have been heard in the continued possession of the sugar colonies in the West Indies, worthless in economic terms since the 1830s, but devoid of any alternative authority to whom they could reasonably be palmed off on.[207] What the British wanted was the maximum of trade with the minimum of territorial possession; naval bases, victualling stations and emporiums like Gibraltar, the Cape and Hong Kong were welcome, as were useful islands like Malta, St. Helena and Bermuda but territorial control was to be avoided if at all possible. Even in India, it was felt that enough was enough and the overwhelming view was that if control in a particular region was absolutely necessary, then 'paramountcy' or 'preponderating influence' – what we would today call 'soft power' - was the preferred option.

Straightforward abandonment of territorial empire was not contemplated because it would create unimaginable upheavals; there were kinship links; the Raj was a major employer both in India and in Britain; the French would take advantage, move in and shut out British trade; there wouldn't be a 'Rupee or a Virgin between the Khyber and Ceylon' (as the saying went) in the general post-Raj scramble; the loss of India might well jeopardise trading interests further east in Singapore and Hong Kong. If any attempt to abandon the empire in a hurry was made, therefore, the first massacre would take place in Parliament and this, the Whig-Peelite-Liberal coalition that dominated the mid-Victorian Parliament, would not risk. The Empire existed as a political *fact* that could not be abandoned without repercussions too dangerous, too complex, too destabilising, too politically damaging to be predicted. So the British became essentially reactive to the question of Empire, defending it where expedient and encouraging piecemeal separation where possible by the granting of self-government and the withdrawal of troops.

This meant, therefore, that if the empire was not to be abandoned wholesale then the routes connecting its constituent parts would have to be defended. In the decades after the Napoleonic Wars this was hardly onerous because the British had the money, the navy and enough of an army to see off potential challengers but beginning with the Crimean War, 1854-56, this all began to change. The patchy performance of the army and Britain's inability to raise sufficient troops conceded leadership of the Crimean War against Russia to

---

[206] Vincent J. (Ed.), *The Diaries of Edward Henry Stanley, 15th Earl of Derby (1826-93), Between 1878 and 1893*, (Oxford, 2003). Entry 11th January 1884. Derby Diaries.
[207] D.K.Fieldhouse, *The Colonial Empires: A Comparative Survey from the Eighteenth Century*, (London, 1966), p. 259.

the French; the Indian Mutiny of 1857-58 advertised British vulnerability further and, when Napoleon III invaded Italy in 1859, fears of French hegemony sparked off a war scare. In 1864, Britain was forced to watch helplessly when Bismarck invaded Denmark against British opposition, an experience repeated in Austria, 1866 and France in 1870. With no large continental style army, Britain could deploy little influence to affect the construction of a new European balance made in Berlin.[208] Meanwhile, across the Atlantic during the 1860s, the American Civil War publicly advertised to all who cared to look that the potential of the United States could at any time be mobilised to mop up Canada[209] and make herself felt as a global maritime presence.[210] Nor had the Russians been idle; if they had turned away from Europe after 1856, it was only to continue their advance to the borders of India. Britain's industrial and commercial lead was also diminishing as Europe and America industrialised,[211] while the revolution in naval design brought on by the change from sail and wood to steam and iron was undermining the overwhelming naval preponderance that Britain had previously enjoyed.[212] By 1870, therefore, many Britons had been shaken out of any feelings of easy dominance and superiority that they might have entertained[213] and forced to recognise that their own security and that of the empire needed to be reviewed and upgraded.

The most important trade routes were across the Atlantic to America and across the North Sea to Germany but the most vulnerable were the routes to India and East. The long Cape route was the most secure for the transport of troops, goods and mails because the Royal Navy could dominate the Atlantic but its very length made it a poor choice for the rapid communication demanded by both official and commercial interests. By far the most popular was the 'Overland' route via Alexandria, Cairo, Suez and the Red Sea. During the 1830s, trials of steam vessel navigation of the Red Sea had begun and by 1839 a regular postal service had been established by which commercial and official mails were despatched according to an agreed schedule. The beginning of a railway from Alexandria to Suez speeded up the passage further (and made it healthier by limiting the amount of time spent in areas visited by the plague) until a journey time of 40 days between London and Bombay was not unrealistic. High value, low bulk freight also began to use the Overland route, especially after the railway was completed in 1858, and during the Indian Mutiny of 1857, troops had also been permitted to cross Egyptian territory on their way to Karachi, Bombay and Calcutta. The weakness in this arrangement was that in time of crisis the link was at the mercy of the Egyptian authorities and – because the mails went to London from Alexandria via Paris – the French. As far as defending this route went, Britain had bases at Gibraltar and Malta, but the Eastern Mediterranean was dominated by the Islamic powers of Ottoman Turkey and her nominal vassal, Egypt.

---

[208] M. Schwartz, *The Politics of British Foreign and defence policy in the era of Gladstone and Disraeli*, (London, 1985), pp. 27-28.
[209] J. Luvaas, *The Education of an Army: British Military Thought, 1815-1940*, (London, 1965), p.109.
[210] See J.T.Scharf, *History of the Confederate States Navy*, (New York, 1996, first published 1887). See also W.F.Moneypeny and G.E. Buckle, *The Life of Benjamin Disraeli*, (London, 1929) Vol.II p.67 for Disraeli's recognition of US power.
[211] Bernard Porter, *The Lion's Share. A short History of British Imperialism 1850 – 1983*, (Longman; London 1984), pp. 75-6.
[212] P. Kennedy, *The Rise and Fall of British Naval Mastery*, (London, 1983), p.7. Also John F. Beeler, *British Naval Policy in the Gladstone-Disraeli Era, 1866 – 1880*, (Stanford 1997), pp.2-3.
[213] W.S.Hamer, *The British Army Civil-Military Relations 1885-1905*, (Oxford, 1970), p.30.

There was also the expansion of the telegraph routes so vital to an expanding commerce to consider. By the beginning of the 1860s, telegraph wires were constructed to link India to Europe via the Persian Gulf and Constantinople and experiments were well underway to lay submarine cables through the Mediterranean and Red seas. By the end of the 1870s, a plethora of telegraph lines existed which connected London and India via France, Russia, Belgium, Turkey, Italy, Germany and Austria, with the most secure being the Falmouth-Gibraltar-Malta-Alexandria-Red Sea-Aden-Bombay submarine cable route. By 1876, messages could be passed by telegraph from London to Bombay in five hours but this route was, again, at the mercy of the Egyptian authorities who could interdict the cable route as it went overland between Alexandria and Suez. This situation was made more serious by the fact that the only secure alternative cable route to India, via South Africa, did not reach past the Cape Verde Islands until the end of 1879, a distance of sixteen days steaming from Cape Town.[214]

The building of the Suez Canal between 1859-69 brought all these security fears into sharper focus. Built by French engineers, using French capital and being a conscious expression of a determination to expand French influence in an Egypt already used to it, the first ship to pass through the canal was the French Imperial yacht *Aigle*.[215] At a stroke the sailing distance between Britain and India was cut in half and seven weeks was cut off the journey time; it was cheaper too - £140 per head in 1843 to £68 in 1875 – which meant that more and more of the lifeblood of British trade would go through an area that was ever more vulnerable.[216] If ever the canal was closed to British shipping then the Cape would become the only viable route for troops, goods and the all-important Bills of Lading and Exchange stuffed into bags aboard the mail steamers.

What about the Royal Navy? Couldn't the empire be defended by Britannia's trident? There is little reason to doubt that the dream of every British admiral was to bring the enemy to battle in a great fleet engagement and deliver a victory to rival Nelson's at Trafalgar, an outcome never in doubt. The reality was rather more prosaic; blockade duty against an enemy fleet unlikely to risk itself against the superior skill and power of the Royal Navy. The real threat was a sustained attack against British commerce afloat,[217] the value of which was both staggering and unprecedented (and if you want this in today's prices, the rough guide to getting them is to multiply by fifty); merchandise exports worth £286,400,000 and imports of £411,000,000 went in and out of British ports in 1880 alone;[218] at Malta 2947 sailing and 1733 steam vessels visited the port in 1871;[219] in 1876 £190,000,000 worth of trade went around the Cape alone.[220] In 1879, the Treasury reckoned that trade going around

---

[214] Carnarvon to Frere, 26th January 1878 PRO CO 959/1 Frere Correspondence; also Frere to Carnarvon 8th March 1877, PRO 30/6/33. The cable from the Azores to Cape Town was completed by Christmas 1879 and the India-Aden-Zanzibar-Durban was completed in 1881. See also Farnie, *East and West of Suez*, p.272.
[215] Hoskins, *British Routes to India*, p. 370.
[216] Capt. H.W. Tyler RE Railway Dept, Board of Trade, "Routes of Communication with India," in RUSI Journal Vol. 10 1867.
[217] J.J.A. Simmonds 2nd May 1877, Carnarvon Papers PRO 30/6/115 Military Memoranda Turkey and India 1877. "The late Duke of Wellington constantly urged the importance of placing our leading commercial harbours…in a state of defence". See also J.C.R. Colomb (Ed), *The Defence of Great and Greater Britain*, (London, 1880). See also 20th March 1878 Colonial Office Circular to all Colonies, CO 885/4/14 June 1878.
[218] Chris Cook and Brendan Keith, *British Historical Facts 1830 – 1900* (London, 1975), pp. 244 – 249.
[219] Customs Statistics and Shipping Returns for the Cape of Good Hope, 1856 - 70. PRO CO 959/1 Frere Correspondence.
[220] Carnarvon to Disraeli, October 1876 (?). PRO CP 30/6/11 Cabinet. Prime Minister 1874 Feb. - 1878 Jan.

the Cape to and from Britain was worth £100,000,000 pa and then three years later upped this figure to £150,000,000.[221] Trade between Britain and India, China and the Far East was worth £66,000,000 pa, exclusive of the value of the ships that carried it – 25,090 merchant vessels registered in Britain, with a further 13,158 registered in colonial ports.[222] Britain's commerce was worth £900,000,000 pa with £144,000,000 worth of freight and shipping afloat at any one time;[223] for comparison, government expenditure was approximately £60,000,000 pa. The capture of even a small proportion of these lucrative cargoes and ships was a temptation to the enemy that could not be ignored and a determined raid would instantly cause insurance rates to rocket, discourage ships from leaving ports and encourage ship owners to put their vessels under neutral flags.[224] The disruption to trade caused by the loss of a bag full of Bills of Exchange could be devastating; the resulting cash flow crisis would bring about a business coronary. For a country that depended on imported food for half its population, this also was a very real concern.[225]

The threat to the shipping lanes came not from the great ironclad battleships but from small, lightly armed, converted merchant vessels acting as 'Cruizers' and from privateers. These vessels, although no match for any regular man of war, were perfectly adequate for the interception of merchant shipping because they were quicker and had a much longer range. A merchant vessel might, under a combination of sail and steam, travel to Australia and back refuelling only once and such a vessel, filled up with coal and ammunition rather than cargo, and resupplied by rendezvous, could keep the sea almost indefinitely, moving at a speed of 8-10 knots, barring accidents. In contrast, an ironclad battleship burned up so much coal that it needed constant re-supply[226] and could barely keep up with cruisers able to steam at *"full speed* for almost as many *days* as our war cruisers can *hours*."[227] Bolting a couple of guns onto a merchant steamer instantly turned it into a viable weapon of war when employed against unarmed steamers and an absolutely lethal one when employed against the 25% of the British merchant fleet that was still under sail in 1879.[228] Just how lethal these vessels could be had been demonstrated in the American Civil War during the celebrated cruises of the Confederate navy.[229] Indeed, the *Alabama* resonates constantly through the strategic thought of the period and its name became almost a household word in political circles. This is actually quite important because these voyages illustrated just how vulnerable the empire and its trade was. Think *U-boats* and you will begin to understand the significance of these commerce raiders.

Lacking a navy upon the outbreak of war,[230] the Confederate states improvised one by converting merchant ships into cruisers and by ordering the construction of specially

---

[221] PRO CAB 7/4 Third Report of the Royal Commissioners appointed to inquire into the Defence of British Possessions and Commerce Abroad, (Carnarvon Commission), 1882.
[222] Colomb, *The Defence of Great and Greater Britain*, p.30.
[223] PRO CAB 7/2 First Report of the Royal Commissioners appointed to inquire into the Defence of British Possessions and Commerce Abroad, (Carnarvon Commission), 8th September 1879.
[224] PRO CAB 7/2.
[225] Colomb, *The Defence of Great and Greater Britain*, p. 23.
[226] T. Symes Prideaux Esq, "On Economy of fuel in ships of war," RUSI Journal, Vol.16, 1873. See also Lt. R.S. Lowrey, RN. "On Coaling ships or squadrons on the open sea," RUSI Journal, Vol. 27, 1884.
[227] ADM 1/8869 p. 28. Also PRO CAB 7/3 Second Report of the Royal Commissioners appointed to inquire into the defence of British Possessions and Commerce Abroad (Carnarvon Commission). March 1882. Part I: The Duties of the Navy.
[228] PRO CAB 7/2
[229] Colomb (Ed), *The Defence of Great and Greater Britain*, pp.75-81.
[230] J.R. Hamilton (late CSN). "The American Navy; its organisation, ships, armament, and recent experiences," RUSI Journal, Vol.12 1869.

designed commerce raiders from shipyards in Britain and France. A host of small vessels scored spectacular successes during the war and the post-war US government sued Britain for $15,500,000 in damages caused by those cruisers built in British ports alone. Although most of the Confederate operations took place in the North Atlantic and along the sea-lanes running between Europe, Brazil and New England, the real potential of these cruisers was demonstrated by the *Alabama* and the *Shenandoah*. Purpose built on Merseyside in 1862, the *Alabama* attacked the US shipping off Tenerife, Newfoundland, Martinique, Venezuela, the Gulf of Mexico, Brazil, the Cape and on as far as the Bay of Bengal and the Sunda Strait before she was finally sunk off Cherbourg by the *USS Kearsarge*. The *Shenandoah* was even more successful. Sailing from Liverpool in October 1864 as a replacement for the *Alabama*, she cruised off Australia taking 9 ships, and then demolished the US Arctic whaling fleet in the Bering Strait, taking 24 ships in a week in June 1865, before returning to Liverpool by way of Cape Horn, and thus demonstrating the global reach that cruisers possessed.[231]

The example of the Confederate cruisers was significant not simply for their exploits but because of the precedent set by the fact that they evaded the Union blockade by building and fitting out in neutral ports. If the British could supply cruisers to the enemies of the United States, then it stood to reason that the United States could supply cruisers to Britain's enemies. This was certainly the view taken by the Foreign Office who, in agreeing to pay US claims for the damage caused by the British built cruisers by the Treaty of Washington, 8th May 1871, 'realised that her [Britain's] conduct had created a precedent for fitting out warships in America or other neutral waters that might be used to destroy British commerce in any future war.'[232]

The effects of extensive and effective commerce raiding would have been enormous. Although the cruisers would probably be defeated[233] and material losses could probably be made good in the long run – and the failure of the U-boats in both World wars to starve Britain into submission indicates that an attack on the food supply to the British Isles would probably not succeed - the moral effects probably could not. It was widely held that "our power in India [and the rest of the Empire] rests as much on prestige as upon the actual strength of our military forces"[234] and such raids would advertise to all who cared to look that the British Empire was a paper tiger rather than a puissant lion.[235]

All this meant that people in London were now having to think about the empire in an entirely different way; new threats from Germany and the USA; Russia advancing on India through Central Asia; and with every shovel full of sand shifted at Suez, this new jugular was exposed to the influence of France. This was a crisis on the routes to India that Britain could not afford to ignore; either she occupied the vital strategic positions, "the strong places of the world"[236] as Disraeli put it, and demonstrated her will and ability to defend them in the belief

---

[231] This section is drawn from J.T.Scharf, *History of the Confederate States Navy*, (New York, 1996, first published 1887). See also National Archives of the USA 1934 M0275/2 and MO275/3 The War of the Rebellion: A Compilation of the Official Records of the Union and Confederate Navies. See also F.J. Merli, *Great Britain and the Confederate Navy 1861 - 65*, (London, 1970).
[232] S.E. Morrison, H.S Commager and W.E. Leuchtenburg, *The Growth of the American Republic*, (London, 1969), Vol 1. p. 771.
[233] OIOC IOR Mss.Eur.D. 604/11 Hartington Papers. *The Defence of India*. Major-General C.M. MacGregor QMG India. Precis with comments by Col. A.C. Cameron, Intelligence Branch March 1885.
[234] CAB 11/81 Report on the General Scheme of coast defence for India, November, 1879.
[235] Many of the cruiser exploits of the Confederate navy and those envisaged by the Russian navy were enacted in WWI by the German navy, especially during the cruise of the *Emden*. See J.Keegan, *Intelligence in War*, (London, 2003), ch.4.

that the responsibilities of empire were justified by the rewards, or she refused and diminished to nothing more than an 'island bristling with bayonets.'[237]

*

## Basutoland

The war that began in 1865 and rumbled on until 1868 between the Free State and Moshweshwe's Basutos produced several unexpected results. The first was that the Boer Commandos proved themselves equal to the task of defeating the Basuto, a task that had so far eluded them. By attacking the crops and grain stores, running off the livestock and, not least, learning the difficult art of storming the hill forts, they demonstrated the will and the ability to reach into just about all parts of Basutoland and although the great fortress of Thaba Bosigo was never taken, no one thought that it was impregnable any more. The second surprise was the inability of Moshweshwe to assemble enough force to defeat the Boers who were still, by any reasonable measure, militarily inferior. In truth, the old man was ailing, his sons were fractious and the weakness of the clan system when placed under stress showed up in a general fracturing of his rule. As a nation, the Basutos were barely a generation old and the habits of precipitate flight in the face of an enemy that had been ingrained during the *mfecane* meant that there was little appetite for a 'backs to the wall' fight when the option of heading down into Natal or the Transkei remained to hand.

This was the difference; the Free Staters had the courage and determination born of desperation. For them, it really was a war of survival and the various terms offered to the Basutos during the conflict reflected this; loss of land, dispossession, the expulsion of the French missionaries whom they blamed for stirring up the Basuto and the breakup of the nation into separately recognised and more easily managed chiefdoms. By far the biggest surprise of all was Moshweshwe's request for Basutoland to be annexed to the British Crown – and the subsequent British agreement to this remarkable proposal.

There was a History to this. Governor Sir George Grey had fielded several such requests during the early 1860s, he being of the opinion that they were not seriously intended. 'Moshesh from time to time sends in letters to this government, vague from him not understanding exactly what he wants, from his ignorance of our customs and vaguer still from his use of figurative language,' he told London.[238] As the war began to go against the Basutos however, Sir Philip Wodehouse (Governor 1862-70) was presented with requests of a more pressing urgency especially as Moshweshwe was already telling the Free Staters that he was a subject of the Queen and his lands under Colonial jurisdiction. Wodehouse regarded this as no more than an ingenious negotiating tactic and was inclined to ignore his requests to come under the British flag as every other governor to date had done. In October 1865, he wrote to London to assure them that he had no intention whatsoever of accepting Moshweshwe's requests only to execute a screeching U-turn three months later. At the beginning of 1866, he announced his view that Moshweshwe's requests should finally be acceded to.

---

[236] W.F.Moneypeny and G.E. Buckle, *The Life of Benjamin Disraeli*, (London, 1929), Vol.II p. 69.
[237] Colomb, *The Defence of Great and Greater Britain*, p. 41.
[238] Grey to Newcastle, 14th August 1861. CO 879/2

Wodehouse was an austere man, with a vast experience of colonial administration in Ceylon and the West Indies and not much given to entertaining the desires of the colonists themselves when they contradicted the interests of the mother country. What he did believe in though was good government based on pragmatic principles and it was this belief that led to his conversion to the cause of annexation. In a despatch to London dated January 13th 1866 he set out the reasons for his conversion.[239] First off, he said, Moshweshwe was actually sincere in his desire to come under British government and in this he was backed by the majority of his tribe, a concurrence without which no such move could be contemplated. 'Matters have been going on in this country from bad to worse for the last ten years,' complained one of the chiefs. 'There is neither government, law or justice in the country. The Chiefs are powerless to govern or to check crime. Everyone does what he likes with impunity.' Here was a heartfelt cry indeed.

Secondly, continued Wodehouse, the Orange Free State was too weak to stand on its own feet which meant a constant dissatisfaction with the Cape government for not going to the aid of the Burghers whenever they got into trouble with the Basutos; as neither side was strong enough to defeat the other this was a situation that would persist until 'the impoverishment of both races' was the result. Thirdly, under present circumstances he believed the Basutos to be capable of increasing in wealth if only they could count on settled government but, with Moshweshwe failing, the prospect of disintegration, civil war and defeat in detail by the Free State looming, good prospects could only be guaranteed by annexation. That defeat was virtually guaranteed was a result of the Sand River Convention between the Cape and the Free State that allowed for the purchase of ammunition by the Free State but not by the Basutos. Last, but not least, the Free State would probably welcome annexation as removing a constant threat and thus allowing them to get on with managing their farms.

London disagreed and said so. In official circles, the view was that empire was a burden and a relic of times past. The Cape was a valuable naval station with some irritating problems attached to it which were to be managed but under no circumstances added to. Wodehouse, however, still believed that annexation was the right thing to do and, his hand strengthened by an outbreak of missionary agitation, submitted his proposals once more. This time he was supported by Lt-Governor Keate of Natal who was concerned that the war between the Free State and the Basutos was spilling over the Drakensberg passes to disrupt trade and deter the arrival of new colonists. Theophilus Shepstone, the Natal Secretary for Native Affairs, had held a meeting with the Basuto chiefs to spell out what British rule meant for them – the Crown would be paramount; smelling-out would be banned; criminal offences would be tried according to British law and civil offences would follow Basuto custom only if the British magistrate agreed – and still they wanted the security and protection of that British rule.

There was another factor that gave great aid to Wodehouse. Between 1866-68, the political situation in London was in great flux as a result of the passage of the 1867 Reform Act which meant that the original refusal of his request for annexation was given by Cardwell (Colonial Secretary 1864-66), confirmed by Lord Carnarvon (Colonial Sec 1866-67), re-considered and reversed by the Duke of Buckingham (Colonial Sec 1867-68), and then handed over to the

---

[239] Wodehouse to Cardwell, 13th Jan 1866. CO 879/2

arch-ditherer Lord Granville (Colonial Sec 1868-70) for implementation. This gave Wodehouse the free hand he wanted and he immediately moved to annex Basutoland as an entity entire and separate from both the Cape Colony and Natal. After that, he imposed a peace treaty on the Free State which required them to give up to the Basuto rather more land than they felt was right by the twin expedients of cutting off their ammunition supply and sending the Frontier Armed and Mounted Police up to the border. That this was done against the wishes of the Colonial Office was evident; W. Monsell, Granville's under-secretary, wanted Woodhouse sacked but was afraid that to do such a thing would open up a whole can of parliamentary worms; 'Certainly Sir P. Wodehouse will do his best to put us in the wrong. With far greater knowledge of the subject than we have, he will write a despatch which, however right we may be, we shall find difficult to answer.'[240]

This would not be the first or the last time that an imperial official would disobey or manipulate the government in London to push his own agenda. Historians call it the 'man on the spot' problem but for the moment it seems necessary to answer two questions. The first is why Wodehouse went to the trouble of disobeying his superiors. There was little in his earlier career to indicate waywardness and given that he was an unpopular governor dealing with a hostile Cape parliament at the time, one might have forgiven him for giving a Gallic shrug and kicking the whole question into the long foie gras. Maintaining Basutoland as a distinct entity irritated those settlers who thought they might like a nice slice of newly liberated fertile land sold for a song by a near bankrupt Free State and certainly, if the British wanted to add further to the grievances of the Boers by cheating them of the fruits of 'their career of conquest...at the moment of its greatest success'[241] then this was a good way to do it.

Wodehouse was an *imperial* administrator though and never lost sight of the fact that he was administering South Africa in the interests of the *empire* rather than the narrow interests of either the Colony or the transient parliamentary arithmetic of the government in London. He was fully aware of the vital interest of the Cape as a naval station and he was fully alive to the consequences of a Boer takeover of a collapsing Basutoland. He was also fully aware of the vital interest of keeping the Boers away from the coastlines so as to control their ammunition supply and fully apprised of their rumoured ambition to push through the Drakensberg and then extend down through the Transkei to take Port St. Johns and so gain an outlet to the sea.[242] It was always the sea! The British would never allow anything to threaten their control of the sea route around the Cape and nor would they allow any power in the interior independent access to the guns, ammunition, trade and foreign alliances that would follow from control of a port.

The second question concerns the decision of the Basuto to seek British protection. The mere fact that they did so has the more rabid Leftie frothing at the mouth in anger, disbelief and rage and then desperately scrabbling around trying to prove that it isn't a fact at all, that they were really conned or conquered, that it's propaganda or that the record has been fixed by

---

[240] W. Monsell 21st June 1869. CO 879/2
[241] WO 106/6135 Precis of Information concerning South Africa; Orange Free State and Griqualand West. Intelligence Branch QMG's Dept 1878, p. 59.
[242] John Benyon, *Proconsul and Paramountcy* p.92.

biased whiteys. It is a fact though and it needs explaining and the best place to look for that explanation is across the border in Natal.

The question of land ownership had plagued the colony of Natal ever since Britain had snuffed out the Boer Republic of Natalia in 1843. This was largely because the Boer victory over Dingane at the Blood River had sent the Zulus north westwards over the Buffalo-Tugela Rivers and thus opened up a vast vacuum into which three main groups of people were sucked. The first were the European settlers, the second were those indigenous clans who had existed on the fringes or had fled from the Zulu *impis* and now began to return, while the third were clans of refugees who had fled from Zululand. Many of these clans were in a shattered state; Natal Secretary for Native Affairs, Theophilus Shepstone reckoned there were at least ninety-one identifiable groups exclusive of the Zulu refugees. In order to deal with this situation Shepstone had developed a system whereby each particular clan was assigned a 'Reserve' or 'Location' where they were allowed to live under their own customs as long as they recognised the Crown, in the person of a Magistrate, as paramount, paid a nominal tax and abandoned obnoxious practices such as smelling-out. Title to land was invested in trustees of whom the chief was the principal, but Shepstone fully intended that this would give way to individual land titles as soon as a class of independent farmers grew up. This was a source of dispute, for many in the Natal government regarded the chiefs as backward, weak and corrupt and felt that the best prospect for development lay in the immediate establishment of a class of independent yeoman farmers rather than waiting for the chiefs to allow it. Refugees entering the colony were treated differently in that they were assigned to a European farmer for a period of three years during which time they would work for keep and wages. This, it was hoped, would avoid vagabondage, teach the refugees the basics of a money rather than a barter economy and equip them with the necessary skills for life in the colony. The lion's share of the land went to the white settlers but as they were vastly outnumbered by both the indigenous and refugee population, they were careful to ensure that all had a sufficiency of land. This was not difficult because there really was a vast abundance of well-watered land available.

The result was that 'our natives have been quietly governed, their confidence has been gained and they are now tractable and obedient, and sincerely attached to Her Majesty's Government.'[243] If this sounds strange to the modern, politically correct ear, it might help to point out that the black population of Natal was reckoned to be roughly 18,000 in 1838 but 180,000 in 1862 which meant that an awful lot of people were voting with their feet in favour of the advantages of settled rule under British auspices. Not surprising really, if the average experience of the average black family had been fifty years and more of *mfecane* and everything that went with it. Settled predictable government; secure title to land; employment opportunities either as a traditional pastoralist or working for a European; the chance of a mission station education; the possibility of setting up in business independently in Durban or Pietermaritzburg; Natal was not paradise and the black population was regarded as 'uncivilised' and unworthy of the franchise, but it was a lot better than anything else that many of them had seen in the last half century. It should come as no surprise then that the

---

[243] Lt-Governor Scott to Newcastle, 4th September 1862. CO 879/5 Papers relative to Native Affairs in Natal, April 1866.

Basutos living next door thought that British rule might be preferable to their present state of affairs. By the Treaty of Aliwal North, 1868, Basutoland became British territory, at the behest of Moshweshwe and the Basutos themselves.

\*

## Diamonds

In 2016, a South African student studying at Oxford University began a campaign to have the statue of Cecil Rhodes removed from Oriel College on the grounds that merely walking past such a statue was likely to cause grave offence to any black student because Rhodes was a white settler capitalist who had ripped off the black people of South Africa. The campaign rapidly gained that necessary and modern mark of idiocy, the hashtag, and the *#RhodesMustFall* movement expanded imperially from the University of Cape Town, where it had succeeded in having the statue of Rhodes removed, and colonised the University of Oxford. The movement failed despite gaining the support of the Oxford Union student debating society because donors threatened to withdraw £100 million pounds of funding if anyone so much as looked at the statue with a crowbar in hand. The student who started this nonsense was named Ntokozo Qwabe and - remarkably – he was attending Oxford on a Rhodes Scholarship. Subsequently, it was revealed that this charming young man had expressed a desire to 'whip the white Apartheid settler entitlement' out of a student who filmed him on his phone during a demonstration at Cape Town University and then reduced a white waitress to tears in a Cape Town restaurant by refusing to tip her until the white people of South Africa returned the land that they had stolen from black people.[244]

It seems to me a pity that the waitress, Ashleigh Schultz, was not up on her South African History for if she had been she might have pointed out that in large parts of South Africa, and especially in the western Cape where this opinionated young man was gorging himself, the land was not stolen by the whites but occupied when the Khoikhoin died out. She might also have pointed out that it was Ntokozo Qwabe's ancestors, the Zulus, who had brought about the single greatest disaster to hit South Africa in the form of Shaka's wars, the *mfecane* and the subsequent depredations of Mzilikazi. She might also have pointed out that if any land was to be given back, then the Zulus would be handing over large tracts in the colonised lands of Zimbabwe themselves and would, into the bargain, be shelling out huge amounts of compensation to the descendants of all the shattered clans that fled to Moshweshwe's protection. In the event, an online campaign raised more than $6000 in tips for Ashleigh Schultz but it would have been rather nicer if she had hit him round the head with a large, heavily bound volume of History rather like this one and told him not to be such a vile ignoramus; it's bad enough that he was a lawyer. South Africa is a product of the History of all its different peoples and they all bear responsibility for it. It isn't a black and white issue. The point of History is to learn from it and move on. It isn't a claim for compensation – otherwise the French would be paying England a millennium's worth of compensation for 1066.

---

[244] http://www.telegraph.co.uk/education/2016/09/23/activist-behind-oxford-university-rhodes-must-fall-campaign-says/

This nonsense is just another symptom of the fact that as soon as you mention diamonds all rational thought goes out of the heads of anyone interested in South Africa and the debate is brought to a grinding halt. 'That's it, then,' says the interested party. 'It's all about the money, innit?' This is usually accompanied by a snort from the standard issue Leftie clone which, though varying in style, rarely varies in content: 'Imperialist capitalist bastards grinding the faces of the poor black workers, mate, innit? Revolution is the only solution…yadda yadda yadda.' Now, it is fair to say that some quite respectable Historians have suspected that British motives in South Africa were conditioned by desires to exploit its potential wealth and motivated by little more than an instinct for aggressive land grabbing and the press ganging of African labour. Arguments for imperial expansion at the behest of capitalist interests have been so popular for so long that they have become sacred cows of political correctness. J.A. Hobson – who doesn't count as a respectable historian but he's often quoted by Lefties - argued during the Anglo-Boer War of 1899-1902 that it was all a conspiracy of (Jewish) business elites while Marx, with his customary idiocy, condemned empire as the product of bourgeois capitalism in his historically illiterate 1848 farrago *The Communist Manifesto* before most of the empires were built. Honestly, it drives me mad because it's all so lazy but also because it is all so completely wrong. So off we go to shoot the fox, gun primed, loaded, double-shotted, extra cartridges stuffed into shooting jacket pockets with a little silver flask of Klippie along to take the edge off the morning.

The Kimberley diamond mine, or The Big Hole as it came to be known, ceased producing diamonds in 1914 and it's now full of turquoise coloured water. It was important at the time because the only other source of diamonds was Golconda in India and thus it spawned a rough and tumble frontier town made up of equal parts mud, corrugated iron shacks, drunken miners, crooks, rebels and rogues from all over the world. Actually, it's curiously unimpressive today because it really is just like any standard issue quarry and you feel that you might just be able to chuck a stone across it but over time it produced 2722kg of diamonds, made the fortune of the titanic figure of Cecil Rhodes, further soured relations between Britain and the Boers and took a giant step towards alienating whites from blacks. What it did not do was prompt Britain into the scramble for Africa - simply because the diamonds were just not valuable enough.

Just to make sure you got that point, I'll say it again; *the diamonds were just not valuable enough*.

The first diamonds were found at Hopetown which isn't much of a place today and was a lot less of one back then. It was known that shiny stones could be picked up along the bed of the Orange River but when in 1867 sharp eyed O'Reilly sent one off to be valued and then flogged it to Sir Philip Wodehouse for £500, interest was sparked. At first, it was thought that the shiny stones had been transported there in the stomachs of ostriches or they had been lost by clumsy Bushmen, a story that gained credence when 'The Star of South Africa' was obtained from a sangoma and sold for £11,000. The word was out and bands of prospectors began to arrive on the Orange, Vaal and Harts Rivers driven in part by the economic depression brought on by another terrible drought in the Cape and ramped up with sheer, slavering greed when it turned out that the stories were true. In July 1871, the first stone was found at Kimberley and for a moment it looked like the rather sleepy, debt ridden colonies of South Africa might finally, potentially, represent an economic asset for the Crown. Certainly there was hope, as a breathless Governor Barkly exclaimed in 1874.

> In transmitting the Blue book of this colony for 1871, I commend my Despatch by stating that the year had been one of unprecedented prosperity. The returns for 1872, which I have the honour to forward, completely throw into the shade nevertheless those for 1871....The total receipts for the Treasury stand at £1,161,548 about double what they were in 1869![245]

Not only that but the increase in shipping at the Cape as a result of this bonanza seemed to be a portent for good things to come; up 20% to 375 British and 107 foreign ships. The coastal trade was up 40% too.[246]

The key word here, however, is 'potentially'. Even with the diamonds, the economy remained pitifully small; brace yourself because I've got to trot out some statistics. Cape imports and exports were valued at around £7.5m each in 1880. This was in comparison to total British merchandise exports of £286m and imports of £411m, foreign investments of £41m and Excise Duties of £44m in 1880 alone. The increase in shipping was also insignificant in comparison, (even when taking into consideration that diamonds come in small packages rather than bulk loads, one might expect a noticeable rise in imported equipment and luxury goods). The figures for Malta – 2947 sailing and 1733 steam vessels visiting the port in 1871 – show that Cape Town was a quiet place indeed.[247] Whatever economic benefits might lie in the future, and even taking into account problems of statistical accuracy, in the 1870s they were not great enough to tempt the British government into a deliberate forward policy that involved war and conquest on anything more than a modest scale. They certainly weren't great enough to tempt the nearby Indian merchants of Mauritius looking to revive their fortunes after the disastrous malaria epidemic and slump of 1875 on that island – by 1880, there were still only eight of them in Durban, five years after they had begun exploring the possibilities of Natal.[248]

So what was the importance of Kimberley? In economic terms, during the 1870s, the answer is; not very much. Over-production depressed the diamond market so much that few people made much in the way of money and as the mine got deeper and the flooding got worse, the costs of production rose to the point where only the consolidation of an effective monopoly by Cecil Rhodes and his partners made Kimberley a going concern; roughly four tons of dirt had to hauled out of the Big Hole for each carat unearthed. This did not happen until the mid-1880s. Some indication of the relative importance of Kimberley might also be inferred from the fact that the railway did not get there until 1885 while another strong indication that for all the noise, Kimberley was not so important, is that when Governor Barkly tried to annex the Diamond fields to the Cape Colony in 1871, he was opposed by 25 votes to 27 in

---

[245] BPP Reports on the State of the Colonies 1874 Vol. XLIV Ser 17, p. 141.
[246] BPP Reports on the State of the Colonies 1874 Vol. XLIV Ser 17 p. 144.
[247] Customs Statistics and Shipping Returns for the Cape of Good Hope 1856 - 70. PRO CO 959/1 Frere Correspondence.
[248] Padaychee, V., and Morrell, R. 'Indian Merchants and Dukawallahs in the Natal Economy c. 1875 – 1914', *Journal of Southern African Studies*, Vol. 17, No.1 (March 1991), p. 82.

the House of Assembly[249] and 6 votes to 13 in the Legislative Council.[250]  Barkly decided, therefore, that the area should be annexed to the Crown as Griqualand West and an Administrator sent up to bring some order to the place in the hope that it could be kept from turning into another running sore of instability, lawlessness and potential war; the claims of the Orange Free State to ownership were dismissed largely because no-one had any confidence in the ability of its administration to manage 50,000 miners of all races, all nationalities and none, many of whom were Fenians, adventurers, complete desperadoes, and absolutely not the sort of people you would want living next door.  The fact that the annexation to the Colony did not take place until 1877[251] - as a direct result of a rebellion among the fractious diggers known as the Black Flag revolt that reduced the town and environs to a state of anarchy (Rhodes was among those arrested but never charged) is more convincing evidence that diamonds were not considered important enough for imperial adventurism.

Even under British nominal (*very* nominal) control, Kimberley remained a running sore.  This was because African chiefs far and wide saw an opportunity to replace their assegais and bows with the firearms that were freely, if illegally, traded there.  Young men from across South Africa were despatched to work in the mines and duly came back armed in plenty, if not always with the most up to date weapons, certainly with the knowledge of how to use them.  Within a decade, the independent African chiefdoms were awash with arms.  This was perhaps the most immediate and important effect of the discovery of diamonds but probably the most damaging effect was the worsening of relations between black and white.  When economic conditions worsened and job lay-offs were in the offing, many white workers who had trusted their whole fortunes to success at Kimberley pointed out that it was not possible for them to return to Britain or Australia or Europe; black workers *could* go home and so, by extension, they should.  One of the roots of the Black Flag revolt, this was the beginning of a long tradition of sections of the white working classes relegating black workers to lower status in the mines; in 1922, the South African Communist Party would respond to attempts by the Johannesburg mining concerns to bring in cheaper black labour with a repetition of the Black Flag revolt and the proud slogan 'Workers of the World Unite and Fight for a White South Africa.' (Shock! Horror! Can a Communist be a racist? Apparently, they can).

\*

## Governing South Africa

It's always been my belief that if you don't know the geography, you can't know the History, and this has been the one of the reasons why I've wandered over much of southern Africa in my researches – others include the vineyards, of course, and better weather in November than dear old Blighty.  When studying the geography, however, one needs to be aware of the distorting effects of maps because the standard projection - Mercator's - is a poor tool for the historian to use because it distorts distances on land and creates false impressions about the relative sizes of different areas; Norway, for example, appears comparable to India, when in

---

[249] Theal, *History*, Vol. VIII, (Cape Town, 1964), p. 368.
[250] Theal, *History*, Vol. VIII, p. 370.
[251] Theal, *History*, VIII, (Cape Town, 1964), p. 423. See also Turrell, Capital and Labour, p.3.

fact it is only one tenth the land area. Tourist guides to South Africa give the impression that the UK (excluding N. Ireland) will fit into the RSA approximately three times; in reality it is five times and of course, this has led all sorts of dingbats to claim that Mercator's projection is a racist plot because it makes Europe and America more important than Africa; 'cartographic imperialism' is, I believe, the phrase used. It is no such thing and the claim is just another of the things that I was expected to swallow during my course in Multicultural Education; all maps that attempt to put a 3D image onto a 2D piece of paper distort in one way or another. Mercator's map is a navigator's map, a seafarer's map, and good luck to anyone attempting to sail round Africa navigating by Peter's projection. Anyway, just use Google maps; unless you think that satellites are racist too.

It's a question of scale too. On a 1:10 000 000 scale map, Port Elizabeth to Grahamstown is the width of a finger nail, to Graaff-Reinet only as far as the first joint on a little finger, while Cape Town and Simon's Town are almost contiguous. Port Elizabeth to Graaff-Reinet is 300km. Bathurst, capital of the province of Albany in 1820, is described as a town by the 1990 Collins Atlas when no one in Britain would recognize this picturesque hamlet with its two pubs, church and corner shop by such a description then or now. (The natural pedant in me noted that The Bathurst Arms had a portrait of Lord Bathurst hanging on its sign when I was there in 2002 – except it was Sir Harry Smith. Given the very good lunch they provided, I thought it ungenerous to point this out at the time. Plus, I was blasted on black Sambuca). Remove the motor car, metalled roads and the railway and the problem of distance and scale expands further. In 1820, there was no road from Port Elizabeth to Grahamstown and the 1820 settlers had only animal tracks and a visual guess as to distance and bearing made from a convenient hill outside Bathurst, to guide them to their allocated farms – there is a thing called the Toposcope there that you can go up and see the problem first hand - while the official map of Natal was claimed by Sir Garnet Wolseley in 1873 to have been drawn up by a drunkard.[252] Zululand didn't get a map until it was invaded in 1879. In 1856, the mail cart from Graaff-Reinet to Cape Town covered the 480km in 81 hours, traveling with only the briefest of stops, but this was a best speed qualified by vagaries of water, fodder, weather and accident. 'Irregularity in the service' commented the historian of that fine town, dryly, 'was normal.'[253] Port Elizabeth could be reached in three days by cart[254] but probably four if mules were used instead of horses.[255] Dick King famously rode the 960 km from Durban to Grahamstown in ten days, a journey that normally took three months, and Harry Smith rode the 900km from Cape Town to Grahamstown in six days in January 1835 with horses laid on along the route,[256] but these were exceptional feats undertaken in wartime.[257] Compare this to Lt. C. Commeline RE, who took five days to move his wagons the 25km from Pinetown to Pietermaritzburg in the rainy January of 1879.[258] More normally, a column of infantry might

---

[252] W.R.Guest, *Langalibalele. The Crisis in Natal 1873-75*, (Durban, 1976), pp. 41-42. See A.Preston, *The South African Diaries of Sir Garnet Wolsley 1875*, (Cape Town, 1971), p. 223.
[253] C.G. Henning. *Graaff-Reinet. A Cultural History 1786-1886*, (Cape Town, 1975), p. 150.
[254] C.G. Henning. p. 150.
[255] Cunynghame, *My Command in South Africa*, p. 47.
[256] Mostert, p. 678.
[257] D. Morris, *The Washing of the Spears*, p. 153.
[258] F. Emery, *The Red Soldier. Letters from the Zulu War, 1879*, (London, 1977), pp. 56-59. Lt. Chard left him behind and thus either saved his life or cheated him of a VC.

be expected to cover 25-35km in a day[259] while a Division of all arms might expect to cover 25km as a fair average on decent roads.[260] In 1875, however, General Cunynghame took two months to move a detachment of the 24th Regiment 960km from Cape Town to Kimberley by rail and ox wagon, an average of only 16km per day.[261] Actually finding out the location of towns or features was a problem; in 1815, there was no adequate map of Britain, let alone South Africa.[262] What this means is that although much has been written about the 'annihilation of distance' during the 19th Century as a result of improved communications,[263] however easier it became to cross those distances in South Africa, they remained formidable.

Problems of scale and distance also impose themselves when population figures are studied; in 1990, the population of the UK and South Africa were approximately 65m and 55m - enough to give Malthus apoplexy; the population of Cape Colony in 1875 was only 721,000 in total,[264] Natal approximately 323,000,[265] with an estimated 100,000 Boers in the Orange Free State and Transvaal.[266] Britain had approximately 32m people living in 7m families in 1871.[267] Durban, Grahamstown, and Pietermaritzburg were really only moderately sized villages with European populations of approximately 2000 souls.[268] In the latter place, 'Government House' was a vicarage and the Legislative Council Building no more than a village hall.[269] Pretoria was no more than a barnyard hamlet, a village of 350 souls, unpaved and strewn about with untidily parked waggons.

Understanding how the British government attempted to control and shape this human geography also requires the historian to consider a differing scale of the effectiveness of established authority. A 21st Century Welshman might expect to be governed by a Parish Council, a District and County Council, a Regional Assembly, a parliament at Westminster and the European Commission in Brussels (for a little while longer at least), while 20% of the working population of Britain is now (2017) employed by the government. In 1871 the British government employed 53,874 people including workmen, dockyard mateys and postal workers (but excluding the Armed Forces);[270] Lord Canning presided over a Foreign Office only 24 strong in the 1820s.[271] The apex of the government was the Cabinet presided over by the Prime Minister, which tended to meet weekly, but could go for months without a session. Added to this was the fact that Cabinets had a variety of challenges to face and there could be substantial gaps between the discussion of South African issues.

---

[259] Emery, *The Red Soldier*, p. 62.
[260] General Sir Edward Bruce Hamley KCB, KCMG. (Commandant of the Staff College 1870-1878). *The Operations of War Explained and Illustrated*, (London, 1878), p. 32.
[261] CO 879/9 Confidential Print Africa. Report of Lt-Colonel Crossman RE on the Affairs of Griqua-land West June 1878.
[262] N. McCord, *British History 1815 – 1906*, (Oxford, 1991), p. 45.
[263] For example, N. Ferguson, *Empire: How Britain made the modern World*, (London, 2004) p.164.
[264] Theal, *History*, Vol.X p.17. Cunynghame placed the figure at just over a million. Cunynghame, *My Command in South Africa*, p. viii.
[265] Theal, *History*, Vol.VIII, p. 174.
[266] D. M. Schreuder, Gladstone and Kruger, (London, 1969), p. 12.
[267] Chris Cook and Brendan Keith, British Historical Facts 1830 –1900 (London, 1975) p. 233.
[268] C. Ballard, *John Dunn. The White Chief of Zululand*, (Johannesburg, 1985) p. 34.
[269] A.Preston, *The South African Diaries of Sir Garnet Wolseley 1875*, p.22.

[270] Chris Cook and Brendan Keith, *British Historical Facts 1830 –1900*, p. 150.

[271] N. McCord, *British History 1815 – 1906*, (Oxford, 1991), p. 53.

In the empire as a whole, the touch of government, as represented by the Colonial Office, was even lighter. Before its reorganization in 1868, it was slow in answering its mail, taking on average 12 days, which was well below commercial standards of practice (surprise, surprise).[272] It had no fixed office hours, a six hour working day and, because work came in cycles, often little for the clerks to do.[273] William Strachey, the précis writer, was rarely seen in the building.[274] Even after 1870 when the Colonial Office underwent a rapid expansion in business with the rapid expansion of Empire[275] and the introduction of the telegraph, the department remained gloriously understaffed - most of the executive work was done by three dozen clerks and the permanent undersecretary.[276] Added to this was the instability of policy inherent in the mid-Victorian compromise between democratic and aristocratic government, which thrust four Colonial ministers into office between 1874-85, each with a different character and approach to colonial and imperial issues, under two different ministries with radically opposing imperial philosophies, led by two strong Prime Ministers with fundamentally opposing views of imperialism. Cabinets were also composed of men with careers to pursue and who were not averse to shifting their grounds when it was in their interest to do so.

Even when the will of the Cabinet was clearly expressed, making that will felt was never simply a matter of pressing a button and watching the machine work. There was always a time lag in communications before the telegraph reached the Cape which could be catastrophic in a crisis; even after the cable reached Cape Town, the Governor often received only précis of the longer telegrams, drawn up by an aide, sent through the Cape telegraph system, and then dispatched by horse to a camp out on the veldt. Also, cables could and did break or were cut. There was also the fact of the Cape parliament to consider which had ideas of its own which often led to two different policies being followed at the same time.

South African local government had always been ludicrously undermanned and overstretched. Under the VOC, the Governor of the Cape Colony, the Llandrosts and Heemraaden, Field Commandants and Cornets spread along the borders on the Orange and Fish rivers represented only the very barest bones of a government; there was little coercive power available to it, even in times of war. Its tax gathering powers were almost nil beyond the immediate environs of Cape Town and Stellenbosch and land regulations and assessments were widely abused. The arrival of the British augmented the effectiveness of government, but even this needs to be kept in perspective; the British could certainly bring decisive force to bear in any area of the colony that they chose to, but the day to day administration of the country was still conducted by too few officials. In those parts of the colony where there were few Europeans, this usually meant a couple of magistrates, a missionary or two and the Frontier Armed and Mounted Police. Governors complained often about the inadequacy of the South African administration; in Namaqualand in the late 1870s, the British government was represented by just one man (with a very inadequate map),[277] while during the 1880s the

---

[272] B.L. Blakeley, *The Colonial Office 1868-1892*, (Duke University Press, 1972), p.23.
[273] Blakeley, *The Colonial Office*, p.25.
[274] Blakeley, *The Colonial Office*, p.27.
[275] Blakeley, *The Colonial Office*, pp.61-3. Letters received by African Dept increased from 2910 in 1870 to 3587 in 1873. As a whole the Colonial Office received 16942 letters in 1878 and 20524 in 1879.
[276] Blakeley, *The Colonial Office*, Ch.II.

Rev. John Mackenzie, was expected to keep order in Bechuanaland with a total force of ten policemen.[278] In the Transvaal and the Orange Free State, the writ of the government was even more limited, while the authority of the African chiefs was still weaker.

The cumulative effect of these factors is to produce the obvious, but vital, conclusion that South Africans existed in a very big country, separated from their neighbours and their government by considerable distances, making decisions often on their own authority and according to no plan but their own. As a result, we have to accept that British policy was often a dog's breakfast because there was little agreement over it within the government and nowhere near the necessary administrative efficiency to make it work if the people who actually had to put it into practice chose not to. If the government in London wanted something to happen and was determined to put the time and effort into making it happen, then generally speaking it could, but this was a rare thing – especially if involved spending money. Any idea that there was some great imperial spider at the centre of a web, spinning out horrible conspiracies for the oppression of mankind, therefore, is just nonsense.

*

## Confederation

For a brief period, however, the government in London *was* prepared put the time and money into making its will felt in South Africa and thus was born the policy of Confederation. The policy failed ultimately but it certainly set a few hares running and brought about several dramatic changes to South Africa in the period 1874-86, not least of which was a substantial addition to the territory under direct British rule. As always in politics, there were a number of motives for this new policy but naked, capitalist exploitation wasn't one of them. This statement will no doubt result in howls of rage and wild accusations from the weak-minded, intellectually lazy and terminally blinkered but before I go into it in a bit more detail, let me point out something so powerful and so obvious that even a Marxist might stop chewing the carpet for a bit and pause for thought.

This is a rough list of the places that the British Empire in Southern Africa impacted on between 1874-86.

Walvis Bay, St. Lucia, St. John's River – annexed as potential ports. Economically, worthless.

The Transvaal, annexed without permission in 1877, handed back in 1881 after humiliating defeat. Economically, pretty worthless.

The Transkei. The Xhosa revolt again and are defeated in 1877-78. *Not* annexed formally until 1886. Economically, pretty worthless. (Cost of war: £1.7 million; tax revenues £16k).

Basutoland 'Gun War' 1879-81. Lost. Economically, as much worth as a Yorkshire Moor, which much of the country resembles. (Cost of war £3 million. Tax revenue £3k pa). 1888, Basuto elect to be subjects of London rather than Cape Town.

---

[277] CO 700/ SOUTHAFRICA12 Map Damaraland and Great Namqualand 1876, showing approximately the position of the principal Stations and localities of the various Tribes.
[278] Schreuder, *The Scramble for Southern Africa*, pp. 92-3.

Zululand, attacked and defeated 1879. Cost of war £5 million. *Not* occupied. Economically, pretty worthless. Annexed 1887 after Zulu civil war.

Bechuanaland, annexed 1885. Economically worthless desert.

This is a fact that we have to start with. Most of southern Africa was economically worthless. If it was possible to make money out of southern Africa, then Africans would have done so already but the reality is that beyond the port facilities and related infrastructure of Cape Town, there was nothing worth the time, cost and effort of conquering. There were no minerals to exploit because gold was yet to be discovered in economic quantities and though the copper up in the Northern Cape had long been known about, it took until 1876 before someone worked out a way to transport it out by rail to Port Nolloth and still make a profit. Farming was only just one step further on than subsistence and diamond mining was risky and largely unprofitable until Rhodes established an effective monopoly in 1888. General commerce was better than it was, but it was small town stuff and nothing to compare with Manchester or Birmingham; the standard of South African offerings for sale at the Cape Town Exhibition of 1877 was abysmal. And, as every capitalist knows, war is a rotten business strategy because there is nothing that isn't cheaper to buy than to get by paying the costs of conquest.

So, what was Confederation all about?

As we have seen, the worries about the security of the empire and the new challenges, both real and potential, from the other great powers were picked up by quite a few military men, colonial officials and assorted politicians after the Crimean War. Roughly speaking, these were the 'Jingoes', a body of opinion who believed that the defences of the empire were in such a ramshackle state that they provided a standing invitation for a rival power to exploit and that something ought to be done to remedy this situation pdq. They also took a different view of the empire than the one prevailing in the 1860s; instead of being a burden that would soon be laid down, they saw it as the potential platform on which Britain could compete with the growing powers of Germany, the USA and Russia; they felt that naval supremacy was at risk due to the change from wood and sail to coal and iron and that the trade of empire was vulnerable to commerce raiders such as the Confederate navy produced during the American Civil War; and being, by and large, capable men of experience, distinction and decision, they also felt that they had the duty to ensure that the politicians did not waste the opportunities or shirk the responsibilities of empire. What animated them was a 'Victorian military millenarianism',[279] a belief that a war for survival with one or other of the Great Powers was inevitable and that urgent, even precipitate action, was needed to prepare for it. They also believed that this war, *when* rather than *if*, it came would be quick and decisive and that victory would go to the state that was best prepared in advance for it. Their motto was *si vis pacem paro bellum – if you want peace, prepare for war*. More controversial was their belief that democratic government was fickle, the Liberal party leader, Gladstone, a lunatic pacifist

---

[279] M.D. Welch, 'Science and the British Officer: The early days of the RUSI for Defence Studies' (1829-1869), RUSI Whitehall Paper, (1998) p.70.

who was quite capable of thinking several impossible things before breakfast – 'some howling fellow…in the front rank of the most ignorant'[280] – and that their expertise gave them the right to ignore democratic control when they considered it necessary.

There were plenty of them too; many were officers trained at Woolwich, others were officials with long experience in India, still more were naval officers and engineers; the Intelligence Branch of the War Office was one of their strongholds (N.B. this wasn't chaps sneaking about with false beards, just officers paid to think about military issues. There was no *secret* intelligence service in Britain until 1907) as was the world's first military think tank, the Royal United Services Institute. General Wolseley and Roberts each had their 'rings' but there were also networks of journalists and academics based in India who were beavering away on defence issues. Among the most influential of those Indian connections were two names who would play significant roles in South Africa over the coming years; Sir Bartle Frere and Sir George Colley.

By the early 1870s, the Jingoes were making their views known in the highest circles and when the first pro-imperial Prime Minister in decades was elected in 1874, they felt that they had gained not just a sympathetic ear in Benjamin Disraeli, but their very own spokesman in the new Colonial Secretary, Lord Carnarvon. Within a week of taking office, the Colonial Office ordered a defence review with the aim of connecting together the various parts of the Empire into one large, self-sustaining community which would act as a guarantor of good government for the settlers and emigrants, a development agency for the indigenous peoples and provide for the defence of both the colonies and the home islands.[281] The Colonial Defence Committee that he set up morphed into the Carnarvon Commission, the hugely influential defence review that played a pivotal role in establishing British defence policy right up to and beyond the First World War. Crucially, although he had no desire to spread the boundaries of the empire wider still and wider for the sake of it, Carnarvon was not opposed to expanding it where some strategic imperative was in operation. Almost immediately, he annexed Fiji; this wasn't out of a desire for more coconuts but for its position on the main sea route across the Pacific from Australia to Canada, where a coaling station would be needed in time of war. When he cast his eye southwards at the most vital of all the ports of empire, he looked at South Africa and did not like what he saw at all. The defences had been left to rot; the old fort and batteries were completely inadequate; Simonstown lacked a magazine dry enough to store powder in; if something like the *Alabama* turned up, there was virtually nothing the colony could do to prevent its banks being robbed, its shipping pillaged and every town or hamlet within a day's march of the coast being torched. Combine this with another Xhosa revolt or trouble with the Voortrekkers and there would be real trouble.

His answer to this was Confederation. The idea was to persuade the Cape Colony, Natal, the Orange Free State and the Transvaal to join together in a federation on the Canadian model and so produce a big, solid, stable, pro-British bastion astride the route to India. Carnarvon had worked on the confederation of Canada back in the 1860s and he saw no reason why the

---

[280] Wolseley to Ardagh 19th July 1892. PRO 30/40/2 Ardagh papers. See also "The National Defences" *The Times* 15th May 1888.
[281] Knox, "The Earl of Carnarvon, Empire and Imperialism", pp. 51 – 52, 61-62.

Afrikaaners, given time and tact, could not be reconciled to British rule in the same way that the French Canadians had been. There was a strong possibility that the Orange Free State might be persuaded at least but whether he was dreaming or not is a moot point; what he did not have was time and this was to prove fatal to his scheme.

\*

One of the things about South African Historians is their astounding narrowness of focus. Back in 2004, I bumped into Professor Shula Marks in the archives in Pretoria – and a damn frosty reception I got too, though not surprising considering that I wrote virtually my whole MA on how she had got virtually everything wrong about the Zulu War – but while managing to dodge the sharpened icicles, I managed to elicit from her the subject that she was researching; women's health issues in the late 19th Century Transvaal. Now, leaving aside the questions of whether this was researchable at all, given the fact that the Transvaal didn't keep many records, or that women's health issues in that particular place were probably not much different from women's health issues in any other distant flyblown outpost of European settlement, it did give me pause to wonder that such a subject should engage the attention of the doyen of South African Marxists when the very much bigger questions of war, peace, apartheid and democracy were still waiting to be described and explained. It struck me that perhaps Apartheid era sanctions had combined with the physical isolation of South Africa to cut off South Africans from the wider world so much that they had gradually come to employ the microscope more than the telescope; they would expend great effort on micro-studies but neglect the big picture. This was brought home to me in a discussion with another Southern African academic who (I shall spare his blushes) corrected my continued references to the Berlin *Congress* of 1878 by insisting that the Berlin *Conference* took place in 1884. Now undoubtedly, the Berlin Conference of 1884 had a big impact on Africa – it is commonly known as the Berlin *Colonial* Conference, so no prizes for guessing what was up for discussion – but he seemed to be completely unaware that the Berlin Congress of 1878 had anything to do with South Africa at all, when it was the thing that prevented the First World War arriving fifty years early.

Connected to this is that when reading South African histories, it's hard not to get the impression that the various British colonial governors are parachuted into the narrative without any attempt to examine their experiences or intellectual baggage. When I began my own Great Trek through the desert of academia, I did so with a desire to understand the causes of the Anglo-Zulu War of 1879. This is by far the most famous of all colonial conflicts and the attention paid to the military aspects has been exhaustive; there are people out there who can tell you where the mealie bags of the Rorke's Drift barricade were manufactured and others who are prepared to argue over the name of the surgeon's dog. What staggered me was that there had not been a full biography of the man who started the war written since the authorised family version came out in 1895, (so I wrote one, *The Zulu and the Raj: The Life of Sir Bartle Frere*). And when I studied the man, his background, interests, previous experience, expertise and concerns, it seemed to me to be blindingly obvious that Sir Bartle Frere's concern was not primarily with South Africa, and certainly not with the Zulus, but with the consequences of what was going on in that Congress in Berlin in

1878. Apartheid seemed to have intellectually isolated South African Historians and blinded them to the fact that South Africa was part of the wider world and what happened out there beyond the misty horizon was often much more important than a farmer's wife up in the Transvaal having a gippy tum.

So, what was going on at that Congress?

In 1876, a toxic mix of religious, racial and national feeling resulted in a series of risings against Ottoman rule in the Balkans which in turn gave the Russians an excuse to intervene on the side of the Bulgars. Apart from liberating the Bulgars and scooping up all the Slavic peoples of the region into their empire, the Russians had their eye on the prize of Constantinople and after defeating the Turks at Plevna in 1877, advanced their armies to within a day's march of the city. This caused a major European crisis because the Austro-Hungarian Empire made it quite clear that they would fight to prevent this, the British followed suit, the French tried to sell their sword to the highest bidder and the Germans panicked at the prospect of the collapse of their alliances with Russia and the Austro-Hungarian Empire. The result was the calling of the Congress of Berlin to stave off what was effectively, as previously stated, the First World War come fifty years early.

For the British, the issue was Constantinople; if the Russians got it they could send their cruisers and commerce raiders into the Eastern Mediterranean to sink British ships going to and from the Suez Canal. If that happened, then the route to India would be severed and so Prime Minister Disraeli went to Berlin with the aim of getting the Russians away from Constantinople and out of the Balkans by teaming up with the Austrians and the Germans. In order to achieve this aim, Disraeli threatened war and Carnarvon ordered the colonies to prepare for it. And the man who Carnarvon chose to go out and secure the Cape route, the route that would become absolutely vital if Constantinople fell, was the imperial big hitter, Sir Bartle Frere.

He could hardly have chosen better. Frere was an Indian administrator of huge experience; he had founded Karachi and rebuilt Bombay; he was an accomplished linguist and sanitary reformer; he had ended the East African slave trade by sending the gunboats into Zanzibar; he was a defence expert, having studied the Confederate raiders first hand, written the plan for the defence of India and promoted his own little band of Scinde Horse officers into positions of influence and authority; he had been head of the Indian Political and Secret Committee for ten years (a fact that he ordered kept out of his biography; I found out about it just after I had published, which was frustrating) and just before he was appointed to South Africa, he had written two major articles on the Balkan crisis. The only niggle in this fabulous CV was that he was known to be impatient of control and had a low opinion of elected politicians. In short, he was a man on horseback who intended to get things done and the job he intended to get done was to prepare South Africa for the war now looming by forming it into a Confederation. Having trawled through every last bit of information available in archives in Britain, South Africa and America I can say this with confidence; nowhere is there one single piece of evidence to suggest that he intended to do this by force. There is, to my mind, not a shred of credible evidence that he intended to subjugate the Xhosa, fight the Boers or invade the Zulus. The only pieces of land he was interested in were the potential ports at Walvis Bay and the St. Johns River, so as to deny them to an enemy navy. The impulse behind Confederation was overwhelmingly concerned with imperial defence and certainly not with ripping off poor Africans for the benefit of capitalist speculators.

As to the long term, *The Spectator* – a journal that was usually extremely sceptical of Sir Bartle Frere - took the view that Frere had no intention of running amok, conquering left, right and centre and then handing over what was left to white farmers.

> He is a very able man, and has, we believe, thoroughly comprehended the "secret" of South Africa, - namely, that that vast dominion must become, and will become, a smaller India, and *not an English colony*, or group of colonies, must, that is, be a "dark man's land," and not *a "white man's land;"* and he will, we do not doubt, if permitted, organise it efficiently upon that basis.[282] (My italics).

The merest suggestion that an overwhelming urge to subjugate, dispossess and generally rip off indigenous folk in the interests of evil, top-hatted capitalist bastards played no part in British policy in South Africa 1874-86 sent the Left into hysterics of course. You might think that I'm throwing my teddy out of the cot in this book but I can tell you, it is nothing compared with the seething rage of the Marxists when they are confronted with the merest possibility that they might just have got things a teeny-weeny bit wrong. The usual suspects were like Olympic trampolinists in the way they leaped up and down whenever their nonsense was challenged. When I was writing about Frere first, back in 2002, I was made to read a book called 'Ploughshare of War' which tediously regurgitated the standard Marxist line and kept up the fine tradition of not looking for, or disregarding, evidence that might contradict the rantings of the old scrounger, Charlie Scuff. The author of this work, R.L. Cope, no doubt keen to impress with his zeal his tutor - another Marxist by the name of Norman Etherington - accused respectable Historians who dismissed the idea of capitalist exploitation being the motor for empire as being 'given to invention', spreading 'distraction and confusion' and being concerned 'only to refute Marx' (Shock! Horror! Heretic! Burn the Witch!). Lord Carnarvon, he said, *was* interested in defence issues but this had *nothing* to do with South Africa because there was *no threat whatsoever* to South Africa at the time. This was just plain wrong and I'm just going to give one quote to illustrate how wrong he was on this; if you want it chapter and verse then you'll need *Imperial Defence and the Commitment to Empire* which goes into this in full academic detail with footnotes. Here is Robert Herbert, permanent under-Secretary of State for the Colonies writing in 1877: 'In Lord Carnarvon's opinion…too much importance cannot be attached to the question of the defences of the Cape against naval attack.'[283] You can't say fairer than that except perhaps to make the observation that if I were to choose a farm implement to stick in the title of Cope's book, I would have gone for *billhooks* over ploughshare every time.

Marks, Etherington, Cope and the rest of this crazy gang much preferred the idea that Confederation was a deliberate policy intended to bring about war with the Xhosa and the Zulus in order to force them into working for white farmers by making them pay a Hut Tax.

---
[282] *The Spectator*, The Coming Zulu War. 1st Feb 1879.
[283] CO 879/12 Papers relative to the defence of the Cape of Good Hope. R. Herbert, CO to WO 4th May 1877.

Think about that for a minute and then see if you could get that idea past your HR department; you couldn't because the idea is as absurd today as it was then. Willing workers are what any business owner wants, not surly individuals so cheesed off that they are likely to bunk off at the first opportunity; the Zulus were already in business as labour recruiters for the colonists of Natal; they and the Xhosa were cattle men not arable farmers and if you think this is irrelevant then I suggest you consult an actual farmer – they had no knowledge of crop rotation, fallowing or manuring[284]; no force was needed to find African workers at Kimberley, just payment in guns; and indentured labour from Mauritius, Zanzibar and India was readily available. And again, the sheer ignorance of Marxist academics as to how business actually operates is revealed in all its glory here; business hates war because business is about risk and *entrepreneurs* are usually interested in managing and reducing risk; *entrepreneur* means 'risk taker' - I know, I'm sorry, but on the off-chance a standard issue Marxist has actually got this far, I thought it best to point out what the word actually means in the vain hope of letting a glim of light into the bleak dungeon of his/her mind; and believe me, as the 24th Regiment found out at Isandhlwana and the Cape farmers had learned from the bitter experience of eight Xhosa wars, war is just about the riskiest activity known to man. (The origin of this old *canard* is, as far as I can tell, a couple of statements from non-Historians in the *Report of the Native Economic Commission* 1930-32). And then, of course, you have to ask the question of whether the penny-pinching British government in London would be interested in the vast expense of fighting several wars in order to help a Cape wine farmer with the vendanges. No; it is just too absurd. The only thing that we can learn from Marxists on this issue is just how far they will go to privilege their religion – oops! Did I really say that? – over actual facts; the First Marxist Commandment is that 'If the Facts Don't Fit the Theory, then the Facts Are Wrong and Need Changing. For them, the answer to any historical issue is always capitalism/racism/sexism/oppression of the working classes and the task of research is to dig up evidence that proves this theology rather than actually discover what happened in the past.

So, back to real History; when Frere went to the Cape in early 1877, his priority was to secure the colony and the route to India against any possible French, Russian, German and American threats and this priority was reinforced constantly throughout 1877, 1878 and 1879 when Russian troops were finally forced to withdraw from the Balkans. The idea that this threat was a chimera is untenable in the face of the mountain of evidence in the Colonial Office, War Office, Admiralty and Cabinet Office records. It was a threat taken so seriously that when Disraeli and Lord Salisbury went off to the Congress of Berlin to threaten war if the Russians did not get out of the Balkans, Lord Carnarvon resigned, horrified at the possibility that the Russians might call their bluff; he knew what just how badly the empire was prepared for war and feared a string of burning ports, indigenous rebellions, cheesed off colonists likely to declare independence in disgust and the collapse of all trade. His successor, Sir Michael Hicks-Beach, held exactly the same opinions.

Frere was steeped in these ideas too but for him personally, the threat had another, crucial, dimension to it. If war was declared, it would be known instantly in London and the fleet and

---

[284] Report of the Native Economic Commission 1930-32.

troops already in Malta would be ready to respond straight away - but there was no telegraph to South Africa. This meant that the first indication that war had been declared in Europe might well be a squadron of Russian cruisers appearing in Table Bay, shelling the harbour and landing marines and in this tense, febrile atmosphere Frere, a man not unafraid to act on his own initiative, developed an unfortunate tendency to move faster than his superiors were comfortable with. Thus did a good man do a bad thing.

Incredible! I hear you cry. Russian marines in Cape Town? Impossible! O'Connor's been in the pub again!

I have to say that this was close to my reaction when I first chanced upon the idea but when I dug into it, I was amazed to find that it was true. The Russians *did* have such plans. They *were* fitting out cruisers in American ports to evade a British blockade. They *did* have plans to send cruisers packed full of marines out from the Far East into the Pacific and Indian Oceans. And they *did* have plans to raid colonial ports in Australia and South Africa in the event of a European war. And both the Admiralty and the Colonial Defence Committee were absolutely *kaking* themselves about these plans. I'm trying not to bore you with footnotes, but given the level of scepticism that the casual reader might greet this bit of news with, I'll point you in the direction of Leonard Strakhovsky's essay entitled *Russia's privateering projects of 1878* in the Journal of Modern History, Vol VII no.1, March 1935; the National Archives at Kew document reference CO 30/6/33 *Correspondence with Governors: Cape: Sir Bartle Frere. Frere to Carnarvon*, 24th August 1877 and also *Frere to Carnarvon, June 1877*; also the Admiralty file at Kew reference ADM 1/8869 pp. 31-33; also at Kew, the Cabinet Office record document reference CAB11/81 *Report on the General Scheme of coast defence for India,* November, 1879; also CO 30/6/122 *Defence of Commercial Harbours and Coaling Stations.* You could also nip down to Kings Cross for a quick squizz at British Library Public Documents CSD 1/5, 24th February 1877, *On the Military Defences of South Africa. A Memorandum addressed to the government of the United Kingdom by Sir Bartle Frere,* (London, 1877). I could go on but I'm going to guess that you might now be willing, if not to take my word wholly for it, to at least give me the benefit of the doubt for what's coming next. To sum up the situation (and give the lie to all that nonsense about starting a war to provide labourers), let's take Frere's own assessment of the vulnerability of South Africa:

> In the Government of the Cape, the largest and most important of this group of Colonies, there is absolutely no military element whatsoever. No effectual measures have been organized for making military defence, whether against privateering at sea or against a Kaffir rising by land.[285]

That this was a concern that stayed right at the forefront of his thinking might be ascertained from the fact that in July 1878, his military commander, Lord Chelmsford, was busy surveying the defences of the Cape rather than, as so many Historians have assumed, cooking up foul and secret schemes for the invasion of Zululand and the subjugation of its people.

---

[285] British Library Public Documents CSD 1/5. 24th February 1877. On the Military Defences of South Africa. A Memorandum addressed to the government of the United Kingdom by Sir Bartle Frere. (London, 1877).

And again, you can find this much ignored and neglected document at Kew; the document reference is CO 885/4 *Thesiger, Memorandum on Defence of Table Bay*, 7th July 1878.

Now, before we go any further, I'm going to answer the question that is forming in your mind: *if this stuff is available, how come no-one else has looked at it?* It's a good question: well done at the back. In the case of Cope, it's because he never looked beyond the CO 879 or WO 32 series of files and never opened the Admiralty files (I'm going off his bibliography here). John Laband didn't see this for possibly the same reason; Historians tend to follow the same paths through the archives; in the not so recent past this was largely because the archives weren't computerised and the indexes were really difficult to search. I suspect the problem may also lie in the methodology in that they both asked why the Zulu War happened and then worked their way *back* from there, and thus accessed only the files that deal with that war. (Why would you want to look in the Admiralty files when the Zulus didn't have battleships? Why would you want to look up the Confederate Navy when you are dealing with Africa?) Doing that would lead them to the view that the Zulu War was a product of the Confederation policy and *ergo* Confederation was the cause of the war and everything that happened in South Africa led up to that war. Fair comment; *except that war was not the aim of the Confederation policy,* a point that becomes more and more apparent when the wider context of British defence policy is taken in to account.

Historians are just as guilty of confirmation bias and seeing only what they want to see as everyone else. Just outside Estcourt and close to the famous bacon factory is a small but substantial fortification called Fort Durnford for which there is no record of its construction and which mystified John Laband and Paul Thomson when they were writing their *Illustrated Guide to the Anglo-Zulu War* back in 2000. What was it for? Built in 1876, it was designed to resist artillery and was far in excess of anything needed to hold back a Zulu impi besides being a very long way from the Zulu border. It was also too large to be defended by the number of settlers in the area, so just what use was it in defending Natal from the Zulus? The answer to this was simple; it wasn't built to defend against Zulus because the British were not interested in fighting Zulus. The fort was part of a series of works, which included Fort Amiel and Fort Mistake up at Newcastle, designed to defend against a *Boer* invasion. An invasion of Natal coming down from the Transvaal and the Orange Free State heading to seize the port at Durban would come down either (or both) Van Reenen's pass or Laing's Nek and would then unite at...Estcourt. Because these two genuinely excellent Historians were looking for reasons for the British to invade Zululand, they discounted the possibility that the British were more concerned with the Boers and had no interest in fighting the Zulus. You can find all the details with copious footnotes in *Imperial Defence and the Commitment to Empire.*

Although I started my researches with the Zulu War, I quickly became fascinated by Frere and following him up, I was led into the whole imperial defence thing; rather than reading *back*, I read *forward*; I did look up the Admiralty and the Confederate navy because that is what bothered policy makers at the time. This difference in method is important; let me give an example. If you want to know the causes of the First World War, you would look back at all the stuff like arms races, alliance systems, colonial rivalries, railway timetables and the

Schlieffen Plan and say it was an *inevitable* combination of whichever ones take your fancy. Except it wasn't inevitable; the war came as a surprise and you can only get the understanding that the First World War was only one outcome of several possibilities by reading forward from (say) 1870 not back from 1914. To people who lived through the First World War, there was no *First* World War; it only got that moniker after the Germans went for an encore in 1939. So in order to understand why things happen in History, you have to read *forward* not *back*. The Zulu War was *only one* result of the policy of Confederation and was far from inevitable; it wasn't even an *aim* of Confederation, nor even *desired* by those who wrote the policy of Confederation; no-one sat down and planned it. It's a question of perspective; if you stand on the border of Zululand in late 1878, you see the Empire bearing down on you at some speed and you are tempted to conclude that this is the centre and aim of British policy. Stand in Cape Town looking at a map of the routes to India on the same day and it really is a place of irritating and distracting secondary importance. Stand in Whitehall looking at a map of the Russian dispositions around Constantinople and Zululand becomes an insignificant irrelevance: *where did you say it was, Carnarvon, old chap?*

Another reason for skimping on the archival thing is that the *paying* interest in the war of 1879 is primarily about that old Michael Caine and Stanley Baker thing and in the dash to get to the exciting bits about pith helmets and assegais, the causes of the war are rather left by the wayside; 'can't you write something with more bayonets and spears in it?' asked one publisher I came into contact with. 'No', I replied, unwilling to compromise my art (and rueing the subsequent loss of income ever since). This goes for the results of the war too; Britain defeated the Zulus in 1879, yet those wicked capitalist, imperialist, land-grabbing, labour-enslaving bastards didn't actually take over the country until 1887, which rather negates the whole Marxist thesis, don't you think? No? Well, you have to admit it complicates the matter – especially as the government in London didn't do the annexing. Hmmm…and there were no pith helmets and red tunics involved in the annexation, you say?....We'll get to it.

Frere arrived in Cape Town in March 1877 faced with a difficult task. The Confederation idea had been mooted and mulled and kicked about for a couple of years now and then rejected by the South Africans. James Molteno, the Cape Prime Minister feared that the Cape would end up paying for the Boer's wars against indigenous Africans while humanitarian opinion feared that the price of Confederation with the Boers would be the £25 property qualification which allowed all races in the Cape to vote. Lt-Governor Bulwer of Natal feared being swamped by the Cape Colony while the Boers distrusted any British proposals on principle. Our old pal and indispensable guide Theal reckoned that Frere had been given an impossible task. Nevertheless, Frere was confident that, *ceteris paribus,* given time and diplomacy he could square this circle and persuade everyone to come together in one big happy family. Unfortunately, he never got the chance because the *ceteris paribus* infuriatingly eluded him as a series of events on the frontier deprived him of the initiative. Instead of gracefully guiding the golden chariot in the direction of peace and harmony, he was forced to run around fighting fires and fretting about a Russian war.

Arriving at Cape Town on 31st March 1877, he had barely got his feet under the table when news of the annexation of the Transvaal reached him on 16th April 1877. The Boers had been engaged on an expansionist adventure north eastwards through the territory of the mPedi in an attempt to gain an outlet to the sea, but Chief Sekhukhune had armed his warriors with modern breech loading rifles and had given them a bloody nose. The treasury being exhausted by the expense of the war, the Transvaal government bankrupt and now in fear of a mPedi invasion, contained enough people willing to privately acquiesce in a British take over to preserve them from the expected massacre, and Theophilus Shepstone, the Natal Secretary for Native Affairs, rode in to offer them a rescue in the form of annexation. Carnarvon had authorised Shepstone to annex the Transvaal if he felt the time was ripe but neither he nor Frere expected him to act so soon and without prior consultation. While Frere was still in transit to Cape Town, Shepstone ran up the Union Jack in a blaze of optimism, ignoring the fact that there were still enough Boers with a vehement hatred of the British to make it an open question as to how long it remained on the flag-pole. Almost immediately a deputation of malcontents, led by Paul Kruger, set off for London and Europe to petition for the removal of British rule, while the President of the Orange Free State formally rejected confederation. Frere was furious and decided pretty quickly that Shepstone needed to be fired but when, a week later, Russia declared war on Turkey, he was prevented from going up to the Transvaal to sort the mess out because his priority was to stay on the vital imperial ground at the Cape peninsular. As far as he was concerned, the only way forward from this was an offer of complete domestic self-rule within a British led Confederation.

What was just as bad was that Shepstone's annexation meant that Britain had now inherited Boer border quarrels the Zulus, which was an unwelcome complication for an already complex problem, but Frere acted immediately to kill off widespread speculation that the annexation of the Transvaal inevitably meant the annexation of Zululand.[286] In this he was in perfect accord with Carnarvon's view that 'it would be most injudicious at such a moment to accept the further burdens and responsibilities involved in the forcible acquisition of a large territory such as Zululand with a numerous and warlike population difficult alike to civilise and control'.[287]

When the opportunity did present itself for him to get up to the Transvaal, another exasperating, unforeseen calamity on the periphery intervened to delay him still further. Setting out for Pretoria in August 1877, he got no further than King William's Town in the Transkei before the decayed Xhosa polity rose in a revolt sparked off by a 'drunken brawl,'[288] Xhosa hatred of the mFengu and a chief, Kreli, who couldn't control his warriors, councillors or people in general (they murdered the respected son of Van der Kemp's slave girl wife)[289] and made worse by yet another prophetess.[290] For the next seven months, Frere was pinned down in the Transkei with Chelmsford while the revolt was put down and by the time the Xhosa were beaten, he needed to return to the Cape to be on hand for if a further Russian

---

[286] Frere to Carnarvon 2nd July 1877 PRO 30/6/33 Correspondence with Governors: Cape: Sir Bartle Frere.
[287] BPP C-1961, p. 60. Carnarvon to Bulwer and Shepstone, 31st August 1877.
[288] Frere to Ponsonby 17th October 1877. Quoted in *Martineau* Vol II p. 199.
[289] Theal, *History of the Cape Colony 1872-1884*, p. 88
[290] Theal, *History of the Cape Colony 1872-1884*, p.61

advance on Constantinople in 1878 led to an outbreak of war with Britain. If this wasn't bad enough, two weeks after Chelmsford finished his report into the defences of the Cape and shortly after Frere had won a desperate bureaucratic struggle with the Molteno ministry over the necessity to centralise control of the armed forces, both imperial and colonial, under his own command, the Natal telegraph told him that in July 1878, the Zulus had committed a series of border violations.

For Frere, this was the last straw. He was convinced that he had been lucky to avoid the coincidence of an African war and a Russian attack in 1877 and was now confirmed in his belief that both Cape and imperial security was dependent on the establishment of a *Pax Britannica* in South Africa. It was a fair conclusion; the Xhosa war he put down to the weak leadership of the chiefs, - 'the gigantic evil to which all this chronic insecurity and warfare is due'[291] – and with problems piling up with the mPondo protesting over the occupation of Port St. Johns, the usual problems of bandits and intermittent instability up beyond the Orange River, a continuing war with the mPedi and rebellion brewing in the Transvaal, he saw the Xhosa revolt being reprised by the Zulus and intended to nip it in the bud. A Zulu war, he reasoned, properly and swiftly conducted, would remove a major internal threat to Cape security, exclude the possibility of a European intervention on the east coast, mollify the Boers by ameliorating their fears of the Zulus and make them more favourable to confederation and, not least, rid the Zulus themselves of a tyrant who barred their path to civilisation and progress. If this was morally dubious, Frere was able to reconcile himself to it by reflecting that when he was in India, Sind had been conquered as a 'useful, humane piece of rascality'[292] by Lord Napier and had prospered under subsequent British rule.

In this conclusion though, he was wrong. The Zulus were no threat to the British at that time and, indeed, enjoyed rather good relations with the settlers in Natal. They traded cattle, recruited Tsonga labourers for them and though continuing to practice such objectionable things as summary justice, smelling-out and raids against the Swazi with no other aim than to wash the spears of younger warriors, they generally kept themselves to themselves. One of the leading chiefs of the Kingdom was the refreshingly unconventional John Dunn, a British trader who had adopted the Zulu lifestyle and had risen to some prominence. Certainly, they were suspicious of the Boers and had several long running disputes with them over territory in the north west of the kingdom, and their relations with the Swazis were usually characterized by enmity, but there had been no real difficulties since Mpande had been put on the throne by Andreas Pretorius in 1840. When Cetshwayo succeeded him in 1873, on the surface things looked set fair to continue. The only cloud on the horizon was the coming of age of a new generation of young warriors who, having been bored rigid by the boasting of their elders, were keen to shut them up by proving themselves in their own right. This was something that they had in common with the Xhosa who revolted in 1877 and went on a pointless spree of almost leaderless, formless violence that lacked planning, preparation or

---

[291] *The Christian Express*, 1 October 1877, p. 1. PRO 30/6/34. Frere sent this article to Carnarvon on 17 October 1877 with the comment "There is much truth in this article...." See also E18/925 p. 245. Correspondence between Sir Bartle Frere and Bishop Colenso December 1878-January 1879, Vol. II, p.68.
[292] Lord Napier quoted in P. Mason, *The men who ruled India*, (London, 1985), p. 145.

hope of success and was duly crushed. That said, it is entirely possible that the wilder spirits might have been contained had it not been for the blundering of Shepstone in annexing the Transvaal.

The new tension on the borders that resulted gave the growing war party within the Zulu kingdom focus and encouragement and also alerted Frere to the fact that Cetshwayo could field an army somewhere in the region of 40,000 strong; and these were not brainless boasting Xhosa boys but much better trained and disciplined warriors who had been brought up in a much stricter form of the age/regiment system than was common among the Xhosa. This meant that when a young Hell's Angel by the name of Mehlokazulu violated British territory to murder his mother, Frere interpreted this – and several related incidents - as indicative of both Cetshwayo's inability to control his people and a Zulu threat to invade Natal rather than just the symptoms of a tense frontier. And in that lay the decision to go to war.

Frere could not go to war without permission from London, however, but that permission was never denied him throughout the southern winter of 1878, even after Lord Carnarvon had resigned and been replaced by Sir Michael Hicks-Beach. Twenty years later, Hicks-Beach was to be a big beast in the parliamentary jungle but in 1878, the big beast was Sir Bartle Frere and the inexperienced young cabinet minister was inclined to do as the legendary proconsul advised. Carnarvon resigned in January 1878 and for a full nine months Hicks-Beach sat back and let Frere get on with the job with his full support and encouragement right up until Frere asked for some more troops to deal with the Zulus. Hicks-Beach took the request to Cabinet on 12th October 1878 and to his dismay found out that Disraeli and Salisbury had no intention whatsoever of backing a war in an obscure corner of South Africa while the Russians were marching on the borders of India and still camped outside Constantinople. Whereupon he did what politicians often do when they misread a situation; Hicks-Beach back-tracked, began distancing himself from Frere and sending contradictory dispatches designed to make it look like he knew nothing of the policy. Frere, in turn, dismissed Hicks-Beach's garbled messages as cold feet, political cowardice and general slipperiness. There has been a lot of gibberish written about how Frere apparently manipulated the time lag in telegraphic communications to ensure he got his war but the reality is that it wasn't until Frere got a partially transmitted telegraph on 30th November that he got the first inkling that Hicks-Beach was serious and this was made even more confusing by the fact that the troops were being sent as requested. By the time he got a clear order forbidding him to go to war on 13th December, he had already presented the ultimatum to the Zulus on the 11th and as far as he was concerned, that was that.

Frere felt that he had grounds enough for war and that he had made his case for it with the strong support of the Colonial Office in general and Hicks-Beach in particular. To throw the whole policy into reverse at such a crucial stage was, to him, simply madness and a prime example of the inadvisability of such interference from afar – a classic case of 'the Man on The Spot' problem. Furthermore, Frere felt that to withdraw an ultimatum once issued would be to destroy any credibility that he possessed with the Zulus and encourage them to think that the British yielded from fear, a result that could only encourage the pro-war party in

Cetshwayo's councils. Frere disobeyed his orders and went to war. Hicks-Beach falsified the records to make sure he didn't get the blame for encouraging him.

The subsequent war would have been confined to the footnotes of imperial History had not Michael Caine and Stanley Baker made a movie of the defence of Rorke's Drift called *Zulu* but it made such an impact that a whole industry of tour guides, military History enthusiasts, wargamers and cinema fans was created. Twenty years after the original *Zulu*, a 'prequel' called *Zulu Dawn* was released and was also great fun although it played faster and looser with the History than the original had; Bartle Frere really was played by an actor wearing an evil top hat and all the British officers were portrayed as blithering idiots eating lunch on a white table cloth while the Zulus were rampaging through their camp. The other thing that made the war worthy of more than a note was that the Zulus won an initial victory at a place called Isandhlwana that set anyone with a dislike of imperialism or the British hyperventilating about 'the worst military disaster *ever*'.

The level of scholarship that has gone into studying that battle is truly remarkable and the excellent Ian Knight (though a Leftie) has built a life time's work on it. I've been over that battlefield several times and it still gives me a thrill each time I go but I can't help but think that things have got a little out of perspective here; are we really surprised that 25000 Zulus were able to overwhelm a thousand Brits? Was it really the worst colonial defeat Britain ever suffered? (My money's on Maiwand, but there you go. Really, I'm not going down that rabbit hole). And was it really proof of the incompetence of those upper-class twit officers in scarlet coats and pith helmets? Reasons advanced for the British defeat at Isandhlwana are legion and I'll give you a selection; lack of screwdrivers to open the ammunition boxes (poppycock), breakdown in the ammunition supply (no), insufficient concentration of firepower (yes), eclipse (no, but there was one), dagga (yes), Colonel Durnford (yes- the main reason for me), a clever Zulu deception plan (no), Zulu leadership (yes), lack of a laager (no), incompetent colonial recce (yes), useless British generals (no), British arrogance (no, despite endless repetition), rank British cowardice (no), Zulus leaving their guns at home (yes; those that did have the sense to bring them to the fray were hopeless marksmen), the contradictions inherent in capitalist, imperialist exploitation (OK, I made that one up). You can take your pick and find plenty of people to agree or disagree with you with varying levels of vehemence, expertise and credulity. There are some great conspiracy theories too; one tour guide told me in all seriousness that Lord Chelmsford was pardoned for the defeat because he was rogering Queen Victoria. He needs his licence revoked, I'm telling you.

To my mind, what makes the battle really remarkable is that defeat for the British was such a rarity as to attract much scrutiny. I mean; here is a fairly (un)comprehensive list of British defeats between 1840 and 1879, Zulus included.
*Gandamack, Taku Forts, Isandhlwana, Hlobane.*
And here is a smattering of their victories.
*Jalalabad, Ghazni, Kabul, Chuenpi* (x2 plus a host of other scraps during the First Opium War), *Mudki, Ferozeshah, Aliwal, Sobraon, Rangoon, Alma, Balaclava, Inkerman, Khushab, Taku Forts,* a raft of fights during the Indian Mutiny, *Rangiriri, Multan, Gujarat* and…and

this doesn't include Napier's expedition to Magdala and Wolseley's West Africa show and…well, you get the picture.
And just to complete it, here are the British victories during the Zulu War.
*Rorke's Drift, Gingindlovu, Khambula, Ulundi* and, we should also mention, *Centane*, where they thrashed the Xhosa in 1878.

So, the Battle of Isandhlwana was little more than a blip and, without being completely heartless about the loss of a thousand men at Isandhlwana, it is worth pointing out that this wasn't Waterloo or the Somme. It's also worth pointing out that the reason why the invasion forces had to retire was not because the victorious Zulus were coming after them but because they lost all their wagons and had to go back to collect more to carry their supplies; the Zulus retired too; Cetshwayo's comment when he saw the casualty roll was 'an assegai has been thrust in the belly of the nation' by which he meant the Zulu nation, not the British; there were three thousand Zulus killed on that bare plain. We should also note that a fair few names on the British casualty roll belonged to men of the Natal Native Contingent (badly trained, badly armed, badly led and so not much use in a fight) and the Natal Native Horse (well trained, well-armed and mounted, well led and very useful in a fight), which tells you something about the dangers of banging on about race to the exclusion of all else.

What happened next? Frere was understandably frustrated at this setback but he left Chelmsford to get on with it and got on with what he considered to be the most important of his jobs – sorting out the Transvaal mess. This was, perhaps, his finest hour in South Africa. Riding alone into a Boer encampment full of armed men on the verge of revolt, Frere met with Kruger and the rest of the malcontents and after a series of negotiations persuaded them to calm down and go home while he told the government in London that unless they wanted a war with the Boers – something infinitely more serious than a war with the Xhosa or the Zulus – then a complete and comprehensive offer of self-government in a loose confederation ought to be made *tout suite*. He even managed to create a good impression with Paul Kruger.

By the 17th April 1879, therefore, Frere was well on his way to achieving the Confederation of South Africa. Over the preceding two years he had managed to put the colonies of South Africa in to a reasonable state of defence, had suppressed a Xhosa rebellion and instituted the rudiments of an efficient African administration among them, headed off a Boer rebellion brought on by the criminal incompetence of Shepstone, and was close to defeating the threat of the Zulu army. There was still work to be done of course, but he had managed to remove the sense of crisis that hung over the region and was well placed to begin the parliamentary and legal processes necessary for Confederation, a policy that many had thought dead before he had arrived. Isandhlwana had been a horrible setback, of course, but it was not a decisive one and, given Frere's experience of the scale of war in India, really rated as little more than an inconvenient skirmish.

The day after his agreement with Kruger, however, Frere received news that after a fierce debate in Parliament, he was to be censured for sanctioning the Zulu war. His prestige and authority were blown apart and any hope that confederation would now go ahead was lost because the government would not sanction his deal with Kruger, nor allow the annexation of Zululand, nor trust him with a threepenny message to the newsagents any more. They also sent out Sir Garnet Wolseley to win the war and sort the political mess out; unfortunately, he turned up too late to prevent Lord Chelmsford winning the final battle and having been forbidden to even think of annexing Zululand, effectively broke it up into a dog's breakfast of thirteen different chiefdoms and called it a peace settlement.

\*

### The Great Gladstonian Disaster

*"Who caused the Boer rebellion?"*
*"I," said the people's Willy,*
*"With my speeches so silly,"*[293]
Rider Haggard.

'Never trust a hippy,' said Johnny Rotten, and he was right. Never, ever, trust an idealist who believes that his ideals give him unimpeachable insight, the right to push those ideals over and past the considered opinions of people of experience and distinction and who will never consider the possibility that he might not just be a little or a lot wrong, but positively howling at the moon. Never, ever, trust a 'man of principle' who says that he is so committed that he's willing to die for them – he usually means he's willing to let other people die for them. And if you are ever so unfortunate as to have one of these monsters fool enough of the people for enough of the time to get themselves voted into office, then take a long step back and watch the bodies pile up. So step forward William Ewart Gladstone, the worst British Prime Minister to disgrace that great office until Tony Blair brought it to a nadir of shameful disrepute.

You either love Gladstone or you hate him. I count myself in the latter camp and having declared my corner, I'll spare you the effort of watching me give the pros and cons and pretending to be sage and measured in my judgement. They should have set the dogs on him. Beaten up at Oxford for being a prig – and never were finer blows more deservingly struck – he decided that the only guiding light he would follow from then on would be the unblemished radiance of his own moral judgement. This was honed by chasing a fallen countess to Italy to confirm that she was up the duff with a child that wouldn't pass muster in the parentage stakes, making a few sympathetic noises about slavery, hanging around with hookers and demi-mondes while being sniffy about his colleagues' mistresses and endlessly badgering his sister about her conversion to Catholicism; he sent her tracts to read which she sensibly used as toilet paper. He was an accomplished hater of people, never passed up an opportunity to ladle out platefuls of the dish best served cold, was utterly unscrupulous in the matter of parliamentary tactics and procedure, not above lying and dissembling like Tony Blair on speed and as woeful a hypocrite as ever disgraced the palace of Westminster. His

---

[293] Quoted in *The Cloak that I Left: A Biography of the Author Henry Rider Haggard by his daughter.* Lilias Rider Haggard (London, 1951).

own side loved him mainly for his ability to induce collective nausea in the ranks of the Tory party.

Disraeli, the Tory PM before him, thought that government should confine itself to defending the realm, maintaining the Queens's Peace, managing the posts and telegraphs, correcting abuses and settling grievances and generally letting people go about their business with as little interference as possible. In terms of foreign policy, he was in favour of maintaining the balance of power in Europe and, as we have seen, allowing the imperialists to improve the defences of the empire but not to the point of letting them run amok. Gladstone's approach to government was almost the opposite; everything must be reformed, interfered with and moralized over – it is to him in part that we owe that great evil imposition on the 19$^{th}$ Century working class, the Temperance movement; from 1881-1961, it was illegal to get a pint in Wales on a Sunday and it was only by good fortune that this outrageous and draconian measure was not extended to England. Gladstone, of course, preferred champagne to beer.... In terms of foreign policy, he believed that there was no problem that could not be solved if everyone got together and had a group hug and perish the thought that a British prime minister ought to act in the interests of the British people. This was what he called a 'Moral' foreign policy. As far as the empire was concerned, he was against it as long as his own pocket wasn't harmed, and stupid enough to think that the toothpaste could be put back in the tube once the imperialists had given it a good squeeze; nor did he care much if a few Africans got shot, ripped off, dispossessed or consigned to the rule of the Boers or the Germans. Never did it occur to him that Africans might be better off under British colonial rule than under indigenous tyrants; if you think this is an outrageous thought then take a look at the choice facing newly independent Ugandans in the 1960s – Idi Amin or Milton Obote; an animal or a cannibal? He was, in short, a disastrous dolt; and if you think I'm being overly harsh, I should point out that the empire expanded more under the anti-imperialist but thoroughly incompetent and idiotic Gladstone than it did under the pro-imperialist and extremely competent Disraeli, which pretty much clinches the argument that the qualifications he possessed to lead a great country would compare unfavourably with those of the Captain of the Good Ship Venus.

Defeating Disraeli in the 1880 election, Gladstone came into office on a platform of reversing imperial policy in South Africa and, specifically, handing back the Transvaal to the Boers. Barely a week after getting his knees under the Downing Street cabinet table, he decided that the political price in parliament of restoring Transvaal independence was too high and so it would not be given back. When the news reached the Transvaal, Kruger shook his head, hitched up his breeches and grumped off to raise a rebellion. Gladstone's response to this was to bury his head in the sand and hope the problem would go away; he refused to discuss South Africa in cabinet for the rest of the year.

The situation deteriorated fast however. In the small European society of South Africa, the uncertain challenges of farming on a dangerous frontier meant that neighbourly and kinship links were maintained at very great distances and at very great intensity. This meant that the grievances of the Transvaal Boer malcontents were transmitted to their relations, business contacts and friends in the Cape, Natal and the Orange Free State. A series of village meetings in the Cape to discuss the Transvaal annexation had resulted in the formation of the *Boere Beschermings Vereeniging* under Jan Hofmeyer and *Genootskap van Regte Afrikaners* under S.J. du Toit, both of which were pledged to defend Afrikaaner interests against what they saw as creeping Anglicisation.[294] The massacre of Slachter's Nek was dredged up to demonise the English as unjust, alien and divorced from the realities and traditions of Afrikaanerdom. Kruger too had been busy reaffirming these kinship links and was in regular contact with Hofmeyer.

Frere, still in post mainly because no-one could come up with a suitable replacement, was aware of this upsurge in feeling and knew that he was losing the political case for an English led Confederation. Even when the Transvaal legislative assembly passed the legislation allowing Confederation to go forward unanimously, Frere was wary because it was thought that the Boers had only voted for it in the belief that they could subvert English domination from within; a Confederation there would be, but under Afrikaaner rather than English influence.[295]

When the Cape Prime Minister, Sir Gordon Spriggs introduced the proposals for Confederation to the conference on the 26th June 1880, Kruger demonstrated how successful his campaigning had been by persuading large numbers of the Cape Dutch representatives to refuse the policy until the independence of the Transvaal had been restored – he sat in the public gallery to watch as Hofmeyer killed Confederation stone dead in the Cape Parliament.[296] The next month, the proposals for Confederation were formally rejected and Frere was finally sacked – and then Gladstone, in an act of pure spite, ruined him by making him submit his travel expenses. On 16th December 1880, Dingane's Day, the old *Vierkleur* flag of the South African Republic was raised and the Transvaal revolted against British rule. In one fell swoop, Gladstone had made such a hash of things as to threaten a collapse in Britain's global strategic position by handing over control of the vital route to India to Kruger and the Boers; it was only the fact that Kruger didn't fully realise the extent of the opportunity that he was presented with that South Africa did not fall completely.

It is popularly supposed that the British defeat at the hands of the Boers at the Battle of Majuba convinced the government in London that the game was up and the Gladstone would actually have to keep his word and restore the independence of the Transvaal but this isn't the case. Gladstone had decided to surrender already – it's all in the CO 879/18 Africa Confidential Print file - and General Colley's decision to seize Majuba was an attempt to gain a bit of a diplomatic bargaining chip. Majuba is important because it's a very big, steep hill that commands the Laing's Nek pass over the Drakensberg from Natal to the Orange Free State and the Transvaal.

It was here, again, that the hazard of war made itself felt. When the Boers realised that Colley had seized Majuba on the morning of 27th February 1881, their response was not to be

---

[294] For example see National Archives of South Africa, Pretoria, KK Official Publications of the Cape Colony Printed Papers Legislative Council Vol. 44 1881 Vol.1 C.1. Petition of the Scriba of the Dutch Reformed Church in favour of making Dutch language compulsory at examination for teachers and middle class certificate.

[295] Lanyon to Kimberley 10th June 1880. CO 291/ 6 Transvaal Despatches 1880 Vol II.

[296] Schreuder, *Gladstone and Kruger*, p.77.

overawed by his presence but to attack up the hill before Colley came off it. Colley's response to this attack was delayed until too late, possibly because he considered the Boer attack to be the work of hotheads who would soon be restrained by their commanders – in theory there was a truce in place and technically Colley had not broken it; Majuba was in *Natal* rather than the Transvaal. Once the Boers reached the lip of this flat-topped hill, the whole British position lay open to them and Colley had conceded the initiative. He was killed and the rest of the force was driven off the summit and the Boers have been hopping up and down with glee about it ever since.

Now, under normal circumstances, and by that I mean when the British government is not in the hands of pusillanimous idealists, the British army would dust itself off, scratch its head, work out what went wrong and then go back and kick some arses. Most people in the army and the cabinet assumed that this would happen if only to restore some pride and allow whatever negotiations that were to take place to do so from a position of strength. But this wasn't Gladstone's way at all; instead he *resupplied the Boer army with ammunition*. I know, you are gasping at the idea that a British prime minister would supply an enemy with the means to shoot British soldiers but it is nevertheless true. The evidence is in that same file. Gladstone even put it in his own diary. And then a couple of weeks later, he did it *again*. He absolutely did it *twice*.

The subsequent deal was a mess; in a rundown cottage at the end of a muddy track at the bottom of Majuba hill Gladstone agreed to complete Transvaal self-rule in return for a nebulously defined British 'suzerainty' which gave theoretical rights over its foreign relations, to be enforced by a single resident, the details to be settled by a Royal Commission. An attempt to preserve effective control over native affairs – there were a million black Africans in the Transvaal - was abandoned, British loyalists abandoned, the green light for Kruger to grab some territory in Swaziland given and Gladstone agreed the terms of what became known as the Pretoria Convention without bothering to submit them to the Cabinet.[297] What was worse was that Gladstone had created an impression in Kruger's mind that the British could always be bluffed, that they would always back down, that they could always be defeated in a war by dealing them a quick knockout blow which would convince the Liberals to run for the white flag, tripping over each other in their eagerness to be the first to surrender. In this last idea, he was right; but only if a slippery old coward like Gladstone was in charge. He would learn something different within a very few years. And it is no credit at all to Gladstone that Kruger did not realise that if he had pushed hard enough and continued to agitate in the Cape, he might well have come close to annexing the Cape to the Transvaal, rather than simply undoing Carnarvon's aim of doing the reverse.

The response across a wide section of opinion was predictable. Queen Victoria was furious. Sir Garnet Wolseley declared that Gladstone wouldn't fight for the Isle of Wight while the Tory leader, Lord Salisbury, accused Gladstone of cowardice. General Sir Evelyn Wood VC, victor of Khambula and the man who had handled the negotiations was ostracised by the army for not resigning. More to the point was the fact that Lord Hartington, the second most important man in the Liberal party was equally disgusted at Gladstone and resolved never to

---

[297] Schreuder, p.158.

allow him to run foreign and imperial policy again without keeping a firm grip on his collar. This, however, would take time to achieve. In the meantime, as a direct consequence of Gladstone's idiocy, disaster would come to Africa because Kruger wasted no time in seizing on the opportunities thus presented to him with a vengeance. Gladstone's cursed and cowardly bullets would not be used against Brits but against the Tswana and the Zulus.

Lord Hartington had a lot of reasons to dislike Gladstone. He thought Gladstone utterly unscrupulous in the way he had pipped him to the premiership; he despised him for sniffing at his mistress while he carried on with Laura Postlethwaite and other ladies of uncertain reputation; he thought he spent too much time with 'catankerous loons'[298] and loud-mouthed Radicals like John Bright; he also preferred first-hand experience and pragmatic solutions to Gladstone's demagoguery, flatulent rhetoric and tortuous logic. He also understood something about the realities of imperial defence, unlike Gladstone who could barely stand to be in the same room as a man in uniform; his private secretary was Reggie Esher, the man who would form the Committee of Imperial Defence in 1906. By contrast, Gladstone appointed Leonard Courtney to be under-Secretary at the Colonial Office, a bone-head who was strongly in favour of Britain withdrawing from South Africa altogether.

*

Interlude in Egypt.

As you have no doubt gathered by now, a central conclusion of my research is that South African affairs were intimately connected with events in other parts of the globe and in order to understand the dog's breakfast that was British South African policy in this period, it is necessary to understand a little of what was going on elsewhere. The Second Afghan War was a similar consequence of Disraeli's decision to allow the Jingoes to adopt a more active or 'forward' defence policy and had several similar results; a proconsul disobeyed his orders and started a war; there were disasters and victories; and Gladstone brought it all to an end in 1881 by a withdrawal that was widely felt to be a humiliation. The worm began to turn, however, over the issue of Egypt and everything that happened in South Africa needs to be understood against the background of what went on there.

During the 1860s Egypt was a country with the potential to grow in prosperity through her agricultural produce, *entrepot* trade, the massive injection of foreign capital provided by the construction of railways and telegraphs and, not least, the development potentialities of the Suez Canal. Unfortunately, her rulers squandered it. Instead of using the opportunity to import modern western business methods based on the creation of business confidence through strict codes of financial probity ("My word is my bond," in short hand), trade was conducted on the labyrinthine Levantine model, where contract law was conditional on personal connections and honest bargaining replaced with the routine dishonesty of haggling.[299] Nor were European standards of official probity adopted; the bureaucracy was quickly corrupted by *wathda* and *baksheesh* with all the inefficiency, waste and graft which went with them.[300] The dreams of wealth encouraged by the opening of the Suez Canal never

---
[298] Lady Salisbury to Beaconsfield relating a conversation with Hartington at Ascot. Quoted in A Roberts, *Salisbury: Victorian Titan*, (London, 1991) p.243.
[299] D.A. Farnie, *East and West of Suez. The Suez Canal in History 1854-1956*, (Oxford, 1969), p.11.

materialised, the Canal Company teetered on the brink of bankruptcy and dividends were not paid between 1869-1875.[301]

What little the Khedive Ismail and his son, Tewfik, understood about modern business practice could be summed up in the realisation that credit could be gained on the security of future taxation. For them this meant that a luxurious life-style and the excitement of foreign conquest in the Sudan could be enjoyed without actual cost to themselves and that debt collectors could be frightened off by armed threats to the canal. As a result, they made the fatal mistake in thinking that they had an inexhaustible line of credit. By 1876, they had bankrupted the country and been forced to sell their last asset, the Suez Canal Company shares to the British government. This left Egypt with a debt of £91 million on an annual income of £10 million and someone had to pay it.

Here then was a dilemma as much moral as financial; should the bondholders in Europe who had lent money to the profligate Khedive take the loss or should the peasants of Egypt be expected to cough up? This was not a simple question of dismissing the bondholders as disgruntled speculators grinding the faces of the *fellahin* into the mud of the Nile. What the bankers of Europe knew was that credit and business confidence were the keys to long-term prosperity and unless some substantial repayment of the debt was made then Egypt would only ever have access to future investment funding at ruinous rates and terms. Cancellation of the debt would, no doubt, be popular but the result would be such a flight of capital as to leave Egypt truly as a desert for the foreseeable future. In Europe, the result would be to rob thousands of small investors of their meagre capital and the collapse of those banks that had invested would bring down many other businesses in their wake, thus depriving potentially thousands more of their livelihoods. In the end, the long-term interests of the unemployed Liverpool docker, the French *rentier*, and the British banker were identical with those of the *fellahin*; what was needed was the restoration and protection of credit and confidence through decent financial management to allow the expansion of economic activity. This in turn meant European financial techniques and therefore European control of Egyptian finances and thereby the greater part of its government.

This presented a second moral dilemma; how far were the *fellahin* responsible for Ismail's debts when they had no say in the government? Representation issues aside, this question was complicated by the fact that the Khedive was hardly accepted as an Egyptian at all by the *fellahin* and much of the officer corps, but rather seen as a Turk who had rifled the treasury without reference or direct benefit to them. In this respect, the short-term interests of the unemployed Liverpool docker and the *fellahin* were not identical at all; the European bondholders, thought the *fellahin*, should get their money from the Turks who had squandered it or from the profiteers on their own exchanges, rather than by squeezing them for more taxes from which they would gain no immediate benefit. Nor was this an academic debate; Ismail's bankruptcy would produce an immediate economic and social crisis in Egypt as troops and civil servants went unpaid, government contracts were suspended or payments

---

[300] A. D. Elliot. *The Life of G.J. Goschen 1831-1907* Vol.I, (London, 1911), p.169
[301] Farnie, p.213.

defaulted upon, and hunger threatened. Unless action was taken quickly the catastrophic financial crash which all feared would be a certainty.

If the situation wasn't bad enough, the Balkan War and the Russian advance on Constantinople made things much worse. The Suez Canal was now vital to British war preparations because it was through that waterway that the British-Indian Army would come to turf the Russians out of the Balkans if they couldn't be persuaded to go peacefully. The result was the imposition of Dual Anglo-French control of the Egyptian government, the removal of the Khedive, a major restructuring plan and by 1880, a return to credit-worthiness. It might fairly be said that Disraeli and his Foreign Secretary, Lord Salisbury, had done a pretty good job of protecting a vital British interest, sorting out a financial mess and setting the country on the road to recovery and indeed they had. It would take Gladstone to undo all this and make such a complete hash of things that within a couple of years British troops would be marching into Cairo.

Gladstone in opposition had had much to say about Egypt and his answer to the problem was 'Egypt for the Egyptians'[302] and a refusal to do anything that might lay 'the almost certain egg of a North African empire.'[303] As usual with his vapourings, none of this meant anything and on gaining power in the election of 1880, he found that his empty idealism clashed with the realities of the situation. Just who were the Egyptians? Were they the profligate rulers? The corrupt but now restructured (unemployed) officials and army officers? Or the *fellahin*? Would the *fellahin* fare better under competent foreign control or under an incompetent nationalist administration? And – far more to the point - just how willing was he to put his principles in operation, cancel the debt and so lose the 40% of his personal wealth tied up in Egyptian bonds?[304] Not difficult that one really, is it?

In late January 1881, the Egyptian army, under the leadership of Colonel Arabi Pasha, revolted against taxation, unemployment and foreign control and the country began to disintegrate. Gladstone dithered, racked by his opposition to the only thing that could prevent Arabi repudiating the debt and occupying the Suez Canal – sending in the troops to prop up the Egyptian government and the Dual Control - and losing a big chunk of his personal fortune. His government began to fall apart too as Lord Hartington demanded action to stop the burgeoning anarchy but was constantly refused. In June 1882, Arabi instigated an anti-European and anti-Christian riot in Alexandria which left fifty people dead; Hartington's supporters insisted on sending the fleet whether Gladstone agreed or not and when Arabi started to build fortifications to threaten the anchorage, Hartington ordered the fleet to blow Arabi out of his fortifications and Gladstone out of control of his Egyptian policy. The army was going to Egypt whether the raddled old hypocrite liked it or not.

Wolseley's campaign went like clockwork. A feint at Alexandria was followed by a shift to Ismailia, the mid-point of the canal, and a march up along the sweet water canal to Cairo where Arabi waited in his fortified camp at Tel-El-Kebir. Wolseley pitchforked him out in

---

[302] Quoted in R. Shannon, *Gladstone:Heroic Minister*, (London, 1999), p.293.
[303] J. Morley, *Life of Gladstone Vol.II*, (London, 1908), p.234.
[304] R. Jenkins, *Gladstone*, (London, 1995), p.507.

thirty-five minutes after a night march and a dawn attack on 13th September 1882[305] and threw a flying column into Cairo to prevent it going up in riot and looting. The Egyptian government was confirmed in office but it was quite clear now where the power lay.

The question of whether Gladstone's heavy investment in the Egyptian debt compromised his anti-imperial policy has been answered with a resounding 'no' by most Historians but I think they are being too kind; whenever I have put the question to my students there has been a resounding unanimity of opinion and you can probably guess what that is. I'm with Lytton Strachey, whose poison pen portrait in *Eminent Victorians,* described the soul of this 'slippery old man'[306] as having a dark spot in its centre.[307] Believe what you like, but he certainly felt no shame at all about the victory: he ordered guns to be fired in Hyde Park and bells to be rung in the churches after Tel-El-Kebir.[308] A cynic might say that he good reason - he had, after all, just made £7,500 (£375,000 approximately at today's prices) on his Egyptian investments.[309] I'm a cynic.

It would be pleasant at this point to report that Gladstone, having learned his lessons and taken on board the fact that as far as foreign and imperial policy was concerned he was as much use as a cow with a musket and decided to leave matters in the hands of those who knew about such things. But no; as soon as the bells had stopped ringing, Gladstone started to insist that the troops come home, the Egyptian government be left to its own devices and the canal handed over to international control and so paralysed Hartington's policy.

The first result of this hands-off approach was that the Egyptian government was allowed to send out what Winston Churchill later called 'possibly the worst army that has ever marched to war'[310] in an attempt to re-assert its control over Sudanese rebels under their Islamic leader, the *Mahdi.* They were massacred on Guy Fawkes Night 1883, in a battle that was said to have lasted only fifteen minutes[311] and left the Mahdi in pole position to strike at the Red Sea ports and so produce yet another threat to the route to India. Gladstone responded to this with yet another outburst of appeasement and demanded that Egypt withdraw from the Sudan. Hartington had other ideas; he had not sent troops to secure the Suez Canal jugular to see the Mahdi establish himself just a little further down this route and pulled out from his sleeve the Gordon Wild Card. This was the second result.

Ostensibly charged with evacuating the Sudanese garrisons,[312] the reality is that Charles Gordon was sent to the Sudan by Hartington in the hope that he would disobey Gladstone's instructions and bring it back under Egyptian control. In this Hartington was hardly

---

[305] WO33/41 Papers 1883 Part 2. 0931 to 0948. Papers in connection with the Egyptian Campaign of 1882.

[306] Strachey, *Eminent Victorians*, p.248.

[307] Strachey, *Eminent Victorians*, p.236.

[308] Shannon, *Gladstone:Heroic Minister*, p.306.
[309] Jenkins, *Gladstone*, p.508.
[310] W. Churchill, *The River War*, (London, 1899), p. 34.
[311] Holland, *Duke of Devonshire* Vol.I, p.410. Churchill said that the army disintegrated after three days of harassing attacks. See W. Churchill, The River War, (London, 1899), pp. 34-6.

[312] Holland, *Duke of Devonshire* Vol.I, p. 417.

gambling because 'Cracked Charlie'[313] had a reputation for erratic behaviour and messianic alcoholism alongside the more useful virtues of charismatic leadership and experience in the Sudan; take a look at the doodles and ramblings in his famous Khartoum journals and you'll be amazed that anyone would put him in charge of a train set. He went south, got himself surrounded by the Mahdi and dug in at Khartoum, offering himself up as the damsel in distress who must be rescued by the knight in shining armour. Hartington polished up his spurs, only to have Gladstone forbid any talk of a 'Gordon Relief Expedition'; as far as he was concerned, Gordon could go hang. It wasn't until the press clamour for the rescue of the 'Christian Hero' grew to monumental proportions and Hartington threatened to thump Gladstone (literally) that an expedition was mounted. It was too late. Khartoum fell and Gordon died before the relief expedition could get to him; whereupon Gladstone sat down and wrote the most odious letter of condolence in History to his relatives.

So what does all this have to do with South Africa? Firstly, it is important because Egyptian affairs dominated things and were seen as much more important than affairs in South Africa but when added to events in South Africa, the results built up a head of steam in the public mind against Gladstone's pusillanimous incompetence; previously he had been known as the Grand Old Man (GOM), now he was known as MOG (Murderer Of Gordon). Secondly, the general disgust as Gladstone's incompetence resulted in policy being taken out of his hands by Hartington and decisions that were not official government policy being made by defence experts. In this way, the empire expanded into areas of South Africa that were of no economic worth but certainly held strategic value because the people guiding the policy were interested in defence not economic gain. Thirdly, the important economic drivers of empire were concerned with trade and the financial system rather than grabbing land and ripping off indigenous people; Britain took Egypt to stop the financial system collapsing, to prevent Colonel Arabi interfering with the cargoes and mails (particularly the vital Bills of Exchange and Lading) that went through the Suez Canal and to ensure that the canal would always be open to use by British troops. Strategic and economic interests were interwoven, but rarely in the way that they have been portrayed by Marxist Historians; troops did not kick down the door so that evil top-hatted capitalists could burgle the house. Please put that garbage out of your mind immediately.

*

### The Boer Offensive: Bechuanaland.

The Pretoria Convention ending the war between Britain and the Transvaal was signed in October 1881 and the Boer assault on the Tswana began before the ink was properly dry. Any idea that the Boers might be restrained by the presence of still powerful British forces in the area was given the lie by Gladstone withdrawing the troops in November 1881 and calling a halt to the upgrading of the Cape Town defence works. As a direct result, Kruger came up with a brilliant way of exploiting the pettifogging legalism that was so often a constraint on British policy. He was determined to expand Transvaal territory just as fast and

---

[313] G. Macdonald Fraser, *Flashman and the Tiger*, (London, 1999), p.49. Possibly a more current nickname in London clubland for him than 'Chinese' – Granville certainly suggested that he was "not a little cracked". Granville to Hartington, 11th January 1884. Reproduced in P. Jackson, *The Last of the Whigs*, (London, 1994), p.152.

as far as he could and he read Gladstone perfectly in believing that if he could offer an excuse for him *not* to intervene in his plans, then the slippery old fraud would bite his hand off to get it. Gladstone was forever banging on about 'international law' as though it actually meant something and so Kruger concocted a set of legal fictions that would keep any number of lawyers willingly bound up in well-paying red tape for any amount of time and offer Gladstone any number of opportunities not to 'suppose that there are producible reasons for apprehending a necessity of some kind for doing something precautionary'[314] – he really did speak like this. Disraeli said he was 'intoxicated by the exuberance of his own verbosity' in a nice bit of satire.

Kruger's trick went like this; organise a trek and send it off to steal some land; claim that the Transvaal Republic knows nothing about it; get the Trek to declare themselves to be an independent republic; claim that the Transvaal Republic knows nothing about it; have the independent republic steal land, overthrow local rulers and put puppet rulers up to legalise their land claims; claim that the Transvaal Republic knows nothing about any of it; get the independent republic to ask for unification with the Transvaal Republic; reluctantly accept.

Did it work? You bet it did. How often? If you go to the Voortrekker monument outside Pretoria, you will see hanging there the flags of the Republic of Stellaland, Goschen and the New Republic and their story is remarkable. What did Gladstone do about this trick? He fell for it. Probably worse, he didn't care whether he fell for it or not.

Beginning almost immediately after Majuba, Boer farmers and freebooters had already begun to make serious inroads into the Tswana lands in the impossibly remote lands north of Kimberley. Here, where rivers ran intermittently if at all, pressure on grazing was intense and instability rife as the loose kinship and tribal networks of the Tswana began to break down as the young men went off to work at Kimberley and the ever disruptive Griqua clans north of the Orange River robbed, rebelled and generally kept the place in a state of disorder. By 1881, the desperate Tswana chiefs began hiring mercenaries and war broke out between the 'pro-Boer' Moswete and Mosweu and the 'pro-British' Mankurwane and Montshiwa while the Boers themselves established the Republic of Goschen in 1881[315] and Stellaland in 1882. Lord Kimberley at the Colonial Office protested about this but Kruger and 'Slim' Piet Joubert simply ignored him on the grounds that if the British were serious then they would cut off the Boer ammunition supply and this Gladstone would never accept because it was effectively, a declaration of war. Result? The Boers kept advancing and the Tswana – who did not get ammunition – kept losing. In September 1882, Mankurwane surrendered his lands to the Transvaal.

Just as Hartington grew angrier and angrier at Gladstone's behaviour over Egypt, Lord Kimberley's fury began to mount over Gladstone's appeasement in southern Africa. It wasn't just a question of ammunition supply; there was some logic to keeping the Boers dependent on Britain in this respect but there was none at all where the matter of money was concerned. The Achilles heel of the Boer republics was their chronic inability to collect taxes and manage some form of national financial stability with the result that Kruger's

---

[314] Shannon, *Gladstone:Heroic Minister*, p.293.
[315] D.M. Schreuder, *The Scramble for Southern Africa, 1877 - 1895* (Cambridge, 1980), p. 90.

government was horribly in debt and dependent on raising loans abroad. Gladstone had already written off a large portion of these debts after Majuba but financial pressure still remained a viable weapon to restrain Boer encroachment; instead of using this influence, Gladstone wrote off another slice of the debt. Whatever Kimberley felt about this was irrelevant; Gladstone ensured that there would be no Cabinet discussion on Bechuanaland affairs for nearly eighteen months and in December 1882, sacked him to be replaced by the dithering Lord Derby.

This decent, but weak man never really understood the forces that he was dealing with, and his diaries give an impression of a man bemused by his predicament, but not really touched by it. He regarded the Colonial Office as virtually a part-time job which came as a welcome diversion from running the family estates; for him ruin and slaughter in South Africa was an interesting problem, but not one that need concern him more than a difficult crossword. He was also a Tory defector who had characterised Disraeli's foreign policy memorably as 'occupy, fortify, grab and brag' and a complete 'soft touch'.[316] To him Bechuanaland was 'absolutely unproductive for the purposes of trade...no value to us for any English or Imperial purposes'[317] – which was true - and he denied that Britain had any responsibilities towards the Tswana – which was also true, if one rules out simple humanitarianism. Dismissing the advice of his own officials that the Boers were 'determined in one way or another to procure the extension of their territories,'[318] were carrying out 'a clean sweep... [in the Bechuana] country of everything larger than a domestic fowl';[319] that they could only be stopped by force, and that if the Pretoria Convention was not to be enforced than it should be abandoned, Derby pottered about doing nothing effectual. This was because Gladstone was indeed planning to abandon the Pretoria Convention and leave the Tswana to the tender mercies of Kruger.

*

### The Boer Offensive: Zululand.

If Gladstone expressed his anti-imperialist morality as appeasement in the Transvaal and the acquiescence in the dispossession of poor black farmers in Bechuanaland, in Zululand he expressed it as a desire to return to the *status quo ante bellum 1879* in an attempt to make personal restitution to a man who he felt had been personally wronged. This man was the tyrant Cetshwayo, a man who had all the flaws bestowed by power unrestrained by law, was happy to practice smelling-out when it suited him and happy to attack the weaker tribes around him; he was definitely not 'a prince of Humanity' as Bishop Colenso's daughter, Fanny, optimistically described him in her long shriek against the war (the old hypocrite Bishop Colenso had backed the war, then changed his mind; Fanny's lover, Colonel Durnford, had been killed at Isandhlwana)[320]. Certainly, he understood the reality of British

---

[316] Conference Paper, 'The View from Knowsley' 19-20th March 2004. John Vincent: *The 15th Earl of Derby.*

[317] Quoted in Schreuder, *Gladstone and Kruger*, p.327.

[318] CO 879/20 Memorandum: Condition of South-Western Border of the Transvaal State and the working of the Pretoria Convention. AWLH 3rd March 1883.

[319] CO 879/20 Memorandum: Condition of South-Western Border of the Transvaal State and the working of the Pretoria Convention. AWLH 3rd March 1883.

and Boer power and was no direct threat to either when Frere miscalculated in 1879, but this did not make Cetshwayo either a martyr or a victim; he was a dangerous man who had come to power in a bloody civil war and whose power to restrain a growing war party in his councils was beginning to slip. Gladstone's pig-headed refusal to muse on the *practical* results of trying to put the Zulu toothpaste back in the tube rather than wallow in the shallow and murky bath of his fluid morality would bring disaster here as well.

The roots of this policy lay in the peculiar circumstances created by Wolseley's post war settlement. After running Cetshwayo to ground in August 1879 (without recourse to genocide, as one writer has ludicrously asserted),[321] Wolseley broke up the Zulu kingdom into thirteen smaller ones in an attempt to get a quick peace and then get home and pass on the poisoned chalice to someone else. The Tlokwa, who had fought for the British during the war, were allocated the lands around Rorke's Drift and John Dunn, Cetshwayo's British born *induna*, was given control of all the lands along the Tugela to form a buffer zone along the Natal border. Further north, the land was divided up among those chiefs who had some reason to resist the re-imposition of a strong, centralised monarchy and who had given some form of material assistance to the British during the war.[322] Cetshwayo was taken to Cape Town to an enforced residence first at the castle and then on a farm on the Cape Flats where he might live in comfortable exile. To maintain the settlement, Melmoth Osborn was appointed as resident in Zululand but without any armed force to make his influence potent.

With the change of government in 1880 came Gladstone's predisposition to restore Cetshwayo to the throne of Zululand. Unfortunately, the defeat and capture of Cetshwayo had unleashed all the separatist, decentralising forces that had existed in the kingdom before Cetshwayo's coronation and the general feeling was that it would be better if Cetshwayo stayed in the Cape. Returning him would have the consequences of either releasing full-scale civil war as he attempted to re-establish his kingdom or, if he was successful, reconstituting the potential Zulu threat to Natal that the war had removed. Alarm bells should have rung in the Colonial Office when Kruger and Joubert began to press for Cetshwayo's restoration in 1881-2;[323] what they wanted was a civil war in Zululand so that they could move on Richard's Bay and St. Lucia to get the port they had always desired. Lord Kimberley was against the plan but Gladstone went ahead and invited Cetshwayo to London in the summer of 1882 to negotiate a new treaty.

The new treaty was possibly worse than the original one,[324] in that Cetshwayo was restored to the central part of his kingdom carved out from territory taken from other chiefs which meant that he would have to fight to assert his authority while the others would have to fight to resist it. At the same time, Cetshwayo was forced to agree to restraints which forbade him to revive the military system and deprived him of the right to regain the royal cattle lifted by the

---

[320] Killie Campbell Africana Library KCAL SR 968.3 Col. Frances E. Colenso, *Sir Bartle Frere's last Attack on Cetshwayo, Sir. H. Bulwer and Bishop Colenso*, (Privately printed, 1882), p.12.
[321] M. Lieven, '"Butchering the Brutes all over the place": Total War and Massacre in Zululand, 1879,' *History*, Vol.84, No.276 October 1999. Professor Laband refuted this argument in detail during a lecture given at the National Army Museum, Chelsea in 2001.
[322] Laband, *Rope of Sand,* pp.337-9.
[323] Laband, *Rope of Sand*, p.349.
[324] Entry 5th January 1883, DD. See also KCAL Africa SR 968.3 Col. Frances E. Colenso, *Sir Bartle Frere's last Attack on Cetshwayo, Sir. H. Bulwer and Bishop Colenso*, (Privately printed, 1882), pp. 5-6.

other chiefs. In short, Gladstone, through his ignorance of the realities of Zulu culture, the brutality of its politics and the changed conditions of post-war Zululand,[325] sent Cetshwayo back to face serious rivals without the means to support his authority, over-ruling Kimberley, who understood exactly what that meant,[326] the Queen,[327] and the Natal officials, in the hope of salving his conscience.

Cetshwayo had no intention of accepting these restraints however[328] and on arrival back in Zululand in January 1883 had, by March, begun to attack his main rival, Chief Zibhebu. The expedition was a terrible failure which resulted in the massacre of his impi in the Msebe valley, and a widespread rebellion. Rather than rein Cetshwayo in at this blatant disregard of the conditions imposed on his restoration, Gladstone then proposed to give him some other territory but then on 21st July 1883, Cetshwayo's forces were decisively defeated at oNdini and he fled wounded into hiding while Zululand sank into anarchy, butchery, murder and theft.[329] Derby refused to intervene on the grounds that it was up to the Zulus to choose their rulers, not Britain or the colonists of the Cape or Natal, a position that brought forth the brilliant riposte from Lt.Governor Bulwer; 'Zulus unaccustomed to elect rulers; dare not express preference, fearing consequences.'[330] Predictably, Gladstone tried to sack him despite the fact that he and Derby admitted to each other that actually Bulwer's predictions about Cetshwayo were 'exactly true'.[331] Gladstone's callousness in this was breath-taking; a further civil war would be less 'evil than our territorial intervention.'[332] For Gladstone, rape, butchery, murder and all the bloody meanness of civil war was a price worth paying as long as he did not have to accept further imperial responsibilities. Derby meekly swallowed the line; for him, shooting meant grouse; he did not mention it in his diary. In the event, the Zulus did settle their own affairs as far as Cetshwayo was concerned; his rivals poisoned him in February 1884.[333] Zululand dissolved into the butchery and hunger of a 'self-destructive stalemate.'[334]

The Boer intervention was not long in coming. In April 1884, Cetshwayo's heir, Dinizulu, was spirited across the border into the Transvaal[335] and the Committee of Dinizulu's Volunteers – a Commando - entered Zululand in May 1884.[336] Dinizulu was crowned by the Commando shortly afterwards and Zibhebu was defeated at the battle of Tshaneni on 5th June 1884. The New Republic was proclaimed – nothing to do with the Transvaal, of course – and Dinizulu ceded over a million hectares to the new Boer state, accepted their sovereignty over the rest of Zululand and gave the Transvaal its outlet to the sea in St. Lucia Bay. Gladstone's

---

[325] For an analysis of conditions see Fynn to Bulwer 29th November 1883, NA ZGH 687 Zululand Correspondence October – December 1883. Henry Fynn was appointed resident with Cetshwayo when Osborn moved to be resident of the Reserve territory.
[326] Laband, *Rope of Sand*, p.353. See also entry 16th January 1883, DD.
[327] Entry 1st February 1883, DD.
[328] Entry 14th August 1882. Lord Kimberley's Journal (KJ). See also entry 14th May 1883, DD.
[329] Derby to Bulwer, 18th September 1883. CO 879/20 African No. 255 Telegrams to and From South Africa 1883. See also entry 14th May 1884, GD.
[330] Bulwer to Derby, 27th November 1883. CO 879/20 African No. 255 Telegrams to and From South Africa 1883.
[331] Derby to Gladstone, 30th September 1883. BL. Add.44141 Gladstone Papers Vol.LVI Correspondence with Derby, 1850 - October 1883.
[332] Gladstone to Derby, 19th December 1883. BL. Add.44142 Gladstone Papers Vol.LVI. Correspondence with Derby, 1883 – 1886.
[333] Osborn to Bulwer 23rd August 1883, NA ZGH 686 Zululand Correspondence August - October 1883. Osborn to Bulwer 8th February, 22nd April 1884, NA ZGH 688 Zululand Correspondence January -April 1884.
[334] Laband, Rope of Sand, p.369. See also Osborn to Bulwer 5th September 1883, NA ZGH 686 Zululand Correspondence August - October 1883; Fynn to Bulwer 29th November 1883, NA ZGH 687 Zululand Correspondence October – December 1883.
[335] Osborn to Bulwer 22nd April 1884 NA ZGH 688 Zululand Correspondence.
[336] Minute paper 1st May 1884, NA ZGH 689 Zululand Correspondence.

anti-imperialism had now succeeded in destroying the Zulu kingdom more completely than anything the arch-imperialist, Sir Bartle Frere, had contemplated and in granting them an outlet to the sea had provided the Boers not just with the opportunity to seek European alliances but also freed them from dependence on the British for their ammunition supply, a luxury not enjoyed since Louis Trichardt trekked to Lourenco Marques in 1837.[337]

Just when you think that things can't get worse, when an idealist is in charge, they always do. This is because they proceed from the theory to the facts rather than the other way around. For Gladstone, the theory was that imperialism was a moral *wrong* and so therefore the opposite – that anti-imperialism was a moral *right* – must also be true. You can hear simple minded people chanting this Manichean idiocy at any Left-wing demonstration and insisting on its essential correctness even when it is obviously and demonstratively wrong. What if, in the circumstances of 1880, imperialism was the best answer to the problem of South Africa even if it might not have been the best answer in 1879? What if Frere had been allowed to get on with Confederation despite the Isandhlwana cock-up and the 1880 election? Imagine; Zululand patched up with mission schools, hospital, magistrates and markets and enjoying a high degree of internal self-government, its young men working for wages and accumulating wealth rather than posing with spears; perhaps the wilder spirits would be enrolled as African Sepoys as Frere wanted? No more smelling-out, no more compulsory military service, no more arbitrary killings and an end to civil war. There is a strong case to be made for leaving the Zulus to their own ways and *not* invading Zululand in 1879 but once the deed had been done, failing to follow up, changing horses in midstream and then washing British hands of the whole affair was absolutely *not* the right thing to do. In this case, *imperialism* was the morally *right* course to take and anti-imperialism simply an evasion of responsibility for deeds done. The problem with idealists is that they do not change the theory when the facts change. And the bodies start to pile up as a result.

*

The Boer Offensive: Back to Bechuanaland.

There had been rumours of German ambitions in southern Africa since 1877 but the activities of a few Hamburg merchants and individual explorers had raised few real fears for the British 'Monroe Doctrine' over Africa.[338] However, throughout 1877-79 Frere warned on several occasions about the possibility of a European powers grabbing a bit of the coastline and teaming up with the Boers[339] and it was this worry that had led him to annex Walfisch bay and Port St. Johns in Pondoland. In July 1880, he returned to the subject again, naming Angra Pequena as the likely site of a Boer-German colony. Lord Kimberley thought otherwise and discounted the warnings.[340] In August 1883, however, Frere's warnings came true when the ex-guano captain, Adolf Luderitz, asked for German Consular protection for his trading post and 215 square miles of territory acquired from the Namaquas at Angra

---

[337] An event marked by an important frieze in the Voortrekker Monument, Pretoria.
[338] J. Charmley, *Splendid Isolation? Britain, the balance of Power and the Origins of the First World War*, (London, 1999) p.193.
[339] Frere to Hicks-Beach 10th August 1878, cited in Worsfold, p. 85; Frere to Carnarvon 24th August 1877, PRO 30/6/33. Frere to Hicks-Beach 5th September 1878. PRO CO 879/14 No.196.
[340] Frere to Kimberley, 19th July 1880. Correspondence respecting a Colony at Angra Pequena, CO 879/21.

Pequena – the town is now called Luderitz - on the Skeleton coast about half way between Walfisch Bay and Cape Town.

Bismarck had no interest whatsoever in acquiring a colonial empire beyond using the possibility of the odd colony to irritate the British and in response to Luderitz's request asked Lord Granville, the Foreign Secretary – a man with as much vim as Lord Derby i.e., none – who actually owned the piece of desert in question. The correct answer was 'Britain' because the whole area had been annexed in 1861, the flag being planted by a certain Acting-Lieutenant Jackie Fisher, but Granville was unaware of this. Derby thought it was beyond his job description to do anything so radical as pass an opinion or make a decision on the subject and the result was, after a year of the usual invertebrate dithering, that Bismarck annexed it along with all the coastline from Cape Colony up to just about two hundred miles south of Walfisch Bay. Granville and Derby meekly accepted it; Derby had even gone so far as to send a gunboat to Angra Pequena to prevent a party of *English* traders throwing Luderitz off what they claimed was their own property[341] while Granville offered to give the Germans everything west of 20 degrees of Longitude and throw in Namaqualand and Damaraland to the south to boot.[342] As far as they were concerned it was all useless desert and the Germans were welcome to it.

What these forerunners of Laurel and Hardy had missed was that Angra Pequena lay at the end of one of the very few practicable routes across Namaqualand, skirting the southern Kalahari and following seasonal river beds along the Kuruman or Molopo rivers to emerge at Stellaland and Goschen. Now the Boers, simultaneously pressing into Zululand and Bechuanaland, had two potential outlets to the sea, one of which was completely outside British control and which, if it could be reached in time, would free them from any residual dependence on the British, especially if they could get a German alliance. The evidence is of course circumstantial, given the patchy records of the freebooter republics at Stellaland and Goschen, that Bismarck, Luderitz and the Transvaal were co-ordinating their activities, but Luderitz made his claim just as the Transvaal was preparing to renegotiate the Pretoria Convention. At the same time, the flag chosen for the Republic of Goschen incorporated the German tricolour for the first time,[343] rather than echoing the Dutch colours more usually employed, which, given that flags are by their very nature loaded with symbolism, provides more evidence of at least a desire to tempt Germany into alliance with the Boers. If Gladstone, Granville and Derby missed the significance of these concurrent developments, very many South Africans did not.

In Bechuanaland, the news of April 1883 that a Transvaal deputation was heading to London to renegotiate the Pretoria Convention sent Mankurwane into a desperate panic to save his country. In June he asked for his country to be annexed to the Cape and served notice that he would fight the Boers to the last if necessary.[344] In September, he asked to be represented at the negotiations in London,[345] but Derby made it quite clear that he could go hang. The deal

---

[341] Admiralty to Derby, 19th October 1883, Derby to Admiralty 22nd October 1883. CO 879/20 African No. 255 Telegrams to and From South Africa 1883.
[342] E.Malet to Granville 24th December 1884. BL. Add. 44629 Gladstone Papers Vol.DXLIV.
[343] All the flags of the various Boer states are hung in the Voortrekker monument, Pretoria.
[344] Smyth to Derby 11th June 1883. CO 879/ 20 African No. 255 Telegrams to and From South Africa 1883.
[345] Smyth to Derby, 27th September 1883. CO 879/ 20 African No. 255 Telegrams to and From South Africa 1883.

was settled in February 1884 without reference to any of the Tswana; the London Convention gave the Boers everything they asked for; a reduction of the debt, an end to British control of native affairs and a new western boundary. The South African Republic was now to all intents and purposes, independent;[346] Derby himself scratched out the word 'Suzerainty' from the preamble and so removed one thin vestige of British control.[347] Almost the first act of the new ZAR was to push on with the offensive in Bechuanaland in defiance of the newly drawn boundary. Kruger went on to a fabulous reception in Berlin.

The publication of this latest piece of shameful appeasement at a time when the Gordon affair was beginning to excite much pro-imperial sentiment, was simply too much and as a result of a public outcry, Derby was pushed into declaring a protectorate that was expressly designed to prevent the Germans and the Boers from linking up. Montsoia wasn't prepared to wait for the news or trust to the word of the people who had promised the protectorate – who would? – and attacked a large Boer camp at Rooi Grond, which was situated officially in the Republic of Goschen, but actually straddled the border with the Transvaal. The attack was successful and half of the township was burnt to the ground. The Transvaal responded with a declaration of war on 24th June 1884 and by the end of July, Montsoia had been defeated and a British police officer and magistrate, Bethell and Walker, murdered in cold blood.[348] This might well have been brushed under the carpet had not the Transvaal declared Montsoia as now under *their* protection, which was a step too far for even Derby coming so soon after the London Convention.[349] The press went crazy too.

*

### The Boer Offensive: Zululand Again.

Bismarck's annexation of Angra Pequena had paid off such dividends in producing a near complete meltdown in British policy that he decided to replicate the situation in Natal. In late 1884 a German intelligence mission[350] led by the traveller, Dr. Einwald,[351] allegedly in the pay of Luderitz, and four German officers, had arrived in Zululand with the blessing of the government of the New Republic ostensibly to inquire into the murder of a German missionary and the confiscation of lands held by some other German missionaries. Einwald had demanded that the lands be restored and asserted to Dinizulu a German right to protect German residents in Zululand. At the same time, he indicated that he intended to urge the German government to set up a settlement in Pondoland. Einwald and Luderitz were mainly interested in St. Lucia Bay and had persuaded Adolf Schiel, Dinizulu's secretary, to whom Dinizulu had originally (allegedly) ceded the area, to give up his claims to them.[352] In early

---

[346] See CO 879/21 African No. 278 London Convention 27th Feb 1884 for the full text.
[347] Roberts, p. 292.
[348] CO 879/23 African No. 301. Bechuanaland Affairs. E. Fairfield. See also "Mr Forster on South Africa" *The Times* 10th October 1884. Walker was said to have been beheaded.
[349] CO 879/23 African No. 301. Bechuanaland Affairs. E. Fairfield.
[350] Secret Memo on German interference in Zululand, 14th January 1885, NA ZGH 693 Zululand Correspondence.
[351] CO879/23 African No.307 General View of Zulu Affairs 1879 –1885 January 1886. E. Fairfield.
[352] Agreement between Adolf Schiel, F. Luderitz and A. Einwald 4th December 1884. National Archives of South Africa, Pretoria. T11 Archief Van de "Nieuwe Republik" (later district Vrijheid in de ZA Republiek) 1884-88. NR 79 Dokumente insake die Akgerwandigde van de N. Republiek maar Europa in 1885, p.15. See also Bulwer to Derby, 12th February 1885. CO 879/22 No.295. Telegrams to and From South Africa Jan to December 1885 and CO 879/22 Africa No.294a St.Lucia Bay and Zululand. Note by the German ambassador and Memo thereon. 7th Feb 1885.

1885, further talks were held between Dinizulu/Schiel and the Germans which clearly envisaged a joint German-Boer occupation of St. Lucia Bay,[353] especially as a German frigate had been reported in St. Lucia Bay in January 1885.[354] At the same time D. Esselen of the New Republic who, by surely no coincidence, had acted as translator to the Transvaal delegation during the London Conference negotiations,[355] and who had then pitched up in London again in October 1884 to protest about British involvement in Bechuanaland[356] (and who had begun surveying the site of a possible town at St. Lucia Bay)[357] went to Germany in June 1885 to pursue the project further,[358] but by this time Bismarck had lost interest. The public outcry at Gladstone and the virtual warfare within the Cabinet at his imperial policy was reward enough and among the many things that Bismarck knew was when not to overplay his hand. Under pressure from statesmen at the Cape, Hartington and a press campaign,[359] Derby was forced to act against his will again and St. Lucia Bay was annexed in December 1884 – without anyone telling Gladstone.

In Pondoland, a similar fishing trip was attempted by the Germans. In December 1883, a report arrived at the Colonial Office indicating that the mPondo were running guns into the port,[360] which was followed in March 1884 with a report that they were in negotiations with a Hamburg firm to purchase 2,000 Snider rifles and 200,000 rounds of ammunition.[361] In August 1884, Chief Mqikela asserted his right to levy customs duties on goods imported through the port or trans-shipped across his territory and demanded that the troops that Frere had stationed at the mouth of the river in 1877 be withdrawn.[362] When considered with concurrent events in Zululand and Bechuanaland, the danger of an African rising being exploited by a German intervention slowly filtered into Derby's consciousness and – remarkably and about five years too late - led him to embrace Frere's policy of annexing the coastlines. Bismarck, understandably, was not convinced by Derby's determination and in April 1885, Mqikela entered into a series of business agreements with the German, Emile Nagel, in which he offered business concessions in return for German protection.[363] Nagel began landing goods at the newly opened Port Grosvenor, a short distance away, only to be prevented by the British resident.[364] This time the Natal government took the decisive action of instituting a blockade of Pondoland through the expedient of detaining ships clearing for Port Grosvenor or Port St. John's in Durban and Bismarck got the message; he backed off and Pondoland was annexed.

\*

---

[353] Osborn to Bulwer 19th March 1885, NA ZGH 693 Zululand Correspondence. See also CO879/22 African No.293 Confidential memorandum for the Cabinet. St.Lucia Bay. RGWH.
[354] H. Shepstone to Bulwer 31st January 1885. NA GH 575 Admiral of the Fleet despatches, Secret and confidential 1882-7.
[355] Entry 28th October 1884, DD. Footnote.
[356] Entry 28th October 1884, DD.
[357] CO 879/23 African No.307 General View of Zulu Affairs 1879 –1885 January 1886. E. Fairfield.
[358] Bulwer to Derby 16th June 1885. CO879/22. See also National Archives of South Africa, Pretoria T11 Archief Van de "Nieuwe Republik" (later district Vrijheid in de ZA Republiek) 1884-88. NR 79 Dokumente insake die Akgerwandigde van de N. Republiek maar Europa in 1885.
[359] See, for example, the Editorial The Times 23rd December 1884 and the letter from AFRICANDER The Times 27th December 1884.
[360] Smyth to Derby, 26th December 1883. CO 879/22 Correspondence respecting the Affairs of Pondoland, Sept 1885.
[361] J.Oxley Oxland, Resident Port St.John's, to Secretary for Native Affairs, 29th March 1884. CO 879/22 Correspondence respecting the Affairs of Pondoland, Sept 1885.
[362] Chief Umquikela to Robinson, 9th August 1884. CO 879/22 Correspondence respecting the Affairs of Pondoland, Sept 1885.
[363] Schreuder, *The Scramble for Southern Africa, 1877 - 1895*, p.151.
[364] E. J. Whindus, Resident Magistrate Port St. John's to under-Secretary for Native Affairs, 13th April 1885. CO 879/22 Correspondence respecting the Affairs of Pondoland, Sept 1885.

## The Boer Offensive Halted. Finally.

The public outcry about Gladstone's failures in Sudan and South Africa wasn't limited to Britain either. The disgust at the constant mismanagement, cowardice and appeasement and the appearance of the Germans at Angra Pequena had achieved the long-desired unity of both English and Dutch sections of the Cape Colony; but they were united mainly in a determination to no longer have their affairs run by the distant dithering of London. Gladstone, Granville and Derby had alienated its leading statesmen and driven the Cape Colony into an independence borne of frustration at the sheer bone-headed stupidity of Whitehall.[365] From now on, the Cape would conduct its own foreign policy and a whole new sub-imperialism was invented.

Step forward Cecil John Rhodes.

The threat of a revolt of the Cape Dutch in support of Transvaal independence had evaporated with the death of Confederation in 1880 and the retrocession of the Transvaal in 1881. True, there were plenty of young, landless hotheads on the frontiers, but the Cape farmers were well aware that the value of their land depended on retaining the benefits of financial and business confidence that came with the British connection and they quickly made their feelings known in the Cape Parliament. Jan Hofmeyer and the Afrikaaner Bond remained influential but both Thomas Scanlen and John Merriman, representing the Dutch and English populations respectively, were firmly against a revolt that would inevitably end in the ruin of the Cape farmers. This was a point that a rising star in the Cape legislature, Cecil Rhodes, had picked up on; in his view the key to the resolution of the situation in Bechuanaland in Britain's favour lay in relative land values under British or ZAR rule.

Rhodes visited Stellaland and Goschen in May 1883[366] and reported a much more chaotic situation there than anyone had really understood. Having been a long-standing resident of Kimberley and implicated in the Black Flag revolt there in 1877, he was ideally placed to make sense of the chaos, and he came away with four main ideas which he communicated to Derby via Scanlen. The first was that most of the freebooters there were actually Cape British rather than Dutch and that the Cape should, therefore, annex it before the Transvaal did. The second was that those Transvaal Boers who were involved would welcome British annexation for the upward move in the value of their landholdings that would result, even though they would not openly voice this desire for fear of offending their kin in the Transvaal and Orange Free State. The third idea was that Stellaland and Goschen lay astride the old "Missionary road" to the African interior and that if the Boers annexed the area than the Cape would be cut off from the fabled riches of the interior. The fourth idea was that 'delay was fatal' and the 'key of the position' was to get Derby to prevent the Boers from expanding.[367] These were all reasonable propositions, except the last, but this changed with the arrival of the Germans at Angra Pequena and the burning of Roi Grond, which made the Cape government much more determined not to be guided by Derby. After the London

---

[365] Schreuder, *Gladstone and Kruger*, pp. 462-3. See also Gladstone to Derby 27th October 1884 Gladstone Diaries.

[366] CO 879/20 African No. 267. Notes of a Conversation between Mr.Scanlen and Mr.Rhodes, 2nd June 1883.

[367] CO 879/20 African No. 267. Notes of a Conversation between Mr.Scanlen and Mr.Rhodes, 2nd June 1883.

Convention of February 1884, Kruger's visit to Berlin, the advance of freebooters into Zululand and the dithering over Angra Pequena, the Cape Government decided on 15th July 1884 that it intended to annex Bechuanaland itself and thus opened a dispute with the Imperial government over whether it would be Cape Colonialism or British Imperialism that undertook the expansion.[368] Their determination to defend their own interests against Derby was made plain when Mackenzie, the British choice, was replaced by Rhodes, the Cape choice, as Commissioner for Bechuanaland. Hofmeyer applauded; this was the Cape acting independently and he was all for it. From this point on, he brought the Bond into a closer alliance with Rhodes than anyone would have thought possible a few years earlier.

Rhodes was a much tougher character than anyone that the Boers had yet had to deal with and from the start he took a stiff line with Kruger telling him that he would resist any attempt to back the Goschen freebooters and that their claim to hold Montsoia under their protection would not be accepted.[369] At the same time he demanded from London that an Imperial force be assembled for service in Bechuanaland, that the mere threat of it would be enough to make the Transvaal back down and that unless it was assembled, there should be no more illusions and Bechuanaland abandoned.[370] This was backed up by a thunderbolt from Hartington which baldly stated that the 'complete abandonment of the Cape colonies…would probably result in a German protectorate;' that the Cape could not be another Gibraltar;[371] that the London Convention must be upheld; that 'it is the undoubted right of the Imperial government to dispossess the freebooters by force if necessary;' and that troops should go at once to annex Bechuanaland and Zululand.[372] The pressure continued to mount when on 9th October 1884 the 'South African Committee' called on the government to act to send troops to both Bechuanaland and Zululand immediately. Failure to act, they argued, would invite Germany to supplant Britain there; its members included several cabinet ministers and MPs, the Lord Mayor of London, H.M. Stanley, Scanlen, Merriman, and FW Chesson of the Aborigines Protection Society.[373] Derby dithered and Gladstone cavilled but at last – at last! – an expedition was authorised to halt the Boer occupation of Bechuanaland. Gladstone, predictably, could not see the problem of handing over the whole kit and caboodle to the Boers and the Germans and actively pushed this treasonous proposal.

Once assembled, the Bechuanaland Field Force led by Major-General Sir Charles Warren[374] was a remarkable expression of the capabilities and latent strength of the British Empire. The core of the force was three regiments of Mounted Infantry, a hybrid unit that combined the mobility of cavalry with the firepower of infantry, which was particularly suited to warfare in South Africa, and indeed, bore an uncanny resemblance to the Boer Commandos. The 1st Mounted Rifles was recruited in England from country areas and sent out to Cape Town as

---

[368] CO 879/23 African No. 301. Bechuanaland Affairs. E. Fairfield.
[369] Robinson to Derby, 12th September 1884, CO 879/22.
[370] Robinson to Derby, 16th September 1884, CO 879/22.
[371] For Frere's restatement of this see "The Transvaal Question" Frere's letter to *The Times*, 29th March 1883.
[372] WO 33/42 Papers 1884 Position of Affairs in the Cape Colonies and the Transvaal. Confidential memorandum by Andrew Clarke, 1st October 1884.
[373] "Mr Forster on South Africa" *The Times* 10th October 1884.
[374] Warren was a firm advocate of intervention. See his letter to *The Times* 21st August 1884.

'volunteers' to be enrolled in South Africa and thus avoid delay by parliamentary scrutiny and objections about their 'irregular' status. The 2nd Mounted Rifles was recruited from Grahamstown and other predominantly English areas of the Cape and led by the remarkable Colonel Carrington, who had arrived at the Cape in 1877 as a Lieutenant of the 24th Regiment and had since been on almost continuous detached service with 'Carrington's Horse,' raised and trained by himself, against the Xhosa, the mPondo and the Basuto. The 3rd Mounted Rifles, 'The Diamond Fields Horse,' was raised from the diggers at Kimberley and, it was suspected, contained more than its fair share of freebooters. In support of these units was a regiment of African Pioneers, whose function was to guard the Lines of Communication against possible Boer raids, a battery of imperial artillery and the Inniskilling Dragoons.[375] Moving forward into Bechuanaland in January 1885, Warren met Kruger at Fourteen Springs on the 24th and 26th January[376] and bluntly told him to withdraw from Bechuanaland or face the consequences. (This place has disappeared from present day maps but it was still around in the early 20th Century and is just south of Vryburg. I know this because I went to look for it and couldn't find it. Having said that, I might have gone past the railway station at Fourteen *Streams*). The symbolism of Warren's escort at the meetings was not lost on Kruger; a squadron each of the Mounted Rifles and the Inniskillings told him that Warren could deploy volunteers every bit as tough and accustomed to the country as the Boers, and back them up with the regular army and, by implication, the imperial treasury. The deterrent effect worked; Kruger protested weakly and, fearing that Warren's real mission was to go on to take the Transvaal, agreed to order his freebooters out.[377] By February 1885, Warren had established military rule over the whole area and stopped the Boer expansion without firing a shot.[378]

For the Tswana, however, the results were less happy; the reluctance of Gladstone and Derby to enforce either the Pretoria or London Conventions until both Mankurwane and Montsoia had been effectively deprived of the power to resist left them devoid of influence in the deal that Rhodes did in Stellaland and Goschen over land ownership. One of the principle reasons for Kruger's defeat at Fourteen Springs was that the freebooters of Stellaland had been bribed into becoming British by confirming their land titles at the expense of the Tswana; had Derby supplied the Tswana with the means to make their own defence effective, they might well have held on to more of their land.

Much the same could be said of Zululand too. Had Gladstone taken a more robust approach to the New Republic then the disaster that followed might have been avoided by the imposition of a more stable settlement of the country. As it was, the price that Dinizulu paid for his throne was so horrendously high that when the Zulus realised what he had given away they revolted yet again. By this time, however, Gladstone was out of office, St. Lucia had been annexed and being in no mood to put up with the claims of the New Republic to a protectorate over the *whole* of the country, the new Prime Minister, the sane and wise Lord

---

[375] WO 33/44 Report of Proceedings of the Bechuanaland Field Force 1884-5, by Maj-Gen. Sir Charles Warren RE, 6th July 1885.

[376] WO 33/44 Report of Proceedings of the Bechuanaland Field Force 1884-5, by Maj-Gen. Sir Charles Warren RE, 6th July 1885.

[377] Methods of Mr.Kruger. Interview with Sir Charles Warren, 26th January 1885. BL. Add.51316 Papers of E.B. Iwan-Muller, Journalist.

[378] Robinson to Derby, 26th February 1885. CO 879/22 African No.295, Telegrams to and From South Africa Jan to December 1885.

Salisbury, ordered that Zululand be annexed to the crown in 1887. The New Republic joined the Transvaal Republic and the Zulus, many of whom were reduced to refugee status in Natal or in a state of starvation, lost their independence completely.

\*

## The Gladstonian Disaster Reviewed.

Gladstone's anti-imperial policy had failed miserably. It had resulted in a disaster for the Zulus and the Tswana and created in Cape colonialism a new sub-imperialism. It had handed over large areas of indisputably African land to the Boers and the Germans. In his overwhelming desire to repudiate the empire, Gladstone had been prepared to see British vital interests in the Cape handed over to first the Boers and then a Boer-German alliance, at certain times, in conditions of near treason. Seeing his policy in South Africa progressively revealed by Cetshwayo, Bismarck and Kruger as hopelessly inadequate in a world where his idiot morality was at a discount, Gladstone's response was to go beyond appeasement to actual encouragement of those who would oust Britain from South Africa and so generated a spirit of near mutiny among both the loyal colonists and his own officials. Yet even then, none of this could alter the logic of Frere and Carnarvon's solution to the problem of South Africa; British control of the coastlines, Boer expansionism contained by British suzerainty, and indigenous African societies settled under enlightened British paramountcy, but not before there had been five years of misery for those least able to defend themselves. And, Dear Reader, please note; there was never a whisper that any part of British policy was about ripping off African land and forcing the inhabitants to labour for evil top-hatted capitalists. British expansion was concerned with strategy and imperial defence - not taking over vast swathes of semi-desert in the hope of filling the pockets of pantomime capitalist villains with oodles of filthy lucre.

\*

## Cape Colonialism

Gladstone's bungling and the Xhosa revolt of 1877-78 brought forth a new form of imperialism which was based not on decisions made in London but on those made in Cape Town and it was this sub-imperialism that drove the annexation of all the lands between the Cape Colony and Natal. The revolt of the Xhosa and their defeat in 1877 brought about a near collapse of anything resembling legal authority, settled government, peace and tranquillity throughout the whole region south of the Drakensberg and north of the sea. Smaller tribes and even smaller clans and sub-branches of clans and tribes, such as the mPondo, Baca, Hlubi, Xesibe, Pondomsi, Tembu, the Griquas of Griqualand East, existed in a state of petty war, the usual cattle thieving, endless disputes over land, the relative standing and status of chiefs, smelling-out and all kinds of unregulated meanness which, to the eye of the government in Cape Town, was indicative of anarchy. Some of the chiefs had formally accepted the overlordship of the Cape, some of the chiefs fiercely resisted the imposition of alien rule, while others still swung whichever way suited them at the time and the Cape, always fearful that a beer drinking or a petty cattle raid could send the whole frontier up again decided that the only way to achieve any sort of settled state was to impose Cape rule over it. This process began with the ending of the Xhosa revolt and though stalled in the first years of the Gladstone government, went on until 1894 when the whole of the Transkei was taken under Cape rule and divided into Magistracies. Theal, who went into exhausting detail when describing this process, was of the opinion that the Cape did this reluctantly and because there was no other choice if these instabilities were not to spill over into the Cape Colony and Natal. He also regretted that it was done without sending in enough white settlers to bring about some material change in the culture, government or economy of the Transkei – what was then known as 'raising up in civilisation' – but duly noted with some satisfaction that the imposition of the law and its enforcement by magistrates, troops and police allowed the population to rapidly increase. Order was also imposed further northwards when, in 1879, it was decided that it was finally time for the Oorlam bandit groups who had plagued the Orange River almost since Van Riebeeck's time to be broken up. Donker Malgas, Klaas Pofadder, Klaas Lukas, Gamka Windwai and Jacobus Afrikaaner were according to Theal who, for once, did not mince his words, an 'utterly worthless collection of human beings' who had refused all restraint, reasonable treatment and appeals to desist. A force of volunteers, white, black, mixed race, regular and yeomanry was got together and the robbers were defeated, captured or dispersed. Colonial rule was not without its imperfections but the imposition of the *Pax Britannica* was a benefit that should not be understated.

\*

### Life and Government under British Colonial Rule.

That there had been a profound change in the circumstances of South Africa by 1886 can hardly be denied. The rule of the chiefs was broken, the Xhosa colonial project had been decisively defeated and the potential threat of the Zulu had been dispersed and substantial portions of land had been alienated. Although African clans and tribes retained a great deal of autonomy in the running of their everyday affairs, the final say on matters of importance lay with either the Boer or the British authorities and as independent political entities, they were now unable to compete with either Cape Town or Pretoria.

In terms of everyday life too, there was a profound change. There was a general disarmament of Africans who were required to hand in the guns that they had bought with money earned at Kimberley, along with their shields and assegais, which hit hard at the warrior status that was central to the age-regiment system. This was as much a police measure as a means to remove the ability of Africans to rebel and resulted in the same furore as meets any attempt at gun control in the USA, but it was insisted upon and carried out to a greater or lesser extent. No-one really wants to admit this, I guess, but it was in some sense a liberating measure; now African men were exempted from automatic conscription as soldiers and freed from both the authority of the chiefs and the regular obligation to prove themselves as men by killing other African men. The age-regiment system would still linger in places but this was the death knell of it as a rigid over-arching social institution.

There was also a profound change in African spiritual life with the coming of Christianity and although the new religion never displaced the vague animism and ancestor worship completely – in many case, it simply complimented it – this was again something new. Whatever one feels about religion, whether the opiate of the people, a ludicrous debate between Lilliputian Big-Enders and Little-Enders, or the true path to glory, enlightenment, rapture and heaven, there can be no denying that it has its benefits as a spiritual comfort, a code for good conduct and (sometimes) a restraint on obnoxious behaviour.   That the Christians campaigned against smelling-out can only be seen as a good thing; during the terrible strife between Xhosa and Zulu that accompanied the last days of Apartheid, the legendary historian and raconteur David Rattray claimed that there had been no violence within fifty miles of his base near Rorke's Drift, largely due to the influence of the churches. This time too conversion was carried on without recourse to persecution and the *sangomas* continued to practice as fortune-tellers, herbalists, rain-makers and healers.   During the 1950s, a famous sangoma by the name of Khotso made himself a millionaire by flogging aphrodisiacs and in 2015, I was pleased to browse through the *sangoma* supply store just around the corner from the Vryburg *Spur*. The biggest surprise I had was in Dundee 2009 when an ANC official explained to me just how I could get wealth and fame by selling my soul to a female water-snake spirit, the *Mamlambo*.  He was serious too (nevertheless, Mugabe still goes to Singapore for his piles).  *Lobola* survived, as did polygamy (the advantages of the variety, in my opinion, being outweighed by the increase in the strife - but for an expert opinion you'll probably need to ask President Zuma, whose six wives all needed new BMWs in 2016 'for security reasons', paid for out of the Joburg police budget, naturally. Sycophancy towards powerful chiefs also survived the imposition of colonial rule).

The arrival of Colonial rule was no doubt painful when cattle and land were confiscated to defray the costs of the war but this did not mean the instant impoverishment of the defeated. The Basutos had positively thrived under the light touch of British rule; they bought guns, saddles and ploughs, bred horses cattle and goats in abundance, sold wool and grain, sent labourers to Kimberley and gained in wealth to the point where by 1881 some of the chiefs thought they could dispense with British control.  They weren't far wrong and when the Colonial authorities turned up asking for their guns they told them to stick it.  What was remarkable about this rebellion was that they were supported by lots of European colonists and Cecil Rhodes himself; the boys had bought their guns with hard graft, the compensation for handing them in was below market value and even Cracked Charlie Gordon told the government where to stick it.  The result was that the Basuto held onto their guns and then pulled off the amazing stunt of freeing themselves from Cape Town control, while at the same time submitting to the control of London, which in effect protected them from the Boers. Result? Independence in all but name. These guys were smart.

A further profound change in African life arrived with the Mission schools which brought widespread literacy and education to cultures that had never been exposed to such things before.  Many commentators are apt to be sniffy about the Missionaries, but the effect of education was to introduce Africans not just to the acquisition of skills useful to a more sophisticated agricultural economy but also to the exercise of the intellect for its own sake. This is something that is often missed largely because few people have actually had the experience of working with or directing people untouched by education; several times I have worked with people whose ability to do new things in new ways has been really badly affected by the lack of any formal education. It isn't their fault and this observation does not mean that everyone who has missed out on formal schooling is thick, but even the most hardened bonehead among the cultural relativists would admit that learning some Reading, Writing and Arithmetic is better for the development of the faculties than staring up a cow's arse for sixteen hours a day as a herd boy; and women would no longer think that menstruation was a result of a bug (amazing, but true). Knowledge of the wider world, the scientific method and literature opened up whole new vistas for those Africans who passed through the training institutions, seminaries and schools that a bewildering array of enthusiastic missionaries set up.

With the railways came all sorts of new opportunities too. African labour was used extensively in the laying of track and new skills were very quickly imparted. This was also true of the mines but it should also be noted that as the track was laid to more and more places, so the economy produced a plethora of new opportunities for trade, introduced new products, new kinds of employment and expanded demand for existing ones. They also offered the possibility of escaping the numbing boredom of rural life to more and more Africans. There is a sort of nostalgia for 'traditional' ways of life that really isn't borne out by the reality; Thomas Hardy's Wessex novels are a prime example of the genre in that he described a rather idyllic English countryside that so many of his audience had abandoned for the towns and the same nostalgia was observed by Orlando Figes when writing about the urban classes in pre-revolutionary Russia. You can see it today when Western Tourists coo at poor people in Third World countries and fondly imagine that the past was a 'simpler' way of life that they have foolishly abandoned. This is, of course, poppycock; urbanisation, capitalism, science, technology and the industrial revolution produced the explosion of wealth, healthcare and education that allowed those same tourists to fill their pockets with enough loot to go pootling around the world in the first place; try persuading a web-designer to swap his latte and workstation for river water and a plough and the nostalgia disappears faster than prosperity in a socialist paradise. That Africans came in at the bottom of the pile is true; but that's where most people start in any enterprise. That they were dragooned into working for the white man is twaddle; there was no need because Indian labourers were plentiful and willing and it was in this period that the colonisation of Natal was begun by Indian workers. By 1884 there were roughly 36,000 Europeans, 27,000 Indians and 360,000 Africans settled there. What is also true is that in large parts of South Africa, it was still possible to live a 'traditional' life if one chose to do so; in the Transkei white people were a rarity.

\*

## Race

There has been a vast acreage written about race and very little of it ever gets past the founding assumption that white people are bad and black people are good. Careers have been built on dredging out tired, specious twaddle from the depths of blinkered academia, duly steeped in post-colonial guilt complexes, twice marinated in political correctness and lavishly funded by governments terrified of being branded as racist. There is a deep weirdness to all this; in 2015, the gloriously right-on actor, Benedict Cumberbatch, was forced to issue an apology for using the term 'coloured' to describe actors who were not white.[379] This is apparently a bad word. What Dr Martin Luther King Jr would have made of it would be interesting to note; he was on the executive committee of the National Association for the Advancement of Coloured People. His dad had been too.[380] When last I looked, Wikipedia had left out all mention of his membership of that fine organisation, which is not just weird but also sinister; are they implying that he was a racist for saying 'coloured'? That same year saw another bizarre development in that Rachel Dolezal, a respected member of that same National Association for the Advancement of Colored People, a university lecturer, activist and apparent black (or perhaps 'coloured') person was revealed to be a *white* person who – wait for it – had once tried to sue a university for discriminating against her because she was *white*. It seems fair to say that she presented herself as black in order to gain some kind of social or career advantage up until the point where someone blew the gaffe on her. Her defence was that 'black' and 'white' are social constructs and you don't actually need black genes to be black. This is self-evidently codswallop and you are going to have to abandon science to argue otherwise.[381] That there are confusing notions of what 'race' actually means today – in the second half of the 19th Century, the term was often used interchangeably with 'nationality' – is, in my humble opinion, almost entirely the result of academic job creation schemes.

So where does all this guff about race come from? Race, ideas about racial supremacy and racial discrimination undoubtedly exist; only a fool would say that they do not. Apartheid was an explicitly racist doctrine but it strikes me as so bizarre a notion that people actually believed this nonsense that it really is necessary to examine where the notion came from. We should, however, start with a few provisos; firstly, antipathy to people of other races has been, and remains, a feature of every society, civilisation and culture in human History; and secondly, people who have no antipathy to people of other races have existed in every society, civilisation and culture in human History; and thirdly, the fact that legal systems have been enacted to legitimise or promote this antipathy does not necessarily prove that those legal systems were anything but the product of organised and vested interests. The short way of saying this is that because Apartheid was legally introduced does not mean to say that all white people in South Africa were in favour of it. There is, in fact, a fair body of argument to say that Apartheid was introduced *against* the wishes of most white people; yup, we'll get to it in due course.

I've already noted that Calvinism was one of the roots of racial discrimination because within that branch of Christianity was the idea that people are divided into the Elect – those pre-destined to go to heaven – and those who are going to the other place. This tied in with other Biblical teachings, especially the story of Ham servant of Noah, who was black and so condemned by God to be a slave. Add this to the Exodus, whereby the Jews (Voortrekkers) escaped from slavery in Egypt (British rule in the Cape) and crossed the desert (the Karoo) to find the Land of Milk and Honey (the Highveldt/Natal) promised to them by God; when

---
[379] https://www.theguardian.com/culture/2015/jan/26/benedict-cumberbatch-apologises-after-calling-black-actors-coloured
[380] http://kingencyclopedia.stanford.edu/encyclopedia/encyclopedia/enc_national_association_for_the_advancement_of_colored_people_naacp1/
[381] https://www.theguardian.com/us-news/2017/feb/25/rachel-dolezal-not-going-stoop-apologise-grovel

brought together, this is a basic narrative that gave religious justification for those Afrikaaners who felt themselves to be among the Elect (and, be honest, who wants to count themselves among the Damned?) to regard black people as inferior. Bearing in mind also the idea of the Boer in permanent mental laager after the Battle of the Blood River and there are the beginnings of a feeling of separateness and superiority.

The next root of this obnoxious weed that we might point to is Social Darwinism. This was the idea that as species of animals compete for existence and so evolve into higher forms from lower ones, so too do the races of Humanity. The fault in this notion is the timescale; evolution in the natural world works on the scale of geological time and a couple of hundred years (i.e., the time in which European peoples established their dominance) just isn't enough. Probably more commonly used as a reason for the difference in material culture, better technology and more sophisticated economy brought by the Europeans was the idea that there was a road leading up from 'barbarism' to 'civilisation' which was similar to the concept of Social Darwinism but owed much more to the notions of Liberal Historians. These fine men held that mankind was perfectible through the advance of material wealth and the perfection of legal systems; it might sometimes be two steps forward and one step back (and at least one writer reckoned that the *Boers* had taken several steps backwards since the Great Trek),[382] but the direction of progress was upwards. Theal was apt to follow this line, as were various writers who took an anthropological approach to the subject. In this respect, black Africans were just lagging behind a bit and could be brought up to speed through education, sanitation, Christianity and general Europeanisation. Dudley Kidd's remarkable 1904 work *The Essential Kaffir* is probably pretty typical of the genre; it makes difficult reading and would never get near a publishing house today but Kidd spent twelve years researching and photographing black South Africans and though he found much that was primitive and repulsive in their habits, he was not without affection for them.

> Quite obviously it is an absurdity, which needs no exposure, to say that the Kafir is in all respects equal to a white man. Would you like him to marry your sister? If you think him quite equal to a white man you should feel no shrinking from this....
>
> ....He is not a monkey or a dog; he is a man. And though he may be a very depraved man, though he may be very ignorant and dirty and objectionable in his insanitary habits and his morals, yet "a man's a man for a' that." This is also quite self-evident. The native is capable of improvement; he can develop, for he has the basal attributes of manhood, though he is at present low down in the scale of civilisation. He has the human qualities of conscience, will, intellect, and affection; he feels many of the emotions which we know; he is a social animal.[383]

If this gets your dander up, it is perhaps well to bear in mind that some of the dimmer types considered on no worthwhile evidence at all, that the position of each race was fixed on the evolutionary scale and that, therefore, black people were incapable of improvement. Whether this was worse than the Left's application of Social Darwinist principles in advocating forced sterilisation, euthanasia and selective breeding to improve the state of the working classes of

---
[382] Leo Amery, *The Times History of the War in South Africa 1899-1900* (London 1900) p.49.
[383] Dudley Kidd, *The Essential Kaffir*, London 1904, p.106.

Britain would make an interesting debate, no? Imagine; Marie Stopes, George Bernard Shaw, Keynes, Beveridge, Harold Laski (Deputy Leader of the Labour Party and sponsor of Marxist Ralph Milliband) The Fabian Society and the *Manchester Guardian* all lining up to tell us why Eugenics is a good idea, why poor people need to have the stupidity bred out of them and why *untermenschen* need to be sent to their deaths.[384] Thank God they were never let loose in Africa; they make the Apartheid mob look positively benign.

A third root of racial thought lay in the fact that victory seemed to justify some notions of racial superiority. Was it not self-evident that Europeans were superior to Africans because they had won the wars, built the railroads and developed the country? This was an argument that was very attractive and it does no one any good to denigrate the achievements of the European settlers because those achievements were real. The fault in it lies with the fact that although European (and particularly, British) society and culture was undeniably more dynamic, more complex, better organised for war and manufacture than African societies, it had nothing to do with race. Kidd gives the example of the African who is sent to fill a kettle but having only ever seen the tea poured out of it, attempts to fill the kettle by pouring water, cup by cup, down the spout; he ain't thick, he just hasn't seen the job done before (my grandmother, born 1899, God bless her cotton socks, thought there were actually little men inside the TV). The British won because they had better guns, logistics, money, transport, organisation, leadership, motivation etc etc, not because there was some little sprinkle of stardust in their genes.

It's probably also worthwhile pointing out that every person who came into contact with Africans formed their own opinion as to the collective and individual worth of them and that those opinions would be a lot more varied than was allowed for in print. A soldier might simultaneously admire the bravery of his opponent yet have contempt for his tactics; an engineer might admire the labour of an African, yet deplore his lack of mechanical knowledge; black and white might interact in formal work situations while spending their leisure time apart. The variations and possibilities were wide. According to his daughter, Rider Haggard considered himself to be the reincarnation of a Zulu. Kipling wrote the immortal line 'You're a better man than I am, Gunga Din,' about a low caste bisti-wallah. No doubt the settlers at Grahamstown were aghast at the stupidity of the Xhosa during the cattle killings and the Voortrekkers up in the Transvaal so disgusted at both the Xhosa and the Zulu that they refused any possibility of equal treatment of black and white – they even wrote it into their constitution – but as to the question of whether all white South Africans were racist in the way we understand it today, the answer is both *yes* and *no*; it depended on the individual and the mores of each group, sub-set, clan, party, or what-have-you. And we should not forget that the enmity that many of the Boers held for the black man was utterly dwarfed by his hatred for the British.

Now all this guff about race might just have remained guff had not the very worst feature of European philosophy been applied to it. This is the idiotic urge to find an over-arching method of organising society according to uniform principles and rational method to the benefit of all; Utopianism. This desire to construct a vision of the perfect society and then

---

[384] https://www.theguardian.com/commentisfree/2012/feb/17/eugenics-skeleton-rattles-loudest-closet-left

impose it on people regardless of whether those people want it or not turned large parts of Europe into a graveyard and an economic train wreck during the 20th Century and the adoption of those Utopian creeds by large parts of the non-European world has had almost uniformly similar results from China to Venezuela by way of Ghana and other points so blighted. The visions of Utopia put forward by the varying versions of Nazism, Fascism, Socialism and Communism all had at their heart the inability to accept and accommodate dissent and, though claiming to be rational and scientific in their analysis and actions, their adherents were utterly unable to accept that they were completely wrong in their analysis of the world, completely unscientific in their actions (if they were scientific, they would have junked the theory as soon as it collided with the facts) and so condemned to disaster. And to this litany of stupidity, mendacity, cruelty, heartlessness, pseudo-science, pseudo-intellectual bollocks, self-delusion and all too often sheer, self-serving cant, we have to add that vision of Utopia called Apartheid. Marx, Hitler, Lenin, Stalin, Mussolini, Mao, Pol Pot, Samora Machel, Kwame Nkrumah, Castro, Hugo Chavez and the ragged racists of Afrikaaner Nationalism all come from the same intellectual stable. They all desire to theorise an ideal world then impose it on all by force, refusing to tolerate dissent and ultimately, employing all the black arts of propaganda, dictatorship, ideological policing, jail, torture and ultimately, mass murder, to keep alive the stinking corpses of their monstrous Frankensteins.

\*

## Some Conclusions

1886 is a good place to pause because it was in that year that the discovery of gold on the Witwatersrand produced yet another series of momentous changes and set another hatful of hares running across the South African landscape. Nothing would be the same after the rise of Johannesburg and the changes to the lives of Africans, the struggle between the British and the Boers followed by the rise of Afrikaaner nationalism need to be considered separately to what had already occurred.

In general terms, the conclusions that we can draw from this brief gallop through History can be divided up under four main headings. The first of these headings concerns the impact of the Dutch East India Company and under this we can fairly absolve them of malign intent in their dealings with the Khoikhoin. They did not carry out a programme of dispossession or genocide and the demise of the Khoikhoin was due to the introduction of European diseases that were only dimly understood by the Europeans themselves. Accepting that some form of interaction with the outside world was eventually inevitable, it seems certain that these diseases would have arrived anyway. The net result of this was that the Dutch Burghers were left with a landscape that was virtually empty and seemingly boundless and they took the view that they had as much right to expand into it as anyone and did so. This was exactly what the Xhosa and other Bantu tribes were doing on the eastern side of the continent.

Secondly, the collapse of African societies during the period after the first conflicts on the Fish River until Confederation came along in the 1870s was largely the result of poor leadership. Where the authority of the chiefs was weak, as in the case of the Xhosa, the people refused to respect agreements regarding borders, cattle or other property, showed little aptitude for the wars that they were too quick to embrace and were far too ready to follow signs, visions and sangomas. Where the authority of the chiefs was strong, as in the case of the Zulu, this was usually expressed in an all too willingness to go to war, with disastrous results for other African tribes, especially during the *mfecane*. Shaka, Dingane and Mzilikazi were all bloodthirsty tyrants who the world could well do without and were, collectively, the greatest disasters to befall the continent during the 19th Century. The Xhosa chiefs were entirely devoid of anything that might be thought necessary or desirable in a leader. In both cases, they showed little aptitude for war against European trained and armed forces and despite one or two successes, were routinely routed. Moshweshwe is the only African leader of note who showed the requisite mettle to keep his people together, adapt, introduce new methods of fighting and display some diplomatic skill. The Bushmen were hunted to virtual extinction by all sides mainly because they were unable to come to some lasting agreement regarding stock theft, hunting grounds and the loss of pasturage to the plough.

Thirdly, both the Great Trek and the collapse of Zululand and Bechuanaland were not caused by imperialism but by *anti-imperialism*. The root cause of these seminal events was the desire of British anti-imperialists – the London Missionary Society especially - to rein in what they thought erroneously as rampant land-grabbing and the ill-treatment of black people. Glenelg's repudiation of Queen Adelaide province after the Boers had been ruined by Xhosa invasion was the last straw for many of them and the main impetus for the Great Trek. Gladstone's hatred of imperialism and his pusillanimous surrender after Majuba allowed Kruger to embark on the destruction of the Zulu and the Tswana and he should have been pilloried for it.

Fourthly, and most importantly, when the alternatives of African leadership or Boer conquest are considered, it is glaringly obvious that the best solution to the problem of South Africa was British rule. The imposition of settled, paternal government under a colour-blind franchise and a flexible and responsive legal system, coupled with the active encouragement of commerce through the development of a global banking and financial system, marine insurance and limited liability companies, plus the spread of sanitation, transportation, technology and education, were blessings previously only dreamed of by South Africans of all hues. And unfashionable as it is to say this, even discounting the appalling times of the *mfecane* and the cattle killings, and the exodus of the Great Trek, black Africans voted with their feet to take advantage of the steady, unspectacular but immensely valuable security of life under British rule. For it was there that you could get on with your work, live your life largely as your talents, capital and opportunities allowed, avoid being smelled-out or forced into the ranks to wash your spear against men you had no quarrel with, and, most valuable of all, enjoy a measure of protection against the ravages of war while expecting some relief when famine or drought struck. The *Pax Britannica* was not by any means perfect but it was better than anything else on offer during the 19th Century and much of the 20th. And looking at Mugabe's Zimbabwe, as well as much else of the post-colonial wreckage of Africa, we might stretch that into the 21st too. If the British record in South Africa was mixed, it was certainly better than the record of the Voortrekker-Afrikaaners and better still than that of the Xhosa and the Zulu.

\*

## Gold

The next part of this book is about the struggle between Nationalism, Colonialism and Imperialism and as those three terms have been so mangled over the years I shall now define them for the South African context. 'Nationalism' means Afrikaaner Nationalism, or the desire of the Afrikaaner people to gain full independence from British control. 'Colonialism' means the desire of the South African colonies to have control over their own government and destiny while maintaining a strong link with the British Empire. 'Imperialism' means the desire of South Africans to keep more or less direct rule from London as an integral part of the British Empire. Of course, there are a million gradations to this but painting with a broad brush stroke is what we are about here and these definitions will do. To illustrate with some big names; Cecil Rhodes began life as an Imperialist, morphed into a Colonialist and was firmly opposed to Nationalism. Jan Christian Smuts began life as a Nationalist and then became a Colonialist with a marked Imperialist bent. Alfred Milner began as an Imperialist and stayed one, even though he thought Colonialism was a good idea. Paul Kruger was a Nationalist and couldn't conceive of being anything other than one. On with the show.

\*

As soon as you mention gold all rational thought goes out of the heads of anyone interested in South Africa and the debate is brought to a grinding halt. 'That's it, then,' says the interested party. 'It's all about the money, innit?' This is usually accompanied by a snort from the standard issue Leftie clone which, though varying in style, rarely varies in content: 'Imperialist capitalist bastards grinding the faces of the poor black workers, mate, innit? Revolution is the only solution…yadda yadda yadda.' Yes, I know; I've already said this about diamonds but you get the same reaction at the merest mention of the gold discoveries on the Witwatersrand in 1886; and it's interesting to note that you get pretty much the same reaction from the ornery old Boers in the bar who went through the Apartheid era Christian-National Education – the two sides aren't really that far apart in their outlook - so let me repeat myself about the value of South Africa in monetary terms.

In general terms, Africa was, and remains, relatively poor because of its geography. There are no navigable rivers; the Orange isn't deep enough, the Zambesi has a little obstacle to navigation in the form of the Victoria Falls, the Congo is blocked by rapids and the Nile has cataracts. This means that there is no cheap means of transportation and so exist vast obstacles to trade. There is also the question of climate; the weather is unpredictable and given to extremes of drought and flood. In 2015, my old pal Thielman sat on his farm in the Free State and watched his neighbour plant three mealie crops, one after the other, and saw each one fail for lack of rain; in January 2018, I drove past the dams beyond the Franschoek Pass and saw them almost empty. They were down to 18% useable capacity and Cape Town was due to run out of water by April; goodbye fruit farming. Despite the interminable blethering about global warming, three year droughts in South Africa are not something that started with the industrial revolution. Add to this vicious diseases like rinderpest and lung sickness which can wipe out a herd in days and you have several more barriers to prosperity.

Africa also happens to be a long way from any markets which means that exports are more expensive; this was a problem that was partly overcome by the development of ports, railways, telegraphs and mails during the 19th Century but it remains a problem today. The Ford plant in Pretoria has a 30% productivity advantage over the Ford plant in Thailand, yet in 2017, it cost $800 more to send the same vehicle to Saudi Arabia than it did from Thailand.[385]

As now, so then. South Africa remained an insignificant country in terms of trade and revenue when compared to Britain. Cape Colony, according to Theal who did his best to put a positive gloss on South African development, enjoyed a revenue of barely £3m pa during the early 1880s, exported around £4m and owed £21m; Natal's revenue was just over £600k, exports £500k and the colony owed just over £3m. I shan't bore you with more statistics, but it is worth reminding you that Britain exported £300m of merchandise alone in 1880. Did gold make South Africa a better economic prospect? Yes, it did. It certainly saved the Transvaal from the bankruptcy that Kruger's incompetent administration had in a near record time reduced it to.[386] Did some people get wealthy on the back of the gold rush? Yes, they did; many of them the members of Kruger's incompetent administration indeed, but what was more important about the gold discoveries in Johannesburg was that it catapulted South Africa into the modern world in a way that no-one could have foreseen. Indeed, it is interesting (but as pointless as parlour psychology) to speculate on just how African societies might have connected into the wider world in the absence of European influence. Would Africa have modernised like Japan? Emerged as a curious hybrid of capitalism and Mandarin rule like China? We cannot know. All we can do is look at Johannesburg and say that it was here that the warriors were turned into miners.

The explosion of Johannesburg, *iGoli*, the City of Gold, from out of the veldt was remarkable. Even today, when you approach it from the south going up the Midlands Expressway it looks like it has come from nowhere and shouldn't really be there at all. There isn't a river for a start and so one of the first rules of human settlement is tossed straight out of the window; the first miners were reliant on well water sold by the bucketful and yet within ten years of the first discovery of gold, there was a fully functioning city with department stores, theatres, bars (lots of them), gas works, a hospital, a railway and a football ground. A thousand miles from Cape Town and five hundred from Durban, it had a population of around 100,000 people divided into roughly 50,000 Europeans, 5,000 Indians, Chinese and Malays, 45,000 Africans and 5,000 mixed-race; probably about 80% of those present were men and mainly at the younger end, which gave the city a reputation for frenetic rowdiness. Looking at the 1896 map, the present-day grid system is discernible but also the fact that the city has specific areas allocated to 'Coolies' (mainly Indians), 'Kaffirs' and 'Natives' – and here, I'm going to abandon the inverted commas because they are patronising and irritating.

That some sort of segregation should emerge was inevitable; birds of a feather flock together and this can be seen in any modern city – there are parts of London SW20 where you can't

---
[385] Greg Mills et al *Making Africa Work*, (London, 2017) p. 144.
[386] Leo Amery, *The Times History of the War in South Africa 1899-1900* (London 1900) Vol.1 p.89.

throw a brick blindfolded without hitting a South African on the back of the head. In the case of Indians, the religious demands of both Islam and Hinduism involve some level of separateness, while different tastes in food, recreation and general modes of living are factors common to all; every expatriate experiences the craving for the familiar things of home (how I missed pork pies in China! - and you need only put a match to the BBQ in SW20 to see South Africans gather like elephants at a waterhole). The problem in Joburg though was the *forced* segregation whereby Africans were kept in compounds, banned from theatres and generally harassed. How much this came about as a result of racial feeling and how much out of sheer pragmatism is a moot point. About 50% of African labourers had been kept in strictly controlled compounds in Kimberley as a means to prevent the theft of diamonds – there was a whole parallel industry of illegal diamond trading and subsequently in Joburg it was estimated that 10% of all gold produced was half-inched – and as a handy way of organising new workers into an entirely unfamiliar environment of clocks, set working hours, machinery, money and canteen food. The same conditions were not applied to European labourers because the Europeans came from an industrial society already, understood the environment and knew just how to tell the boss where he could stick his compounds. We can only guess at the bewilderment of the unskilled, uneducated African man, deprived of his land during the Boer invasions, his chiefs dead, drunk or deposed, coming from a rural backwater of cattle and mealies into a city the like of which he could never have envisaged and full of 'magic' that his sangomas had never dreamt of, then going down a deep hole to sweat in the dark heat of the low oxygen environment with people who spoke a different language, using machinery and tools the like of which he had never seen; perhaps the only thing that was familiar was the compound, where there remained some semblance of communal village life. But it was still segregation, if in cases, rather paternal; in 1890, the Cape Town compounds that serviced the harbour and docks were established both 'to protect the worker from …social evils in the town, to protect the town from the workers.'[387]

What we do know, however, is that when those African labourers went down the mine and into the compound, they were no longer calling the shots in South Africa and were ever more subordinate to the dominant British and Afrikaaner influences. In a remarkable history of Johannesburg entitled *Johannesburg: Out of the Crucible* written in 1940, black people get barely a mention until page 161, that is, until 1902; in 1899, the author reckoned there were 110,000 Africans at the mines; it is as though they have been airbrushed out of the picture almost.[388]

The people who were front and centre of the picture in Joburg at that time were the *Uitlanders*, foreigners of mainly European extraction who came to work in all the professions that a busy city requires but especially prominent in the mines. One of the great fallacies of Marxist history is that capitalism and industrialisation is seen as a process of dragging workers out of rural idylls and chaining them to cotton looms rather than a dynamic process that did away with the routine poverty of agricultural un- and under-employment, provided regular work and wages, a higher standard of material welfare and, what's more, the

---
[387] Quoted in, Paul Maylam. *The Rise and Decline of Urban Apartheid in South Africa*. African Affairs, Vol. 89, No. 354 (Jan., 1990).
[388] Hedley A. Chilvers. *Johannesburg. Out of the Crucible*. (New York, 1940).

opportunity to empower and advance yourself and your children by industrial training. The trained, experienced mechanic, miner, boilermaker, plate-layer, railwayman and toolmaker were all in great demand throughout the industrialising world and this, combined with cheaper sea passages, recruitment and emigration schemes, meant that a class of skilled workmen were not chained to any employer or even any country and thus washed around the world to wherever would pay them. Cornish miners could be found in Australia, the Americas - South America adopted the *empanada*, the pasty specially designed for eating down a mine from the Cornish - as well as in South Africa; British workers provided the foremen and skilled labour that built the railways of South Africa and much else besides. There were whole classes of men who tried their hands at the mines and industrial ventures around the world before pitching up in Johannesburg; MacMac pools reflects the number of Scots up at the Pilgrim's Rest diggings. Some of these men were, as we have seen at Kimberley, adventurers, mercenaries and desperadoes who were never more than two meals away from starvation and so provided a ready pool of potential gunslingers, freebooters and land-grabbing crooks eager to participate in the post-Majuba chaos in Bechuanaland and Zululand. Others were more respectable types; Christopher Bethell was a man who had been rusticated from Cambridge and sent out to the colonies by his Yorkshire gentry family to redeem his foolish youth. He worked variously as a hunter, trader and policeman before marrying a Tswana girl and fighting the Boers. (He was the model for the eponymous hero in my novel *Pelly's Quest*: get it while it's hot).

What drove them to set out on such adventures when Europe, on the verge of the late Victorian/Edwardian *belle epoch* in the 1880s, provided a wealth of opportunities in all sorts of new professions? Many, like Cecil Rhodes, were Dick Whittingtons out to seek their fortunes. Others just felt the call of the wide blue yonder and were prepared to give up established careers for the challenge – that would include Rhodes' familiar, Leander Starr Jameson – still others joined family members already established. Russian Jews arrived with the pogroms of the 1880s, sailors came ashore and never went back; there were still pockets of grinding poverty in Europe that fed the waves of emigration to the Americas and some, few, ended up in South Africa too. Indians came as indentured labour for the sugar plantations and as merchants and traders and stayed. These were all familiar stories but what was different about Johannesburg was its size and concentration. What was more striking was that these Uitlanders came with Anglo-Saxon ideas of law and liberty and rights and demands for the vote; *No Taxation Without Representation* and *Reform!* were written through their bones like sticks of Blackpool rock.

As far as Kruger and the Trekboers were concerned, Johannesburg was a foreign country that had come up out of the veldt like a noxious weed only fifty miles from Pretoria and they were ill-equipped to deal with all the challenges that came with it. Indeed, before 1881, it is possible to see something heroic in the Boers. The Piet Retief generation who had trekked away from British rule went out onto the veldt and competed on more or less equal terms with their African rivals but after they regained their independence at Majuba, this becomes more difficult. There was little that was heroic in the assaults on Bechuanaland and Zululand and in the ascendancy of Paul Kruger there was much that was ugly. His hatred for the British was more or less fixed; his hatred for black people had been acquired at the Battle of

Blood River and ever since he had held to the principle of getting his revenge in first, of grabbing whatever came within reach and making sure the blacks were knocked down, kept down and prevented from ever rising again. Among his supporters, this sense of being in permanent laager, of being permanently on the watch for signs of black rebellion was common and in it lies the roots of *Swart gevaar*, the fear of the black man, that was such a feature of Apartheid.

However, it is important not to tar all Afrikaaners with the same brush. There was actually a Progressive Party led by 'Slim' Piet Joubert – don't get carried away by the title; *progressive* was a very relative term – which sought better relations with both Britain and the Uitlanders. The majority of Afrikaaners had *not* trekked out of the Cape Colony but had reconciled themselves to the British connection and were playing an increasingly important role in its government and politics. In the Orange Free State too, there were very many Afrikaaners who viewed their brethren to the north with some suspicion and distaste while in the towns of the Transvaal, new classes of people were arriving, many of them Uitlanders with different ideas, more liberal dispositions and often better educated; it is a fair comment to say that when the Transvaal was annexed in 1877, there was a sizeable minority of its citizens who were in favour of it and many of these were the small town dwellers of more recent arrival. It is hard to be precise about this, but reading through the contemporary literature it is possible to glimpse a certain dissatisfaction with Kruger and his old Trekboer cronies as being dinosaurs who were looking increasingly irrelevant in the modern world. Kruger, for example, believed the world was flat, that giraffes were really camels because they weren't mentioned in the Bible, that firing a rocket into a likely looking cloud in order to start the rain was a direct provocation to God (as was music outside of church); it was widely believed that rinderpest and locust attacks were Acts of God (this last was actually debated in the *Volksraad*)[389]; at least some of the deaths in the concentration camps of the Anglo-Boer War were due to the insanitary practices of the Boers from the boonies. Again, there is more than a suggestion in contemporary accounts that avarice, peasant nastiness, sharp practice and brutality were at least as common among the Trekboers as the regular and routine hospitality they displayed towards the stranger 'provided he did not stay.'[390] In contemporary South Africa, it is the residents of the Free State who are the butt of jokes about rustic, bovine, boorishness but I suspect that it was Kruger and the old Voortrekkers who were increasingly on the receiving end of such jokes during the 1890s.

As a guide to the Uitlanders, there isn't a better one than Percy Fitzpatrick, who we might fairly describe as being a Catholic, Irish-British-South African clerk, storekeeper, transport rider, journalist, conspirator, gaolbird, author, MP for Pretoria, zoologist and citrus farmer. The author of that great ripping yarn, *Jock of the Bushveldt*, he is now famous for being the originator of the Remembrance Day two-minute silence but at the time under consideration he was deep in the machinations of the Reform Committee, which aimed at no less than the overthrow of the Kruger government and the bringing of the Transvaal back under the British flag. His book *The Transvaal From Within* is quite striking because much of what he wrote

---

[389] Leo Amery, *The Times History of the War in South Africa 1899-1900* (London 1900) Vol.1 p.129

[390] Sarah Gertrude Millin, *General Smuts Vol.1* (London, 1936) p. 20.

was echoed within the Colonial Office files and you can't help but feel that his views were influential there. It was written in 1899 and published during the Boer War when everyone wanted to know why that war had come about. In laying out the case for the Uitlanders, he had a pro-British imperialist point of view, but he does seems to have tried to maintain some balance and most of what he wrote rings true enough to be taken seriously. He didn't like Kruger though, seeing him as venal, duplicitous and dictatorial and charged him with only rebelling against the 1877 British annexation of the Transvaal after he had had his repeated requests for a pay rise turned down by the British authorities. Kruger was certainly an old troll, but this is stretching it too far. The journalist Leo Amery's charge that Kruger was dismissed from his post for unofficially *adding* £100 to his salary seems much more likely.[391]

There were some charges that do stick though. The first was that the Transvaal government was so broke that it couldn't pay its own officials and this resulted in widespread corruption. Smuggling was the first indication that something was rotten but more serious was the issue of 'registration'. In 1882, Kruger had rigged the franchise law to prevent anyone but the old country Boers exerting real power. The towns were effectively disenfranchised and the period of residence needed to qualify for the vote was extended to five years; those five years dated from the moment of registration in the Veldtcornet's register and very often there was no register, no literate Veldtcornet to register with and so no way of proving residence (in 1891 when the Johannesburg Veldtcornet died, it was found that he had not bothered to keep a list of names of the thousands of people who had registered).[392] In effect, anyone who arrived in the Transvaal after 1882 faced major practical difficulties in getting the vote. Added to this was an intensification of racial feeling against anyone of British origin in the country districts as a result of the annexation, war and retrocession, which meant that those Veldtcornets who were inclined against the British could make sure that registration didn't take place at all. So was born the great African tradition of rigging elections.

It was also the case that although Kruger thought himself to be a hell of a sly old fox when it came to relieving others of their money, he had until this point only been up against Africans unfamiliar with the money economy, peasants and the self-flagellant Gladstone. When the money started rolling in from the goldfields, he and the rest of the Volksraad found themselves way out of their depth when it came to dealing with all the paraphernalia of modern capitalism and so recruited a whole load of Germans and Dutch – collectively known as 'Hollanders' – to help him. This help manifested itself rather along the lines of how the Gupta family instructed President Zuma in the finer arts of corruption; they filled his pockets, filled their own even more and left the taxpayers with the bill. The Netherlands Railway Company was a case in point; when granted the monopoly over all the Transvaal railways, this fine example of honest endeavour managed to spend £124,000 on construction before any construction was done; whole sections of track were contracted out to be built at £23,500 per mile when the real cost was nearer £8,000; dressed stone was shipped out from a quarry in Holland for the Komati bridge when there was plenty of rock to hand. They also acted as agents for the raising of loans to the state, for which they awarded themselves a commission

---

[391] Leo Amery, *The Times History of the War in South Africa 1899-1900* (London 1900) Vol.1 p.62.
[392] Leo Amery, *The Times History of the War in South Africa 1899-1900* (London 1900) Vol.1 p.135.

of 10%, and agents for the collection of Customs duty which they also skimmed mercilessly. When the Uitlander taxpayers complained the Company responded with a blizzard of paper which, in Percy's fine phrase, 'left the unfortunate Volksraad members absolutely stupefied where they had formerly only been confused.'

No matter, everyone knew how to quiet any misgivings; in 1890, Barend Vorster, a member of the Volksraad managed to get himself the contract for the Selati railway by bribing a goodly portion of the Volksraad, Kruger included. He then sub-contracted the construction at a cost of £9,600 per mile to a company which, within two days, sub-sub-contracted it at £7000 per mile; and behind this outrageous scam was the Netherlands Railway Company, which netted just over £500,000 from the deal.

Old Percy also brought up the question of the Dynamite monopoly. This product was absolutely vital to the working of the mines and a monopoly for its *manufacture* had been granted before the gold at Johannesburg had been discovered. The fact that the chap with the concession got to sell the product for a 200% premium on what it cost to import the stuff was not thought particularly important because no-one really thought there would be much demand for it and if a local industry could be encouraged then, all well and good. This changed when demand skyrocketed; what didn't change was the monopoly. Only when it was revealed that the dynamite wasn't being manufactured at all, but actually *imported*, was the concession cancelled, which Percy claimed was the only time that Kruger did anything for the Uitlanders; and then Kruger reinstated it, handing the contract to a partner of the original swindler, at the behest of his Executive Council crony, JMA Wolarans, who was skimming a shilling a case, or £10,000pa as payment for his influence. At the best of times, the competence of the Transvaal administration was notional; but now it was corrupt as well; and completely under the patronage of Kruger himself to boot, with one in five Boers being on the official payroll. And increasingly, the Uitlanders began to say that as they paid 90% of the taxes (which were four times as high as they were in Australia and roughly eight times higher than in England) and most of the bribes, and had to put up with high food and fuel prices because everything had to be carried in via the inflated tariffs of the Netherlands Railway Company, they ought to have a say in how that money was spent. They wanted the vote.

Thus it was the franchise issue that really rankled. As we have seen, Kruger had already made it difficult for an Uitlander to get the vote but in 1890, he mangled an already improbably complex franchise law so that an Uitlander would have to wait for 14 years before he might reasonably expect to get it – and Percy, himself, wouldn't get it because he was a Catholic and only Protestants were eligible. In 1894, the law was rigged again so that an Uitlander would not get the vote until he was forty years of age and had duly acquired the personal permission of no less a person than the President in person. Reading through the way in which these laws were produced is quite hilarious if you like that sort of thing – it makes Tony Blair look honest and straightforward – but basically the aim was to make it impossible for the Uitlanders to vote because if they were allowed to vote, Kruger would instantly be pitched out on his arse - as indeed would Tony Blair have been in 2005 if he hadn't prevented the Electoral Commission from redrawing the boundaries throughout his disgraceful tenure of office.[393] This was a point that many members of the Volksraad understood and many of them took the view that if the Uitlanders were denied rights for much longer there would surely be a rebellion and on the back of that rebellion would come British troops and British rule: 'Kruger and his Hollanders have taken our independence more surely than Shepstone ever did,' declared one old Boer.[394] Just to make sure everyone got the message that no backsliding would be tolerated, Kruger then rigged the 1893 election to ensure that he stayed in office; and this was the real point because if the franchise was conceded, Kruger as already stated, would lose the election but this did not mean that the Transvaal would instantly become British because quite a few of those Uitlanders were American or Irish or Cape Dutch. Rather the likelihood was that Piet Joubert would become president and from that point some sort of reconciliation with Britain would become possible. Just to restate; Britain had no interest in taking over the Transvaal as long as it refrained from intrigues with the Great Powers, got on with making money and stayed away from the coastlines.

From Kruger's point of view, the Uitlanders had no right to the vote because they were, as their name suggests, foreigners, who came uninvited and who were free to leave at any time and the sooner the better; he once addressed a crowd at Krugersdorp with the memorable greeting 'Burghers, friends, thieves, murders, new-comers and others'[395] which was nice. Neither were they part of the *volk* who had struggled through the Great Trek, fought the endless wars against black Africans and then won their independence at Majuba. Even worse; they were mainly *British*. This argument ignored the fact that large parts of the Transvaal actually belonged to other people at the time of the gold discoveries (and before and subsequently) and that even if legal claim could be established on the basis of Gladstone's surrender and the retrocession after Majuba, the moral claim was actually quite dubious being based on not much more than 'we stole the land first'. In reality, Kruger's rule rested on nothing but corrupt patronage and his oft repeated threat to bring in the backwoods Boers to keep all those Coolie, Kaffirs, Cape Boys and uppity Uitlander interlopers, and anyone else who disagreed with him, in their place because, for him, Africa was for the Afrikaaner and he was *the* Afrikaaner. As Flora Shaw, journalist, imperialist battleaxe and wife of Lord Lugard (of Nigeria fame), said: 'what he endeavoured to preserve was not so much the liberty and independence of the Transvaal…as the continued predominance of the faction whose leader he had been for twenty years.'[396] Now, admittedly, Flora Shaw was not above fibbing when it suited her so we have to be rather cautious in taking her word for anything, but on this occasion I think we can accept that what she says is a pretty fair comment.

*

---

[393] http://littlejohn.dailymail.co.uk/2011/09/after-13-years-of-labour-gerrymandering-the-boundary-commissions-proposals-are-modest-to-say-the-lea.html Also: https://www2.warwick.ac.uk/fac/soc/pais/people/kettell/cloud/election2005.pdf
[394] Leo Amery, *The Times History of the War in South Africa 1899-1900* (London 1900) Vol.1 p.144.

[395] Leo Amery, *The Times History of the War in South Africa 1899-1900* (London 1900) Vol.1 p.136.

[396] Leo Amery, *The Times History of the War in South Africa 1899-1900* (London 1900) Vol.1 p.144. Flora Shaw wrote the relevant chapters in this book.

Rebellion was brewing indeed and at the back of it was the titanic figure of Cecil Rhodes. Every time I think about this man I come away with a different opinion of him because he was so contradictory in his actions and opinions. You can label him as a rogue, a pirate, a philanthropist, a visionary, the defender of African land and voting rights – who stole Mashonaland and was in favour of flogging Africans; who wanted a colour bar but had no time for 'race feelings';[397] an unashamed imperialist – who supported Home Rule for Ireland and funded the Xhosa language newspaper *Izwi Labantu* which was instrumental in setting up the South African Native Congress, forerunner to the ANC; a financial and business genius – who missed out on the Joburg gold rush; and a whole lot else besides. There are those who say he was gay, fond of young men and point to his nursing of Neville Pickering as he lay dying and the fabulous rows he had with those men in his entourage who went off to get married; and yet the Polish adventuress, Princess Radziwill, who did her best to marry him and then blackmail him, never made this charge. He was certainly charismatic and inspired absolute devotion in many of his supporters and hatred among those who weren't; *Trooper Peter Halkett of Mashonaland* was the writer Olive Schreiner's shriek against him (given her previous relationships, I can't help wondering if this was in revenge for possibly being turned down by him). He was not fond of the scroungers and loafers that always congregate around money and under no circumstances could his business relations with men like Rudd, Beit and Barney Barnato be described as anything but hard-nosed and pragmatic; he wasn't above bribery though and had half the House of Lords, any number of newspaper owners and even S.J. du Toit, the founder of the *Bond*,[398] in his pocket. He was not dismissive of academics but he preferred men of action and in Leander Starr Jameson, the model for Kipling's *If* and a man built from teak and steel, he found his particular favourite. He didn't believe in God but rather admired the Salvation Army; preferred a bed roll on the open veldt to the palace he built himself at *Groote Schuur* and he died in a shabby cottage overlooking the sea at Muizenberg. He wouldn't stay in a decent hotel when he went to London but put up at a fleapit called the Burlington Hotel; in Kimberley he lived in a tin shack; for all his wealth, he acted as though money didn't matter to him. He was also a serial Will writer and left eight of them behind, all of which were full of dreams of an ever-expanding empire, the re-unification of the USA and Britain – the Cape to Cairo railway was only the start – and controlled by a band of brothers who were all to be educated at oxford – the famous Rhodes scholarships. Above all, he believed that South Africa could only be ruled if the Brit and the Boer combined.

At the time of the Johannesburg tensions, Rhodes was head of the British South Africa Company – legally empowered to do anything up to and including arresting God and invading the moon - Prime Minister of Cape Colony and, fresh from his triumphant destruction of Lobengula's tyrannical rule in Matabeleland and Mashonaland and his carving out of Rhodesia, probably the most powerful man in southern Africa. Rhodesia lies outside the scope of this book but it is worthwhile saying that if the Pioneer Column that he sent up beyond the Limpopo looked remarkably like a trek backed up by a Commando, it wasn't sent

---
[397] Sarah Gertrude Millin, *General Smuts Vol.1* (London, 1936) p.221.
[398] Lindie Korf, *D.F. Malan: a political biography*. University of Stellenbosh Ph.D Thesis, 2010.

against some poor defenceless Africans but against an absolute bastard whose father, Mzilikazi, had stolen the land and who had then begun a reign of terror on the Shona peoples that the son happily maintained. Lobengula was no victim when Rhodes' Maxim guns did the world a favour by wiping out the murderous thugs of the Matabele impis. What Rhodes learned from the episode though was that the Pioneer column technique might work equally well in the Transvaal. This isn't to say that Rhodes was the instigator of the rebellion – far from it – but he was certainly in cahoots with it.

The promoters of the rebellion were the Reform Committee, among whom Percy Fitzgerald could be found acting as secretary, who wanted the franchise above all else. That this would mean British rule was something else that they knew, but this did not appear to them to be unreasonable considering present arrangements. Made up of various 'leading citizens', they were given some backing from the mining companies but, by and large, the Randlords were far too cautious to get seriously and decisively involved; such a gamble would be catastrophic for business if the plot failed. Even Rhodes – whose brother was on the committee - was wary and though everyone, including the British Colonial Secretary, Joseph Chamberlain, was aware what was afoot, no-one really wanted to be the one to fire the starting pistol. It was also a dog's breakfast of a plot; arms were smuggled in, but in insufficient quantities; plans were discussed to seize Pretoria fort and liberate the arsenal but there doesn't seem to have been much serious organisation at work; many Uitlanders disliked Kruger but, being Americans and Fenians, were less than enamoured of coming under the Union Jack; others were earning good money and couldn't give a fig; others were beered up; worse still, the plotters consisted of a committee of around sixty members, which pretty much guaranteed that nothing would work.

Like the Battle of Isandhlwana, the blame game for why the Jameson Raid failed has provided Historians both amateur and professional, Conspiracy Theorists, Anti-Imperialists, Afrikaaner Nationalists and Uncle Tom Cobley and all, with plenty of material for an entertaining parlour game. Who knew what, when and who saw which telegram at which place, at what particular time, is material that can be mangled and manipulated to praise or condemn whoever takes a particular Historians' fancy. Getting a clear picture isn't helped by the fact that in the Parliamentary Inquiry that followed all the main protagonists lied like a New Labour Spin Doctor in possession of a dodgy dossier. Old Percy maintained that the plan was for the Reform Committee to organise a big meeting on or about the 6th January 1896 at which the Reform Manifesto would be presented to Kruger's Government as a sort of ultimatum. He maintained that the arms smuggled into Johannesburg were only for self-defence if, as expected, Kruger responded with violence. Only then, and only if Kruger did respond with violence would Jameson's forces be called in. He put the blame fairly and squarely on Jameson for jumping the gun on his own initiative. The inquiry concluded that Rhodes and Jameson were to blame (true), that no-one in the Colonial Office including Joe Chamberlain knew anything at all about it (hmmmm…) and that High Commissioner Hercules Robinson was a doddery old fool who should have known what was going on and ought now to be put out to grass (also true).

It seems clear that Jameson is guilty as charged. He did jump the gun, some say as a result of reading a biography of Clive of India. It's reasonable to speculate that his success in leading the Pioneer Column to defeat Lobengula's Matabele made him over-confident. He was also a gambler and his luck had so far held up to a remarkable extent. This might also have led him to act without the sanction of his boss, Cecil Rhodes, who really did not give his authorisation. That said, Jameson's own judgement that if he had succeeded all would have been forgiven is like most of the things that remarkable man said, bang on the button.

Jameson crossed the border, according to Percy, without the knowledge of the Reform Committee. He also crossed the border with only 450 of the 800 men he was expected to bring because at the last moment a large number of troopers refused to follow him when he could not produce a legal order for them to mount an armed invasion. Within a very few miles and a very few hours it was clear that not only were the commissariat arrangements inadequate, that re-mounts and food supplies were inadequate but also that alarm bells were ringing in the offices of Cecil Rhodes, Sir Hercules Robinson and the Colonial Office in London at this illegal and risky - to the point of foolhardy - forward movement. Alarm bells had already rung in Kruger's office and his commandos were gathering much more quickly than Jameson had allowed for. The Reform Committee panicked and began sending messages to Jameson to turn back and to Kruger saying they knew nothing of his actions. To say that this was a highly original version of events given by the Reform Committee would not be an understatement. Much of Percy's book is a long whine against the accusation that Johannesburg ought to have been renamed *Judasburg* for its abandonment of Jameson. The projected rising in Johannesburg fizzled out after Kruger made promises to hear the demands of the Reform Committee, which he never intended for a moment to meet, but which did allow the more pusillanimous among the committee members to grasp at the opportunity of backsliding. Again, it is hard not to get the impression that the committee was amateurish, organised more on the lines of a cricket club and about as serious about bringing about revolution as the Johannesburg Ladies' Sewing Circle. They sent no aid to Jameson.

Jameson did his best. In fact, when faced with forces that began to outnumber him to an order of magnitude situated in positions of great strength, it was he who overrode the advice of his military commanders to press home an attack that was doomed to fail. Later on at Doornkop, which is today just by Soweto, surrounded and pounded by artillery, he was forced to accept failure and he duly surrendered. He and his men were rounded up, the officers arrested and the men put over the frontier while the Reform Committee members, much to Percy's disgust, were also rounded up and incarcerated in the Pretoria *tronk*. Percy was of the opinion that the Reform Committee had done no wrong and were actually to be commended for their restraint and for negotiating with Kruger in good faith. Butter would not melt in his mouth.

Mind you, just because the Reform Committee was guilty did not automatically mean that Kruger was innocent. He immediately disregarded the surrender arrangements under which Jameson had laid down his arms and then went after the Reform Committee in a legal process that was of the distinctly Australian marsupial variety. British lawyers chosen by the Reform Committee were prevented from addressing the court; the only judge available to hear the case (because most of the other judges were to be called as witnesses) was a chap called Morice who was of distinctly liberal tendencies. This was clearly unacceptable to Kruger so a hanging judge who hated anything English was imported from the Free State. On top of this the Transvaal operated two different legal systems – the constitution of the ZAR and Roman Dutch law – and the defendants were not told which system would operate. The council for the prosecution then offered a deal that if the defendants entered guilty pleas they would be given purely nominal sentences. To this Percy and Co. agreed only to find that when they did plead guilty the prosecuting council pressed for the harshest possible sentences. On top of this, evidence which would have been of benefit to the defence was reserved, disclosure was abandoned and affidavits produced from one of Jameson's dimmer officers which he could not remember signing. When sentence was passed, four of the leading members – including Rhodes' brother - were sentenced to death; a sentence delivered by the judge with a broad grin, while the rest were fined £2,000 and given two years each. This was the sort of justice that British people could expect under Kruger. Percy might have been guilty but this was like sending Pablo Escobar to be tried by the Cali Cartel. Even the Afrikaaners, who were utterly disgusted by the Raid, were appalled at the sentences and a petition for the sentences to be overturned was immediately got up and the Mayors of 200 towns across the Cape and Free State went up to Pretoria to demand an amelioration.

Nevertheless, the Jameson Raid had been a disaster. How great a disaster was described by one of Britain's leading Jingoes, Leo Amery, who in his no nonsense way declared that Kruger had been on the point of being overthrown by a combination of Uitlander pressure and the Joubert's Progressive Party yet:

> Dr. Jameson had, by one act of supreme folly, won back for the President the confidence of his burghers, crushed the resistance of the Uitlanders, and dissipated all prospects of future revolt; put out of court and almost ruined Kruger's one great political opponent [*Rhodes was forced to resign as Cape Prime Minister*]; hopelessly embarrassed the Imperial Government; and fanned into fierce flame throughout all Afrikanderdom the hatred of England which for the last ten years had gradually been falling to sleep.[399]

One writer reckoned that the real wound caused by the raid was that Rhodes was found to be deep in it and he was the one Englishman that the *Bond* was willing to trust. As a result:

> They did not see that Rhodes was not anti-Boer – merely anti-Kruger. Rhodes became to the Boers, not the enemy of the government, but the enemy of the nation.'[400]

And what went for Rhodes, went for the rest of those *bladdy Rooineks*. Certainly, it was this incident that led a young prodigy by the name of Jan Christian Smuts to tear up his Cape British nationality and head for the Transvaal.

---

[399] Leo Amery, *The Times History of the War in South Africa 1899-1900* (London 1900) Vol.1 p.180

[400] Sarah Gertrude Millin, *General Smuts, Vol.I* (London, 1936) p.61.

\*

## The Causes of the Anglo-Boer War 1899-1902.

For the past forty years or so the standard work on this subject has been Thomas Pakenham's *The Boer War*. Written in 1979 by a socialist government minister, the 8th Earl of Longford, who had tried to refuse his title (but kept the castle) and who had, almost by definition therefore, swallowed the Marxist view of empire, it was indicative of the full-blown academic and cultural assault on the idea that the British Empire had anything positive about it. Previous to this there had, of course, been a great deal of debate about the origins and nature of the Empire and James Morris (now Jan, having transitioned: can a Transgender person be sympathetic to imperialism? Apparently, they can) wrote a really good trilogy about the Empire entitled *Pax-Britannica* in which, through a series of sympathetic word pictures, he drew a glorious panorama which wove together the varied experiences, eccentricities, personalities, impacts and influences, gains and sacrifices made by, as well as the hard realities, on and of the Victorian Empire. He did not shrink from criticism where criticism was due but he was also alive to the many creditable things that were achieved in by the bewildering array of imperialists, philanthropists, Benthamites, educational and sanitary reformers and what-have-you. His judgement was roughly that there was more positive than negative in the Victorian Empire but that even so, the negatives as well as the positives should be put under the microscope. All in all, he held to the idea that while there was good and bad in the Empire, it had had its day by 1945 and was justly and sensibly wound up. In 1972, the BBC used his book as one of the bases for a 13-part TV series *The British Empire* but, quite predictably, took out all the sympathetic stuff and laid huge emphasis on the bad stuff. So much so that a public outcry – which included objections from the brilliant historian of India, Philip Mason and equally brilliant Lord Blake, made them re-cut several episodes.[401] One commentator said it should have been re-christened 'Monty Python's Flying Empire'. It made no difference in the long run; an organisation that tolerated its drama department to be almost entirely run by the Workers Revolutionary Party and needed regular MI5 involvement to stop it being handed over to the Bolsheviks completely could simply not be trusted to come up with anything fair-minded regarding the Empire. And the farrago that was the 1996 BBC series *Rhodes* shows that the tradition has been maintained – they actually went so far as to accuse Rhodes of being a paedophile. Pakenham was firmly in this anti-imperial camp.

This revulsion at the British Empire by the Britain's intelligentsia was a remarkable aspect of the times. Despite the fact that under the Labour Government of Wilson, Callaghan and Healey the evidence of the failure of Socialism that lay right under their noses in the form of unburied bodies, rubbish piled head high in Leicester Square, a hundred NHS hospitals closed at the behest of the IMF, the only organisation willing to lend money to the bankrupt British Government after Sterling collapsed; despite the fact that the Labour Government was closing coal mines at a rate that was only marginally below the galloping rate of inflation; that public utilities were at the point of collapse and that Nationalised Industries barely

---

[401] http://hansard.millbanksystems.com/lords/1972/jul/06/bbc-and-british-empire-series

qualified for the title of being either National or Industries being for the most part run by chaotic unions whose greed and idleness knew no bounds; and despite the fact that on the other side of the Inner German Border a huge Soviet Army was waiting its opportunity to sweep across Europe and add the Socialist Republic of Great Britain to its list of impoverished, enslaved and oppressed client states, the British intelligentsia – 'the people, who, admiring only their own cleverness, despised real goodness, real thought, real wisdom' as someone said, in another context[402] - decided that Socialism was a better alternative than the old British way of Liberty, Parliamentary Democracy and Capitalism. For them the old certainties of the British people and pride in their history had to be removed if ever the Socialist Nirvana was to be achieved and so the assault on the British Empire as something that the British could point to with some pride began.

Now, History as I have said is as much about Historians as it is about things that have happened in the past so it's time to actually look at the kind of History that Pakenham was pedalling. It is important to do this because the picture he paints of the Boer War has hardly been challenged in the past forty years and his book is still on the shelf in book shops far and wide. It is a picture of a rapacious and aggressive Imperial bully picking a fight with two small, independent, peaceful republics who wanted nothing more than to be left alone to get on with a life of bucolic bliss. The war was fought to steal Boer gold and for no other reason. It was an unjust war fought by stupid, blimpish Generals leading bewildered Tommies to slaughter at the hands of sturdy, patriotic resistance fighters. As the war dragged on and the monstrous Imperial Colossus ground forward, these same fine resistance fighters resorted to guerrilla tactics which again ran rings round stupid, blimpish Generals and bewildered Tommies, until finally, the dashing freedom fighters were unfairly defeated by barbaric methods which included the herding of Boer women and children into concentration camps where they died in droves as a result of British incompetence and criminal neglect.

This, of course, was a familiar narrative and fitted right into the 1960's notions of the First World War being one of 'lions led by donkeys', of indiscriminate pointless slaughter which solved no problems and ended in the unjust and unnecessary humiliation of Germany at the Treaty of Versailles. Indeed, by 1970 it seemed that the History of the First World War was no longer being written by Historians but by a handful of poets who barely sold a book in the 1920's and taught by English teachers who never ventured past the 1916 Battle of the Somme. It was, in fact, 'Blackadder History' and as far as accuracy went it was, in the words of Captain Edmund Blackadder himself, 'Bollocks'.

When I read Thomas Pakenham's book as an undergraduate, I found it to be as unconvincing and unreliable then as I know it to be now. Its cardinal errors were of exaggeration and careful exclusion of evidence that didn't fit the picture. He spent page after page dissecting British defeats in glorious, technicolour detail just to prove how crap we were and then glossed over the victories, but more importantly, he never really answered the question that formed in my mind as I was reading and which was as applicable to the First World War narrative as it was to the Boer War; if the British were so utterly useless how on earth did we win? Looking at his other book, *The Scramble for Africa* published in 1991, the omissions

---

[402] Smuts. Quoted in Sarah Gertrude Millin, *General Smuts* Vol.II (London, 1936) p.174

regarding South Africa are so important that one can only treat the rest of his work with extreme caution. In the particular case of the Zulu War, no mention of Frere's status as a defence expert was made; there was no explanation of Carnarvon's resignation over the Bulgarian crisis; nine pages were devoted to the British defeat at Isandlhwana, none to the victories at Khambula and Ulundi; no mention either of Zululand between 1879-1906 and thus no mention of the Boer invasion, while his treatment of the concurrent assault on Bechuanaland was skated over as though the desert there was covered in thin ice. Pakenham wrote *The Boer War* in the 1970s and if he had tried to write that book in the 1990s he would never have got it into print. This was not because of any thoughts that his anti-imperialism or general denigration of the British would be questioned but because in the intervening years the whole question of Apartheid had cropped up. From the mid-1980s onwards it became increasingly impossible to say anything nice about a white South African. Indeed, the satirical TV show *Spitting Image* carried a musical sketch in which the chorus was *Oh You'll never meet a nice South African*. This meant that although the bad bits about the Brits were still fine, Pakenham's lionisation of Kruger and the Boers simply wouldn't pass muster. It stayed in print because no-one wrote anything that could seriously challenge its place on the bookshelves.

As we have seen, South African academics played a large role in opposing Apartheid by working to undermine its historical justifications. Much of this opposition was based abroad but as the end of Apartheid approached, those South African academics who had remained began to look at the future and realised that for them it might not be so rosy. This was because post-colonial Africa had form when it came to universities. Amongst the many evils that the hated imperialist colonisers had inflicted on Africa – like sanitation, science and medicine – was a collection of rather good universities. Bangui, Makerere, Dar-es-Salaam, Lusaka, Accra – which boasted J.D. Omer and Conor Cruise O'Brian – Nairobi, Algiers, Ibadan, Dakar and, possibly the best, Lovanium, in the Congo. Each one of them collapsed under post-colonial rule through that peculiarly African blend of bare-faced corruption, monstrous mismanagement and plain stupidity.[403]

At Wits, Rhodes, University of Cape Town, Stellenbosch and the University of Natal therefore it became a racing certainty that tenured positions would be under threat from black claims for positive discrimination in favour of those who could claim historical disadvantage. They also realised that the management of those universities would come under black control and this too added a level of uncertainty. Furthermore, there would be major demands for an increase in the number and proportion of black students. All these things were perfectly reasonable in theory but in practice – and no-one, *no-one* dared to whisper it - this meant unqualified and inexperienced management, staff appointed on the basis of their relationship with the ANC rather than any academic ability and large numbers of students who had neither the ability or the education to qualify for university. No academic wants to teach large classes of dumb students - if they did they would work in secondary schools. Seeing which way the wind was blowing a huge number of South African academics took the opportunity provided by the lifting of sanctions in 1994 to make a run for it, alongside all

---

[403] RW Johnson, *The African University? The Critical Case of South Africa and the Tragedy at the UKZN.* (Cape Town, 2012).

those other white South African professionals who had sellable skills that would be welcomed abroad rather than denigrated and restricted under the new regime. In 2000 John Laband packed his bags for Canada after the university authorities had floated plans to make him teach Business Studies. Thus did South Africa, and KwaZulu-Natal particularly, loose a brilliant academic and the leading expert on the History of the Zulus themselves.

The effect on South African academic output has been catastrophic and the only half-decent general work on the Boer War published in nearly two decades is Bill Nasson's *The War for South Africa* which came out in 2000 and doesn't do much more than re-state Pakenham's Brit-bashing. Where he does break new ground, he does so by showing how badly the black and coloured populations were treated during the war (Bill Nasson is coloured) but this was best done in his earlier work, *The War of Abraham Esau, 1899-1901* written in 1988. And, of course, the participation of Blacks in the war is played down because, of course, the ANC does not like to be reminded that solidarity in the 19th Century anti-colonial struggle was not, well, very solid. What I'm really saying is that the narrative of the Boer War hasn't changed in a generation and that is a bad thing because that narrative is wrong in a lot of respects.

\*

If you are sitting in a bar in South Africa you can usually illicit the accusation – actually, most of the time you don't even have to illicit it; it comes for free - from some ornery old Boer that Britain started the Second Anglo-Boer War (1899-1902) in order to get its grubby little hands on all that filthy lucre in Jo'burg, so I'll deal with this straight away. This fine myth has several elephant-in-the-skirting board-sized holes in it; first off, it is always cheaper to buy what you want rather than fight to conquer it; secondly, just when relations between Britain and the Transvaal were hitting a new low in 1896, gold was discovered in the Klondike in Canada, which was already British and then in 1898 on the verge of the war, more of the stuff was found on the equally British Yukon; thirdly, because the mines on the Joburg reef were deep, the gold was difficult to get out and so only the biggest companies with access to finance, capital and expertise could operate there and those big companies were based in Britain *ergo* Britain already owned the gold mines; fourthly, if Britain invaded to get the gold mines then the ZAR would probably blow them up or flood them and thus destroy the profits for any number of years afterwards. 'It is notorious,' said Sir Alfred Milner, the British High Commissioner and the man who Pakenham blamed for starting the war, but in this case stating the bleedin' obvious. 'That many capitalists regard political agitation with disfavour because of its effect on markets.'[404]

This sort of twaddle isn't limited to ornery old Boers either. Bill Nasson (of Stellenbosch University) declared in one of those witty little jokes that are deployed as a clincher for his argument that 'had the Witwatersrand become famous for asparagus there surely would have been no war crisis'.[405] An absolute rib-tickler, that one; just the sort of killer wit that we might expect from someone whose collection of essays *History Matters* includes a gushing tribute to old Stan Trapido, in which he manages to slip in the stiletto that 'it is quite

---

[404] Leo Amery, *The Times History of the War in South Africa 1899-1900* (London 1900) Vol.1 p.248.

[405] Bill Nasson, *The War for South Africa* (Cape Town, 2010) p.61

remarkable that Stan Trapido rose to become so eminent an historian without ever producing an authored book of his own' (*bitch!*);[406] who dismisses his fellow historians as writing 'numbingly dry products' aimed only at each other, (but doesn't name names, which is, of course, handy – Stellenbosch is a *very* small town);[407] feels the need to tell us that he was Head Boy at his old school and includes a poem in the collection that wasn't written by him, but *dedicated* to him;[408] and who wrote satirical pieces anonymously under the name *Maki Saki* – the name derived from those two brilliant satirists and commentators, the Edwardian *Saki* (HH Munro) and the present day *Taki*. Take it from me; he isn't in their class. His argument was that possession of the Transvaal gold was vital to Britain's position as the financial centre of the world through the maintenance of the Gold Standard. Er…Bill, mate. We came off the Gold Standard in the 1920s and London is still at the centre of the financial world. What matters in the financial world then and now is *credit* – the reasonable belief that a loan will be repaid - and *confidence* that all those Bills of Exchange and Lading would be honoured. Also; see point one, two, three and four above. So, taking these three things into consideration, we have to look for a better reason than filthy lucre for the fact that Britain and the Transvaal did go to war in 1899.

Now, of the many things that the British Empire was good at – ending slavery, combatting piracy, spreading science, technology, medicine and sanitation, Critall windows, corrugated iron, tongue and groove wood, enabling trade through global banking and communications, setting up examination boards so that Bill Nasson could get his A Levels and go to university in England (bit of gratitude might be in order here, Bill), ie., producing many of the things that make life liveable and generally enriching the world – perhaps the most striking thing is the way in which it created records. It seems that in between sinking gins, oppressing the natives and scheming up plots to grind the faces of the poor into the dust at the behest of evil capitalists, every official generated an annual acre of paperwork which found its way into the archives of the India Office, the Foreign Office, the Colonial Office, the Admiralty, the War Office and all sorts of sundry government departments. This was brought home to me when I worked in the rather dismal Chinese city of Yichang and stumbled, quite by chance, across the old British Consulate there. Tempted by the thought of what it must have been like to live out there in the 1870s, I looked up this forlorn outpost at the National Archives in Kew and was rewarded with the discovery of a beautiful, hand painted map scroll which showed a fantastic walled city full of pagodas and peach gardens and gaily painted boats plying their trade across the Yang-Tse river. I also found the Consul's records; one of his jobs was to report on trade opportunities, general conditions of the area etc etc and reading through them I came across a startling serendipity. Like me, he thought the place was a dump too and spent a long time appealing to his superiors for a better posting; what he would have made of it after the Communists wrecked it during the Cultural Revolution and then rebuilt it in the style of a crappy 1960s council high rise estate is probably predictable. As a footnote to this story, I once saw some grovelling little BBC pseudo-historian interviewing a Chinese museum curator and feeding him the line about how bad the 19th Century British antiquarians who

---

[406] Bill Nasson, *History Matters: Selected Writings 1970-2016* (Cape Town, 2016), p.10.
[407] Bill Nasson, *History Matters: Selected Writings 1970-2016* (Cape Town, 2016), p. 208.
[408] Bill Nasson, *History Matters: Selected Writings 1970-2016* (Cape Town, 2016), p.263.

collected up Chinese records were for taking them away and putting them in the British Museum. Never once did this BBC bonehead point out the obvious – that if the records hadn't been in the British Museum then they wouldn't exist because the Communists would have destroyed them during the Cultural Revolution. So, another great service rendered by the British Empire is ignored and/or denigrated.

The point of this diversion is this; if you want to know what happened in just about any particular place at any particular time then it's a pretty good bet that the archives have a wealth of information to guide you. I know, I'm labouring this point but really, you really don't have to rely on some ornery old Boer in a bar, Bill Nasson or - God Help Us – anything the BBC churns out – because, in this particular case, the Colonial Office did all the hard work for you and produced a document entitled *Africa (South) No.518 (Confidential) The Case Against the Transvaal 1896* and the file number at Kew is CO879/56, popularly known as the *Africa Confidential Print*. What this shows is that someone was building a case for war with the Transvaal for quite a long time – five years and possibly more - before the war actually began in 1899 and was doing a pretty thorough job of it, having trawled through the records going back to Majuba in 1881. In this respect, Kruger was quite right in suspecting that the British were considering war as an option; what the horrible old troll didn't realise was that to a large extent it was his own behaviour that was exasperating the British and encouraging them to take up firmer policies. It is also vital to point out that this document was drawn up when there was a real possibility that war would result as a result of German interference in the fallout from the Jameson Raid. It does *not* prove that there was a dastardly British plot afoot to bring about a war willy-nilly because this is not how the government worked back then. The Colonial Office bureaucracy certainly held views, as did the Colonial Office minister but it was the Cabinet and the Prime Minister that held the real power and unless they could be persuaded into war, then there would be no war. If you doubt this, go back to what happened when Hicks-Beach tried to persuade Disraeli and Salisbury to embark on a Zulu war in 1878.

The charge sheet begins with the rehearsal of some old grievances against the Boers going back to the Anglo-Boer War of 1881. These included firing on white flags, abusing truces and shooting prisoners, all of which were seen to be against the rules of 'civilised' warfare. These claims were pretty common knowledge, largely credible but were probably the result of Boer ignorance of what the rules of civilised warfare as seen from Europe actually were. I'm being kind here. The next charges related to the Boer incursions into Bechuanaland and Zululand as evidence of a level of land-grabbing duplicity that went well beyond even the wide pale of what was considered acceptable in southern Africa. Again, as we have seen, these charges were pretty much true but Kruger could hardly be blamed for taking advantage of Gladstone's criminal incompetence and Lord Derby's blithering idiocy.

From this point on, however, things change because when Kruger's capers were brought to an end in Bechuanaland and Zululand by the application of British force, that was supposed to be the end of Transvaal expansionism and Kruger was supposed to have agreed to desist. Unfortunately, only a little while later, the Transvaal Boers began to cast their eyes towards Swaziland and related areas in the North-East where the last opportunities to gain independent access to the sea lay. This guaranteed trouble with the British who would not allow him the opportunity to free himself from dependence on British arms or the opportunity to seek overseas alliances.

The method employed to subvert that state of Swaziland and the surrounding minor chiefdoms was to maintain Chief mBandini in the state of drunkenness to which he had become accustomed and then extract all sorts of concessions from him while he was under the influence. Trekboers were already encroaching on Swaziland in search of winter grazing, apprentices and cattle that didn't belong to them; Kruger ludicrously claimed that Swaziland had belonged to the Transvaal previous to 1881;[409] we tend to think of Swaziland as being a mountain kingdom today but at the time its borders extended down as far as the town of Piet Retief situated in rolling grassland. More sinister were the attempts of Kruger's agents to get the king to put his heir under the protection of the Transvaal and to hand over the Land Registry and the collection of revenue to them. By 1890, they had so infiltrated the administration of the country that they reckoned they could get Britain to let them incorporate the whole lot, lock, stock and smoking barrel directly into the ZAR. In this they were mistaken and in 1893, Britain issued the nearest thing to an ultimatum without firing it from a cannon to Kruger to pull his horns in or get them snapped off. Swaziland retained its independence under British protection but only by the skin of its teeth and at the price of handing over virtually its whole administration to the ZAR; on the official CO map of 1898, the country is shown as *actually being part* of the ZAR. That Kruger was allowed to get away with so much is due largely to the baleful appeaser Gladstone, who expressed his fervent anti-imperialism by handing over black people to whoever wanted them as long as they didn't come under the British flag; he was back in office, again disastrously, between 1892-94.

Still, Kruger carried on, this time in the Trans-Pongola territories where he hoped to bully three minor chiefs into handing over control to the Transvaal by allowing a couple of particularly nasty types by the name of Ferreira to act as though they owned the place. Each time the British or colonial government objected, Kruger fobbed them off until eventually in 1895 (once Gladstone had been shovelled off into retirement), a British protectorate was declared over all the land from Zululand to the Portuguese frontier, which effectively cut Kruger off from the sea; his last hope was Kosi Bay, up on the Mozambique border. 'There is no bound to the rage of Kruger....' said one informant, when the news was received that the Brits had got there first. In his *Memoirs* Kruger had the bare-faced cheek to claim that this was an outrageous act because Britain 'had no more claim upon them than upon the moon.'[410]

Next up was the question of 'commandeering'. Lacking much of a formal structure for warfare, the Commandos had previously relied on the Veldtcornets calling out able-bodied men for military service and pressing transport and supplies into service. In 1894, in the process of suppressing the rebellion of Malaboch, Kruger had the cheek to demand that although the Uitlanders had no say in the government, they did enjoy the privilege of paying taxes for the war, handing over transport, money and supplies to the Veldtcornets as and

---
[409] P. Kruger, *Memoirs* (Toronto, !902) p.201.
[410] P. Kruger *Memoirs*, (Toronto, 1902) p.224.

when required and actually physically serving in the Commandos. Needless to say, this brought about several protests, the principle one being that the Brits were getting visits from the Veldtcornets while the Afrikaaners were not. When the British government intervened, Kruger first attempted to sell the idea that only *coloured* British citizens or protected persons would be 'commandeered' but this was unacceptable and in 1895, Joe Chamberlain told him that no British subjects whatsoever would be treated in this way.

The next section dealt with intrigues with foreign powers. According to treaty the Transvaal was entitled to deal with foreign powers but the final say rested with Britain. However, the wording that had been born of Derby's bungling and Kruger's haggling ability meant that the Transvaal had long exploited any gap in the text wider than a fag paper to gain advantage. Fixed in Kruger's mind was the idea that the most likely way in which he could assert his entire independence from British control was by enlisting the help of a great power. This in practice meant Germany and he had long co-ordinated and co-operated with German interests and ambitions in South West Africa, in Zululand and in the Portuguese colony at Delagoa Bay. Under Bismarck, however, any hope that German troops would come flocking to the aid of the Boers was a pipe dream. Under Kaiser Willem II the same could not be said. Starved of oxygen at birth and brought up by martinets the Kaiser had come to worship militarism and was increasingly enamoured at the prospect of a glorious war of conquest against anybody, anywhere and at any time, a tendency which was only held in check by his more sensible ministers (and they were few indeed). In short, he was a dangerous megalomaniac who intended to disrupt the fine balances that had kept Europe from a general war for almost a century because he thought war was a glorious adventure. With the failure of the Jameson Raid, the Kaiser had sent Kruger a congratulatory telegram and had encouraged a lot of wild talk about landing German marines at Lourenco Marques and marching them up to garrison Pretoria. This turned a little local difficulty into a full blown international crisis in which Germany was forced to back down because the Royal Navy had the ability to sink those marines before they ever came within sight of Afric's fabled shore. Unfortunately, Kruger read – actually, he being functionally illiterate, he had to have things of import read *to* him[411] - the situation wrongly and believed that this was the future; as soon as Britain got into difficulties with another great power, he thought, his opportunity would come. In reality, Britain would never give up her dominance of South Africa as long as the Cape route to India and points east retained its vital significance.

What was also included under this head was the increasing efforts of Kruger's Transvaal to draw the Orange Free State into an offensive and defensive alliance which could only be directed against Britain. Previously, the Free Staters had been extremely sceptical about any of Kruger's schemes and had much preferred to keep on friendly terms with both the British and their Afrikaaner cousins down in the Cape. The Jameson Raid had, for the time being, changed all that and the Colonial Office officials working on this paper were very worried by the prospect of the OFS being absorbed by the Transvaal in the not too distant future, a possibility that they could not view with equanimity.

---

[411] Sarah Gertrude Millin, *General Smuts, Vol.I* (London, 1936) p.68.

Transvaal native policy came next and here the Colonial Office officials evinced a hard-headed disgust at Kruger's behaviour. Things had always been bad in the Transvaal, they argued, referencing David Livingstone and both Khama's and Sekhukune's complaints in the 1870s. These officials were men not in the pocket of missionaries – far from it - but who felt, as any decent liberal minded person would, that the ill-treatment of non-white residents in the Transvaal had just gone too far. At the time of the Retrocession in 1881, the protection of natives had been reserved to the British Government but this was something else that the bigot Gladstone and the hapless Derby had subsequently handed back to the mendacious Kruger. The result was that Native Commissioners were appointed by the Transvaal who, in theory, were supposed to protect and represent African interests, but in practice began to prey on Africans with a vengeance. This was done in any number of ways; bogus fees and fines were levied at inflated rates; taxes were extracted from chiefs at will; when the chiefs lacked the cash to pay such fines the Native Commissioners undervalued the livestock offered in payment, which allowed them a five hundred per cent profit at sale. Forced labour was also extracted; when the railways came the notorious Abel Erasmus of Lydenburg made the chiefs in his area provide workers for which he charged the railway company £1 per person and then took half their wages. When those chiefs who objected went to law and won their cases – and this is proof positive that there were plenty of Afrikaaners who were disgusted at the behaviour of the Native Commissioners - Kruger intimidated the courts, paid the fines of those Boers convicted and then reserved all cases involving disputes between employers and employees to the Native Commissioners, thereby removing the protection of an independent judiciary. Those chiefs who still complained were apt to find themselves on the receiving end of a Jim Crow lynch mob. Boer rule of black Africans was, according to the Rector of the Lourenco Marques Cathedral, 'candid but brutal and a proof of their invincible ignorance of the elements of good government'.[412]

In 1894, Maloboch, declared the Colonial Office officials, had been goaded beyond endurance by the Native Commissioners and had rebelled. The Commandos went out, duly defeated him, apprenticed the women and children and threw the men in Pretoria jail. There, without anything approaching adequate food or shelter from the bitter Highveld winters, they were left to die in droves. At the time, the British agent in Pretoria did his best to intervene on Maloboch's behalf but the Jameson Raid cut the ground from under him and it was the imprisoned members of the Reform Committee who then bore witness to the terrible deprivations inflicted upon the Africans. Many stories of corruption and atrocity committed during the Maloboch rebellion had leaked out and the British agent had demanded a tribunal or a trial so that the evidence could be heard. Kruger refused and stalled in the clear hope that any and all the complainants would be dead before their cases could be heard. By 1896, according to the Colonial Office, at least half of those incarcerated had indeed died.

Next on the list – and it may or may not be significant that this item comes below complaints about the treatment of Africans – was *Attacks on British Commercial Interests*. This began with the attempts of the Netherlands Railway Company to put the Cape and Natal railways out of business by refusing carriage for their goods except at ruinous rates (roughly double

---

[412] Rev J.H.Bovril, *Natives under the Transvaal Flag* (London 1900) p.13

what they charged for freight coming in from Lourenco Marques). When the Cape refused to pay the extortionate charges and instead unloaded their goods at the Vaal River and sent them on by ox waggon, (it was still cheaper than risking 'fever and Portuguese administration')[413] Kruger closed the crossings – this was known as the Drifts Crisis – until London made it known that there would be trouble unless the Cape railways were allowed to go about their lawful business unhindered. As usual, when faced with a policy of firmness, Kruger took one step back in the hope of taking two steps forward at a later date. Next came the iniquities of the Dynamite Monopoly, by which the cost of this vital mining explosive was doubled for corrupt reasons already mentioned by Percy Fitzpatrick.

The corruption of the Transvaal government was up now and a series of (to the modern, cynical eye – mine – hilarious) cases of petty malfeasance were related, which included Kruger, the original rotgut in the body politic himself, ripping off the government for travelling expenses that the British government had actually paid; building plots in Johannesburg meant for diggers being illegally acquired by members of the Volksraad, a practice then justified by Kruger on the grounds that as officials had no pensions, some corruption was justified; among the most egregious thieves was F.Eloff, Kruger's son-in-law. The Selati Railway scheme was also mentioned, pretty much in exactly the same terms as Percy Fitzpatrick described it and the case of Judge De Korte, who was in the habit of 'borrowing' money from litigants, was aired. The government commission appointed to inquire into his case admitted that his actions were 'in some ways…incompatible with the dignity of the bench' but let him off anyway.

The judgement of the Colonial Office revealed in this document was that the Transvaal was corrupt, chaotic, brutal and unlikely ever to stick to any agreement with Britain that it put its name to, a judgement from which it is hard to demure especially as many of the charges were made by the Transvaal Afrikaaner press itself and backed up by the British Agent in Pretoria Sir Jacobus de Wet – a Cape Dutch 'Africander' exasperated by Kruger's hatred of Britain, his constant aggression against Africans and the sheer corruption of his government.[414]

Two years later, in May 1898, the Colonial Office came back with *The Case Against The South African Republic Part II* in which the original charges were reviewed with the despairing conclusion that nothing effectual had been done by Kruger and his cronies to check corrupt abuses, address the grievances of the *Uitlanders* or desist from a foreign policy aimed at gaining a port and a European ally. Instead, things had gone from bad to worse; Africans had long complained that the police regularly treated the Pass Laws as an opportunity to extort bribes in the same way that the present day SAPS use alleged traffic offenses to rip off motorists (I once got shucked down in the Joburg airport parkade, believe it or not); petty infractions could result in fines of a month's wages or more plus flogging and the *tronk*. Mixed-race citizens from the Cape – then known as 'Cape Boys' - were being particularly harassed despite being entitled to the same rights and privileges of white British; they were made subject to the Pass Laws and made to wear a brass badge advertising the fact

---

[413] Leo Amery, *The Times History of the War in South Africa 1899-1900* (London 1900) Vol.1 p. 154.

[414] De Wet to Lord Rippon, October 1894. CO879/56 Africa (South)No.532.Secret papers Relating to the South African Republic

(an attempt to impose Pass Laws on the white British had failed due to Imperial protest).[415] A popular and successful mixed-race tailor by the name of P.J. Daniels was incarcerated for no reason that anyone could see while mixed-race coachmen were arrested for driving their employers' carriages without a pass. When it was revealed in the Daniels case that the police were carrying out an entirely illegal campaign against the Cape Boys, and after representations from High Commissioner Milner, the Pass Laws were amended to exclude those who, on production of a certificate (£3pa, thank you), could prove they had 'attained a higher degree of civilisation'; a small but welcome dent in the view of the more Neanderthal Afrikaaners that 'a Kaffir was a Kaffir whether educated or not'.[416] No sooner had this form of harassment ended than the police started again, this time picking on British Indians for good measure, banning them from hiring cabs, evicting them from their homes and relocating them to Locations, banning them from walking on pavements and from having front doors that opened onto the street (why?). Promises were extracted from the government that these regulations would be reviewed, but the writer of this document, laying on the sarcasm, held out little hope of a decent result.

> Dr Leyds promised to consider the matter, which will no doubt enjoy the very mature consideration which all grievances and complaints of British subjects, however pressing, are privileged to receive.[417]

There were further complaints about government attempts to restrict English language education. This was more complex because while the government had a right to expect immigrants to learn the language of the host country if they were ever to be assimilated, many of the Uitlanders saw no benefit in their children learning Dutch when they did not intend to settle in the Transvaal once their fortunes were made while others insisted that as English was the language of business, it was vital for children to learn at least equal fluency. In practical terms too, English teachers were being passed over in favour of those recently arrived from Holland.

Press Laws were becoming ever more tyrannical too with the censorship of telegrams becoming so extreme that many editors were reduced to having to cross into British territory to send them, while the independence of the Judiciary, never very strong at the best of times, was being further undermined by Kruger's attempts to gain control of them; people were appointed to senior legal positions despite having no legal qualifications in a move that makes us draw the inevitable comparisons between him and virtually every other African despot to be released from the onerous impositions of British rule. In yet another echo of today's South Africa, it was also noted that the potholes in the roads were not being repaired, the job having been tendered out corruptly. The behaviour of the Native Commissioners, of whom a certain Piet Cronjie was notorious, was getting worse and worse despite the impoverishment of many Africans brought on by an outbreak of rinderpest.

Under the heading of *General evidence of unfriendliness*, a whole number of transgressions were noted, including Kruger's grandson insulting the Queen to a British official while

---
[415] Rev J.H.Bovril, *Natives under the Transvaal Flag* (London 1900) p.8
[416] CO879/52 *The Case Against the Transvaal Part II.*
[417] CO879/52 *The Case Against the Transvaal Part II.*

wearing his uniform; when a complaint was made, an understanding was given that Lieutenant Eloff was drunk at the time and would be punished – the punishment turned out to be a major promotion. Other complaints included high taxes on food which, the country Boers being by and large self-sufficient, fell upon the shoulders of the mainly British *Uitlanders* and hit them twice because the Boers sold their surplus at famine prices.

The final heading was concerned with Kruger's large purchases of armaments which, the Colonial Office felt, could only be aimed at Britain and which led the writer to draw several conclusions.

> The Boer Government of today is in fact the rule of a corrupt oligarchy based on the military force of the most ignorant part of the population....and there is no prospect of improvement in either the external relations or the internal condition of the Transvaal until the present system, which is based on force, is crushed by greater force, either from without or within.[418]

Eighteen months before the war broke out, the lines had perceptibly hardened.

\*

Your mother told you that you should always tell the truth. So did your teachers/vicars/imams/rabbis and so does the Law. The great philosopher Immanuel Kant conjured up a whole theory to back up your mum and called it the *Categorical Imperative* whereby he argued, basically, that as we are moral creatures so we should always act morally by telling the truth....and yet....I wonder if he was ever asked the question: *does my bum look big in this?* The temptation in this case is to tell the questioner what they want to hear rather than what you think is the truth and as a dilemma, it takes some beating. I mention this because when I went for my Masters' Degree *viva* I was presented with a straightforward, very simple question which, like an awful lot of very simple and straightforward questions was absolutely loaded with consequences. You know the type of question; you have been asked it at job interviews, in the witness box (perhaps even the dock), on pleasant evenings pregnant with possibilities and upon the answer depends your livelihood, your freedom (possibly) and your prospects of immediate or future happiness. It is always presented as a binary question and although a proper answer would require a long exposition loaded with nuance, caveat and escape clauses, you are required, always, to choose between two stark alternatives and at that point you ask yourself: *should I tell them what I think they want to hear or do I tell them what I really think?* And it is always a bugger to decide between the two.

I wrote my Masters' Degree on the causes of the Anglo-Zulu War of 1879 and, as you might have gleaned, I went through a fair bit of grief because I was challenging Marxist orthodoxy and, being at a pretty Leftie university, pretty much drowning in Marxists. I had also invested a lot of time, money, effort and *amour proper* into achieving that degree and the thought of failure gave me more than a few sleepless nights so when the examiner asked me *that* simple and straightforward question, it is fair to say that I gulped a bit. The chap in

---

[418] CO879/52 *The Case Against the Transvaal Part II.*

question was Professor Iain Smith, certainly among the world's leading experts on the Boer War, and so no slouch, and the killer question came out like a coiling serpent ready to squeeze the dreams out of me.

'Was the Zulu war about *power* or *money*?' he asked.

The answer was *power*, of course. A large chunk of the thesis had been devoted to taking apart the Marxist 'Land and Labour' school and junking the statistical basis of their claims so obviously I was going to answer truthfully...and then the thought suddenly occurred to me that I was sitting in front of a chap who's work I was unfamiliar with, who might possibly be – and on past experience of university lecturers probably *was* – a wild-eyed Marxist fanatic and therefore not likely to appreciate the actual truth. Should I take the easy and obvious route, therefore, display my Che Guevara tattoo and don my Lenin cap and say '*Money* - it's like, er, capitalist exploitation, man; grinding the faces of the poor and dispossessed like, er, man, etc etc.'?

It did go through my mind. The number of jobs I've missed out through being truthful has come very close to convincing me that honesty is never the best policy (and certainly never where bums and new outfits are concerned).

'It's *power*,' I said. 'It was the vital necessity to control the route to India.'

Fortunately, Iain Smith was not a raging Marxist and his 1996 book *The Origins of the South African War 1899-1902* did an excellent job in demolishing Leftist arguments about gold grabbing capitalists and asserting that the contest in Southern Africa was about *power* not money, so I was home safe (and Kant was thereby vindicated) and drinks all round. Phew.

And Iain Smith was right too. The conflict *was* about power, about who would be dominant in Southern Africa and about what the future of Southern Africa would look like. Would the vision of 'Africa for the Afrikaaners' shape the future or would the *status quo* of a British bastion on the route to India be maintained? It was the stark question that John X. Merriman, Cape parliamentarian and future PM of the Cape had asked back in 1885: *was England or the Transvaal to be the paramount force in South Africa?*[419]

One of the accusations regularly levelled at Historians who don't subscribe to the view that the Boer Republics were victims of the British Imperial bully is that they only use 'Jingo' sources. This line of approach is one that is, as we have seen, shared by the Marxists; if you don't like the conclusions drawn from the available evidence, then discredit the sources. It's the kind of *ad hominin* attack that is often the resort of axe-grinders and grievance-mongers because, of course, *every* source comes with baggage and it is the job of a Historian to assess both the *weight* and the *quality* of the available evidence as fairly as possible. This process is also affected by the access to available evidence and it's fair to say that before the IT revolution of the 1990s that access was often difficult to, well, access. This meant that the main sources for Historians were often newspapers, memoirs, edited collections of private papers, Victorian and Edwardian tombstone biographies all of which were problematical

---

[419] Quoted in Leo Amery, *The Times History of the War in South Africa 1899-1900* (London 1900) Vol.1 p.86

where objectivity and completeness were concerned. As far as government records were involved, the standard source were the Parliamentary 'Blue Books'. These were collections of papers, telegrams, correspondence etc which were ordered by Parliament for the information of Parliament in which ministers were duty bound to provide a fair selection of the available material on any particular subject. Detailed and valuable, they were, but they did not tell the whole story because some things needed to be kept secret (*pace* conspiracy theorists) and ministers were not above releasing papers that supported their view of things and keeping back some of the more embarrassing bits. Departmental files were not released *in toto* even though much of what appeared in the Blue Books came from them and Cabinet Papers were regarded as *Top Secret*. Historians working before (roughly) 1990, therefore, laboured under more than a few handicaps.

The IT revolution changed a lot of this and there is nowhere better to see this than at the UK National Archives in Kew. Whereas under the old system, when the archives were based at Holborn, it might take hours, days or even weeks to find a document or file and then even more frustrating hours fiddling with microfilm or microfiche before something useful and interesting might be found, today you can have order any document going back to the 10th Century and have it on your desk in fifteen minutes. It is *amazing*. What's more, when I first started using this fantastic resource I had first to struggle through the catalogue, fill in an order form and then read like a wild-eyed maniac and scribble notes at speed (pencils only allowed in the Reading Room on pain of death) because I only had so many hours in a day. Nowadays, I search the catalogue on line, order online, stroll in and *photograph* the documents, transfer them to my laptop and take them home to consult at my leisure. One day all the documents will be online but that will take a while as they have nine miles of shelves down there and (so one curator told me) no idea what's in half of the boxes; they found a mummified rat in one medieval scroll and declared that, as it had eaten so many of the public records, it had thereby achieved the status of actually *being* a public record and accorded it its own file number. Those dudes need to get out more. In short, the fact that a source is generated from within British government files does not necessarily make it a 'Jingo' source and therefore unreliable; what it does do is provide an insight into the views and discussions going on within departments and within the government, into what has been called the 'official mind'.

What this means is that much of what was written before (again roughly) 1990 and anything that deals with policy that was written after that date which does not access these archives needs to be handled with caution. This does not mean that it has no value but it does mean that the big questions of war and peace can only be partially answered without looking at the now declassified files. This is one reason why I am suspicious of Bill Nasson's restatement of Pakenham's thesis that the Boer war was all about the gold; going off his bibliography, he doesn't seem to have consulted any of the relevant archives. Pakenham, of course, didn't have that access.

That said, contemporary commentators were very often close to the action and can tell us quite a lot about how things were viewed from that particular end of time's drainpipe. Leo Amery, the staggeringly clever British journalist, and eventual First Lord of the Admiralty and Colonial Secretary, wrote the *Times History of the War in South Africa*, finishing the first volume before the war had properly got going, and is a good source on several counts; firstly, he had first-hand experience of South Africa in the run-up to and opening stages of the war; secondly, because he was completely open about his conviction that Britain was justified in going to war; and thirdly, because he was utterly scathing about aspects of British military planning, preparation and Generalship. Indeed, Amery, is one of the founding fathers of the 'bonehead generals and dumb donkey Tommies' view of the war, a myth that he deliberately constructed in order to shock Britain into building an army commensurate with its size. Why it's necessary to exercise caution with him is that he was also one of the sources for the 'Boer Superman' myth (a myth created after the war by Afrikaaner Nationalist politicians and a slew of unreliable memoirs), because he was also a complete Social Darwinist who believed that war was a type of natural selection necessary to strengthen the 'race' and that a good war against a people as tough as the Afrikaaner 'race' could only do the British 'race' a power of good. Not only that, but because the Afrikaaners had also been purified by war, they were a much more valuable addition to the British Empire than a collection of 'pansies, dandies, obvious Onanists, Softy-Cecils, defectives physical, moral and mental, cads, boundahs, and pacifists' (this isn't a direct quote but read any Edwardian popular fiction and you'll get the point). One of the later volumes was penned by Erskine Childers, author of *The Riddle of the Sands*, who was also consumed by the prospect of a millenarian war with Germany; and if you read anything by the equally *Boys Own* rip-roaring yarn-spinning John Buchan, you'll see straight away that the 'Teuton' race was seen by large sections of the British public as the looming threat. Yet another member of this Rogue's Gallery was Charles à Court Repington, a brilliant soldier ruined by an inability to keep his trousers on who, along with the rest of Amery's gang, wanted to exaggerate the poor performance of the Army in order to make the case for reform and expansion. If you are looking for Jingo sources well, here they are and they make uncomfortable reading for any self-respecting, G&T-swilling, Boer-bashing Jingo.

Finding reliable contemporary Boer sources and commentators is more problematical, especially if your command of Afrikaans goes no further than the necessary ability to order beer in a bar and swear. Certainly for the period of the 1880s, the Transvaal didn't keep many records and the ones that I have seen were a complete dog's breakfast; literacy levels were generally not very good and the one man who might have really told us what was going on – Kruger himself - produced a memoir in 1902 that was remarkable mainly for the whining tone of the habitual criminal caught at three in the morning coming out of a house that isn't his own with a bag full of items that he can't provide receipts for, followed up by pot-and-kettle insults, wild accusations, conspiracy theory paranoia, false martyrdom, special pleading, selective presentation and sheer fabrication. *A Century of Wrong* which came from the pen of Transvaal State Secretary Reitz, a man just educated enough to prove himself a fool, aided by Smuts, isn't much better; he began this 1899 polemic with the accusation that Britain aimed to *exterminate* the Afrikaaner people and the equally bogus claim that the Dutch had originally arrived at the Cape in search of freedom of conscience;[420] what van Riebeeck would have made of that old pony, we can probably guess. The claim that Dingane murdered Piet Retief on the say so of 'some Englishmen'[421] and the accusation that Sir Bartle

---

[420] Reitz, *A Century of Wrong* (London, 1902) p.4.

Frere was intending to use the Zulus to invade the Transvaal[422] is the sort of twaddle that in these days would only be found in the sub-scrotal regions of the internet and though he tried to give this anti-historical account of Anglo-Boer relations a veneer of respectability by referencing Theal and Moodie, (but then ruined it by adding in another shriek from Olive Schreiner) it remains a perfect example of utter balderdash. It isn't possible to deny that the Boers had a case in 1899 but it is no wonder they failed to make it if Kruger and Reitz were the best they could hire to make it. The pair of them sound like the bully who having been threatened with a thrashing in the schoolyard rushes inside to complain to Miss. We might excuse Kruger for his literary failings on the grounds that he had not had much in the way of formal education (and it looks like he pinched plenty of material out of *A Century of Wrong*) but Reitz was a lawyer who had studied at Edinburgh and should have known better. Smuts *did* know better and came to hate that he was associated with it. How he kept a straight face when berating Britain for 'the illegal appropriation of other people's property,'[423] is beyond me – but then, as noted, Reitz *was* a lawyer. I do love his coining of the phrase 'atrocity-mongering'[424] when referring to the Rand newspapers though; the editors were the ones he tried to jail. The discontent of the Uitlanders he put down to drink and high altitude (the first charge might be partly true) and when he gets on to 'Capitalistic Jingoism', it's hard not to be transported back (or forward) to 1970s polytechnic student radicalism especially when he blames the corruption of the Transvaal administration on the Randlords; and then claims there was no Afrikaaner corruption because the Volksraad were blameless, moral men of impeccable credentials. Reitz's contention that Britain's grievances against the Transvaal were *all* 'of an imaginary character'[425] is the sort of comedy that deprives the rest of his points of any credibility at all.

The preface for *A Century of Wrong* was written by W.T. Stead who, as a long experienced newspaper editor also should have known better than to get involved with this remarkable production especially when Reitz had been instrumental in getting newspaper editors arrested, aggressively censoring the press and effectively killing off freedom of speech and association for the Uitlanders under the guise of maintaining order. Stead had a track record of good investigative work and could be found on both sides of the imperialism debate; he had employed Alfred Milner as an assistant and was a supporter of Rhodes until he fell out with him; he hated Joe Chamberlain and ruined his fellow imperialist Sir Charles Dilke with a bogus sex scandal; he was a supporter of Irish Home Rule but ruined C.S.Parnell with a genuine sex scandal but even this chequered past couldn't make this document a reliable account. What was remarkable about it though was that after ninety-eight pages of specious twaddle about how for a century the poor, blameless Boers had been harried from pillar to post when all they wanted was to live a pastoral life free from all that horrible capitalist development, Reitz (you really wouldn't want to hire him as your lawyer) gave the game away.

---

[421] Reitz, *A Century of Wrong* (London, 1902) p.13.
[422] Reitz, *A Century of Wrong* (London, 1902) p.30
[423] Reitz, *A Century of Wrong* (London, 1902) p.42.
[424] Reitz, *A Century of Wrong* (London, 1902) p. 77.
[425] Reitz, *A Century of Wrong* (London, 1902) p. 65.

> As in 1880, we now submit our cause with perfect confidence to the whole world. Whether the result be Victory or Death, Liberty will assuredly rise in South Africa like the sun from out the mists of the morning, just as Freedom dawned over the United States of America a little more than a century ago. Then from the Zambesi to Simon's Bay it will be "Africa for the Africander."[426]

And this remarkable production, we should note, was written while peace negotiations were still under way! What made this statement even more remarkable was that it echoed almost the exact words of a similar statement made by S.J. du Toit, a Transvaal statesman and founder of the *Bond*, after the signing of the London Convention of 1884 when Gladstone and Derby had surrendered to Kruger for the second time.

> The South African flag shall yet wave from Table Bay to the Zambesi, be that end accomplished by blood or by ink.[427]

Nor was it just ballooning away on the *stoep* after a few too many *mampoers* or simply the delusions of 'Jingo' sources: as W.T.Stead himself wrote in 1897 'the Boer ideal was 'Anti-British Federation'....to destroy British supremacy in South Africa.'[428] In 1952, Smuts' own son rather gave the game away too by confirming that his old dad had a 'careful plan drawn up' which was:

> for the Boers to strike down swiftly at Durban and the other ports upon the outbreak of hostilities, in order to prevent the British landing reinforcements. That phase completed, the mopping up of troops in the country would begin.[429]

Here then, we can start to look into the reason for the war. Sweeping away all the special pleading, Marxist clap-trap and tendentious re-writing of history we can see that the war came about as a result of two competing and fundamentally irreconcilable visions of the future of southern Africa. The Transvaal hoped for a union with the Orange Free State, followed by the shaking free of the Cape Colony from British control – it was to be the 'Third Republic'- by a combination of parliamentary action, the subversion of the Cape Dutch, and the confinement of British control to the naval stations at the Cape. This in turn would line up Bechuanaland, Basutoland, Rhodesia and Swaziland for absorption leaving only the more problematical Natal to be dealt with. This was a colony that unlike the Cape - where only about a third of the European inhabitants were of British origin or descent – had a European population of determinedly British intent and loyalty although there was still a significant Afrikaaner minority to be found there. In order to achieve the union and/or conquest of these territories, Kruger wanted a port through which he could draw his arms and ammunition freely but more importantly he desired the removal of any last vestige of the British suzerainty which prevented him from gaining the thing he desired most of all on the diplomatic front, a European ally. From that point on, he need only wait for the British to get into difficulties with France or Germany in Europe or perhaps a Russian march on India

---

[426] Reitz, *A Century of Wrong* (London, 1902) p.98.
[427] Leo Amery, *The Times History of the War in South Africa 1899-1900* (London 1900) Vol.1 p.78.
[428] Quoted in C. Ash, *Kruger's War* (Pinetown 2017) p.86.
[429] *Jan Christian Smuts by his son*, p.90

which would necessarily denude the British South African colonies of troops, attention or parliamentary political will to resist and he could send in his commandos to take control. The timescale was not predictable, of course, but given the turn of the century tensions in Europe it was a fair bet that an opportunity would arise sooner or later. Naturally, he hoped to be alive and leading the way in person but there were plenty of 'Young Africanders' coming up who adhered to this vision; if anything, they were rather hot headed about it all and apt to overestimate their strength and be impatient and he felt it important to damp down their ardour from time to time. The big fly in the ointment was, of course, the presence of the Uitlanders who Kruger regarded as nothing more than a fifth column.

For the British, nothing had changed since 1806 and nor would it change until India regained the independence that the men who ran the Raj believed they held in trusteeship. Control of the routes to India was a vital interest which, if lost, would dismember the empire and the clear-sighted and determined imperialists would no more accept the loss of South Africa than they would the Isle of Wight. Every military or naval study ever carried out or contemplated had made it perfectly clear that neither Cape Town nor Durban could be another Gibraltar and the thought of an Afrikaaner Union of South Africa under German or French protection was something that would not be tolerated. Britain wanted the *status quo*. If Kruger stayed within his borders, accepted the very mild conditions of suzerainty and minded his own business, there would be no need for conflict. Even the Uitlander issue need not be unsurmountable, just as long as Kruger stopped interfering in the affairs of the Cape Colony and gave up his constant quest for a port. There was nothing in the Transvaal that Britain wanted that couldn't be bought on the open market and certainly nothing worth the cost, effort and inconvenience of a war.

*

1896 was the year that things began to move towards a crisis. The Jameson Raid had convinced many in both the Republics and those among the Cape Dutch that Britain did have aggressive designs while the effect in Britain of the Kaiser's telegram sharpened up minds in Whitehall and brought a new determination to pay more attention to what was going on at the Cape and to ensure that vital interests were protected. Rhodes fell; Sir Alfred Milner went out as High Commissioner, Reitz gave up his Presidency of the Orange Free State to the virulently anti-British Marthinus Steyn and went up to Pretoria to serve Kruger; the issues on which the two main protagonists chose to engage were those of the Uitlander franchise and Suzerainty.

For Milner and Chamberlain, the franchise was the way in which the more unpalatable policies in the Transvaal could be changed by peaceful, constitutional means. A simple franchise which gave the Uitlanders reasonable representation and a reasonable number of seats in the Volksraad would do. No one was talking about mass democracy here and there was certainly no intention to extend the vote to the black population *en masse*; universal male suffrage was still a long way away from British parliamentary democracy largely because the Victorians believed in representing interests rather than numbers; Manchester had MPs not because it had a large population, but because it represented the interests of the cotton industry; Joe Chamberlain had his seat in parliament because he represented the business interests of Birmingham (he came from a screw manufacturing family); the 'people' were therefore represented indirectly, so the theory went. The ideal would have been a franchise similar to that enjoyed in the Cape Colony – colour blind and based on a property qualification which excluded the riff-raff and rabble and ensured that only those who worked or ran businesses had the vote. Recognising that this was probably an impossibility, given Boer determination to prevent non-whites attaining more than subordinate status, Milner and Chamberlain would probably have accepted anything reasonable as a means of getting a foot in the door. It was a reasonable proposition to suppose that if the Uitlanders got the vote then Kruger would be voted out, Piet Joubert voted in and the deadlock would be broken. What would happen from there was anyone's guess but it would at least open the door to change and better relations.

Kruger saw the franchise issue in very different terms. For him it was not so much as a foot in the door but the thin edge of the wedge and he believed that if the Uitlanders got the vote then not only would they vote him out but they would then go on to vote for Union with the Cape and thus extinguish the independence of the Republics. In this he was guilty of assuming that the Uitlanders were all in the pocket of Milner and Chamberlain and this was very far from the truth. Although the majority of Uitlanders were British by descent, there were large numbers of Irish, Americans, Russian and Polish Jews, Germans and other Europeans who could not be automatically expected to vote on Chamberlain's whim. There was a strong possibility that large numbers of them would do what electorates often do, that is vote with their pockets, or vote on local, Joburg issues, such as reforming the corrupt, partisan, clodhopping police and cracking down on the illegal liquor trade; these were big issues at the time. The mine owners would probably have welcomed British rule as it would cut down on the bribes that they had to pay to the *Volksraad* to get anything done but it was probably also the case that if they could achieve a third of the seats there then they would be happy; their interests would be represented and they could set about getting rid of the dynamite monopoly and sorting out the Netherlands Railway Company. The result of this was that when negotiations took place between Milner and Kruger at the Bloemfontein conference in early 1899 and throughout the southern winter, Kruger made an offer of the franchise to those who lived in the Transvaal for seven years and only four seats in the *Volksraad* and then made it conditional on Britain giving up her Suzerainty.

Milner was in favour of a five-year residence qualification and this Pakenham misrepresented as a miniscule difference which an intransigent, arrogant proconsul of Empire chose to go to war on. The key issue was trust; if Milner had been negotiating with anyone but Kruger it is entirely possible that both Chamberlain and Milner would have accepted the deal but Kruger's record as a negotiator was one of wriggle, bad faith and the dogged pedantry of the barrack room lawyer. His aim was always to get rid of the Suzerainty and hedge about any franchise reform with provisos that could be mangled and manipulated later to allow him effectively to refuse the vote. When, in July 1899, he offered four seats in the *Volksraad* to Joburg, he then instantly added fifteen to the backwoods constituencies that he controlled. When the details of the seven-year deal were looked at, the small print showed that Kruger could refuse the franchise to anyone he didn't like. This meant that the only way in which Chamberlain and Milner could reasonably expect Kruger to adhere to the spirit as well as the letter of the law was to retain the Suzerainty for if the Transvaal became fully legally recognised as a sovereign state then Kruger would be freed from any restraints at all. 'Sovereignty' means that a country recognises no authority higher than itself and is free to pursue its interests as it chooses, where it chooses and when it chooses, accepting restrictions of treaty or international law only so long as it chooses to and insofar as stronger powers can enforce those restrictions. 'International Law' is a term that provides work for all sorts of lawyers and diplomats but it is in reality a fig-leaf to cover the law of the jungle; no lawyer's quibble ever stopped an invading army. If the suzerainty was given up, then Kruger would be free to seek his German alliance – and he would very probably get it. That, in itself, would mean Britain going to war with the Transvaal to enforce its control of the routes to India.

That Kruger, the president of a small, land locked, rather inconsequential state occupying marginal land felt able to resist the demands of a Great Power was largely because he thought he could count on the support of the Cape Dutch. This was a reasonable supposition. Since the annexation and retrocession of the Transvaal, there had been a resurgence of Afrikaaner nationalism through southern Africa and this had made itself felt largely through the influence of the *Bond*. Set up by S.J. du Toit, Jan Hofmeyr, F.W. Reitz and others, it was part political party, part secret society and part social organisation; it was initially violently Anglophobic and had as its avowed aim the union of South Africa under its own flag. It also had a tendency to regard any Afrikaaner who didn't agree with its aims as being a virtual traitor, a tendency noted and repudiated by more than a few influential Afrikaaners including President Brand of the Orange Free State who, in 1883, declared it to be 'a device of the devil'.[430] Brand's successor was Reitz, who in turn was replaced in 1896 by fellow Bondsman, Steyn. Most of the 'Young Africanders', of whom the most prominent was the States-Attorney, Oxford educated lawyer Jan Smuts were also enthusiastic members of the *Bond*. Tied up intimately with the *Bond* was the Dutch Reformed Church which promulgated its aims through the pulpit throughout the Free State, Natal and the Cape; among a community as religious and as poorly educated as Afrikaanerdom, (Smuts got his rapid promotion because it was reckoned there was only one other member of the Transvaal *Volksraad* with the literacy level to do the job), this had a powerful effect which in turn was reinforced by much of the Afrikaans language press. In the Cape parliament, Jan Hofmeyr quickly attained to the position of kingmaker mainly by toning down the wilder spirits of the Bond and pushing the idea of a South African union which would include the English as well as the Dutch; Rhodes was willing to work with him on this basis too. In the run up to the war, the Prime Minister was William Schreiner (Olive's brother: 'So tell me, Miss Schreiner, how did you get your ground-breaking anti-British literary work published?') of the South African Party, which was linked to and enjoyed the support of the *Bond*. It was also notable that the 1898 translation of Reitz from the Free State to the position of Transvaal State Secretary appeared to mark a change of policy which aimed to replace the 'Hollanders' in the administration with pure-blood Afrikaaners, the sons of Cape parliament and Free State *Volksraad* members and not least, with the distribution of favours to Progressive Party members, to tie in all the leading Afrikaaner families of southern Africa to a dependent relationship with Kruger.[431]

---

[430] Quoted in C. Ash, *Kruger's War* p.100.

If this wasn't enough to bolster Kruger's confidence, he had also spent a considerable amount of money, time and effort in backing the Transvaal Secret Service's efforts to prepare the way for a rebellion in the Cape should war break out. As early as 1895, arms and ammunition were being smuggled into Rhodesia and when the Matabele revolted against British rule in 1896, they did so armed with rifles brought in from the armoury at Middelburg. Guns were run into border areas and as far south as Paarl in the Cape while right up until the outbreak of war attempts were made to exploit the devastation of a rinderpest outbreak to turn Tswana and Basuto against the British by claiming that the measures necessary to control the disease (extermination, principally) were really a plot to deprive them of their cattle wealth.

Finally, he was convinced by his reading of the international situation that when push came to shove, the other Great Powers would take the opportunity to clip the lion's mane, if he provided one. This, on the face of it, was a reasonable proposition given the support obtained from Germany since the Jameson Raid, the ratcheting up of colonial tensions between Britain and France in Egypt and West Africa, and the near constant disputes between Britain and Russia over Central Asia and the Indian frontier. In fact, like most of Kruger's calculations they were the fatally flawed products of an intellect limited by lack of formal educational and intellectual training and a deep ignorance about anything beyond the little world of southern Africa.

Kruger's hatred of Britain and everything British blinded him to some important realities. The first was that he was intellectually outmatched by Chamberlain and Milner. Like Kruger, Chamberlain had come from relatively humble beginnings but had made his name in business as an astute analyser of problems with a mind incisive enough to come to counter-intuitive conclusions; in many ways his methods anticipated the author of *Scientific Management*, F.W. Taylor's methodology; studying the type of labour and the age and sex of the workers involved, he proved to his own commercial satisfaction that *reducing* the workers' hours resulted in higher productivity and thus higher profits and acted accordingly, much to the joy of all involved and, incidentally, undermining the dismal stereotype of capitalist bastard-grinding-the-faces-of-the-poor (even though he did wear a top hat, wore a monocle, sported wing collars and an orchid from his own greenhouses in his buttonhole). So successful was his approach to marketing that, despite a wall of protective tariffs, the Americans paid him to stop exporting to their market. Retiring from business in 1874, as Mayor of Birmingham he virtually rebuilt that city through slum clearances and the provision of gas, clean piped water and street lighting, before being elected to parliament in 1876. There he reformed the Liberal party organisation, was schooled in the minutiae of departmental administration as well as the snake-pit of parliamentary politics and became, during the 1880s, Gladstone's Commons spokesman on South African affairs and an extraordinarily effective mounter of parliamentary ambushes; over the Zulu War debates, he once reduced the Commons to a riot. Like many other Liberals, though, it was Kruger's outrageous behaviour in Bechuanaland and Zululand and Gladstone's bungling appeasement of it that turned him from his theoretical anti-imperialism to an understanding that theory and reality in southern Africa were two very different things. The fact that he split with Gladstone over this and other affairs can only

---

[431] Leo Amery, *The Times History of the War in South Africa 1899-1900* (London 1900) Vol.1 p.221.

count in his favour (and if Beatrix Potter thought he was wonderful, we can only take this as evidence that his judgement was good). After this, the Conservative PM, Lord Salisbury, sent him on a diplomatic mission to the USA and Canada where he added the skills necessary for the international snake-pit to his CV. It was during this period that Chamberlain's attention was turned towards the Transvaal and to Cecil Rhodes, whom he distrusted intensely and whose Chartered Company for the conquest of Rhodesia he did as much as he could to limit but without success.[432] What Chamberlain's education and experience show us is not that he was without flaws, but that he had both a breadth and depth of intellect that attracted the attention of Gladstone and his infinitely more cerebral and competent nemesis, Lord Salisbury, and which was applicable in a range of circumstances to a range of problems. More than this, though, was that he was a great pragmatist in that he saw problems as things to be solved in a practical manner, rather than according to high-falutin' theories; if it worked, it worked. He understood business and so understood that a war in South Africa was undesirable on those grounds alone but he also understood how to conduct negotiations and having dealt with a wide range of business people, trade unionists, diplomats, politicians, civil servants and imperial officialdom, he had a pretty good idea of what he was doing. Kruger, throughout his dealings with the Colonial Office, simply could not see that Chamberlain was not just a creature of Rhodes (or *vice versa*), or that perhaps there might be some nuance to the 'policy of firmness' or, essentially, that his long and inferior experience of dealing with Afrikaaner village politics did not outweigh Chamberlain's. He thought he could outwit him.

And, of course, Alfred Milner was a lot smarter than Kruger but in a different way. He was a brilliant Oxford scholar, passed the bar, immersed himself in social and educational reforms, mastered the intricacies of government finance at the Treasury which led to a posting to Egypt to run the finances there. In 1894, he was brought back to run the Inland Revenue (bastard!) and then, in 1897, Chamberlain asked him to go out as High Commissioner to replace Sir Hercules Robinson. Rather austere and cerebral, he believed in the idea of an elite civil service guarding the state and advancing the interests of the people and was rather suspicious of democracy – as we have seen, this was not an uncommon view and was related to Plato's idea of the country being run by a Philosopher King aided by Guardians to prevent the plebs making a cock-up of it all; what he would have made of the dog's breakfast of social democracy is probably easy to divine. The point is that Milner, like Chamberlain, was vastly and widely experienced, extremely clever and unimpressed by Kruger's supposed peasant craftiness. Both men read Kruger's approach as that of the baker who thinks selling short weight is a clever way to do business and then, mistaking the customer's raised eyes and weary dismissal of the cheap pettiness involved, takes it as proof that he's a sharp operator.

There's a great description of the meeting between Milner and Kruger at the Bloemfontein conference in *Grey Steel*, H.C. Armstrong's biography of Jan Smuts, and I shall quote it at length as it highlights the differences in personality and outlook between the two men:

---

[432] Dictionary of National Biography.

> Across the table the delegations faced each other: Milner, carefully dressed, tall, erect, dignified and vigorous, the Proconsul of a great Empire, with clear cut features and the voice and the manner of an aristocrat. Kruger, sagged down, crumpled up in his chair, his faded frock-coat buttoned up tight, his enormous body grown shapeless, slack, unwieldy and monstrous with age and disease, a fringe of unkempt beard below his chin, his face worn into deep creases and lines, his eyes narrow and crafty, the mouth large and crooked, repellent in its ugliness, the ugliness of a worn gargoyle, yet giving a man a sense of vast strength and determination; a rugged, brutal, powerful, dirty old peasant, yet a personality accustomed to power and being obeyed.[433]

Good, eh?

Furthermore, just as Kruger could not conceive of any negotiation with the British that was not, in the modern parlance, a 'zero sum game', neither could he conceive that the British wanted a mutually beneficial deal at all. 'It's my country you want!' he is said to have shouted at Milner at the end of the Bloemfontein conference. He would have had no reply had Milner responded by saying 'Whatever for?' Milner's actual reply was: 'I assure the president that I don't want to take away his independence.'[434]

Hovering in the background was the spectre of Majuba and Gladstone's cowardice. 'If politicians are to be held responsible for the natural consequences of their actions, however long deferred,' wrote Leo Amery in 1900. 'No small share of the guilt of the blood shed in the present war lies at Mr. Gladstone's door.'[435] He was right. One of the leaders of the 'pro-Boers' in parliament undermining Milner and egging Kruger on was John Morley, Gladstone's grovelling biographer, another was Leonard Courtney, who Gladstone had appointed to the Colonial Office before Majuba. At bottom, Kruger's overwhelming belief was that if the British Army could be given a sufficiently hard, fast, early blow by burghers well-armed and trusting in God, then the effete politicians of London would give him what he wanted. Despite all the evidence to the contrary, despite him being faced down by Sir Charles Warren at Fourteen Springs in January 1885, despite the fact that Lord Salisbury was in charge and not Gladstone, despite the fact that Britain had recently wiped out the stain of Gladstone's abandonment of Gordon by marching up the Nile and avenging his murder at Omdurman and despite the fact that the Royal Navy could prevent all the navies of the world ferrying all the troops of the world to his aid, Kruger believed that when push came to shove, the British would fold. In a sense, therefore, this wasn't Pakenham's 'Milner's War' or even as Chris Ash argued so powerfully in his 2017 work, 'Kruger's War'. It was Gladstone's War.

*

Militating strongly against the idea that the war was cooked up to order by Chamberlain and Milner (with a dash of Rhodes thrown in) is the fact that at the time British foreign and imperial policy was firmly under the control of Lord Salisbury. Salisbury is hardly known

---

[433] H.C. Armstrong, *Grey Steel. A Study in Arrogance* (London, 1945) p.55.
[434] Quoted in Sarah Gertrude Millin, *General Smuts, Vol.I* (London, 1936) p.94.
[435] Leo Amery, *The Times History of the War in South Africa 1899-1900* (London 1900) p.72.

today but he must surely be counted alongside the greats of Disraeli, Churchill and Thatcher for his long service and sure guidance during the latter part of the 19th Century. Clear sighted, pragmatic and long experienced, he had witnessed the transformation of Europe by German unification, dealt with the problems of India and Ireland and steered the country through the shoal waters of what has since become known as 'Splendid Isolation' and which is short-hand for 'keeping Britain out of Germany's entangling alliances'. His model for relationships with other countries was 'a mutual temper of apathetic tolerance'[436] and his approach to foreign affairs was ideally 'to float lazily downstream, occasionally putting out a diplomatic boat-hook to avoid collisions'[437]. He was also suspicious of imperial proconsuls, soldiers, businessmen, any sort of enthusiast or idealist – especially Gladstone – and anyone, like Chamberlain, with grand visions of reinvigorating what the latter thought was an empire on the cusp of decay. One biographer, Paul Smith, accorded him recognition;

> for performing with patient and undramatic skill the formidable task of defending the worldwide interests of a satiated power without open conflict with powers less replete or onerous commitment to any ally. Peace was an integral part of his matured strategy of Conservatism.[438]

A desire for peace did not, of course, prevent him from being willing to wage war to protect Britain's vital interests and he had demonstrated his willingness to do this in his endorsement of the permanent occupation of Egypt and booting the French off the Upper Nile during the 1898 Fashoda incident. This did not mean he was a rampant empire builder - it was he who had tried to rein in Sir Bartle Frere at the time of the Zulu War and Lord Lytton's 1878 invasion of Afghanistan - but it did mean that he intended to maintain what had been built already. It is, of course, true that Salisbury was increasingly ill from the spring of 1898 and that he was forced through ill health to delegate more than he wanted to at this time, but this necessary delegation in no way extended to him handing over decisions of war and peace and nor did it impair his ferocious intellect.

Of course, ever since the Jameson Raid the question of the Transvaal had been moving up the agenda but he was still of the opinion that the *status quo* ought to be preserved. Salisbury was the Prime Minister of a country with a strong democratic element to its constitution but this was something that Salisbury accepted without much enthusiasm, rather like the British weather, and so he could not be persuaded to go to war to get universal male suffrage for Uitlanders when he viewed it with such suspicion at home. There were limits to his patience with Kruger's assertive and aggressive nationalism though and he saw the dangers of this getting out of hand, especially as Milner seemed to be getting increasingly hot under the collar; Salisbury had had plenty of experience of 'prancing proconsuls' acting on their own initiative and was determined to strangle any such impatience with the telegraph wire. It was for this reason that he insisted the matter be dealt with strictly according to government hierarchy, that is, with Milner at the bottom of the heap, Chamberlain in the middle and the

---

[436] Dictionary of National Biography
[437] Dictionary of National Biography
[438] Dictionary of National Biography

Cabinet very firmly at the top. He personally approved every communication sent to Kruger before it was sent.[439]

With the failure of the Bloemfontein Conference in May/June 1899, Milner became more convinced that the end result must be war; Chamberlain thought so too but was less enthusiastic about the prospect while Salisbury remained rather more optimistic; they all agreed, however, that Milner's policy of firmness was the right one and that the pressure should be piled on Kruger to come back to the negotiating table, principally by the despatch of troops to the Cape and, if that didn't work, by ultimatum. Salisbury was also of the opinion that neither the Cabinet nor the public would support a war on the Uitlander issue and though the former might be persuaded to accept one, the latter would not. It was for this reason that Chamberlain published Milner's alarming despatch of 4th May 1899, in which he claimed that the Uitlanders were like desperate Helots clamouring for succour from H.M. Government and that the refusal to come to their aid was undermining British prestige, and began schmoozing various newspaper editors.[440] This seemed to be producing results because during July the rumour got around that Kruger was about to offer the seven-year franchise but back-dated to 1890, an offer which both Chamberlain and Salisbury were minded to accept as long as it was an offer made in good faith. When Smuts (who didn't qualify for the franchise himself) made the offer to the British Agent in Pretoria on 12th August, it turned out to be even better; a five-year franchise and ten out of thirty-six seats in the *Volksraad*, use of English there and an Arbitration Commission on any franchise issues, but still insisted on the end of Suzerainty as the *quid pro quo* (even then there were plenty of petty obfuscations about the *exact* conditions of the franchise).

Turning the screw seemed to be working and so on 28th August, Salisbury responded by accepting all the good bits but refusing to compromise on Suzerainty. On 2nd September, Kruger withdrew the offer and so Salisbury turned the screw again, this time by sending out 10,000 troops to double the number already out at the Cape - but it would be at least a month before they could be landed at Durban. It was, however, indicative that Salisbury would go to war unless Kruger backed down. That said, any war that Salisbury started could not possibly be embarked upon until much greater forces than this could be assembled because British forces were still outnumbered by at least 2:1 and possibly 3:1. Salisbury was still negotiating.

The same could not be said of Kruger; if he could get what he wanted without fighting he would do so and he was prepared to signal his military preparations to turn a screw of his own but he seems to have decided on war some time quite shortly after the failure of the Bloemfontein conference. The difference between the two positions also lay in the fact that as Salisbury's hand strengthened and looked set to strengthen ever further during July and August 1899 as he deployed the ever greater resources of the Empire, Kruger's gradually weakened as his support bled away. The first blow came on 14th July when Jan Hofmeyr, leader of the *Bond* in the Cape told Smuts that if war broke out, Kruger could expect only *moral* support from that vital constituency, the Cape Dutch farmers. These were men of

---
[439] A. Roberts, *Salisbury: Victorian Titan* (London, 1999) p.732.
[440] A. Roberts, *Salisbury: Victorian Titan* (London, 1999) p.722.

weight, property and horse sense who understood the benefits of a predictable legal system where property rights were respected and contracts could be enforced; who understood the benefits of being connected in to the British commercial world; who realised that any war would likely be fought over their crops and farm yards and that any rising might well encourage brigandage on a grand scale from *bywoners*, vagabonds and lawless blacks or coloureds; whose products and produce had been on the receiving end of Kruger's outrageous tariffs; who looked up at Pretoria and didn't like what they saw in terms of corruption and mismanagement, fellow Afrikaaners or not. In short, Hofmeyr had been moving in the direction of Rhodes for a long time and now saw the future as a united South Africa under the protecting wing of the British Empire, rather than the very disunited dog's breakfast that waited any extension of Kruger's chaotic rule. Then from Europe at the beginning of August came a steady stream of telegrams from the Transvaal's Agent Dr Leyds warning him that though France and Germany might be well disposed he could 'expect nothing from the Great Powers'[441] while on the 11th fifty Afrikaaner members of the Cape parliament told Kruger he must re-open negotiations. On August 28th, Cape Prime Minister William Schreiner, a man who had done everything he possibly could to avoid hostilities despite a fair amount of vilification from all sides and who had, right up to the end, acquiesced in the importation of armaments to the Orange Free State through the Cape ports, declared that if war did break out the Cape Colony would stand apart and aloof from the struggle.[442] Bang went Kruger's hope of a rising in Cape Colony and bang went any hope of aid from Europe and so bang went any hope of winning a war with Britain – unless, of course, Salisbury was another Gladstone, which, of course, he wasn't.

In reality, Kruger had no more intention of enacting meaningful franchise reform than he had of moving to China. Both Salisbury and Kruger knew the issue was not about the franchise or about suzerainty or any of the other issues laid out in that long charge sheet drawn up in the Colonial Office. It was about whether South Africa would continue under British paramountcy or whether it would be part of an Afrikaans Republic 'stretching from Table Bay to the Zambesi'.[443] The Smuts proposals, along with several other schemes, were simply distractions to buy time for his military preparations to be completed and, not least, for the grass his commandos would need for forage to grow.

*

The war was not inevitable. No war ever is. It is only when a politician makes a conscious choice to put the resolution of a dispute to the hazard of the bullet that wars begin. Military preparations are often used to indicate, intimidate or threaten but they can always be halted. Soldiers might chafe with impatience to be at the enemy, newspaper editors might rage and rally like dunghill roosters while their hacks gather like stormcrows and railway timetables might itch to be out of the secret cupboard and into the signal box but it takes a politician to start a war. Someone has to sign the paper, give the nod, cry 'havoc' and let loose the dogs. Once that permission is given then things change however; once the machine starts rolling

---

[441] Leo Amery, *The Times History of the War in South Africa 1899-1900* (London 1900) Vol.1 p.315
[442] Leo Amery, *The Times History of the War in South Africa 1899-1900* (London 1900) Vol.1 p.339
[443] Smuts to the Transvaal Executive, 4th September 1899. Quoted in C. Ash, *Kruger's War* (Pinetown 2017) p.150.

forward it becomes very difficult to put it in reverse without ripping out the gearbox and leaving yourself at the mercy of the enemy's juggernaut. This war was no different to any other.

From the British point of view, this war was no different from any other because we went into it with insufficient forces, insufficient kit, insufficient planning and insufficient organisation. This was not the fault of the Armed Forces but the fault of the Treasury who despite having all of them, to a man, learned Latin at school and possibly studied it to an extremely high level at Oxford or Cambridge, had never been able to translate the phrase *si vis pacem, paro bellum*. In the long ignoble history of British armed forces being sent into battle without decent boots, decent swords, decent APCs, enough artillery or sufficient body armour at the behest of puffed up grinning monkeys, I can think of only one instance where the Treasury made a positive contribution to the first duty of government *viz*, the Defence of the Realm. This was the decision in the mid-1930s to allow the development of the Spitfire – and they only did this because it was cheaper than buying bombers. *Si vis pacem, paro bellum*; if you want peace, prepare for war. It remains untranslated to this day.

That the British Army was well aware of its own shortcomings is not particularly well known and I confess it was only when I was asked to write the official history of the Royal United Services Institute in 2008 that I became aware of just how much effort had gone into the study of the military art by hard thinking military intellectuals in the period after the Crimean War of 1854-56. Indeed, if I may quote myself:

> The fact that Britain had an army to send to South Africa in 1899 at all was due to the exertions of the defence establishment and its centre in RUSI. In 1879 the despatch of eight battalions to fight the Zulus had stretched capacity to the utmost, a lesson that was repeated again in Egypt in 1882, but not remedied until Salisbury's Conservatives came back into office after 1885. By 1898, despite the fact that defence expenditure had been doubled and now made up 40% of the government's budget, the amount spent only added up to 2.5% of Britain's net worth, which still left Britain with an army about half the size that it needed to be if it was to fulfil its imperial and home defence functions.'[444]

The RUSI had been instrumental not just in driving forward the spending on defence but it was also responsible for testing out new ideas on warfare brought on by the development of new technology, especially those questions posed by the development of long range artillery, magazine rifles and smokeless powder. The 1891 Prize Essay competition was set on *The Tactical Operations of the Future (Including Questions of Supply and Transport of Ammunition) as Affected by the Introduction of Magazine Rifles, Machine and Quick-Firing Guns, and Smokeless Powder*. There was also a long running debate about whether cavalry should retain the role of shock troops charging with lance and sabre or stack the cutlery and become rifle armed Mounted Infantry. The Intelligence Branch of the War Office also did sterling work in developing military thought and providing useful information but what no-one could persuade the government to do was establish a proper, permanent General Staff to

---

[444] Damian P.O'Connor, *Between Peace and War: British Defence and the Royal United Services Institute 1831-2010* (RUSI, 2011) p.103.

provide detailed contingency planning. Instead, the army was forced to rely on a long-standing and particularly brilliant talent for improvisation and the battlefield experience that its regimental officers had acquired over years of slugging it out with Pathans on the NW Frontier and any number of denizens of other hot, inconvenient and troublesome frontiers. The truth was that there was really nothing wrong with the British Army that couldn't be fixed by adequate funding and, then as now, a really thorough *Auto-da-fé* in No.11 Downing Street.

This had important effects on policy right from the outset simply because Salisbury, like many other politicians past and present, had a tendency to think that all one had to do was press the button marked 'War' and soldiers and sailors would appear like magic from the toy cupboard, do what they were told to do and then get back in their boxes and leap back on the relevant shelf. Being a long time sceptic of the military establishment, Salisbury had a tendency to disbelieve what the soldiers and sailors told him and then profess himself surprised when they informed him what couldn't be done. During the 1878 Balkan Crisis he had disregarded anything the soldiers had told him about the vital necessity of defending Constantinople right up until the last moment and during the 1895-6 Armenian Massacres, he had railed against the Admiralty's refusal to see the Mediterranean Fleet sunk by attempting to force the heavily defended Dardenelles, accusing them in the process of worrying about the paintwork on their shiny boats.[445] This was also the case in South Africa when he expressed complete frustration at the news that, with the best will in the world, there was no way the army could ever be ready for a war in South Africa before December. This was, of course, partially his own fault because he had repeatedly refused War Office requests to allow adequate preparations to be made for such a war, principally on the grounds that he really did not believe that there would be one right up until the end of September when Kruger made it clear he was going to start it.

The key source for the military preparations during the run up to the war is Major General Frederick Maurice's massive tome *History of the War in South Africa 1899-1902*. This was the British official history of the war compiled in 1906 by one of Britain's leading military intellectuals and Professor of History at the Staff College and although there will be those who dismiss it as a 'Jingo' source, this can only be done if you have never read it because his brief was to produce a 'warts and all' account of the campaign from which officers could learn the necessary lessons and to do so without cheesing Britain's new Afrikaaner subjects off. If anything, he was rather more sympathetic to the Boer side of things than was perhaps just and the publication of the first volume provoked a fair amount of protest from the British side; later volumes didn't pull their punches either, even though a more 'Boys Own' style was detectable in parts. So, when Maurice declared that there was an 'unwillingness of Her Majesty's Government to believe in the necessity for war'[446], I'm prepared to take him at his word.

In 1896, the Intelligence Branch of the War Office was told to start investigating the military capabilities of the Boer Republics and to begin map surveys of northern Natal. These were

---

[445] A. Roberts, *Salisbury: Victorian Titan* (London, 1999) p.608.
[446] F. Maurice, *The War in South Africa 1899-1902* (London, 1906) Vol.1 p.1.

reasonable precautions and resulted in the compilation of *Military Notes on the Dutch Republics of South Africa* which discussed in some detail the resources, likely plans and tactics of the Boer forces plus the water, rail, road and forage situation should an invasion of the Republics be envisaged. When a copy of this was captured by Boer forces at the beginning of the war the famous newspaperman W.T.Stead, and every Brit-basher and conspiracy theorist since, seized on this as proof of a cunning plot to overthrow the independence of the Republics. It wasn't; the Intelligence Branch had been producing information like this for years and ever since 1874, each of the colonies were required to provide an annual defence analysis. The thing that the soldiers wanted most of all – a proper topographical map survey done to a scale that would be useful to a soldier – they didn't bother asking for because they knew it would be refused on the grounds of expense and because it would be seen in Whitehall as a provocative act.[447] This is the sort of stuff that costs lives; when the British Army went to relieve Ladysmith it did so from maps cobbled together from farm surveys and word of mouth, on which hills were shown without contours and with blanks that might well have been filled in with 'Here be ye dragons'.[448] The defeat at Colenso was due to a vital ford and commanding hill being marked wrongly on the only available map and the Irish Brigade were massacred because of it; the failures at Spion Kop and Vaal Krantz were due mainly to maps that failed to show that both positions were overlooked by other hills and were thus untenable and the price was a lot of Lancastrians.

This was only one of many frustrations that the military had to endure. Throughout 1896-7 requests to reinforce South Africa were refused and in 1898 when the Officer Commanding South Africa reported that the Cape would fall to any attack made upon it, he was ignored. Similarly, the military pointed out that any war in South Africa would require vast numbers of transport animals and that as these could not be magicked out of thin air, someone ought to start buying them up; the request was refused. When preparations were given the go-ahead during the spring of 1899, they were then halted after the Bloemfontein Conference as, yet again, the possibility of war was discounted. It wasn't until July that orders were sent out to bolster the defences of Kimberley and Rhodesia and do something about the transport situation, but then at the end of the month a request for poles for ox-wagons was refused. The first indication that the possibility of war might actually be a racing prospect came at the beginning of September when C-in-C Sir Garnet Wolseley told the government bluntly that defeat was on the way because their bungling hesitancy had conceded the initiative to the enemy. A week later, reinforcements were ordered from India and on 20th September the War Office was authorised to tell the Admiralty that they might need to hire some ships to take an Expeditionary Force out to South Africa; this didn't become an order until the 30th. Still, just to labour the point, this still did not mean that war was inevitable, just that a Boer victory might be marginally more difficult to achieve; these were *defensive* preparations and damned inadequate ones at that. The British government had no intention of starting a war and it only dawned on them that one was going to start towards the middle of September, which was about a week before Kruger mobilised his commandos.

---

[447] F. Maurice, *The War in South Africa 1899-1902* (London, 1906) Vol.1 p. 14.
[448] A Duminy, *Mapping South Africa* (South Africa, 2011) p. 113

For Kruger, preparations for war were rather simpler. He had bought masses of arms in Europe and had shipped them in either through Delagoa Bay or through the Cape ports. He had prepared the ground for a rebellion in the Cape through the *Bond*, his Secret Service and the supply of arms to sympathisers. His diplomacy had brought the Orange Free State into an offensive and defensive alliance that could only have Britain as its target and unlike the British, he could assemble masses of mounted infantry and a fair amount of artillery at any point on his borders within a week. The only danger lay in a hostile Joburg and this he took steps to neutralise by arresting two newspaper editors and the leader of the Uitlander Council on 1st September on charges of High Treason. This was the signal for English people to get out and 30,000 of them duly sold what they could, locked up what they couldn't and took the train to Natal and the Cape. 78,000 blacks, Indians and coloureds followed suit and Joburg shut down and the mines ground to a halt. The only thing that held him back now was the state of the grass and this had been prepared by burning off the old growth much earlier than usual in order to ensure a good strong regrowth with the coming of the rains. By the middle of September, he was ready and on 26th September a draft ultimatum was cabled to the Orange Free State, on the 27th the Commandos were called out, on the 29th the military took control of the railways and those Uitlanders who hadn't already left Joburg were expelled.

Even then, it was not too late. The Natal Colonial forces mobilised on the 29th; on the 5th October the Cape Colonial forces were partially mobilised; on the 6th British troops began to embark for the Cape and on the 7th a British Army Corps was mobilised but there was still room for negotiation because those troops were not expected to arrive until the first week of December and, as everyone in the British Army knew (having boned up on *Military Notes on the Dutch Republics of South Africa*), this was still nowhere near enough troops to invade the Transvaal. What made the war certain was the Boer ultimatum issued on the 9th October and the Declaration of War two days later and to say that Kruger had no choice but to press the Big Red Button is just not true.

As we have seen, key props of his position had been knocked away with the refusal of the *Bond* to instigate rebellion and the melting away of the mirage of foreign support. Kruger's support from the Orange Free State was always more provisional than he believed and the ultimatum had gone through the Bloemfontein *Volksraad* with the narrowest of margins; the Free State had always enjoyed friendly relations with the British at the Cape and regarded a war as unthinkable before Reitz and Steyn thought it. With the mobilisation of British forces, Kruger was now presented with a narrow window in which to strike in the hope of victory because that victory would become more and more elusive with every boot that crunched down the gangplank at Cape Town, Durban and Port Elizabeth. Under pressure from the Young Afrikanders, from the newspapers that he had himself whipped up, from the Commandos he had himself called up, from the party that he had built up over twenty years and whose very foundation stone was anti-English, Kruger knew that to back down would mean, at the very least, his own fall amid catcalls and accusations of cowardice, the destruction of his reputation and his pride, and his replacement by Piet Joubert; and Piet Joubert was much more inclined towards a compromise with the British. If Kruger gave in, there would probably be peace, personal humiliation and a franchise reform that he believed (absurdly) would mean the end of the Afrikaaner *volk*; so he chose war. He chose to put his faith in the God of Battles that a highly selective memory could remember as being always on his side (*pace*, the mPedi of 1877 and the Bechuanaland Field Force) since he was fourteen at the Blood River; he put his faith in the Majuba miracle and gambled that it would be repeated. He let his hatred of the British blind him to the disparities in power of a couple of small Republics and a Great Power and letting fall his Bible, he succumbed to the temptations of the older Gods of the Dutch; Odin, the *Valkyrie* and thus, the *Gotterdammerung*. Smuts put it best:

> South Africa stands on the eve of a frightful blood-bath out of which our *Volk* shall come…either as…hewers of wood and drawers of water for a hated race, or as victors, founders of a United South Africa, of one of the great empires of the world…an Afrikaans republic of South Africa stretching from Table Bay to the Zambezi.'[449]

\*

### The South African War

In 2014, Chris Ash, amateur historian and Boer War enthusiast, released *Kruger, Kommandos and Kak* (updated and re-released in 2017 as *Kruger's War)*, a highly polemical and exceedingly witty debunking of the many myths he had come across during his twenty years residence in South Africa. It was a very good book, well researched, thoughtful and all the better for standing well outside the rather sterile academic consensus; it sparked death threats, a Facebook pillorying and a one-star review of his work on Amazon by none other than Fransjohan Pretorius, Professor of History at (where else) the University of Pretoria: how dare this iconoclastic rebel, interloper and dissident question the likes of those intellectual giants Pakenham and Nasson? This, of course, is all first rate evidence of how hard his work hit home; a selection of the wilder insults are featured on his Blog under the title 'Entertaining Fan Mail' but you can also find his response to Fransjohan Pretorius there. In my humble opinion, Ash's judgement is more reliable than the good professor's, despite all the huffing and puffing and bizarre speculations about what lies beneath a Scotsman's kilt, but what really struck me about his work is just how much his experience of researching South African history chimed with my own. In particular, his description of just how viscerally held are the myths surrounding the war which we have already alluded to – heroic Boers, victims of imperial mendacity, etc etc – and just how defensive many Afrikaaners are about them. Indeed, *offensive* about them; in 2017, I was sitting nicely, minding my own business, drinking beer and eating *braii* in a wonderful open air restaurant just south of Lamberts Bay when a chap, overhearing my accent, came over, plonked himself down, assured himself that I was English and then said:

'Your country really fucked mine up.'

'Recently?' I replied.

He meant, of course, during the Boer War, a war that ended when my Grandfather was two years old.

---

[449] Smuts to the Transvaal Executive, 4th September 1899. Quoted in A. Roberts, *Salisbury: Victorian Titan* (London, 1999) p.734.

'Thanks,' I said, after enduring the usual tirade about gold, concentration camps and the mighty Boer warrior. 'And you work for the Tourist Board, do you?'

It was the same with my old mate Thielmann, when I first met him. To begin with, he could hardly bear to speak to an Englishman because according to family legend, the British had shot his Grandmother's cow in 1901. Frankly, I found all this a bit mystifying; obviously I'm interested in History but I don't hate the Germans because they dropped a bomb on *my* Grandad in 1940 (or so my Mum told me) so what's the big deal? Thielmann himself couldn't understand why I, *we*, the British, didn't think it was a big deal until he went to England to visit his daughter who was working in London. The next time I saw him, he was sitting at the bar at his place wearing a *British Army rugby shirt - complete with the royal insignia!* He admitted, rather sheepishly, that he had enjoyed the visit, that further, his daughter had married a British soldier who played rugby for the army – hence the shirt – and then, through gritted teeth, that that same girl had sworn allegiance to the Crown and taken British citizenship. Nevertheless, he had had a smashing time seeing the sights, thought the English were wonderfully hospitable and friendly and would love to go back. This was something of an epiphany.

'Does this mean the Boer War is finally over, Thielmann?' I asked.

'*Ja*,' he replied. 'Now I know why you are not so bothered about the Boer War. If you fought the French for a hundred years, how will you remember us for fighting for just three?'

Klippies and cokes all round. This is how it should be. No country has a monopoly on righteousness, bravery, competence or mendacity and if there is a particular Hell reserved for politicians who let slip the dogs of war for no sufficient reason then it's probably in need of an extension. History should enable us to learn from the wit, wisdom, success, failure and general experience of the past rather than become a tool of the axe-grinding grievance monkey or the bludgeon of the Marxist Utopian. Myths are OK: as long as you don't believe them or make them the basis for death threats or political action. Or disturbing me when I'm eating *braii* on a sunny day by the seaside.

\*

Most histories of the Boer War run along a well-worn groove which begin with the Boer investments of Ladysmith, Kimberley and Mafeking, then go on to a blow-by-blow dissection of the three British defeats at Colenso, Stormberg and Magersfontein during what was known as 'Black Week' to prove how useless the British Army was and how stupid were its Generals. After that, a sort of 'battle fatigue' sets in and although Spion Kop is gone into, just to underline British incompetence, there is precious little about what else was happening; what else was happening was that the British Army was comprehensively kicking seven buckets of the brown stuff out of the Boer armies at Paardeberg and Tugela Heights. Next comes the relief of Ladysmith, which seems to happen as if by a miracle, followed by those of Kimberley and then Mafeking, which also seems to be accomplished without serious effort or prolonged fighting. After that a guerrilla war breaks out in which even more useless Tommies and bonehead Blimps are tied up in knots by the wily Boer until the dastardly Lord Kitchener decides to starve all the Boer women and children to death in concentration camps thus forcing the heroic resistance to a noble, but unbeaten, surrender. Under Apartheid, the National Party went to great lengths to inculcate this version of History through their Christian-National Education curriculum, thus creating the Boer War Bore in the process. Much of the foundation of this version of events is rooted in Maurice's *History* because he was so concerned to ensure mistakes were acknowledged and learned from; also from Leo Amery's *Times History*, which overstated British mistakes and did a notorious hatchet job on General Buller in particular in order to build the case for a reform of the army to make it bigger and introduce a General Staff. Pakenham and the likes seized on the criticisms, but didn't make much of the positives that both of the previous authors pointed out, to provide us with *Blackadder* history. And, of course, if you are going to write history then you need sources and unfortunately, when it comes to Boer accounts, we have plenty of good ones on the experience of being in a Commando but not much on the grand strategy side of things, so this version of events tends to stick.

I'm not going to follow in that comfortable fur-lined rut. I'm going to start not with the incompetence of British Generals but with the absolutely mind-boggling hopelessness of Kruger and the Boer Generals.

Let's start with a bit of military theory; in any battle, be it great or small, there is an area called the 'vital' ground. This is a piece of Real Estate which, if the enemy gets control of, you are done for and you either retreat, surrender or die. On the strategic scale in South Africa, the vital ground was Cape Town; if Kruger could get his Commandos down there then the wavering Cape Dutch would come over to him and Britain would be forced to accept terms. If Cape Town was lost to a United South Africa, there would be as much chance of recovering the South African colonies by force as there was of recovering the American colonies.

In 1899, Cape Colony itself was only lightly and inadequately defended and would be so until the British Army arrived in mid-December. Those units that were deployed were scattered across the main railway routes south from the Orange Free State without hope of support from either the coast or each other; Stormberg, De Aar, Naauwpoort and Orange River Station (around 4000 men in total) were the only decently held outposts between Kimberley and Natal and behind them were just a couple of hundred men of the Royal Munster Fusiliers at Stellenbosch – 650km/400 miles away. These were mere 'tripwire forces' whose function was to signal to the Boers that an invasion would be resisted; Maurice was quite right in saying that they 'would be cut off and crushed in detail in the case of serious attack or of a rising in their rear'.[450] The only place where there was something approaching a decent Field Force (this is an all-encompassing term used in the British Army to describe a collection of troops cobbled together at the last moment for an ill-defined and often improbable purpose) was over in Natal. The Boer armies had all the advantages of superior numbers, superior mobility and longer range, more modern artillery and could therefore expect to swoop down on the Cape encountering no serious opposition until they came within range of the Royal Navy which was capable of defending Cape Town for a while - but not for long - as every

---

[450] F. Maurice, *The War in South Africa 1899-1902* (London, 1906) Vol.1 p.51.

study since van Riebeeck's time had shown that the Cape could not be defended from an attack from the landward side.

So Kruger decided to do the exact opposite and attack Natal with a view to landing a knockout blow on the forces there and galloping down to occupy Durban in the hope that this would convince the Cape Dutch to rebel and convince the British public that the cause of South Africa was lost. Kruger, therefore, expected Britain to surrender when she still held the vital ground, had an Army Corps at sea and on the way, while he simultaneously held down a rebellious English population in Natal sheltering under the guns of the Royal Navy. And this is without considering the attitude of the rather more pro-British than pro-Boer Zulus next door. If you want stupidity, this is it.

And it doesn't end there either. Another vital military principle is that of 'Concentration of Force'. This means that if you go to a fight, you go mob-handed towards the vital ground, in overwhelming numbers if possible, and you don't split your forces up chasing sideshows. Instead, a force of perhaps 4-6000 men was sent to besiege the 3000 man garrison of Kimberley; certainly it made sense to screen off the town but the vital ground was further south at Orange River Station where the railway went over the river; whoever held that post commanded all points northward. And if it made poor sense to commit those forces against Kimberley, it made even less sense to send Piet Cronjie with 7000 men and ten guns to besiege Mafeking which was even further up that same railway line. When you look up Kuruman on a map, the absurdity of sending a thousand men to besiege what is very much the arse end of nowhere becomes nothing less than stark. Add to these, the 1500 men sent to patrol the border with Rhodesia – a border that was impassable to an invading army of any size (which didn't exist anyway) – that's 15,000 men out of a total of perhaps 50,000 available sent on wild goose chases. When the decision was made to attack Natal, only 21,000 burghers were sent in that direction which left the balance – another 14,000 - doing nothing very effective at all, when even that number sent down towards the Cape would probably have been decisive. Please note that the numbers are approximate; the Boers did not keep many records.

The most important military principle is known as the 'Selection and Maintenance of the Aim' and it means that before you start a war or an attack, you have to decide what you want to achieve and then once the enterprise is underway, to avoid being distracted from it. This concept was unknown in the Transvaal and the Orange Free State. That there was a *political* aim was clear – to invade British territory, beat the British Army and then amid the acclaim of a popular rebellion graciously hand down terms. This, however, is not the same as a *strategic* aim. A strategic aim is the foundation for an overall concept of how the war will be actually fought, and directs where forces will be committed and what objectives will be set for the various commanders. Various German Staff officers had tried to drum this into Kruger's head in the period before the war and Smuts, being the exception that proves the rule, had come up with a plan for a Blitzkrieg on Durban and Natal, but these efforts were wasted. Kruger had been a successful Commando leader in his time but he was utterly ignorant of the wider practice of warfare. As far as he was concerned, the Boers had only to shoot a sufficient number of Tommies and the war would be over; it didn't particularly matter where those Tommies were shot as long as they were shot in large numbers and as the largest numbers of Tommies were to be found in northern Natal, where the grass was nice and green and near to Majuba, they would do. As a result, there was no strategic direction to the war, no realisation that the vital ground was Cape Town, with Durban a high but secondary priority, and no attempt to think through and implement a decent plan. Thus, President Steyn of the Orange Free State was allowed to send his forces to Kimberley in the hope of slurping up the diamond wealth instead of pinching the whole of the West off by taking Orange River Station, all the while standing on the defensive at Norvals Pont, Bethulie and Aliwal North where the crossings of the Orange River provided the gateway for a Blitzkrieg on the Cape.

What this all meant was that if Tommy Atkins declined to oblige Kruger by being shot down in suitably large numbers in suitably short order, the Boers would lose the war because as soon as that Army Corps reached the ports of Cape Town, Port Elizabeth and Durban then all hope of a quick victory would be gone. From then on, all the Boers could do would be to go onto the defensive and hope that either British public opinion or a twist in Great Power relations might alter the situation so profoundly that Lord Salisbury would come grovelling to the negotiating table. In short, Kruger would be dependent on the actions of others for his victory rather than his own efforts and this was a tried and trusted recipe for defeat.

The plan, such as it was, began to unravel almost immediately. On 12th October, the Commandos crossed into Natal and headed down the passes towards the important railway junction of Ladysmith where the lines from the Transvaal and the Orange Free State united before heading straight down through Colenso, Estcourt, Pietermaritzburg and on to Durban. It's about 150 miles/250km, all downhill, with plenty of water and good grazing and, as the British had been so convinced that there would be no war, (the railway tunnels had not been mined or blown), easily do-able in the six weeks before the Army Corps could be landed. British forces numbered roughly 12,000 strong, a tough enough nut to crack, but because the Governor of Natal had insisted that the coal supplies at Dundee were to be protected, they were hopelessly out of position, surrounded on three sides by Boer territory and forty miles from Ladysmith. So with all these advantages, the Boers took five days to cover the distance from the top of the passes to Dundee, a distance of 130km/80 miles, largely because many of the burghers had allowed themselves to be distracted by pillaging Newcastle and robbing the surrounding farms. And in the first major engagement of the war, the Battle of Talana Hill just outside Dundee, Tommy Atkins served notice on General Piet Joubert that he would not consent to be shot down in large numbers, nor run away at the first whiff of grapeshot; around 3000 of them fixed bayonets and assaulted the hill and the attacking force of around 5000 Boers retired in some disorder. Two days later, the veteran Gordon Highlanders and Devons, fresh from the NW Frontier, and ably assisted by the Uitlanders of the Imperial Light Horse handed the Commandos another lesson at Elandslaagte, and then withdrew into Ladysmith. Not that it was all one way traffic; a couple of days later, the Boers cut off a battalion at Nicholson's Nek and swept up 900 men into the bag but enough had been done to confirm Piet Joubert's doubts about the wisdom of this war. When he decided to lay siege to Ladysmith, he went further than simply confirming those doubts – he threw away all hope of victory. The correct thing to do was to leave a sufficient force behind to keep the British from moving – say 8000 men? – and then claim a victory and ride hell for leather for Durban, because in front of those 12,000 riders were only perhaps 3,000 soldiers and volunteers spread out across the colony. Instead, the Boers sat outside Ladysmith, paralysed by another defeat when an attempt was made to storm the town on the 9th November, and wondered what to do for fifteen days until a council of war decided that they should, perhaps, carry on doing nothing effectual but also ride for Durban at the same time after all; but in numbers that were completely insufficient for anything more than reconnaissance and plundering. On the 22nd, a confused night action at a place called Willow Grange convinced Joubert that he was dangerously exposed and ought to retire and thus the main Boer effort became the siege of Ladysmith. They had abandoned their aim; the main thrust of a flawed strategy was brought to a halt. A week later, the British Army started landing at Durban.

At Mafeking, repeated attacks failed to make much impression on the defenders while at Kimberley, no serious effort was ever made to take the town. Only a belated effort was made against the Cape itself, when the leftovers from those sent West, North and East – indeed in any direction but the important one – crossed the Orange and advanced down the railway to Naauwpoort and Stormberg, where they too sat down and handed the initiative to the British. The only positive effect of this non-strategy was getting the British press worked up because Cecil Rhodes was confined in Kimberley and General Buller was ordered to relieve him as soon as he could. This meant that Buller's strategy had to be changed from concentrating all his forces in Natal to an advance on two fronts, but this was no real hardship as any advance was dictated by the railway routes up which all the supplies would need to come anyway.

The advance from the Cape towards Kimberley began on 21st November and by the end of the month the Boers had been defeated at Belmont, Graspan and the Modder River putting the British Army in the Western theatre within easy reach of its objective. The first week in December also saw Buller on the Natal front ready to attack the Boer positions at Colenso in an attempt to relieve Ladysmith, while in the Central theatre, General Gatacre moving up from Port Elizabeth and East London, prepared to re-take Stormberg. In each one of these areas, the British Army was defeated and the three Boer victories at Magersfontein, Colenso and Stormberg sent the press into a panic at what they christened 'Black Week'. The defeats were due largely to the lack of adequate maps (Colenso and Stormberg), geography (Colenso was a natural fortress) but also to the new realities of magazine rifles and smokeless powder that the British military intellectuals had been working on for some years previous. Much hot air has been expended on the effectiveness of Boer marksmanship, and indeed, many of them had a great deal of experience hunting game but the Commandos also had their fair share of Joburg costermongers and counterjumpers who probably didn't know which end of the Mauser was the dangerous bit, so the effectiveness of Boer musketry needs explaining.

Basically, the standard model of attack in the British Army began with a thorough reconnaissance conducted by the cavalry to discover the enemy positions, followed by an advance by the infantry in extended order – men in a series of lines with anything from three to ten paces between them and roughly a hundred yards deep – supported by artillery deployed well forward but just outside rifle range. When contact was made, a firing line would form into which more supports would be fed while attempts were made to go around one or both flanks. When the enemy began to crack, bayonets would be fixed and the position taken by storm, after which the cavalry would pursue the broken enemy. Now, obviously, there were a wide range of variations on this theme but it'll do for our purposes. The problem arose because magazine rifles allowed for a much greater rate of fire and smokeless powder allowed for a greater concealment of the enemy; from this time onwards, battlefields begin to look empty because to reveal yourself was to risk becoming a target. Not only that, but the extension of the line meant that command and control became ever more difficult and in the absence of any reliable form of real-time communications, the ability of an officer to control the battle became ever more diminished; the earlier scarlet uniforms had been adopted so that a General could tell where his troops were at a distance but they had long been given up - if ever a battlefield guide tells you the British advanced shoulder to shoulder dressed in the famous scarlet and white pipe-clay crossbelts, ask for your money back because he's ballooning; the army wore khaki to allow for better camouflage; the Boers didn't bother with uniforms.

As to marksmanship, well, when I was taught to shoot by the British Army I used a 7.62 SLR which was designed to hit an individual man-sized target at 300m and which could cause grief at 600m if seven or eight of us fired at it simultaneously. Throughout the Boer War, British soldiers were killed at much longer ranges than this but this was only partly due to marksmanship; the key factor was that *thousands* of rifles would be directed at those advancing infantry men and those hundreds and thousands of rifles would be rattling off shots at a rate of 5-10 per minute. It was the *weight* of fire that counted more than individual skill at that range.

The other key factor in all this was that the longer ranges of magazine rifles made close reconnaissance by cavalry virtually impossible and when this was combined with the lack of decent maps, attacking – always a hazardous business - became much more so. And as the Boers were holding onto British real estate, it fell to the British to do the attacking while the Boers dug in or concealed themselves in thornbush and krantz; this is how they earned their nickname of *Rock spiders.* And what was sauce for the goose was sauce for the gander; whenever the Boers attacked, they experienced exactly the same conditions and casualties. There was, however, one crucial tactical difference; when the British won they *pursued*; when the Boers won, they stayed put and patted each other on the back and so guaranteed that they would lose eventually. This is what happened during Black Week; the Boers stopped the British but never turned defeat into a rout by an effective pursuit. Piet Joubert threw away this last and unexpected opportunity to push on to Durban after Colenso. Piet Cronjie (whom Maurice, in an uncharacteristic blast, described as having 'a full share of the stoutness which had delivered his European forefathers from the hand of Spain ... leadened with a stupidity which was to drag himself down to ruin')[451] declined to pursue on the grounds that the British would either go away or come back in exactly the same way because, being *unable to march*, they would never leave the railway line that his position at Magersfontein commanded. Neither did he do anything to secure his supply line to Bloemfontein which other, more able, commanders pointed out to him, was wide open. The only forward move that was made was the occupation of the dusty dorp of Uppington, a place so remote it's a

---

[451] *Maurice,* Vol III p.146.

wonder anyone knew it was there – look it up on a map – and being 400km/250 desert miles west of Kimberley, of no military or strategic value whatsoever. And there was a rearward move in the Central theatre to boot, where Sir John French drove the Boers back from Naaupoort during a brilliant campaign on the Great Trek routes.

*

'We are not interested in the possibilities of defeat,' said Queen Victoria to Foreign Minister Arthur Balfour, calming everyone down after Black Week. 'They do not exist.' And they did not; Lord Roberts and General Kitchener came out to take overall command while Buller was left to concentrate on Natal. The troops which were expected at the beginning of December began to arrive in numbers and more followed from Britain, India, Australia, New Zealand and Canada so that eight weeks later, on 11$^{th}$ February 1900, when what Chris Ash christened the Boer 'Black Month' began, Roberts had assembled the 6$^{th}$, 7$^{th}$ and 9$^{th}$ Infantry Divisions plus a Cavalry Division ready for the move on Kimberley; Lord Methuen's 1$^{st}$ Division in reserve and ready to march on Mafeking; another Division to make sure the Cape stayed quiet and guard the railways; two powerful Divisions on the Orange River at Colesberg; and Buller still had the 2$^{nd}$ and 5$^{th}$ Divisions, plus two cavalry Brigades south of Colenso; and these were just the main units – there was a whole host of Colonial Volunteers, Mounted Infantry units, Engineers, balloon, pontoon, telegraph and railway repair sections, Naval Brigades, ammunition columns, scouts and, the answer to all problems in war (as in life), masses of artillery.

And if this wasn't enough, there was always more. From the outset, it was decided that as this conflict had acquired the character of a war between the British 'race' and the Boer 'race' it had better be won by one or the other of them without recourse to help from other races. The 200,000 strong professional British Indian army was therefore excluded – as were the non-white contingents offered from various parts of the Empire - and it was decided not to bring in the black people of southern Africa on the British side, the latter for fear of what these 'savages' – and by this time, the word had dropped any romantic eco-pixie overtones that it had once had – might do once let loose. This did not mean that this was a 'White Man's War' or that black people regarded the whole thing with anything more than anxious indifference because both sides employed black, coloured and Indian people as transport riders, grooms and labourers; in several cases armed black units were formed but they were far from common and generally, the convention was accepted and adhered to, as was the general agreement to respect the borders of Basutoland, right up until the end of the war. Nevertheless, this vast pool of potential warriors was always available to the British if they were needed.

The only serious weakness in this array lay in the matter of animals; transport animals were in short supply and ox-wagons were slow and cumbersome but what went for the British went for the Boers too and in some respects the British were better off because they did not bring their families along with them and so add niggly kids and worried women to their burdens. Both sides were in some respects tied to the railways but again the British were rather better off in this respect because they controlled more lines and, as these lines had been built with lateral connections, were able to shift forces from one theatre to another in a way that was denied to the Boers. When it came to horses though, the Boers had a major advantage because their animals were bred to the country and in better condition because they had not undergone a long sea transport. The horses that were shipped in from Argentina, the USA, Britain, Canada, Australia, India and Hungary all arrived in poor condition through lack of exercise, never had enough time to acclimatise before they were loaded onto rails for the journey northwards and were prone to diseases that had long been bred out of South African horses. The wastage rate was often as high as 10% from these causes alone and over the course of the war 206,603 horses and 91,769 mules (used for supply and towing guns) were provided by the remounts department. What this meant was that Sir John French's Cavalry Division was seriously weakened by being mounted on horses that were in a large number of cases not fit for the work involved.[452]

The British had one other advantage that Kruger, Steyn, Joubert and Cronjie were missing; a plan. Originally, the idea was to drive straight up the railway from Cape Town, Port Elizabeth and East London to Bloemfontein and hence, on to Pretoria but the press panic in Britain meant that for reasons of political expediency and general public morale, Kimberley and Ladysmith should be the principal objectives. This meant that Roberts would take a diversion from the direct route, relieve Kimberley and then march down the Modder River to Bloemfontein. There he would rendezvous with forces coming up the line of the railway from Port Elizabeth and Colesberg while in Natal, Buller would batter away at the Boers on the Tugela in order to pin them in position. Ladysmith would fall the moment that Roberts advanced from Bloemfontein when the Boers there realised that he was behind them. After that, all the forces would unite and head for Pretoria in a march that would take them 1500km/950 miles from their point of disembarkation at Cape Town and 600km/380miles from Durban. For a more meaningful comparison, it takes a straight seventeen hours at 70mph to drive from Pretoria to Cape Town, black top all the way; my Missus did it. In the end, Roberts chased Kruger all the way to Komatipoort, which is a distance of 2000km/1250miles and which by way of comparison beats both Napoleon and Hitler's marches on Moscow into a cocked hat for sheer distance and logistical difficulty.

In some ways, Buller had the tougher task because the Boers holding the line of the Tugela River at Colenso occupied a natural fortress made up of a chain of steep, riven, rugged hills which provided sweeping views virtually all the way to the coast. This allowed the talented Louis Botha, who had replaced Piet Joubert injured by a fall from his horse, to see just exactly where the Brits were planning to attack and thus allow him to move his forces along the reverse slopes of those hills to any threatened point. A further characteristic of this tumbled geography is the number of false crests which meant that the British infantry might struggle up a slope, take it at bayonet point, only to find themselves overlooked by a second crest bristling with more rifles. And this unmapped jumble was seventy miles steep and deep and only ended at Harrismith at the top of the Drakensberg. Nor could it be outflanked, as Buller found out after the failed attempts made at Spion Kop in late January and Vaal Krantz in early February 1900. It would have to be taken head on and on 14th February, this he proceeded to do; there are those who say Buller was a dunce but during the sixteen day Battle

---

[452] *Maurice* Vol.IV p. 651.

of the Tugela Heights he found a way and forced the Boers out of their stronghold step by grim, bloody step. His method was to take the hills one at a time, running up a hundred guns to blast a way through and then sending the infantry forward. If the infantry stalled, then the direction of the attack would be shifted and those guns would blast another hole through which even more infantry would go. It was simple, brutal and effective and two weeks later, Ladysmith was relieved.

Roberts had not only the luxury of manoeuvre but also the advantage of facing the stalwart but dim Piet Cronjie rather than Louis Botha. On the 11th February 1900, he began his forward march, first outflanking the Magersfontein position on the east and thus getting astride Cronjie's supply line and then sending Sir John French and the Cavalry Division to gallop through a gap they had found in the Boer lines right into Kimberley. Cronjie didn't notice or react until it was too late whereupon Roberts chased him down the Modder River to Paardeberg, surrounded him and after a few days siege, forced him to surrender on 27th February. Kimberley and Ladysmith relieved, two Boer armies shattered and Bloemfontein ripe for the plucking; Black Month was well underway.

Pausing for a week to rest his horses, which were now in a shocking state – over 500 had simply been ridden to death – and resupply, Roberts then set off for Bloemfontein. The Boer army dug in at Poplar Grove, then Abram's Kraal, then Driefontein, and though now led by the relatively more talented Christian de Wet and Koos de la Rey, simply melted away in a demoralised panic; even Kruger himself, all *sjambok* and Holy Wrath, couldn't prevent the rout. Even de Wet, in his self-congratulatory, petulant and unbelievable memoirs, described his force as 'a disorderly crowd of terrified men blindly flying before the enemy.'[453] On the 13th March, Roberts entered Bloemfontein while the two Divisions based on Colesberg crossed the Orange River to invade the Free State from the south. Black Month ended with the complete subjugation of one of the Republics and the disintegration of perhaps half of the total Boer fighting strength. Not bad for boneheaded Tommy Atkins and his blinkered blimpish Generals.

The victories kept on coming. Lord Methuen began his march north towards Mafeking which his subordinate Colonel Mahon relieved on the 17th and by the middle of May, Roberts was in Kroonstadt – Orange Free State capital No.2 – while Buller was punching the retreating Boers up the Drakensberg, taking Newcastle back on the 18th May. Two weeks later, Roberts won the Battle of Doornkop which opened the way into Joburg and led Kruger to abandon Pretoria in the first stage of his long run to the border of Portuguese Mozambique. After Bloemfontein fell, Koos de la Rey did his best to impede Methuen's advance but was defeated at Israel's Farm while de Wet began raiding Roberts' supply lines, which was a perfectly sensible thing to do, before taking the truly bizarre decision to take 10,000 men to spend sixteen days besieging the strategically, politically, economically and militarily insignificant dorp of Wepener which, despite outnumbering the defenders 5:1, he failed to take. Many of the men under his command were those who had surrendered, given up their weapons and taken the oath of allegiance to Britain.[454]

---

[453] Quoted in Ash, *Kruger's War* p.297.
[454] C. de Wet *Three Years War* (New York, 1902) Ch.11

In May, Mafeking was relieved and in June Pretoria fell, its fortresses handing over their keys without the firing of a shot; on the 12th the Boers were defeated at Diamond Hill just to the east while in July a steady string of victories across the two Republics culminated in the surrender of Prinsloo's 4000 men at Brandwater Basin hard against the Basutoland border; many of those who had escaped then voluntarily gave themselves up at Harrismith.[455] In August, Lord Methuen captured de Wet's wagons while Buller defeated Louis Botha once more at Bergandal and again the following month at Paardeplaats. By the middle of September it was all over, with Kruger fleeing to Lourenco Marques, Sir John French pouncing on Barberton to liberate most of Botha's transport, £10,000 in gold, forty-four locomotives, two complete trains, herds of sheep and oxen, supplies of all kinds, a hundred burghers (and releasing a hundred British POWs to boot). The last corner of Republican territory was abandoned when the British occupied Komatipoort, where they found:

> …an immense and chaotic occupation of mass of stores and railway material. Nine miles length of rolling stock, including eighty engines, blocked the lines and sidings, some burnt, some loaded with stores, some derailed. On the Lebombo hills, commanding the railway, a 6-in. gun lay blown up; the station itself had been destroyed by fire which still fed upon the piles of coal and other inflammables stacked in the yards. Everywhere was destruction and filth….[456]

It was, said Maurice, 'an emblem of the debris of a cause.'[457]

*

It was all over: or rather it should have been. The Boers had been out-generalled, out-marched, out-fought and their armies ground to fragments and reduced to inflicting guerrilla pinpricks and calling them gashes. Kruger had fled to Europe while Steyn was in hiding somewhere on the veldt. Roberts had declared both Republics annexed and had already indicated the mild nature of the occupation by releasing those burghers who had surrendered, sending them home to their farms and back to civilian life, on the relinquishment of their weapons and the taking of an oath of allegiance. They had fought with honour and would be treated with respect; many Free Staters had been against the war to begin with and now looked forward to getting back to normal; Roberts had been cheered on his entry to Bloemfontein and de Wet reckoned that Kroonstad was a place full of people 'all too ready to do me an injury';[458] the principal pre-war opponent of Steyn, J.G.Fraser, was already co-operating with the British authorities to bring some sort of normality back. The Progressives of Piet Joubert's party would also be likely to accept a suitably mild peace deal and as soon as the gold mines could be started up again, the Transvaal could get back to business as usual. There would be a British Governor and there would be franchise reform to bring it in to some sort of alignment with the electoral systems of the Cape; no one was talking about enfranchising the black people, but coloured people and the property qualification would probably have to be swallowed. What would come to an end was an aggressive foreign

---

[455] *Three Years War* Ch. 17.
[456] *Maurice* Vol.III p.419
[457] *Maurice* Vol.III p.420
[458] *Three Years War*, Ch.12

policy, the tyrannies of the Native Commissioners and the corruption of Kruger and his backwoodsmen but that was it because all the British wanted was control of the coastline to protect the route to India and lots of happy, settled subjects growing crops, making money, deciding local issues pretty much for themselves and not being a burden on the British taxpayer.

It was not to be because at a series of Councils of War before and after the fall of Bloemfontein in March 1900, the decision was taken to continue the war. This was one of the great turning points of South African history, as great perhaps as the decision to embark on the Great Trek, for it was on this that ninety years of Afrikaaner grievance, victimhood, Apartheid and bitterness were built. Piet Joubert, Kruger, Steyn, de la Rey, de Wet and several others took part in the debates and amid much common sense about the reorganisation of the Commandos, the tightening up of military discipline among them and the forbidding of large trains of wagons stuffed full of camp followers, they took the truly terrible decision to prolong resistance in the hope of European intervention. At that particular moment, it seemed that the idea had some mileage in it; there were still men in the field and if Roberts' advance on Pretoria could be stopped by raiding his supply lines then perhaps time might be bought for that European intervention but as soon as Pretoria fell in June, it could not be regarded as anything other than the fantasy it was. And when Kruger went to Europe on board a Dutch cruiser in November 1900, the Kaiser refused to receive him and thus, as he admitted, left him in no doubt whatsoever that no help was coming.[459] At that point the old troll should have asked for terms but his blind hatred prevented him from thinking straight and he thus condemned his country to all the miseries of a guerrilla war that he knew he had no hope of winning. He chose *Gotterdammerung*: or rather, he chose *Gotterdammerung* for the Afrikaaner people while he went sight-seeing in Europe.

And a guerrilla war is perhaps the worst form of war because it is, in many ways, a civil war. From this point on Afrikaaners would fight Afrikaaners, as men who had served loyally on Commando now saw the futility of further resistance and then joined with the British against those they saw as fanatics. The breakdown of all law and order provided opportunities for criminals, freebooters and all sorts of petty meanness and revenge on every side; de la Rey's wife complained of losing all her cattle to black African thieves.[460] Across large parts of the country low level strife would enter into even the smallest dorps as cattle were lifted, coloured and African communities were raided and in turn retaliated and the war became a matter of small patrols of greater or lesser discipline, petty theft, civilian sniping and military reprisal, crop and farm burnings and the sweeping up of horses, cattle, sheep and mules. Commando leaders careered about the veldt with no chance of defeating the British, claiming success when they took a supply column from an army that had thousands more, when they ambushed a platoon from an army that had thousands more, when they evaded a capture that would come with time; as de la Rey would later say of himself;

---

[459] Kruger, *Memoirs* p.326.
[460] Mrs General de la Rey, *A Woman's wanderings and Trials during the Anglo-Boer War* (London, 1903) p. 13.

And what real advantage had accrued from his successes in the veldt? What had followed on them? All his cattle had been taken away, some three hundred of his men had been killed, wounded, or taken prisoner.[461]

Theirs was the victory of a cat on a hot tin roof and no more. And a legacy of tears and bitterness was created which, fortified by a 'stab-in-the-back' myth created by nationalist Afrikaaners after the war, is the bedrock of all those bar room accusations of British oppression and brutality and one of the foundation stones of Apartheid.

There are several keys to a successful insurgency and the Boer resistance lacked most of them. The most important is outside assistance to provide secure base areas where arms, training and supply can be organised; this could never be achieved while Britannia ruled the waves and British territory surrounded the republics. Next comes a political programme around which a sizeable disciplined minority can unite and impose their will on the majority; it's probably fair to say that most burghers in the republic were in favour of independence but not at the price of total ruin; and disciplined unity was never the strongpoint of the individualistic Boers. Nor was there much hope that the Cape Dutch would rise after Bloemfontein fell and nor was there any real political direction to the campaign. After this, a resistance must find some way to negate the force of a stronger enemy so that battles can be fought on their own terms; after some initial success, this advantage evaporated as the British changed their methods and became just as adept at veldt warfare as the Commandos and in greater numbers and equal skill. Finally, there must be some mechanism developed which is capable of undermining the enemy's political will to continue the struggle and although there was a group of 'pro-Boers' in Britain, they never commanded a fraction of the support that they claimed and which subsequent historians have accorded them.

The guerrilla war began just as Roberts began his march on Pretoria but at the start it was only a subsidiary tactic until Kruger fled and the country came fully under British dominion. De Wet who opened the campaign with a spectacular *ruse de guerre* at a place called Sannah's Post was quickly driven into a corner at Brandwater Basin, where 4000 of his compatriots surrendered, and then hunted and harried all the way to the Western Transvaal where he established a tenuous base in the rough scrub of the Marico and the Magaliesburg (present day Sun City and thereabouts). Understanding the changed nature of warfare, the British quickly adapted by breaking up the large Divisions and Brigades into smaller, mobile columns, usually between one and three thousand strong (sometimes smaller), often organised and reorganised on an *ad hoc* basis to suit local conditions; in short, Commandos. They were made up of a mix of cavalry, mounted infantry, the Imperial Yeomanry raised from the British countryside, locally raised colonial scouts from Joburg, the Cape, Natal and other colonies - backed up by the Bully Beef and Bayonet stoicism and dogged bloody-mindedness of the infantry of the Line plus Maxims and artillery. Being every bit at home with horse and gun as the Boers, the men employed were of similar metal, being born to the farm or the country, but with the advantage of having professional leadership and better logistics. And what leadership! For skill, experience and flexibility there was nothing to match it from top to bottom. Roberts had made his name by kicking the Afghans' arses from

---

[461] Quoted in C. de Wet, *Three Years War* (New York, 1902) Appendix C.

Kabul to Kandahar during the 2nd Afghan War while Buller won his VC leading a Commando against the Zulus in 1879; Milner and Kitchener had worked hand-in-glove in Egypt and the Sudan campaign; Smith-Dorrien had survived the massacre at Isandhlwana and Ian Hamilton had been present at Majuba; what Fred Carrington, Baden-Powell and Herbert Plumer didn't know about campaigning on the highveldt wasn't worth knowing; Johannes Colenbrander, a Cape Dutch loyalist had commanded a Zulu impi; while Allenby, French and Rawlinson would go onto hold high command and become household names during the First World War, there was a host of lesser known Colonels and Majors who proved themselves worth their Commissions day in and day out in command of columns; Broadwood, Babington, Scobell, de Beauvoir de Lisle, Thorneycroft, Kekewich, Sir Bindon Blood (Churchill's old boss from the North West Frontier) are just a few; and Douglas Haig, who, as the victorious commander of the British Armies in 1918 would ride down Whitehall on a white charger to the acclaim of hundreds and thousands of grateful citizens only to have his reputation trashed in the 1960s by a handful of doggerel poets and a hatful of pacifist English teachers; he thrashed one Commando leader after another. The only advantage that the Commando leaders retained was a knowledge of the country and a sympathetic civilian population, but these were finite resources; the Intelligence Branch, led by intellectuals such as G.F.R. Henderson (Oxford, Sandhurst, Tel-El-Kebir, Citations for Bravery, Professor of Military History, author of *Stonewall Jackson and the American Civil War*) steadily gathered field intelligence from the constant patrols that harvested local knowledge, geographical information, rumours, complaints, grievances and scuttlebutt from loyalists, prisoners, coloureds, blacks, 'hensoppers' – literally 'Hands-uppers' or surrendered Boers – cheesed off farmers and the usual snitches.

Having opened the guerrilla war, de Wet was now to find himself on the end of it. By the end of October, he had been beaten from pillar to post, failing to take the railway dorp of Frederikstad, losing his wagons on the 27th October at Rensburg Drift and what remained of his artillery on 6th November during the rout at Bothasville - all of which the old fraud glossed over in his memoirs. Taking the decision to double-back south, he was back in the Orange Free State in December – or Orange River Colony as it was now re-named – being chased by Thorneycroft and a host of other columns preparatory to his grand plan to invade the Cape Colony and foment the long hoped for but still elusive Cape rising. So effective was the pursuit that de Wet was forced to abandon this plan and break up his Commando into ever smaller units to avoid capture. This tactic is often quoted to show just how brilliant de Wet was but hiding a couple of thousand men in the rolling country of Southern Africa really is no feat at all; the Zulus had hidden 25,000 men a couple of miles from the British camp at Isandhlwana in 1879 despite the best efforts of the colonial reconnaissance forces (men who knew the country). In the lands up against the Basutoland border, places like Bethlehem, Vrede and the Golden Gate, it was the simplest task; I once saw a convoy of 4x4s drive into a hollow outside Vrede and disappear so completely, I thought the grass had swallowed them up. Towards the end of December he sent two small Commandos over the Orange River led by J.B.M. Herzog and Kritzinger only to find that the Cape government was immediately able to raise 10,000 volunteers to defend the towns against them and that the possession of the railway network allowed the British to concentrate column after column after column to chase him. The invasion came to nothing but a dusty and pointless tour of sparsely populated areas of desert and scrub before Kritzinger broke up his Commandos between Willowmore (where a rock has today been unflatteringly painted and named Malema after the Mugabe-wannabe leader of the Economic Freedom Fighters) and Steytlerville (the place with the gay German Cabaret) in a *sauve qui peut* to get away from Haig. De Wet finally managed to mount his invasion of the Cape on 10th February 1901, but the new commander in South Africa, Lord Kitchener, was well warned and was already engaging his rearguard as he headed south. The railways were once more pressed into service and the columns entrained and shifted more rapidly than any Commando straggling along with herds of sheep for food could hope to move. As soon as de Wet crossed the Orange, Plumer was onto him and what followed was a miserable straggle and headlong flight through terrible thunderstorms that turned the Karoo desert into bogs, forced him to abandon supply wagons and ammunition and advertised publicly to any burgher still hankering after a bit of trouble that de Wet was a busted flush rather than some sort of Scarlet Pimpernel. Field intelligence never lost touch with his flight westwards to Prieska – another dusty dorp such a long way from Cape Town that one has to question whether de Wet knew where Cape Town was at all – nor his doubling back towards Hopetown where, on 22nd February, an absolutely chin-strapped Plumer, riding three-quarters dead horses and absolutely and completely out of supplies, routed him and took all his guns. Dodging out from under the blow once more and abandoning his dismounted burghers, de Wet fled back along the Orange until, finding a little known drift, he managed to get his bedraggled tail beneath his hindquarters just long enough to get over it. Plumer pursued him for another twelve days before torrential rains and de Wet's dispersal of his Commandos brought the whole sorry episode to an end. Rather than acknowledging his staggering incompetence, de Wet claimed that his escape was due to Divine Intervention[462] – but then, of course, he was the sort of leader who needed it.

Bloody-minded stubborn defiance is fine quality to have; I'm a big fan of it myself. Without Winston Churchill's 1940 bloody-minded stubborn defiance in the face of Lord Halifax's appeasement, the demands of the Left to end the imperialist war against their fellow travelling Nazi chums in the Nazi-Soviet Pact, we would hardly be sitting here, feet up, glass in hand, making best use of the marvellous freedom to say and write whatever we think by ballooning about the world in the hope that civilised discourse might thereby alleviate some of its problems. Rather we would be either shivering to death in a dreadful Arctic Gulag as we mused on the delights of Socialism in One Country or kowtowing to some awful lederhosen-wearing Gauleiter banging on about the superiority of Aryan National Socialism while he gasses the Jews and we are left hoping that we get an Italian Dictator as our next ruler in the vain hope that perhaps slovenliness will temper despotism. *That said*, de Wet should have given up at this point. Firstly, because (unlike Britain in 1940) he had no hope of help from allies – if he read the papers he would have been aware of a joint Anglo-Russian-German-American-French and Japanese alliance forming against the Boxers in China; secondly because all the evidence so far pointed to peace on easy terms; thirdly, because there was absolutely no hope whatsoever of a rising in the Cape; fourthly, because he had been beaten in the field more times than he had had biltong for dinner and he had

---

[462] *Three Years War*. Ch.26.

absolutely no chance of winning the war; fifthly, Kitchener had just asked for, and got, an extra 30,000 mounted troops which was probably a number equal to or greater than the number of guerrillas that the Boers could field *in toto* and twice the number of prisoners already in the bag. And Kitchener *was* offering peace terms to General Louis Botha up at Middelburg which, though emphatically *not* a Majuba Miracle-style surrender, was an honourable *paix des braves*.

Roberts had called on the Boers to surrender in September 1900 after Kruger had decamped while Kitchener had been trying to get a peace deal from December onwards when he encouraged the formation of a Peace Committee in Pretoria and then allowed its members to go out to the Commandos and pass on the offer. Botha and Smuts had been in favour of talks when Pretoria fell but most of those who went out to the Commandos were berated as traitors and imprisoned; their leader Meyer de Kok was tried for treason and executed (Amery and Childers rather approved of this) while the emissary to de Wet was flogged and then murdered (which Amery and Childers decided was something that shouldn't be gone into *too* deeply in case it reflected badly on these marvellous new additions to the Empire).[463] In February 1901, Kitchener tried again at Middelburg when he offered Botha self-government under the British flag (after a certain period under direct government), funds for reconstruction, equal status for the English and Dutch languages and enfranchisement for whites and coloureds but not blacks. Botha was for taking the deal but he found his own government stubborn and de la Rey opposed. Steyn and de Wet were absolutely opposed (de Wet had blown up a train on his way to the peace negotiations)[464] and so, on his own initiative, rejected the terms and recommended the burghers reject them too, gratuitously adding the wholly untrue statement that the British wanted 'the destruction of our Afrikander people.'[465] This was yet another failure of a pig-headed leadership motivated only by hatred; what more did they want? All that Britain was asking for was that the Republics refrain from mistreating the natives (white and black) and stay away from the coastlines, yet these men, who we can only call unreasonable fanatics by this time, chose to fight to what they were prepared to call 'the bitter end'. They had failed in all their aims yet they still clung to them when all hope of success had gone and in this they failed in their duty as leaders of the *Volk*. Another terrible year of war beckoned. Amery's comment on this was about right:

> When the Boer leaders finally surrendered the terms of peace included not a single concession which the British Government would not have been prepared to grant after the fall of Pretoria, nearly two years earlier, or would not have granted if the war had continued to the capture of the last burgher.[466]

And Amery would have been absolutely spot on if he had added that the British Government would have offered these terms in 1899 to *avoid* the war had not Kruger's blind hatred and insistence on full sovereignty led him to start a war whose aim was the expulsion of Britain from southern Africa.

---

[463] Amery, *The Times History* Vol.V p.93.
[464] C. de Wet, *Three Years War* (New York, 1902), Ch.28
[465] Botha's communication to the Burghers 15th March 1901 quoted in *Maurice* Vol IV, p.527
[466] Amery, *The Times History*, Vol.V p.vii

\*

Lord Roberts had thought the war was over when Kruger fled and that the mopping up of diehards could be left to his deputy, Lord Kitchener. There had been a certain amount of guerrilla activity ever since de Wet had begun his attacks against the railways after the fall of Bloemfontein but it was generally thought that this would now cease. Proclamations were issued which guaranteed property as long as the oath of allegiance was held to and bade everyone get on with their lawful business. As the number of attacks began to increase, these proclamations became harsher in tone and reprisals were taken, mainly in the form of confiscation of livestock and the burning of farms and crops of those who had actively assisted the rebels; this was, of course, entirely justifiable, especially if the farms belonged to surrendered burghers who had been released on oath. When attacks against the railways were made, these reprisals were escalated into punishment of those in the neighbourhood who, it was assumed, must have helped the raiders; this was not justifiable by any stretch of the law. Though the burning of villages was regarded as acceptable practice on the North West Frontier of India, largely because conflict was usually the result of incursions into British territory, the idea of collective punishment went completely against the grain of English law, custom and practice and the practice was heavily criticised. This did not stop mistakes being made or indeed, vengeance being taken by those Natalians and Cape Colonials whose own farms had been looted and burned by the Boers in the earlier phase of the war but the practice also resulted in men going back to the Commandos out of sheer frustration. Unfortunately, it was a military necessity because many of the farms burnt were the supply and intelligence centres for the Commandos.

There was a further problem in that those burghers who had surrendered were subjected to a fair degree of intimidation by the Commandos in the field, often by threats to their families. Steyn was adamant that anyone who showed any inclination to impede the republican forces in any way whatsoever should face imprisonment or death; Botha believed that he had the right to conscript burghers at will and burn their farms if they would not; Smuts and de la Rey were not above executing those who had surrendered; de Wet's defence of recruiting oathbreakers in his memoirs gives some sense of the rage displayed towards those who were not convinced of the war's utility – he branded anyone who took the oath as a coward. This meant that anyone not minded to re-join the Commandos was caught between a rock and a hard place and, in the absence of Imperial forces to protect them, usually elected to go back to war. What was more, as the war dragged on the Commandos gradually changed from being full of respectable burghers fighting for their country to being increasingly staffed by 'the poorest and most ignorant class of *bywoners*…stealing and looting from the farmers who have surrendered' as Paul Botha, ex-*Volksraad* member for Kroonstadt complained.[467] Their treatment of blacks was notorious right from the beginning. Here is General Ben Viljoen persuading a Zulu to help him during the retreat from Elandslaagte:

> "If you will show me the way to the Biggersbergen I will give you 5s. on account." My amiable and dusky friend insisted on 7s. 6d., but after I had intimated that if he did not accept 5s. I should certainly burn his entire outfit, slaughter all his women and

[467] Quoted in C. Ash, *Kruger's War* p.326.

kill all his cattle, he acquiesced. A young Zulu was deputed as my guide, but I had to use my fists and make pretty play with my revolver, and generally hint at a sudden death, or he would have left me in the lurch.[468]

Bill Nasson's account of *Abraham Esau's War* was seminal in revealing the terrible brutality to which the Commandos would go to dissuade coloured people from aiding the British in what was, to all intents and purposes, an undeclared war between poor whites and poor blacks in the countryside. Here a coloured blacksmith, Abraham Esau, working out in the dusty dorp of Calvinia was the victim of continued pillaging by Free State forces and was thus swept into leadership when rumours of a Boer approach led the local people to demand weapons for self-defence. When these were refused, he formed a rag-tag militia with improvised arms and with predictable results when faced with occupation in January 1901 by a couple of Free State Commandos. The population was quickly reduced to conditions akin to slavery, the sjambok was wielded without much discrimination and Esau was arrested. Dragged before the Veldtcornet, he was lashed, beaten, dragged behind a horse for five miles, beaten again and finally shot the day before British forces chased the Boers out of the town.

Despite the obvious difference being that Britain won the war, it has become commonplace to see this phase of the war as being something akin to the American experience in Vietnam but the reality is rather different. What was happening was a general breakdown of law and order, the destruction of any sort of personal security for life or property and the disruption of farming and commerce on a grand scale by British forces, Boer forces and the many banditti that took advantage of the situation to engage in robbery, muder and general freebooting. What had begun by the Boers as a war of conquest now became a devil's trident of civil war, civil breakdown and guerrilla war and nothing that Botha, de Wet, de la Rey, Smuts or any of the other irresponsible leaders of the *Volk* could do would change things. And every month, the British ground them down a little more in a thousand patrol actions, a thousand farm burnings, a thousand skirmishes; figures for the first quarter of 1901 showed that 1888 Boers were unnecessarily killed or wounded while 223 either surrendered voluntarily or were taken prisoner; for the second the figures were 1143 and 982; for the third 946 and 5281 respectively; and for the fourth quarter 715 and 4073. Mile by mile, the protection of the railways was improved by the building of blockhouses and the construction of barbed wire entanglements, by the use of armoured trains and the deployment of Railway Guard companies and Railway Repair units, so that British logistic security and strategic mobility was protected and that of the Boers restricted. Slowly but surely, both the Bitter-enders and their supports drained away.

One of the unseen consequences of the guerrilla war was the question of civilian refugees. Whenever a farm was burned, a destitute family was created and it formed no part of the British plan to wage war on women, children and the aged but no provision had been made for this situation because no-one envisaged a guerrilla war. This situation was complicated by the willingness of the Commandos to abandon their families to the care of the British (Kruger included: he left his wife behind when he ran for Holland) and while Roberts had, at first, tried to organise transport for them to remove to Republican held areas, the practice was

---

[468] Ben Viljoen, *My Reminiscences of the Anglo-Boer War* (London, 1912).

halted because the families were abandoned a second time. The first responses were *ad hoc*; makeshift camps were set up on the outskirts of military posts, followed by the establishment of bigger ones on the outskirts of the towns where they were quickly filled up by families of surrendered or loyalist Afrikaaners. After the rejection of his peace overtures at Middelburg, Kitchener then took the decision to depopulate the veldt by bringing Boer families in off the farms and so deprive the Commandos of supplies and as the war degenerated into miserable and formless civil strife, the numbers of both the refugees and the incarcerated increased. This was a recipe for disaster because the army was having enough difficulty feeding itself and because many of the Boers from the Boonies were unused to living in large concentrations that required a higher degree of sanitation than the family *windpomp* and *kakhuis* they were used to. Disease was already rife among the troops – the dreaded Enteric – and when a measles outbreak struck, the results in the camps were devastating. The resultant scandal brought about the appearance of that most formidable weapon of British social reform – the Ladies Committee – and conditions were rapidly ameliorated but not before there had been terrible mortality. This was to lead to all sorts of accusations of vile British brutality after the war but we'll leave the task of sorting out that myth from reality for a later volume. Suffice it to say that Kitchener had offered Botha a deal at Middelburg whereby he would leave the farms alone if the Commandos would do likewise; Botha refused, leaving Kitchener with little choice but to send the unfortunate people involved into the camps.

The establishment of the camps, by relieving the Boers of the responsibility of feeding their families, also contributed to the one remaining advantage that the Boers possessed – their mobility – and it was this that led to the construction of Kitchener's blockhouse lines. Originally intended to protect railway bridges and culverts, these were small pre-fab forts manufactured by the Royal Engineers for the knock down price of £16 a go which could be erected and improved quickly and then held by a token force of ten or so men. Connected together by barbed wire, supported by trenches and laid out so that rifles and guns from one fort could support its neighbours, they were never designed to prevent the movement of Commandos but rather to impede and report it. A herd of cattle could be driven against the wire to breach it, but a wagon could not cross the subsequent trench and a force of riders could not gallop past without being noticed and their whereabouts telegraphed back to HQ. Huge strings of these forts were laid out; the Harrismith to Bethlehem line was fifty miles long with 134 blockhouses and two fortified posts garrisoned by 1894 men or thirty-eight men to the mile.[469] Commandos could and did cross these lines almost at will – but never without being noticed and thus giving away their position and direction of travel. Commando communications between the different parts of the country also suffered so that few men knew either the movements, plans or state of their compatriots in other parts of the country. The wire was gradually strangling them.

All this had its effect and in May 1901, Smuts, Louis Botha, Reitz and what remained of the Transvaal government met at Ermelo to discuss the situation and came to the unanimous decision that peace must be concluded and that someone must go to Europe to consult with Kruger. This was to be done whether the Free State government agreed or not and President

---

[469] *Maurice* Vol. 4 p.572.

Steyn was duly informed. Steyn was livid and demanded that all talk of peace should be scotched until de la Rey and de Wet had been consulted and only then should the two governments meet to discuss the way forward. More farms burned, more burghers were shot, wounded or surrendered, more Afrikaaners were consigned to the camps and when a telegram came from Kruger on 5th July telling Botha to fight on, the same futile process of the cat burning its paws on the corrugated iron roof went on for another eleven months. In July, the Free State government itself was scooped up by a column with Steyn running for it *sans broekies* while throughout that southern winter the Commandos were driven out of the Cape, Botha was defeated in Natal, de la Rey's attacks were beaten off at Moedwill and one by one the Commando leaders were captured.

In September, Smuts (now, finally, as a General, eligible for the Transvaal franchise) invaded the Cape where lay, as Maurice put it, 'the forces of money, brains, organisation and a statesmanship only awaiting the proper hour to reveal itself'[470] but this was just another futile dream. Any appetite for rebellion among the solid Cape farmers had long drained away; they had witnessed the stream of troops, they had read about the endless defeats and learned of the terrible nature of the war from refugees and relatives in the camps or fleeing to the Cape; smallpox and the plague had broken out in Cape Town; they knew what a burning field looked like and knew just what it would take to rebuild a 16th Century farmhouse; and Schreiner's ministry had fallen, to be replaced by the pro-British Gordon Spriggs and the declaration of martial law. In October, 1901, a delegation of Afrikaaner clergymen had urged Steyn to take his Commandos away from the areas occupied along the Orange River and this was significant because the church had been one of the main fomenters of rebellion before the war had started.[471] Something else was happening too; the National Scouts had been formed from surrendered Boers – including de Wet's own brother - convinced that the war was pointless and willing to take up arms against their former comrades to make sure it came to an end much sooner than later. The mines on the Rand were re-started and the Uitlanders were going home; an increasing number of burghers were beginning to regard the Commandos as no more than foolish diehards and banditti. The end was nigh.

Smuts struck towards Port Elizabeth in yet another one of those terrible strategic blunders which guaranteed defeat; here again Maurice was rightly scathing of Smuts:

> ...the country was too difficult, the barriers too numerous, the hostile communications, lengthy though they were, too well guarded, and the objectives too few. It was comparatively easy for the British commanders to cut up the terrain into so many enclosures, and so quickly to transfer the fencing, that the commandos, though they might long escape actual arrest, were always either in prison or flying from one corral to another.[472]

Even if Smuts had actually taken Port Elizabeth, it would have made no difference because that city was still a long way from the heartlands of the Cape. His decision to send a couple of Commandos down the Atlantic seashore was undoubtedly a correct one – *if* he had made it

---

[470] *Maurice* Vol. IV p.349
[471] *Amery* Vol. V. p. 538
[472] *Maurice* Vol. IV p.349

the main thrust, *if* it had been attempted at the beginning of the war – but by now, with the limited resources available it was utterly hopeless. In October, Commandant Saloman Maritz ran down through Clanwilliam to Malmesbury, the centre of the great granary of the Swartland, with a ragged band only 500 strong, but the British columns were already coming up and the only recruits he could find had neither horses nor arms; an attempt to get them by raiding the garrison at Piketberg ended in failure. Losing touch with his subordinate Commandos, Maritz fled north to besiege…Tontelbosch Kolk, fifty miles north-east of Calvinia, a place that was so useless and so far in the middle of nowhere that the garrison was in the process of packing up and going home when this Boer Napoleon laid siege to it. Down to 400 men by this time, Maritz was then shot and chased off by a relief column. Smuts was reduced to trying to raid a convoy going into Calvinia from Clanwilliam; I've driven that road and if you can't mount a successful ambush there, then you can't mount a successful ambush anywhere; Smuts failed and his desperate band fled.

Nor did Boer successes make any difference. On 7th March 1902, de la Rey famously ambushed Lord Methuen's camp at Tweefontein and took him prisoner while at the end of the month, he captured another convoy but none of it made any difference because, one by one, over the summer of 1901-2 the Commandants were rounded up, their laagers captured, and those who were left driven into ever more marginal areas; de Wet put his defeats down to having sinned against the Lord; by April 1902, Maritz was capturing Springbok and Smuts was besieging Okiep. Why?

The great South African short story writer, Herman Charles Bosman, gave the answer and in doing so summed up the absurdity of the Boer position at Okiep, and everywhere else, from Middelburg onwards.

> Eventually Herklaas van Wyck reined in his horse. His hand shielding his eyes, he gazed for a long while at the place where the sea and sky met on the horizon. He had known two years before that the Boer War was lost for the Transvaal and the Free State. One last hope had returned to him, early that morning, when he had caught sight of the ocean. That hope, too, had vanished now. He realised that he would not be able, with the handful of burghers under his command, to invade England….
>
> 'It's no good, kêrels,' he called out above the roar of the waves and the wind. 'We'll have to go back again. There's no drift around here where we'll be able to get our horses through.'[473]

The game was up.

Negotiations began in April 1902 when safe passage was granted to Steyn, de Wet, de la Rey, Schalk Burgher and Reitz to meet at Pretoria to discuss terms with Kitchener and Milner. Steyn, fanatically and fantastically stupid to the last, demanded independence; Milner offered the Middelburg terms and when news came in that de la Rey's Commando had been hammered at Roodewal, the delegates asked for an armistice which would allow them to consult Kruger and the burghers in general. Kruger was ruled out but the second request was

---

[473] H.C. Bosman, *A Boer Rip van Winkel*.

partly acceded to and a national convention was arranged for May 15th at Vereeniging where representatives of the burghers still on Commando would be given immunity and free passage to make their deliberations; those who weren't representatives would still be waged war upon until the 12th. Reitz, Botha and Burgher were of a mind to accept a peace and sensing this, Steyn stomped off in disgust and took no further part in accepting the inevitable while de Wet rode up and down the ruined farms, splintered trees, burned out grassland and wasted orchards of the Free State on a Free Pass exhorting what was left of his men to stand firm and continue the fight.

Smuts, rather more cerebral than the blinkered, boastful de Wet, was given passage by sea to Cape Town to attend the conference, joining 59 other representatives, most of them Commando leaders, and played a crucial role in persuading the Free Staters, who de Wet had only allowed to attend on condition that they rejected the peace terms, that they could vote as independent men, rather than mouthpieces of de Wet. He also pointed out that the principal object of the war – the seizing of Cape Colony by rebellion and the expulsion of British influence – was beyond failure. Though many other delegates pledged resistance, few held out hope of ultimate victory. Many voiced fears that the black people they preyed on for supplies were become restless – a Zulu impi had wiped out a laager at Holkrans – even though de Wet talked balderdash about the Basutos being friendly; and the scorched earth plus the continued attrition tactics that had put half the Commandos in the grave or jail already could only grow worse. Reitz came up with the idiotic idea that Britain could be bought off by being handed the goldfields and in doing do proved just how unfit for the work of a statesman he was. Louis Botha laid out the real situation:

> The blockhouses were an intolerable obstruction, and were likely to prove the ruin of the commandos; food was scarce; horses were weak and few; the sufferings of the women were terrible, now that the British had ceased taking them into the concentration camps; foreign intervention was a dream; a general rising in Cape Colony was out of the question; the enforced abandonment of so many districts had allowed the British to concentrate their efforts in crushing force on the remainder; lastly - weightiest reason of all perhaps with the speaker - their own people were turning against them. "If we continue the war, it may be that the Afrikanders against us will outnumber our own men." By all means let them cede the gold-fields, "that cancerous growth," if such a partial cession was possible; if not, let them save their country by making the best terms possible. Terms might still be secured which would save the language, customs and ideals of the people. The fatal thing was to secure no terms at all and yet be forced to surrender.[474]

De la Rey nailed it. Fight to the bitter end? This *was* the bitter end. De Wet still thought that God would save them but went along with Smuts, Herzog, de la Rey and Botha to talk to Milner and Kitchener on the basis not of surrender and annexation but of the acceptance of a protectorate and an alliance with Britain: Smuts and Herzog the lawyers were behind this pretzel logic of course. Milner (also a lawyer) and Kitchener kicked it straight into touch; surrender and annexation it would be on the Middelburg terms modified in the detail but not

---
[474] *Amery* Vol V. p. 589

the substance. This was a reasonable deal and probably better than any conquered (or near-conquered) nations could reasonably expect to get; the delegates were sent back to Vereeniging with instructions to accept or reject the deal within three days or face the renewal of the war.

The debate that ensued was one between the pragmatists who recognised that they could not long resist the might of British arms and should get a deal while they were still in the field - the Commandos were cracking; the country was devastated; help from Europe had failed and the Cape had not risen; it was time – and the fanatics who simply refused to face facts, de Wet being chief among them. His alternative was resistance based on the continued hope of European intervention and, even less likely, that of the Divine, until Britain offered better terms. His speech to the convention betrayed a complete ignorance of the political world beyond the Vaal and the intellectual vacuity of the conspiracy theorist. One of his supporters offered up the touching view that 'it was in the Hands of God – He would take care of it. Right must conquer in the end';[475] General Muller thought that another Covenant with the Lord on Blood River lines was the way forward. Steyn refused even to hear the word 'peace' uttered and resigned as President of the Orange Free State (and then surrendered in order to get treatment at a British hospital: thus did the second of the two prime movers of this pointless, destructive and depressing war abandon his people at the moment when the really hard decisions had to be faced). Botha, Smuts, both of whom had had their earlier fanaticism tempered by Buller's Maxims and Lee-Metfords and de la Rey (who had actually gone to war with his own pet prophet but had since come to the realisation that the Bible was no protection against a 4.7inch gun) prevailed. The terms were accepted on a vote of 54:6. The war was over. The Boers were beaten.

\*

\*

## 1066

It is certain that Kruger never read Clausewitz *On War* and a pretty fair guess that it was a mystery to Botha, de la Rey and de Wet. Smuts probably had come across him but as he had no real hand in the direction of the Boer war until the end his erudition was redundant. Sir Alfred Milner, educated in Germany and steeped in an atmosphere of debate around military reform, Home and Imperial defence, conscription and Imperial Federation almost certainly had read Clausewitz and taken his most famous dictum to heart: *War is the continuation of politics by other means.* Milner had come to South Africa with an imperial vision, the Confederation of the country into a British-led bastion on the route to India and a full part of the Imperial family of nations, all to be achieved through peaceful persuasion, using the Uitlander franchise to undermine the Kruger regime and allowing the natural run of commerce to create a body of interest that would see more advantage in the British connection than in a backward and corrupt Boer republic. When Kruger's ambition of

---

[475] *De Wet* Appendix C.

'Africa for the Africander' boiled over into aggression in 1899, Milner's aim did not change, but the carrot turned into the stick.

Once Bloemfontein had fallen, Milner wanted to go back to dangling the carrot but the Bitterenders, now pursuing no aim but a vague desire for the preservation of their independence, meant that the stick would still be plied, liberally and with gusto but whereas the Bitterenders had no strategy to bring about the achievement of their aim under the changed and unexpected circumstances of defeat, Milner did. The aim was still Confederation but his reading of Clausewitz allowed him to understand and put into practice the principle that military force is only one part of the toolkit of politics. The defeat of the Commandos would be accomplished as much by politics as by war and that defeat would begin with the restoration of normality to Joburg; the mines would be opened up, the Uitlanders returned and the railways and associated infrastructure protected. Milner had no doubt also studied the previous experience of Sir Bartle Frere, the last proconsul to attempt Confederation, and his approach to the delicate matter of how to conquer and then reconcile a nation to that conquest, was almost identical. 'The essence of the whole business,' Frere had written in 1865,

> is first to put down all violence with a strong hand; then, your force being known, felt and respected, endeavour to excite men's better nature, till all men seeing that your object is good and of the greatest general benefit to the community, join heart and hand to aid in putting down or preventing violence.[476]

So, while Milner left Kitchener to apply the strong hand, he would concentrate on restoring normality first to the Rand and then, using the surrendered Boers, to spread that normality out to the farming areas, until the Commandos would be forced to realise that the destruction of their own country could only result in the erosion of the unity of their own people and the emergence of an Uitlander-Hensopper alliance. This policy of development would also lift the new colonies onto an entirely different level of existence, as contented, prosperous, loyal entities thriving under British and Imperial institutions. The strategy, of course, went right over the heads of the Boer leadership who continued to gallop about in marginal areas on pointless errands of destruction but by the end of the war, the Rand mines had been restored to a third of their productive capacity and 45,000 people had returned to work there, helped by a Refugees Aid department which disbursed substantial grants, handed out cooking pots and beds and generally helped to get those former residents of Joburg back on their feet; 10,000 children were back in school too. A Personnel and Property Inquiry Department was set up to restore to their former owners the vast amounts of property that the Boers had looted as well as locating missing persons; the reunions were no doubt joyful. On top of this, the mines were brought under the control of the Joburg municipality and made to pay rates (plus a 10% tax to fund reconstruction).

Elsewhere, the ramshackle civil service was reformed, the utterly disgusting prison administration turned out and a Public Health Department begun; the 'medieval horrors of the

---

[476] Frere to Lord Elphinstone, Governor of Bombay 28th May 1855, quoting his mentor General Sir John Jacob. IOR MSS EUR F.75/7 No. 49. John Jacob Collection.

lunatic and leper departments'[477] were thankfully ended and a Public Works Department was opened; these were things that had been accomplished a generation ago in Britain and since proved their worth. Legal reform was not neglected, the Transvaal constitution was torn up and a system of justice was instituted which did away with Kruger's kangaroo courts; Posts, Customs and revenue collection were organised; the scourge of rinderpest was addressed by the Bacteriological Department rather than, under the former system, prayers. The Education Department was particularly successful in starting schools in the camps and shipping out teachers from Britain and the Empire to add to the Dutch staff who were already there; the potential for reconciliation as Boer women met British women, and Boer children learned English from British teachers, was here enormous. And education was not limited to children; the Agricultural department sent many surrendered Boers out on tours to Canada, Australia and New Zealand to study modern farming methods. Reconciliation would also go alongside the eventual repatriation of Boer prisoners and camp inmates to their farms and a register was established among them to ascertain the nature and state of their needs and the resources of livestock and seed corn that they would need to re-establish themselves and by April 1902, the Repatriation Department was more or less ready to dole out whatever was needed from the captured supplies. Milner's strategy worked: one of the Commando delegates at Vereeniging paid unwitting tribute to it when he declared that 'If we continue the war, it may be that the Afrikanders against us will outnumber our own men.'[478]

When the surrender came, the focus of the administration shifted to the immediate problems of repatriation and resettlement. Virtually the whole *volk* was in British hands; 110,000 in the camps, 4,500 serving with the British Army, 7,000 PoWs in jail or on parole in South Africa and another 24,000 in camps as far apart as Ceylon, St. Helena and Bermuda. Perhaps only 30,000 men, women and children were self-supporting with another 20,000 still on Commando. In addition, almost 100,000 black Africans had also been kept in the camps and these too were sent back to the farms as stockmen and labourers, while at the same time 200,000 British, Australian, Canadian and New Zealand soldiers were on the ration strength and waiting to be repatriated. And the result of the Bitter-enders resistance meant that the whole infrastructure of rural life lay in smoking ruins. If reconciliation was to be achieved then Milner would need to be open handed as regards the practical wants and needs of people who would face a mighty struggle to start their lives again and in this, he was not found wanting: he would, he said, 'not stand fiddling over small economies while people starved.'[479] Clothes and blankets were handed out to returning prisoners; transport animals, carriages and military stores were issued by local committees; the blockhouses and barbed wire became building materials and stock fences; tools, food, everything from 'ox-wagons to wooden legs'[480] were either issued free or supplied at cost price; those who didn't have money had access to soft loans on easy terms; pretty much everyone who applied got £25, roughly the equivalent of six months wages for an average English working man. When a family was ready to return to its farm, they went with tools, a wagon, livestock, seeds, bedding, tents and a month's rations all paid for by the British taxpayer and when it came time to plant, the

---

[477] *Amery* Vol VI p.30
[478] *Amery* Vol V. p. 589
[479] Milner quoted in *Amery* Vol VI p.145
[480] *Amery* Vol VI p.48

government got over the shortage of plough oxen by sending out teams to break enough ground on each farm to provide enough of a crop to keep famine away for a year; in the event a drought caused the first crop to fail, so the British taxpayer fed them for another year. In the end, direct relief, loans, payments for requisitions, compensation for damages caused added up to over £20 million; even black Africans got £300,000; considering that the Boers had started the war, that the Bitter-enders refusal of terms at Middelburg had prolonged the war unreasonably and that there was no Treaty obligation to pay anything over £3 million whatsoever, this was both an act of astounding generosity on the part of the victors and an indication of the lengths Britain was prepared to go to achieve reconciliation. In addition to this, Britain guaranteed a loan of £35 million to pay off the debts of the Boer Republics, compensate the colonists of Natal for the damage the Boers had done in the invasion of 1899, buy up that locomotive of corruption the Netherlands Railway Company, extend the railway network and provide public works. It did Britain no good; according to Amery, the Boers quibbled, cavilled and considered themselves to have been bilked. I'm tempted to add *as usual*.

Much the same could be said of the attitude of the Boer leadership. When the tattered remnants of their battered armies surrendered, the Boer leadership was treated with every consideration and courtesy. When Denis Reitz, son of the man who had penned the Boer Ultimatum, went with Smuts to the peace conference at Vereeniging, he noted the individual kindness and the guards of honour provided by both great and small and, not least, the clean sheets and good food provided in the First Class section of the ships and railways he was transported on. When the Commandos surrendered their weapons, the British provided them with rations and offered a *paix des braves* piss-up afterwards – though Reitz junior noted that his father's Commando broke their rifles rather than hand them over; this sort of behaviour was to be expected from a sour-faced clod like Reitz senior though. As far as the British were concerned, the defeated Boers were now fellow citizens rather than conquered subjects and they accepted that they would come very quickly to form a political party which might oppose the policies that Milner was to impose upon them. It had been part of the deal that self-government would be returned to South Africa as soon as was practicable on pretty much the old terms; as long as Britain controlled foreign policy and the Boers didn't treat the Natives too badly, they would be left alone. It was Britain's fervent hope that Boer, Briton, the rest of the Europeans (and in due course, the black Africans) would come together and form a new South African identity in the same way that Canada and the Australasian colonies were in the process of achieving.

Such an opposition already existed in the Cape parliament and though the Schreiner ministry had hardly been whole-hearted in support of the war effort, and the Bond even less, Joe Chamberlain had resisted all calls to suspend the Cape constitution because he believed that parliaments were entitled to do and say whatever they thought best as long as they stayed this side of treason. This was deep within the British ideal; banging up political opponents in jail was both tempting and satisfying but it was really no solution in the longer term and the attachment to *habeus corpus* was profound. The British Empire was not the Russian Empire and though it would no doubt have saved a lot of time and heartache to have carried out a Katyn-style massacre on the Bitter-enders, it went against the instinctive British values of fair play, tolerance and not being beastly. Indeed, the fact that Milner and Kitchener had dealt with the Boers remaining in the field, rather than those who had recognised reality and gone home, had effectively recognised them as the *de facto* leaders of the Afrikaaner people in the Transvaal and the Free State. It was therefore in no small measure the attitude of Botha, Smuts, de la Rey, de Wet and the other Commando leaders that needed to be changed if reconciliation was to become a reality and it was hoped that a display of magnanimity would achieve it. In this, the British were to be sorely tested.

From the outset greed, bad manners and stupidity were the characteristics displayed by the Boer Bitter-ender leadership. They began by demanding that only they and their adherents should be entitled to a share of that £3 million *ex gratia* payment. Then they were in the forefront of those complaining about the slowness with which British public servants - who were still a generation or two away from mastering the arts of handing out taxpayers' money without scruple, receipt or good reason - handed out the vast largesse coming their way. Reitz refused to sign the oath of allegiance despite having signed the instrument of surrender and, stamping his little feet, chose exile instead. In June 1902, Botha, Smuts, de Wet and the other generals went on a tour to Europe with the dual aims of raising a large Widows and Orphans fund and seeing Kruger; and then, when presented by public demonstrations of support by the Bond at the Cape and then by the pro-Boers in Britain, they preened themselves so fabulously that they felt entitled to snub the King-Emperor himself when, after receiving them on his yacht, he extended an invitation to them to attend the Coronation Naval Review. They pleaded a prior engagement and went to Holland.

Pride cometh before a fall. Despite the fact that Kruger had failed in all his aims to create a Greater Afrikaanerdom and had left the country defeated, occupied and in ruins, they still thought that his advice was worth listening to and sent in a list of demands to the British government that could have been written by the busted flush himself: complete amnesty, massive compensation, reinstatement of all republican officials, restoration of the Vryheid district from Natal to the Transvaal. Kruger thought this was 1881 not 1902 and the generals agreed. Chamberlain was not Gladstone though and they were sent away with a flea in their ears. They then issued an appeal to the 'Civilised World' which neglected any mention of British generosity, ramped up all sorts of bogus accusations against the British and portrayed themselves, once again, as poor helpless victims of the imperial bully rather than the defeated representatives of two acquisitive, aggressive minor republics. All this achieved was to undercut any sympathy that the British pro-Boers were able to garner for them and as they went off to Paris and Berlin in the hope of tugging on the heartstrings of those who had promised so much and provided so little in their hour of need, they began to look like nothing more than bogus beggars panhandling on a street corner; they came away with a few farthings, a couple of spare *sous* and the odd *pfenning* but nothing more. The biggest donation of £20,000, almost 20%, came from the Carnegie Trust, but only on the proviso that it should not be used for any anti-British purpose. The total raised was roughly 4% of the £3 million that Britain had already promised. *Pride cometh before a fall* and money talks; in this case it shouted in Louis Botha's ear that the only viable future for the Afrikaaner people lay in being part of the British Empire and he and Smuts decided to listen to it. Back in England in November, he suddenly became anxious to explain away the Continental tour.

Chamberlain reacted with a generosity they did not deserve and told them their people would be succoured, their country would be re-built but that it would be under the British flag – and he was coming personally to see that this was done. When he got to the Cape in January 1903, Botha, Smuts, de la Rey and Piet Cronjie appeared with him at a public banquet to signal that reconciliation was their chosen route and a couple of days later in Pretoria, Smuts assembled a hundred leading Boers, and in order to let them know in person who they were dealing with presented Chamberlain with a repeat of the demands that they had made back in September. Chamberlain told them not to be so ungrateful, that they would get a fair hearing for fair grievances but the surrender terms would be adhered to and that was that. It sank in finally that the pusillanimous spirit of Gladstone could not be conjured up from his mouldering grave no matter how hard the pro-Boers chanted their invocations of appeasement; Chamberlain and Milner were given a round of applause led by Botha himself. Even the boneheaded de Wet was forced to come to this conclusion when in February 1903, he and Barry Herzog, the future founder of the National Party, attempted to give Chamberlain a good slagging off by presenting him with an insulting address claiming that only the Bitter-enders (ie., him) should get that £3 million. It wasn't to be expected that the de Wet would be any more successful in debate as he was in invading Cape Colony, but even the lawyer Herzog couldn't hold a candle to the experienced parliamentarian and Chamberlain 'in the most scathing fashion proceeded to pull the charges to pieces.'[481] The deputation applauded Chamberlain; de Wet never mentioned it in his memoirs; Herzog spent two hours trying to calm Chamberlain down.[482] The war *was* actually over.

Politics wasn't though; when Chamberlain offered Smuts, de la Rey and Botha positions on the Transvaal Legislative Council they refused on the principle that until the government was elected, then they would decline to take responsibility for any decisions made. Our old friend Percy Fitzpatrick took the offer though and so brought the voice of the Uitlander into the government for the first time; virtually its first act was to bring in a system of elected local government. The Bond remained suspicious, though Hofmeyr also accepted that the war was over too, and when the drought of 1903 hit, Afrikaaner politicians of many hues took the opportunity to blame the resulting hardship on the British government.

This was politics as usual, even if the whining was utterly undignified, and made worse by the fact that there was plenty of work available on the Rand where the reluctance of black Africans to go back to the compounds until the wages went up had created all sorts of opportunities for white labour. In the Afrikaaner mind, however, this was 'Kaffir' work and if the mines needed labour then black Africans should be forced to do it; while the old Uitlanders were not averse to a bit of hard graft, they were used to supervisory roles and the increased wages that went with them. As far as the mine owners were concerned, not even skilled white labour was the answer because the low grade nature of the ore meant that it was quantity not quality that was the key and their answer was to bring in Chinese labour. This, to understate the situation, was not a universally popular view, the general feeling being that complicating the racial picture in South Africa any further would be unwise, yet everything

---

[481] *Amery* Vol VI p.93.
[482] http://www.pelteret.co.za/content/000162/A-Blink-in-History-the-visit-of-Joseph-Chamberlain-to-Bloemfontein-February-1903.pdf

depended on the productivity of the mines. They were the key to industry, to prosperity, to raising the taxes necessary for development, to providing the economic underpinning to the coming Union. Milner was straight out for Chinese labour but he realised that he could not proceed in advance of a Transvaal public opinion that was implacably hostile and organising itself into the White League. Here was the first clash brewing between benevolent colour-blind capitalism and racist Trade Unionism. (And as that is the sort of sentence to get the Trots leaping up and down with rage, I'll just tie the bunjee and invite them towards the abyss by saying that the White League were joined by the African Labour League shortly afterwards. And then I'll invite the Trots to step fully off the platform by saying that the white miners went on strike in November 1903 against the employment of *Italians*).

Alternatives were tried; navvies from England were brought in to lay the railways but they proved to be four times as expensive as black Africans; indentured labour was sought from India but the Raj refused to supply Indians on the terms offered; Africans from different parts of the continent suffered from diseases that they were not exposed to in climates warmer than the bracing cold of the Joburg winter; TB was rife and a killer; conditions in the compounds were improved in an attempt to get the horrendous death rates down from 120 per thousand to 30. None of them worked and by the end of 1903 the pressure of financial facts and economic reality resulted in the Chamber of Mines getting their way, having sponsored a petition in favour of Chinese labour which drew 45,000 signatures or 50% of the white adult male population of the Transvaal (which says something about the limits of the acceptance of Social Darwinist theories of race). In February 1906 the necessary legislation was passed and the way opened for the importation of Chinese indentured labour.

As I've said elsewhere, I spent six happy and profitable years as an indentured servant in Abu Dhabi in the 1990s and hundreds of thousands (millions?) of workers all over the world have been indentured. It isn't slavery and the experience depends entirely on the nature of the deal but the common features are that it is entered into voluntarily, is for a fixed period of time, with stated benefits and penalties and includes the costs of passage. When the labour recruiters headed for Hong Kong and China in 1904, the deal on offer was neither the best nor the worst but it was certainly attractive. Workers were engaged for three years, were restricted to the job they were recruited for – unskilled labour on the Rand – and they would be returned to their place of origin at the end of the contract. This last stipulation had been insisted upon to prevent the Chinese from settling in South Africa as the Indian indentured labour had done and far from being a heartless capitalist imposition, it represented quite a hefty extra expense to the mine owners who would have to pay the cost of those passages. Without it, however, the White League would have gone out on strike and brought the mines to a halt. None of this stopped the Liberals in Britain from whipping up vile charges of 'Chinese Slavery' against the government in one of the most vicious and cynical political campaigns in British history, nor prevent British working men protesting about the under-cutting of wages by introducing starving Chinese peasants just to fill up the pockets of greedy capitalists.[483] One of the more bizarre scare stories put about was that Chinese labourers were to be imported into North Wales to work in the slate quarries. Needless to say, once the

---

[483] See *The Spectator* http://archive.spectator.co.uk/article/15th-october-1904

Liberal government got into office in 1906, partially on the back of this campaign, they ended the scheme and in doing so prevented thousands of poor Chinese from getting a job; they even offered to pay the fares home of those 'slaves' who wished to terminate their contract early; few took the opportunity. (And at the same time, as the 1906 *Report into Poor Whites* revealed, destitute white children were being indentured across Cape Colony as a means of getting them into employment and out of the orphanages). Meanwhile, by 1905, 50,000 Chinese had taken up the offer and were busy down the mines, the gold was coming up, and like miners everywhere, the Chinese were spending it in the local economy. Even the white miners were happy because they were now promoted to supervise the Chinese workers. The threat of recession receded.

The Rand was the key, but Milner was interested in developing the country as a whole and in the period between 1905-7, he doubled the length of the railway. This, of course, was a major stimulus to production in areas that had previously had only restricted access to markets but it was followed in short order by the replacement of forty drifts by bridges, the extension of the telephone and telegraph network, improvement of water supplies and a massive building programme on anything from schools to jails, the most famous result of which was Herbert Baker's magnificent Government House at Pretoria. On a more prosaic, but no doubt equally welcome level, the British garrison at Potchfstroom also paid for a golf course, whose 19th hole was a spittoon in the local hotel bar. It isn't too much to say either that Milner's agricultural reforms laid the foundation of a new and more prosperous future for the countryside which within a very few years would challenge the mines for their dominant position in the economy.

Looking back on Milner's tenure as a whole, you just can't fail to be impressed. The transformation he effected was remarkable and, whether they liked it or not, the Afrikaaners were now living in colonies that were far better than the republics they had thrown into the balance against the weight of the British Empire. There was a functioning and honest government, a growing economy and an improved agricultural sector, an education system which encouraged reading beyond the limits of the Bible, a transport system which promised routine communication at speeds in advance of the ox-wagon and the pont at the swollen drift and a network of telephones and cables that connected more of the two colonies into the wider commercial world (and up them came the all-important Bills of Exchange and Lading). There was also a recognition that the problems of the 'races' and nationalities would also need some creative thought if a harmonious and specifically South African nationality was to be created; and this meant black African, Coloured, Indian and Chinese as well as Boer and Briton. In a world where we see politicians routinely confining themselves to footling around the edges of a focus group or tinkering with the details of an agenda set by mendacious journalists, Milner painted with a broad brush stroke and, mimicking the Lawrence brothers in the newly conquered Punjab during the 1840s, he employed energetic and intelligent young men who were likewise unafraid to take a decision and make a mistake; they were mocked as his 'Kindergarten' but they were better than anything produced by the British system between Churchill and Thatcher and considerably better than the old muffs, crooks and intellectual dwarves of the Blair years. As Leo Amery said at the time:

What was achieved in that brief space was not a mere series of useful reforms but the creation of a new country. The Transvaal and Orange River Colony of 1905 differed almost as much from the Boer Republics of six years before as the Canada of to-day differs from the old Canada which passed away with Montcalm. Upon that work South Africa can no more go back than England could have gone back upon the Norman Conquest.[484]

*

## More Conclusions

The first and most obvious conclusion that we must draw from this most tumultuous period is that economics was not the driving force of the conflict. Marx was as wrong as ever and those Marxists who adhere to this most flawed of ideologies were wrong then, wrong today and will continue to be wrong in the future. The same can be said of those Afrikaaner Nationalists who bore tourists to death with the same tune. The war was not driven by British desires for gold but by the age old need to control the route to India.

The second conclusion goes to the question of leadership or lack thereof. I have been scathing about African leadership for good reasons but now the same judgement must be applied to the Boer leadership. Being a leader involves formulating an aim and a vision, being realistic and pragmatic about how that duty may be discharged and, when the facts change, adapting to them. All these things were conspicuously absent from the leadership that took the Boer Republics into the disastrous confrontation with the British Empire. Kruger was unable to cope with the new situation produced by the eruption of Johannesburg out of the veldt, unwilling to rein in his territorial ambitions and dismissive of the realities of British power and the international situation both before and during the war. Nor was he ever able to convincingly formulate a strategic plan for the war that he started and never had the statesmanship to accept that dealing with defeat is as much a part of leadership as any other challenge. Only with the emergence of Smuts and Louis Botha after the war do we start to see real statesmanship.

Thirdly, the condition of near-complete ruin that large parts of South Africa found itself in by 1902 was entirely the responsibility of that bad leadership. While there is much to admire in termas of bravery and tactical ability in the way that the Afrikaaners fought their battles, the decision to fight on long after the war had been lost was a bad decision and the scorched earth and concentration camps that followed would have been avoided if the terms offered by Kitchener at Middelburg had been accepted. These terrible wounds were self-inflicted ones.

Fourthly, although the voice of black Africans virtually disappeared during the years 1886-1902, the people themselves had not gone away. Rather, something of a metamorphosis was occurring in the mines of the Rand and whole new classes of people with all sorts of new ideas were poised to emerge. This would provide challenges to African leadership across the racial spectrum during the coming years but it was not inevitable that Apartheid would be the outcome.

---

[484] *Amery* Vol VI p.149

Finally, the reconstruction of South Africa undertaken by Milner brought an improvement to the overall administration of South Africa that Kruger had been unable to contemplate by dint of his narrowness. This represented an enormous magnanimity on the part of the British who might well have been tempted to keep the two republics in a state of grinding poverty and weakness, annexing territories that they deemed useful and establishing Johannesburg and the mines as a separate Crown Colony. That they chose not to do this was one of the stronger indicators that the British wanted to maintain the idea that the empire was to be based on consent, acquiescence and mutual self-interest rather than the mailed fist. However much the Boers cavilled and however shell-shocked the black Africans were, in 1906 the best solution to the myriad problems of southern Africa remained British rule. The coming years would also bear this reality out.

Printed in Great Britain
by Amazon